# A View from the Palatine:

The *Iuvenilia* of Théodore de Bèze

# MEDIEVAL AND RENAISSANCE

# TEXTS AND STUDIES

VOLUME 237

> Vos docti docta præcingite tempora lauro:
> Mi satis est illam uel tetigisse manu.

## THEODORVS BEZA
## VEZELIVS

Bèze at age twenty-nine, from the first edition (1548).
The legend reads,
"You learned, encircle your learned brows with laurel;
For me it is enough just to have touched it with my hand."

# A View from the Palatine:
## The *Iuvenilia* of Théodore de Bèze

Text, translation, and commentary

by

KIRK M. SUMMERS

Arizona Center for Medieval and Renaissance Studies
Tempe, Arizona
2001

*A generous grant from
Pegasus Limited for the Promotion of Neo-Latin Studies
has assisted in meeting the publication costs of this volume.*

**Library of Congress Cataloging-in-Publication Data**

Bèze, Théodore de, 1519–1605.
  [Poems. English & Latin]
  A View from the Palatine: the Iuvenilia of Théodore de Bèze / text, trans-
lation, and commentary by Kirk M. Summers.
     p. cm. — (Medieval & Renaissance Texts & Studies ; v. 237)
  Includes bibliographical references and index.
  ISBN 0-86698-279-5 (alk. paper)
  1. Báze, Thâódore de, 1519–1605 — Translations into English. 2. Latin
poetry, Medieval and modern — Translations intro English. 3. Báze, Thâó-
dore de, 1519–1605 — Criticism and interpretation. I. Summers, Kirk M.,
1961– II. Title. III. Medieval & Renaissance Texts & Studies (Series) ; v.
237.

PA8475.B8 A27 2002
871'.04--dc21                                                    2001022525

∞
This book is made to last.
It is set in Garamond,
smythe-sewn and printed on acid-free paper
to library specifications.

Printed in the United States of America

*Carissimae venustissimae*

*amicae et uxori,*

*Tatianae*

# Table of Contents

# *Preface*

Historians of sixteenth-century Neo-Latin literature have long noted the need for a critical edition of the poetry of Théodore de Bèze. The last printed edition was published by Alexandre Machard in 1879, which makes the text accessible, but lacks a critical apparatus. Commentaries are almost nonexistent as well. Machard's notes, on the whole, would not fill up one page. L. Maigron's 1898 Latin dissertation on Bèze's poems (*De Theodori Beza poematis*) takes an impressionistic approach for interpreting the poems, along the lines of nineteenth-century theoretical conventions. He trots out a seemingly random selection of poems, to which he applies a patronizing critique that amounts to little more than blustering. If a poem is, to his mind, charming and well-executed, and free from any hint of immorality or exaggeration, Maigron gives it the highest praise. But should a poem stray from the somber path of virtue, or include references to Greco-Roman divinities, Maigron becomes scandalized and wags his finger, so to speak, to scold the author and admonish the reader.[1] More valuable has been the contribution of F. Aubert, J. Boussard, and H. Meylan in 1953, whose study of the Orléans manuscript containing some of Bèze's early poetry has made the task of the present edition somewhat easier to accomplish.

---

[1] Examples abound. I translate one succinct instance from page 83: "It was more agreeable and elegant when he was declaring that Candida has better looks than can be painted on canvas. But what is more inappropriate for a liberal and good man than that epigram on the statue offered to Francis I by Lorenzo? We can only consider him to be a sorry and contemptible sycophant when he was so brash as to write that Venus herself descended from the sky, having left Mars and Jupiter, because she considered the French king greater than all three of those ("quod regem Gallicum maiorem et polo et Marte et Jove ipso haberet")."

Although they shy away from philological observations, Aubert et al. do provide the historical and biographical context that elucidates several poems in the published version. None of the scholars mentioned so far, however, writes in English, so that speakers of that language without knowledge of Latin or French are still barred from comprehending or enjoying Bèze's poetry. Likewise, aside from the occasional appearance of individual poems in an Englished anthology or in specialized articles, none of the poems has ever been translated into English.

It is my aim to remedy this woeful state of affairs by providing a critical edition with translation and commentary. I have presently set my sights on reconstructing only the 1548 edition of Bèze's poetry, which was published when he was twenty-nine years old and is often for that reason referred to as *iuvenilia*. After the publication of that slender volume, Bèze's life took a dramatic turn that compelled him to flee Paris and join the reformed movement in Geneva. Later editions of his poetry change as his ideology changes: the Muses of Helicon give way to the Holy Spirit. What had initially been an attempt to rival the classical poets on their own terms evolves in later editions into a passion for inspiring others to a life of holiness and devotion. Nevertheless, the two states of Bèze's poetry are in constant dialogue with one another, so that even the later, Christianized editions have significant bearing on our understanding of the first. Though he expurgated many of the original poems, enough remain in an altered state to reveal to us the issues that concerned Bèze as he revised that first edition. He cleared up problems of scansion, reworked infelicitous turns of phrase, and removed paganisms. In some instances titles are expanded to clarify the circumstances. Some of these changes are a response to technical and academic criticisms, others to moral criticisms.

One may rightly wonder why Bèze's poetry has not received much attention up to this point. I suspect that those who have studied Bèze have been put off by his *volte-face* in 1548. His sudden transition from a mostly secular poet to an ardent Calvinist discourages interest in his earlier writings and adds to the complexity of his work. The number of varied strands that must be pulled together before one can come to grips with what he wrote is daunting: the classical influences, the historical context of sixteenth-century France, other contemporary Neo-Latin and vernacular poets, Calvinist theology, and Renaissance humanism, to name a few. My own deficiencies in some of those areas will be all too apparent as one reads through this edition. Others will undoubtedly be able to say more about Bèze's relationship to his fellow vernacular poets, for instance, than can be found here. Nevertheless, it has been my hope that the qualifications I do bring to this task, namely, a classical training combined with studies in Calvinist theology and a strong attraction to the writings of Renaissance humanists, would allow me to produce a foundation on which others might build according to their own expertise.

To establish the text of the present edition, I have compared the fundamental editions, together with a few minor ones that happened to be available to me.[2] The editions required for establishing the text are the first edition of 1548, the second authorized edition of 1569, and the third authorized edition of 1597. The rest of the editions that made it into the apparatus are those of 1576, 1580, 1713, and 1779. The 1576 edition follows the 1569 edition closely, with some variants that I have noted throughout the apparatus. Three of the editions I consulted were meant to be reprints of the first edition: the 1580, surreptitiously printed in Bèze's lifetime; the 1713, which was printed in London; and the popular 1779, which also contained the poems of Buchanan and other Neo-Latinists. And yet all three editions exhibit novelties and odd deviations from the first edition that either highlight problem areas in the 1548 edition or indicate what editions were used for particular anthologies. The 1599 edition adheres so closely to the 1597 in regard to the original core of poems that it does not contribute anything of importance, and so I have excluded it from the apparatus; it will undoubtedly be useful for establishing the text of the later Christian poems in a future project. The woodcuts of *Religio* and the family coat-of-arms that are included here both come from the 1599 edition. Of the few extant copies of the 1547 *plaquette*, written by Bèze and dedicated to members of Francis I's family, I was able to consult the one in the Newberry Library (Chicago), which is the only copy in the United States. I make note of variants in that text in the apparatus at the appropriate places. I do not include Machard's edition in the apparatus, but I do make note of some of his edition's puzzling textual deviations in the commentary.

Here a word should be said about the aims of the commentary itself.

---

[2] T. Thomson ("Poemata") has set out the case for what editions would be needed to complete such an edition, and Gardy, *Bibliographie*, is also helpful in that regard. I am aware, too, that in his two-volume 1983 Oxford dissertation ("A Critical Edition of the *Poemata* [1548] of Theodore de Beze") Thomson created a critical edition of Bèze's 1548 edition (with an introduction in English, but no English translation), but I have not been able to gain access to it to compare it to my own. While I am confident that our independent efforts achieved similar results, for me the commentary and translation have been an integral part of the process of coming to terms with Bèze's text.

My primary goal is to give the reader some appreciation for the profundity that I myself have found in these poems. It has long been fashionable in academic circles to dismiss the efforts of the Neo-Latinists out of hand, which partly explains why so few of them have received proper editions. As this dismissiveness applies to Bèze, one can expect to find scholars claiming that the *sylvae* are mere schoolboy exercises, the *elegiae* nothing but trite nonsense, the *epitaphia* hollow sycophancy, and the *epigrammata* self-indulgent and feeble attempts at imitation. Furthermore, the whole collection might be discarded as a vain and meaningless attempt to recreate the feel of certain classical models. I, however, have not accepted those widely-held presuppositions. James Hutton is right when he remarks (*Greek Anthology in France*, 117) that Bèze is among the most original of the Neo-Latin poets, and I think it is clear that his poems are the product of an acute intellect. Therefore, I have given every effort to uncover the abundant treasures hidden in each poem. There is always the danger in such enterprises that the commentator will read more into the text than is really there, or will seem to be limiting the meaning or gist of the poem to one possibility. Though I may be guilty of the former at times, I do not accept the presumption of the latter: I hope that this edition will spur further studies on Bèze's poems, not discourage them. But aside from the identification of each poem's main thrust, I have concerned myself with other matters as well in the commentary. I thought it important first of all to indicate material from the classical period that elucidates obscurities, clarifies the meaning of a difficult piece of Latin, or points to a possible source for an idiom or aphorism. I also perused as widely as possible Bèze's Neo-Latin contemporaries, especially those within his circle, for material that might parallel, echo, or explain a certain verse; these authors are noted in the bibliography. The volume of contemporary writings is so immense, however, that quite naturally this aspect of the study is not as exhaustive as one might wish, but I hope that it will ignite enough interest among other scholars to undertake the task.

In my effort to unveil the depth and breadth of Bèze's poetry, I have added in the commentary observations on various literary devices, word plays, and elements of structure, insofar as I think they have some bearing on the meaning. Matters of sound and rhythm will best be appreciated by reading the poems aloud in the original, though occasionally I have seen fit to comment on those too. As a final note, I have given attention to identifying historical and mythological people and events. I have not wasted time explaining who Heracles was, or others whose credentials are well-known, yet for the personages that I suspect a general reader may not know I provide a brief explanatory note. I should add that I consider the translation as part of the commentary. For that reason, I have not attempted to turn Bèze's poems into English ones of my own making, but have opted instead for a prose rendering. I realize that there are certain benefits to a literal translation, but I have recoiled from it, because Latinized English merely repeats the alien expressions of the Latin in a different guise. I have taken the liberty, therefore, to express Latin idiom with English idiom, and Latin tone with English tone, while resisting the urge to stray too far from the original. The balance, however, is delicate and difficult to maintain consistently.

I cannot conclude without mentioning the many people and institutions who helped bring this work to fruition. Back in 1982, during a Greek class with Professor Mark E. Clark, quite by chance I was introduced to the name Théodore de Bèze for the first time. It was Professor Clark who initially nudged me down the path that eventually led to this present volume. Several years later, under the guidance of Professor J. K. Newman at the University of Illinois, I gained insights into reading Latin poetry that greatly influenced my interpretation of Bèze's poems. Dr. Leslie S. B. MacCoull at Arizona State University painstakingly read one of the final drafts of the manuscript and made many insightful comments that I have incorporated into the text. Three institutions have been extremely helpful in providing support for my work. In the summer of 1996 the Research Grants Committee of the University of Alabama provided me with a fellowship so that I could devote all my energies to writing on the *epigrammata*. Then in 1998 the Newberry Library in Chicago offered me the Lester J. Cappon Fellowship in Documentary Editing, for work in residence, without which support this project could never have been completed. Not only does that library possess all the editions of Bèze's poetry that I needed to consult, it also gave me access to a vast corpus of Neo-Latin literature and historical documents, while offering me the chance to collaborate with scholars of other institutions with whom I otherwise would have had no contact. Also, in the summer of 2000, the American Academy in Rome graciously permitted me to utilize their library and facilities so that I could fine tune the classical aspects of the commentary. Finally, I must extend the deepest thanks to my wife, Dr. Tatiana Tsakiropoulou-Summers, who, despite the demands of a full-time teaching job and her unswerving devotion to our two young children, unselfishly and patiently read early drafts of the manuscript and cleared it of many embarrassing gaffes and idiosyncrasies. I hope the fact that this volume is dedicated to her will repay in some small measure her constant love and support.

# Key to the Commentary

| | |
|---|---|
| ABM | Aubert, F., J. Boussard, H. Meylan, "Un premier recueil de poésies latines de Théodore de Bèze," *BHR* 15 (1953): 164–91, 257–94 |
| *AJP* | *American Journal of Philology* |
| *BHR* | *Bibliothèque d'Humanisme et Renaissance.* |
| *Corr.* | Théodore de Bèze, *Correspondance. Recueillie par H. Aubert, publiée par H. Meylan, A. Dufour, et al.* (Geneva, 1960– ). 20 vols. to date, covering 1539–1579 |
| *DOP* | *Dumbarton Oaks Papers* |
| *IJCT* | *International Journal for the Classical Tradition* |
| *IL* | *L'Information littéraire* |
| *JEA* | *Journal of Egyptian Archaeology* |
| *JRS* | *Journal of Roman Studies* |
| Orléans ms. | Manuscript 1674 of the Municipal Library of Orléans |
| *RE* | *Real Encyclopädie der classischen Altertumswissenschaft*, ed. A. Pauly, rev. G. Wissowa, W. Kroll, K. Mittelhaus, and K. Ziegler (1893–1978) |
| *Rend. Linc.* | *Rendiconti della reale accademia dei Lincei* |
| *TLL* | *Thesaurus Linguae Latinae* (Leipzig, 1900– ). |
| *WJA* | *Würzburger Jahrbücher für die Altertumswissenschaft* |

If a book or an article is used once, it receives a full bibliographical entry *ad locum*. All other entries refer to authors appearing in the bibliography.

At the beginning of each commentary I have noted which editions do not include the poem under consideration, and which anthologies do.

The anthologies are keyed to the bibliography. For example, the follow-ing entry,

> "Missing in 1597; Heywood, *Pleasant dialogues* ..., ed. Bang, 267",

means that all editions consulted (1548, 1569, 1576, 1597, 1713, 1779) contain the poem *except* the 1597 edition, and that Thomas Heywood's *Pleasant Dialogues* includes the poem on page 267 of the edition listed in the bibliography. If no entry appears, the reader can assume that all edi-tions contain the poem, and that no anthology does. I have provided the information so that with one glance the reader will be able to view the *fortuna* of any given poem.

Most Latin cited in the commentary is translated, but occasionally I have chosen to leave a passage untranslated, either because of its short-ness and obvious sense, or because I provide the gist of the passage in my discussion of it and a full translation is not necessary.

## Meter

In the commentary I have identified all the meters, with the excep-tion of the more easily recognizable dactylic hexameters and elegiac couplets. Some general observations can be made about the remaining meters. In regard to the phalaecian hendecasyllables, Bèze tends to open the lines with a spondee, as Martial did, but unlike both Martial and Catullus, he frequently breaks the normal pattern of putting a caesura at the fifth or sixth syllables to accommodate unusual words. Elision is also more common than in the lines of Martial. In constructing the relatively rare iambic quaternarius, Bèze allows many variations and resolutions. Iambic feet become spondees or resolve into tribrachs, dactyls, or ana-paests, while the pure iamb expected in the last two syllables sometimes gives way to a final anceps.

# INTRODUCTION

Si quid agam quaeris, nihil prorsus, nisi quod aliquoties nugor
cum Musis meis, deinde animi gratia in Palatium[1] ventito. Ibi
omnium hominum mores velut in amplissimo theatro intueor.

[If you want to know what I am doing, nothing much, except
that sometimes I play around with my poetry, then for relaxation
I go to the Palatine. There I watch the pageant of people's lives,
as if I'm in a vast and spacious theater.]

Bèze to Maclou Popon, 7 December 1539

Théodore de Bèze (or Theodore Beza)[2] was born on 24 June 1519
in the town of Vézelay in Burgundy, France. His ancestors, accord-
ing to his own characterization of them, were noble and good, free from
any hint of scandal and known for their generous donations to the
Church. His father was Pierre de Bèze (1485–1562), a licentiate in law
and bailiff of Vézelay; his mother was Maria Bourdelot, an intelligent
and godly woman of a noble family.[3] He had two uncles who were well

---

[1] Presumably by "Palatine" he means the Palais-Royal and its environs.

[2] Early in his life, until about 1539, Bèze used the French and Latin spellings of his
name: Dieudonné and Deodatus.

[3] She died very early in Bèze's childhood. Later, Bèze dedicated this touching epitaph
to her (Maigron, *De Theodori Bezae poematis*, 12): "Vixdum vivere coeperam puellus, |
Mater, vivere quando desiisti: | Ut te vix ego dixerim parentem, | Vix tu me quoque filium
vocaris. | Hinc lustris tibi quinque iam sepulcri | Sub hoc pondere frigidi peractis, | Nunc
primum Aonidum favore fretus, | Heu mater, cineres tuos saluto. | Felix ah nimium futu-
rus olim, | Si natus citius forem vel ipse, | Vel tu mortua serius fuisses!" [Barely had I
begun to live as a little boy, mother, when you ceased to live: I barely had time to call you
my parent, and you barely had time to call me your son. Hence now that five lustrums

placed within the Church and government: Nicolas (1469–1532) was abbot of Cervon, priory of Saint-Eloi-lès-Longjumeau, and councillor in the Parlement of Paris. Claude (d. 1553) was abbot of Froimont near Beauvais. It was the former uncle who first noted the young Bèze's talents and unwittingly set him on the path that led to Geneva. When Bèze was not yet three years old, Nicolas convinced Théodore's parents to allow him to take the precocious child to Paris, so that he could provide him with the best possible upbringing. His mother reluctantly agreed. In Paris, Théodore had access to all the privileges of high society. His mind was naturally sharp, yet, despite his uncle's care, he was a sickly child, and therefore was slow to develop physically. Throughout his childhood he suffered terribly from illnesses and at the hands of a Paris surgeon, whose Renaissance cures were doing more harm than good. Nevertheless, in December of 1528, to the surprise of everyone concerned, Nicolas sent the boy to Orléans to live with the German scholar Melchior Wolmar, who was quickly gaining a reputation for his ability to educate young boys in polite letters.

Bèze would later look back on his arrival at Wolmar's house as his "second birthday." Under Wolmar's tutelage Bèze was introduced to Latin, Greek, and other subjects proper to a humanistic education, including law. More importantly, Wolmar taught Bèze to read the Scriptures from a new perspective, and to look on certain Catholic doctrines and institutions with a critical eye. Of all the subjects it was in Latin where Bèze most excelled. When in 1530 Margaret of Angoulême, sister of François I, invited Wolmar to join her court at Bourges, Bèze followed him. By this time, Wolmar had come into such demand for instruction in Greek that another young student, with whose life Bèze's would eventually be inextricably bound, chose to study that language with him. Here, in the house of his teacher, Bèze first met Jean Calvin. Later, in 1546, Calvin dedicated his commentary on II Corinthians to his former Greek instructor. There were other luminaries that Bèze met at Bourges, most notably Conrad Gessner, whose scientific and medical writings were to hold primacy in sixteenth-century France.

After the Affair of the Placards on 18 October 1534, which turned the tide of public opinion against Protestantism, Bèze's life dramatically

---

have passed since you've lain under the weight of this tomb, alas, mother, I pay my respect to your ashes, relying on the good graces of the Muses. Ah, too happy I would've been, if only I myself had been born sooner, or you had died later!]

changed. Although Wolmar had kept his Protestant leanings a secret, he still feared that he would be discovered and imprisoned for heresy. Therefore, he took advantage of an invitation to return to Germany to teach law and literature at the University of Tübingen. Bèze would have followed him gladly, but his father refused it, and instead ordered him to return to Orléans to take up the study of law. Bèze obeyed sadly, and in 1535 found himself again in Orléans, this time at the university. He admits later that he gave himself half-heartedly to the study of law, preferring instead to concentrate on his poetry, to which he was drawn by a natural impulse, and to fraternize with other humanists in that city, including Jean Dampierre, Germain Audebert, Hubert Sussaneau, Maclou Pompon, and others who were to make their mark in French politics and literature. It was during these years that Bèze composed the bulk of the poems that later found their way into the published edition of 1548.

Despite the distractions and the lack of motivation, Bèze was able to obtain his license in law in 1539, at which time he departed for Paris where a life and career were already being prepared for him. Unbeknownst to him, he had received two benefices worth seven hundred crowns a year, and learned that many more were being held in reserve for him. Those benefices, together with the allurements of Paris, the fame he was gaining for poetic composition, and the many offices and honors being laid before him, caused Bèze to hesitate to undertake a course of action to which he had been long resolved. For, as soon as his affairs were sufficiently in order, he planned to repudiate the papal religion, along with the benefices, to reveal a secret marriage that he had undertaken with a certain Claudine Denosse, and to depart Paris for the house of Wolmar at Tübingen, where he could openly espouse the reformed faith.

For a time, however, Bèze lived happily in Paris as he came into contact with some of the leading figures of the day. Through his friendship with the poet Jacques Peletier, famous for his translation of Horace's *Ars Poetica*, Bèze came into contact with future members of the Pléiade, Pierre de Ronsard and Joachim du Bellay. He was joining them and others in intellectual discussions at the house of the printer Michel de Vascosan during the period 1547 to 1548. The future Protestant printer, Jean Crespin, was one of the witnesses to his secret marriage in 1543. Bèze also knew the poets George Buchanan and Salmon Macrin.[4]

---

[4] In the preface to the 1569 edition of his poetry, Bèze describes his lifestyle and

These friendships, among others, were indicative of the fact that Bèze was associating with many free-thinkers, especially those who resisted the repressiveness of the Sorbonne. And like many of his free-thinking contemporaries, Bèze was appalled by that institution's execution of the printer Etienne Dolet, and he expressed his views on the matter openly in an epitaph. Some years later, Etienne Pasquier would remark on Bèze's leading role in resistance to obscurantism:

> Ce fut une belle guerre que l'on entreprit lors contre l'ignorance, dont j'attribue l'avantgarde à Seve, Beze et Peletier, ou si le voulez autrement, ce furent les avantcoureurs des autres poëtes. Après, se meirent sur les rangs Pierre de Ronsard vendomois, et Joachim du Bellay angevin ... (*Recherches de la France,* vi.7)

We are fortunate that the chance survival of Bèze's unpublished poetry, written during the Orléans and Paris years and later thought by Bèze to be "either lost or in the hands of some friend," fills out the picture of his life in those days. Sometime around 1544, his old companion Germain Audebert, recently returned from a trip to Italy, compiled a collection of Latin poetry that had been written by the *sodalitium* in Orléans. Bèze's poems comprise the greatest part of the collection and include some pieces that later make their way into the 1548 edition, as well as some that were never published. The unpublished poems in the manuscript confirm much of what we can reconstruct from other sources about Bèze during this period, as its editors have noted. We see him following the humanists' disputes, such as the battle over Ciceronianism, and taking sides himself; he supports the royal family while obliquely expressing contempt for the Sorbonne; he gives tribute to the most prominent scholars of the day, including Erasmus and Guillaume Budé; he is interested in major political figures and religious themes; and he has a fondness for weaving together pagan motifs with Christian ones. In short, he is, as the Jesuit Maimbourg describes him in his *Histoire du Calvinisme* (Paris, 1682), loved by the great, polished and cultivated in every way, and well-read in a variety of subjects.

---

associations during this period: "When I had returned to Paris from Orléans, and there, as it were, in the most prosperous gymnasium of the whole world, met with those with whom I engaged in intellectual pursuits of every kind, as much as I could I continued to write poetry as a means of escape from the more serious pursuits. At the risk of causing envy, I can say that the most learned men of the academy, whom I had as my friends, received my poetry with such favor that when I wrote the poem on the birth of François II, they all agreed that I was a first-rate epigrammatist."

Notwithstanding Bèze's involvement with Paris's elite circles and his association with the leading humanists, it is evident from many poems that his dissatisfaction with the status quo was ready to boil over at any moment. Meylan ("Conversion de Bèze") argues convincingly that Bèze's break with the Roman Catholic Church began as early as 1535, sparked by his reading of one of Bullinger's tracts while in the house of Wolmar. He continued to waver in his intention to renounce Catholicism, however, even as late as 1548. In an autobiographical letter to Wolmar, he describes the situation in vivid terms:

> Furthermore, the same most kind Father effected my determined rejection of that paltry glory and the honors held forth to me, to the wonder of my friends and the reprehension of most of them, who jocularly styled me "the new philosopher." Meanwhile I was still stuck in the mire. My friends urged me finally to embrace some kind of life. My uncle placed everything at my disposal. On the one side, conscience pressed me and my spouse called on me to fulfill my promise. On the other, Satan was cajoling me with his serene expression. My income increased when my brother died. In a sense, I lay incapable of coming to a decision in the midst of this mental solicitude.

During these long years of internal struggle, Bèze was continually sending samples of his poetry to Wolmar at Tübingen, from whom he had long been separated. Wolmar in turn was sharing the poems with his own friends, most notably the Dutch humanist Joachim Camerarius. Both of these preeminent scholars were enthusiastic about the talent they saw in the young Bèze, and Wolmar, whose opinions Bèze respected immensely, was constantly encouraging him to publish them. Friends in Paris and Orléans echoed that sentiment. Some time in late 1547 or early 1548, Bèze appears to have received a letter from Wolmar that expressed such praise for his poetry, while at the same time adding the approbation of Camerarius, that he, in his own words, "rashly gathered those *nugae* into a bundle" and sent them to the publisher. To their head he added a dedication to Wolmar in which he thanks his former teacher for his instruction and expresses his hope that the authority of Wolmar's opinion will lend some weight to what he himself presents with a measure of uncertainty. The true value of the dedication for us, however, is that it reveals what little movement Bèze is making toward executing his resolve even in mid-1548. Bèze is much more interested in indulging his poetic talents and receiving accolades for them from other

humanists than in confronting his convictions or promoting a new relig-
ious outlook. In the preface to his 1569 edition Bèze himself admits that
he was motivated out of vain need for glory and recognition: "Tum igi-
tur mihi nescio qua inanis gloriolae spe ducto, partim praeceptoris de me
optime meriti desiderio satisfacere vel maxime cupienti, excidit libellus
ille, accipere me puderet ..." In fact, the positive reaction from men of
letters was swift in coming. Bèze reports, for example, that the celebrat-
ed Italian poet and Catholic reformer Marcantonio Flaminio hailed the
collection of poems as a sign that "at long last the Muses have crossed
over the Alps and gone into France."

In general terms the poetry of this first edition can be described as
playfully risqué to a degree not unlike many of the classical poets,
whom Bèze acknowledges that he is imitating:

> Proposueram autem mihi in bucolicis et sylvulis quibusdam scri-
> bendis imitandum poetarum omnium principem Virgilium, gra-
> vius nihil dum meditans; in elegiis autem Ovidium, cuius ingenii
> ubertate magis quam Tibulli munditie capiebar. In epigrammatων
> vero lusibus, quod scribendi genus praecipue quadam ingenii pro-
> clivitate amplectebar, Catullum et Martialem usque.

> [I had decided that in writing certain bucolics and *sylvae* that I
> should imitate Vergil, the best of all the poets, while contemplat-
> ing nothing more serious. And in elegies, I imitated Ovid, whose
> rich talent I was enjoying more than the neatness of Tibullus. But
> in the playful banter of epigrams, the genre that I embraced
> wholeheartedly out of a certain inclination of my talent, I imi-
> tated Catullus and Martial throughout.]

Like many of the so-called love poets, both of antiquity and among his
contemporaries, Bèze includes a cycle of love poems devoted to amo-
rous escapades with a fictitious girl named Candida, although they in no
way comprise the bulk of the poems. Even so, the subject matter is of-
ten racy and edgy, and filled with invective: shameless prostitutes chased
by gnarled old men, pompous poets inflated with self-importance, her-
maphrodites and fools lifted from some Plautine comedy, to name but
a few. Bèze himself would later regret the volume, saying that the very
recollection of those poems makes him blush and admitting that he was
not sufficiently circumspect in his youth.[5] Even Badius, his publisher,

---

[5] Preface to the *Abraham Sacrifiant* (= *Corr.* 1:200) and preface to the 1569 *Poemata*, (=
*Corr.* 10:89).

asked the readers of Bèze's Christian play *Abraham Sacrifiant* (1550) to excuse the "vers lassifs" and "rithmes impudiques" of his 1548 collection.[6]

It would not be entirely accurate to say that Bèze's earliest production is entirely devoid of religious feeling. In *sylva* 3, a poem addressed to personified Night (specifically, Christmas Eve), he invokes "chaste muses" to help him compose a sacred song about the birth of Jesus. He begins the poem with a recognition that secular poets usually praise the night as a time for wooing their girls, but he, as a poet-priest (*vates*), will concentrate his efforts on matters of divine significance. At the end he speaks of the "religion of our pious fathers," and casts aspersion on the unholy rites of Cybele and Dionysus. *Sylva* 4 is a lengthy poem that reviews the story of David's sin with Bathsheba and his subsequent penitence. Here classical myth is mingled in odd ways with Old Testament narrative: Cupid attracts David's attention to Bathsheba's beauty; Yahweh calls a council of the heavenly hosts on Mount Olympus; Tartarus demands the punishment of David. Still, the poem crescendos into a frustration of Cupid's power through the repentance of David, and, by implication, the triumph of Christianity over paganism. Even among the epigrams, where Bèze often strays into various off-color themes, we find a beautiful poem about worshiping God in simplicity and with a pure heart (*epig.* 33).

Bèze must have known that some of the poems he included come dangerously close to a denunciation of the papal religion, and that he would have to answer to the authorities for them. We can never know, however, what sort of reaction officials of the Church would have had in regard to the poems *per se*. Almost immediately after the book's publication, a severe illness struck Bèze down and finally sparked his determination to follow his conscience. He describes his conversion experience in this way:

> Post infinitos et corporis et animi cruciatus, Dominus fugitivi sui mancipii misertus ita me consolatus est ut de venia mihi concessa nihil dubitarem. Meipsum igitur cum lachrymis detestor, veniam peto, votum renovo de vero ipsius cultu aperte amplectendo denique totum illi meipsum consecro. Ita factum est mortis imago mihi serio proposita, verae vitae desiderium in me sopitum ac sepultum excitaret, et morbus iste verae sanitatis mihi principium

---

[6] The entire poem is given at *Corr.* 1:188.

esset: adeo mirabilis est Dominus in suis [cf. Ps. 67.36, 92.4] una eademque opera simul et deiiciendis et erigendis, vulnerandis et sanandis.

[After infinite tortures of mind and body, the Lord, pitying His runaway slave, so consoled me that I entertained no doubts of the concession of His pardon to me. Therefore I renounced myself with tears, I asked for forgiveness, I renewed my vow openly to embrace His true worship—in short, I consecrated myself wholly to Him. Thus did it come to pass that the image of death, seriously confronting me, excited in me the desire of the true life that lay dormant and buried, and that disease was for me the beginning of a true soundness. So wonderful is the Lord in that He casts down and raises up, wounds and makes whole again His children by one and the same stroke.]

Bèze had scarcely gained the strength to walk again when he fled Paris with Claudine Denosse and made his way to Geneva, where he arrived in late October 1548.[7] He was drawn there, undoubtedly, by the presence and inducement of Jean Crespin, who preceded him as a fugitive, and by a desire to present himself to Jean Calvin. From there Bèze made a trip to Tübingen to see Wolmar, after which he intended to join Crespin in the printing business at Geneva. On the return trip, however, Bèze was entertained by the Swiss reformer Pierre Viret, who persuaded him to take the position as professor of Greek at the Academy of Lausanne.

It was at this stage in his career that Bèze began a number of ambitious writing projects and made important contacts. At Lausanne he wrote his most noted work, a lively tragicomedy entitled *Abraham Sacrifiant*, in French verse,[8] the reading of which, Pasquier comments, "made tears fall from my eyes" (*Recherches de la France*, vii.615). At the same time, Calvin was encouraging Bèze to complete the translation of the Psalms begun by Clément Marot, since that author had completed only the first fifty before his death. The resulting metrical collection served as the Huguenot psalter for many years to come. In addition to

---

[7] The Parlement of Paris condemned Bèze as a heretic and confiscated his property (31 May 1550). A special royal mandate restored it to him in 1564.

[8] Ed. K. Cameron, K. M. Hall, and F. Higman (Paris, 1967).

teaching Greek at Lausanne, Bèze lectured in French on the New Testament, particularly on Romans and the epistles of Peter. These lectures provided Bèze with material that eventually figure in his massive Latin translation of and notes on the New Testament, first published in 1556, and running through several editions, up until 1598. In the notes, Bèze draws detailed analogies from classical and Jewish literature and language to justify his own Latin translations as opposed to those of Jerome and Erasmus. He also collates numerous manuscripts, including the odd Codex D (Codex Cantabrigensis or Codex Bezae),[9] to establish the Greek text, which he provides along with his translation. Later, the King James translators would rely on Bèze's Latin translation as the basis of their own English one. During these years Bèze also traveled to Germany in an official capacity with Guillaume Farel and John Budé (son of the famous Guillaume Budé), and while there had the opportunity to confer with Philip Melanchthon.

In 1559 Bèze accepted an invitation from Calvin to come serve as rector of the newly established Academy of Geneva and to assume the pastorate of one of the city's congregations. Bèze, now in his fortieth year, was being groomed to become Calvin's successor as head of the Reformed movement. Although in the years between his arrival and Calvin's death in 1564, Bèze spent much of his time in France supporting the Huguenots, he and Calvin became more and more intimate, to such a degree, in fact, that it was understood by all that Bèze would someday succeed him. The city council made the succession official shortly after Calvin's death, and the presbytery of Geneva chose Bèze as their moderator, a post which he held until 1580 when he retired of his own accord. Meanwhile, in 1569, Bèze published his second, much expurgated edition of poetry, with all the Candida poems struck out, along with any other lewd or suggestive ones. Those he replaced with poems of a religious nature, many of which honor prominent leaders in the Protestant movement or criticize the papal religion. Any reprint of the 1548 edition during his life time was completely surreptitious.

By 1597 the afflictions of old age began to wear the reformer down. Rarely did he speak in public after that, though it must be noted that he

---

[9] A bilingual, fourth- to fifth-century manuscript the provenance of which is disputed (though it was probably made in a strongly Latin-using area, possibly Berytus), the codex had been found in a monastic library in Lyons when the Huguenots took that city in 1562. See D. C. Parker, *Codex Bezae: An Early Christian Manuscript and its Text* (Cambridge, 1992).

continued to serve as a figurehead and to write poetry. In 1599 the last authorized edition of his poetry issued from the press. In December of 1600 he traveled a short distance to Luisel with other deputies of Geneva to meet with Henry IV, to whom Bèze delivered an oration and wrote verses. Henry presented Bèze with a gift of five hundred crowns. His earliest biographer Antoine de la Faye (*De vita et obitu*, [Geneva, 1606]) recounts that in 1605 he slipped away quietly into death, after years of decline, and after a lifetime of service to the Church. He had written nearly a hundred tracts and treatises, defended reform doctrines in numerous colloquies, been friend and advisor to men and women of the highest station, and carried on a considerable correspondence, the reprinting of which has already extended into twenty volumes, with more to come.

At this point we must return to the 1548 edition of poetry, which took on a life of its own after its publication and particularly after Bèze fled to Geneva. Bèze's sudden departure from his offices in the Church, together with his espousal of the new doctrines, did not exactly warm the hearts of conservative clerics and Catholic defenders in the Sorbonne. They began to cull his poetry for evidence of immorality with which they could undermine his prestige and authority. In particular, they hoped to demonstrate that Bèze had chosen to leave the papal religion not for intellectual reasons, but because from his youth, as his poetry reveals, he had cultivated a lifestyle of debauchery and self-indulgence. He was not so much *protesting* the Church, they claimed, as acting according to his own depraved impulses. Others fabricated the details of his youth when they discovered that his poems were short on specifics. The resulting *querelle* over Bèze's poetry and the lifestyle in which it was spawned receives considerable attention in Machard's introduction (following closely the discussion of Pierre Bayle, *Dictionaire historique et critique* [numerous editions]), the highlights of which are worth reviewing here.

The first assaults on Bèze's character in reference to his poetry are described by Bèze himself in the prefatory letter of his 1569 edition. He writes,

> Ad nostra poemata revertor. Clamitant boni cacolycae sive apostaticae fidei defensores, nempe Ecebolius ille Balduinus (duobus fictitiis geniis septus, quibus Gabrielis et Michaelis nomina fabricatus est) et bonus ille fraterculus Claudius de Xainctes, Sorbonicae illius cloaecae, quod ille Romanae curiae Glaucia, Bezam

a pueritia imbibisse vatum impudicitiam et impudentiam, totam-
que aetatem explendis suis libidinibus et cupiditatibus, ac descri-
bendis suis amoribus (agnoscis lector, Sorbonici oratoris δεί-
νωσιν) denique ulciscendis rivalibus suis exercuisse; quem etiam
in meretricem, in lenam, in cinaedum denique transformant. Istis
haec eadem crimina ex intima usque Polonia, velut echo quae-
dam, responsat bonus ille Cardinalis, quem ominis, opinor, causa
Hosium vocant. Cedo vero, quibus tandem argumentis tam
graves isti accusatores nituntur? Versiculos meos citant, nec enim
aliud, Deo sit gratia, possint proferre, ne si quidem testes emptos
undique conquisierint. Atqui primum omnium, in tam exiguo
libello paucos prae aliis amatorios versus invenient, et eos qui-
dem, si paucissima quaedam epigrammata excipias, licenter potius
quam obscoene scriptos, in quos etiam age, quandoquidem ita vo-
lunt, inquiramus. Uxorem mihi, ea quam illa tempora ferebant
ratione, ut alibis plenissime exposui, quatuor circiter annis ante
voluntarium meum exilium despondi, genere quidem imparem,
sed ea virtute praeditam mulierem cuius me poenitere ab eo tem-
pore minime oportuerit.

[I return to our poems. Certain wolves in sheep's clothing, or,
more accurately, apostate defenders of the faith, Ecebolius Bald-
win (protected by two fictitious spirits, under the pseudonyms
Gabriel and Michael) and that good little brother Claude de
Sainctes, who is to Sorbonne's sewer what Glaucia was to Rome's
curia, claim that Bèze imbibed the immodesty and impudence of
the poets from boyhood, and that he spent his whole life fulfill-
ing his own pleasures and desires, describing his love affairs (you
know how that orator of the Sorbonne exaggerates), and, finally,
taking revenge on his rivals. They transform him into a prosti-
tute, into a pimp, into a sodomite. The good cardinal, whom
they ominously call Hosius, echoes their accusations from deep
within Poland. But on what are these important gentlemen bas-
ing their arguments? They cite my verses, since by God's grace
they cannot produce any other evidence, even if they look every-
where for bribed witnesses. But first of all, in so slight a book
they will find relatively few amorous verses, and they, with a few
exceptions, were not obscene so much as loose. But since they
want to look at them, we should too. During the time they are
talking about, four years before I went into exile, I had taken a

wife, as I have fully disclosed elsewhere. And she was indeed un-
equal in birth, but her excellent virtue never made me sorry.]

Already in 1569 Bèze can point to numerous people who have criti-
cized him in print. Claude de Sainctes (1525–1591), professor of theology
at the Sorbonne, launched an *ad hominem* attack against Bèze in his
*Examen calvinanae et bezianae doctrinae* of 1566, to which Bèze respond-
ed with a treatise of his own; de Sainctes's criticisms were even harsher
in his *Responsio ad apologiam Th. Bezae editam contra Examen doctrinae
calvinianae* of 1567, which then provoked two more published responses
from Bèze Even earlier, though, François Bauduin (1520–1573), a juris-
consult from Arras who taught law at Heidelberg from 1556 to 1561 and
appears at one time to have wanted to accommodate Reformed doctrines
within the Catholic Church, wrote two treatises against the Calvinists,
one of which drew an angry response from Bèze in 1563 (*Ad Francisci
Balduini apostatae Ecebolii convicia Theodori Bezae responsio*). Two stu-
dents of Bauduin returned fire against Bèze in turn (Bèze is wrong to
believe their names are pseudonyms for Bauduin): Michael Fabricius
published a work in 1564 entitled *Responsio ad Calvinum et Bezam pro
Francisco Balduino Iuriscons. cum refutatione calumniarum de scriptura et
traditione*, while his nephew, Gabriel Fabricius, published a work in
1567 entitled *Responsio ad Bezam Vezeliam Eceboliam*. In the latter work,
which is written in the style of Menippean satire, the author applies
only feminine names to Bèze, making him out to be a woman of the
worst repute.

Still more criticisms were leveled against Bèze by Conrad Schlüssel-
burg, a divine of the Confession of Augsburg, in his *Theologia Calvinis-
tarum libri tres, in quibus ... demonstratur, eos de nullo fere doctrinae
christianae articulo recte sentire ... collecti opera*, 3 vols. (Frankfurt, 1594).
Although Catholics led the charge against Bèze from the outset, there
were others such as Schlüsselburg who wanted to see him discredited
enough to follow their lead. Bèze had always included the Lutherans
among the adherents of the true faith, but even so, many resented the
fact that in theological debates Bèze criticized them sharply, particularly
in regard to the question of the real presence in the Lord's Supper.
Schlüsselburg charges that Bèze excuses his poetry by saying that it was
just urbanity and youthful playing, when in fact Bèze drew his inspira-
tion from his acquaintence with the whorehouses and seedy side of
Paris.[10] Finally, an unknown author of the work *Passevent Parisien*

---

[10] A certain Gulielmus Reginaldus (William Rainolds), author of the unfavorable biogra-

*respondant à Pasquin Romain*, published in 1556, calls Bèze "the master of kisses" while hurling all kinds of invective against him and Candida.

In the prefatory letter of his 1569 edition, Bèze enumerates and reacts point by point to his detractors' accusations, all of which they had drawn from the information found in his poetry. In short, he scoffs at their identification of his wife Claudine with Candida, the love interest in his poems, whom he says merely stands as a fictitious literary figure created according to the practice of the ancient poets. Not only is the actual Claudine chaste and exemplary, her life does not match the description of Candida as presented in the poems. He cites as an example the fact that in one poem Candida is described as pregnant, though Claudine had never been pregnant and in fact was unable to bear children. His enemies also claim that he carried on a homosexual relationship with Germain Audebert, as could possibly be understood from *epig.* 90, yet they fail to take into account that the poem could be portraying brotherly love (as is explicitly stated in the similar *eleg.* 4), nor does it shame them, according to Bèze, to ruin the reputation of a man of such integrity and standing, who currently holds a high office in Orléans, by "turning him into an Adonis."[11] Furthermore, Claude de Sainctes uses the third elegy, where Bèze mentions a certain Publia, to accuse him of seducing the wife of a Parisian man.

While Bèze is quick to deny the charges of immorality, he will accept the criticism that he was too loose and careless in the things he wrote during years of youthful indiscretion. But he also points out that, aside from the fact such fictions are empty and unbefitting a Christian, it is a well-established principle of this type of poetry that "while the page is licentious, the poet's life is good" (from Martial 1.4.8), by which he means that such poetry should not be read as autobiography. At any rate, he goes on to say, his critics are only being hypocritical, since they condemn in him what they condone in others. No one in the high schools or pulpits of Paris interprets writers so naively. And even modern poets such as de Ronsard and du Bellay are tolerated, no matter how

---

phy of Calvin entitled *Calvino-Turcismus, id est Calvinisticae perfidiae, cum Mahumetana collatio, et dilucida utriusque sectae confutatio, quatuor libris explicata* (Cologne, 1603), repeats the attacks on Bèze's character made by Schlüsselburg.

[11] An allusion to Schlüsselburg, *Theol. Calvin.*, lib. 2, fols. 92–93: "Certo constat Theodorum Bezam a pueritia imbibisse vatum impudicitiam, et impudentiam, totamque aetatem explendis suis libidinibus et cupiditatibus, ac describendis suis amoribus et ulciscendis suis rivalibus exercuisse, atque in meretricem lenam, et cynedum transformatum esse. De quo item constat et hoc quod obscenissimos versus scripsit ad Germanum Audebertum Aureliae, et eundem tanquam Adonidem a Theodoro Beza factum esse."

much debauchery they describe in their poems. They are even elevated to the stars, so long as they adhere to the papal religion. To drive home the point of his critics' hypocrisy, Bèze added a poem to his 1569 edition (page 21), in which he condemns the character of his enemies by turning the tables on them:

*In cucullatos Bezamastigas*

Quod facit ipsa libens, gens caelo invisa soloque,
    Et raso cunctis vertice nota cohors:
Hoc iuvenis temere Aonidas per devia sectans,
    Lusisse ex aliqua parte quod ausus ego,
Clamat grande nefas, et quae sibi vera patrare
    Fas putat, in reliquis nec simulata probat.
Et merito. siquidem hos demum haec fabrilia fabros,
    Seria seu fuerint, seu simulata, decent.
Immo quae iuvenis ludebam crimina, certe
    Huius contages sordida gentis erant.
Cuius ut effugi afflatum, mutatus eodem
    Tempore, damnavi quae placuere prius.
Ecce igitur, nunc sacra fero mutata prophanis,
    Seria pro fictis, proque iocis lacrymas.
Sed quid si haec etiam carpat gens improba? nempe
    Certa bonis laus est, displicuisse malis.

[*Against the Hooded Beza-bashers*]

Those who belong to a brood hated in heaven and earth, a cohort known to all by their shaven heads, shout that I have committed an outrageous sin because, rashly following the Aonian Muses through their byways in my youth, I dared trifle in the very things my critics do readily and eagerly, and acts they consider appropriate for themselves meet their disapproval when others merely pretend to commit them. And rightly so, since these tools, whether real or imagined, only befit these craftsmen. Yes, the sins I played with in my youth were surely the foul infection of this race. When I fled their influence, and was changed at the same time, I condemned the things that formerly pleased me. Look, then, I have exchanged profane things for sacred things, falsehoods for serious things, jokes for tears. But what if that wicked brood carps at these new poems? Fine, for there is one sure praise for the good, and that is to displease the bad.]

After the publication of the 1569 edition, with its prefatory letter responding to the various charges and its poem against "the hooded brood," Bèze enjoyed only a brief respite from the controversy about his early days in Orléans and Paris. In 1580, a Parisian man by the name of de Bolsec, who made a reputation for himself by attacking the morals of Genevan reformers, published his *Histoire de la Vie, moeurs, doctrine et déportement de Théodore de Bèze, dit le spectable grand ministre de Genève.* He makes the claim that Bèze's Candida was really Claude, the wife of a tailor in Paris, and that the husband himself had consented to Bèze's carrying on a sordid affair with his wife. Although de Bolsec had no real evidence, from then on the story of the tailor's wife is much repeated. Most notably, Florimond de Raemond, in his *Histoire de la Naissance de l'Hérésie* (Paris, 1605), gathers up the calumnies of the past, and adds the witness of a certain Mathieu de Launay, a man who had wavered between Catholicism and the Reformed Church. He gives a lengthy story of intrigue and treachery on the part of Bèze, naming the street on which the tailor lived, and adding all sorts of details about how Bèze tried to cover up the story with payoffs from the Church's coffers. The story is then picked up and repeated numerous times throughout the seventeenth century by Catholic writers, including Louis Maimbourg in his *Histoire du Calvinisme* in 1682 (3:217).[12] Maimbourg vehemently rehearses all the charges of his predecessors, and in particular de Raemond's story:

> C'est pourquoy comme il vit qu'il estoit cité à comparoistre au Parlement pour rendre compte de cette infame poësie, il se cacha pour se garantir du feu, et après avoir vendu son prieuré de Longjumeau, et quelques autres petits bénéfices que son oncle Maistre Nicolas de Beze luy avoit résignez, il s'enfuit à Genève avec sa Candida, c'est-à-dire, une certain Dame Claude, femme d'un tailleur de Paris qu'il avoit débauchée, et qu'il épousa du vivant de son mari, commençant ainsi à Genève sa nouvelle Réforme par un adultère continuel, et par un mariage monstrueux

---

[12] As one would expect, the response from the Protestants to this negative work was swift in coming: Pierre Jurieu, *Histoire du Calvinisme et celle du Papisme mises en parallele, ou Apologie pour les refoormateurs, pour la reformation et pour les reformez, . . . contre un libelle intitulé l'Histoire du Calvinisme par Mr. Maimbourg* (Rotterdam, 1683).

qui le rendoit digne de mort selon toutes les loix divines et humaines.

Such charges of adultery and sodomy persist in many other authors as well (François Garasse,[13] François Eudes de Mezeray,[14] Adrien Baillet,[15] et al.). Cardinal Richelieu, for example, writes in his *La Méthode des Controverses*, (II. x:321–22 [Paris, 1663]), that among his colleagues Bèze had earned the nicknames "Shame of France" and "Sodomite." But Bèze had his defenders too. Mostly, they point to Bèze's own denunciations of his early work as they appear in various prefatory letters. They argue too that the indecent poems are few when compared to the vast number of poems of an excellent quality and content. The indecent poems are explained away as indiscretions of someone who was less than twenty years of age when he wrote them.

One notes certain trends in this *querelle* as reported by Bayle and Machard. The stimulus for it was ecclesiastical politics, so that just as surely as all Bèze's detractors turn out to be Catholic, so also all of Bèze's defenders turn out to be Protestant, with the occasional Lutheran exception. Bayle, *Dictionaire historique et critique*, makes the interesting observation that if Bèze had used his considerable oratorical and literary skills in service of the papal religion against the Protestants, then without a doubt the Protestants would have used his poetry against him, while the Catholics would have defended him.

Such was the spirit of the times. Perhaps of greater interest to the modern reader are the judgments of humanists who did not concern themselves with the moral content of Bèze's poetry. We have noted already that the Italian poet Flaminio proclaimed the highest praise for the 1548 edition. Other poets and humanists, such as Dampierre, Buchanan, and Salmon Macrin, give Bèze high marks at a time when his religious beliefs were not at issue. Du Bellay includes Bèze in a select group of contemporary poets whose expressions of love he hopes will inspire his own:

---

[13] *La doctrine curieuse des beaux esprits de ce temps, ou prétendus tels, contenant plusieurs maximes pernicieuses à la religion* (Paris, 1624).

[14] *Histoire de France*, 3 vols. (Paris, 1667–1668).

[15] *Des Enfants devenus célèbres par leur études ou par leurs écrits, traité historique* (Paris, 1688), and *Jugements des sçavans sur les principaux ouvrages des auteurs*, 9 vols. (Paris, 1685–1686).

*De amoribus poetarum. Ad Gordium*

. . .

Quicquid ipse Marullus et Petrarcha,
Quicquid Beza canit, canit Macrinus,
(ut nostros quoque nominem poetas)
Ronsardus gravis et gravis Thiardus,
Mollis Baifius, mihi (si quis
Probatos locus inter est poetas)
Optarim veteres meos calores . . . (*Delitiae*, i:449)

Jean Girard echoes du Bellay's sentiments in the introduction to the
hendecasyllabic verses of his 1584 edition of poetry, and prays that he
may obtain the fame that Bèze and others have achieved:

Quidquid sit, haec nativa scribendi carminis facultas, et (si Musis
placet) facilitas, eò me circumduxit, ut ipsius exagitandae me
neque pudeat, neque pigeat in tam conspicuis, et fama super ae-
thera notis exemplis. Istuc te, Beza, Buchanane, Stephane, Hospi-
tali, Aurate, à Quercu, et quotquot estis animae in Helicone
caelestes, advoco vos; manus vestras exosculor, aeternùm vivite;
vestrae in senecta scriptiones meum satis fatum probabunt: et in
poesiomastigas, consilium invenerint.

It is clear that Bèze inspired many poets of the day, whether they
pay homage to him or not. Etienne Pasquier nearly plagiarizes Bèze at
times, as I note throughout the commentary, but he decides not to ac-
knowledge him as an influence, for whatever reason. Sainte-Marthe, in
a poem addressed to Bèze's old friend Germain Audebert, mentions
Bèze in passing, along with Macrin, Dorat, and Muret, as the product of
a more polished age:

*Ad Germanum et Nicolaum Audebertos patrem et filium*
Quo te prosequar, Audeberte, versu?
Linguarum o decus, o pater leporum
Secli munditiae politioris,
Quod Bezas tulit et tulit Macrinos,
Auratos tulit et tulit Muretos . . . (*Opera* [1616], 259)

Sainte-Marthe appears to be interested in naming poets with whom
Audebert had some association. From the pen of Montaigne, who was
writing about the same time, we are presented with a somewhat differ-
ent list of poets rating as the best of the sixteenth century. There, in

*Essay* II.17, while recounting men of virtue and ability who lived in his century, he mentions Bèze as belonging to an elite and talented group: "It seems to me that poetry too has flourished in our century. We have a wealth of good craftsmen in that trade: Dorat, Bèze, Buchanan, L'Hôpital, Montdoré, Turnebus." This is a very small list for Bèze's name to appear in. One wonders about Marot, Muret, and Salmon Macrin, to name a few. To be sure, Julius Caesar Scaliger does not include Bèze among the chief modern poets in his *Poëtices* (1594),[16] but that may be because he died eleven years before the appearance of Bèze's second edition. His son Joseph, however, knew Bèze in his latter years and at his death was one of those who eulogized him in the *Epicedia* of 1606 (see Appendix 2). While the hyperbole innate to the genre is everywhere apparent in Scaliger's epitaph, and given that he is more interested in Bèze as a theologian than as a poet, it is nevertheless worth noting that in general terms he thought highly of Bèze's skills as a writer (esp. lines 103ff.). Furthermore, the many appearances of Bèze's poetry in the anthologies and in the imitations of English writers, as noted throughout the commentary here, indicate that he was still being read and admired long after his death. At any rate, there seems to have been a fairly uniform agreement among those who were not motivated by ecclesiastical controversy that Bèze ranked high among the French Neo-Latinists. One can only speculate how his talents might have developed had he continued in the vein in which he had begun.

Whether Bèze's poetry is still worth reading today or not is left up to the reader to decide. Nowadays, sadly, the study of Latin is not cultivated by Renaissance scholars as widely as it should be, and that alone may account for the relative neglect that Bèze's poetry has suffered in the last hundred years or so. Some of what he wrote will seem at first glance to be bound up in a particular time and space, and therefore not immediately relevant to this age. Yet, as we are reminded by the quote that begins this very introduction, this is not so much a book about Bèze and his feelings or aspirations, or even about his friends, although they are often named; rather, it is a book about the one constant that allows such a collection of poetry to span the centuries and speak to us even today, and that is human nature. Here, in this dusty, long-neglected *libellus* of poems, one discovers the familiar and timeless "pageant of people's lives" as seen by the observant eye and keen mind of one of the most remarkable figures of the sixteenth century.

---

[16] See I. Reineke, *Julius Caesar Scaligers Kritik der neulateinischen Dichter* (Munich, 1988).

# A View from the Palatine:

## The *Iuvenilia* of Théodore de Bèze

Theodorus Beza Vezelius
Melchiori Volmario Helvetio, praeceptori suo
S(alutem) P(lurimam) D(icit)

Etsi totum hoc scribendi genus a multis et gravibus et eruditis homi-
nibus reprehendi solet, numquam tamen hoc a me potui impetrare,
ut in eo excolendo operam aliquam non ponerem, sive ita cogente animi
impetu quodam, sive quod hanc exercendi styli speciem numquam vel
ineptam vel inutilem esse putavi. Ad haec accessit gravissima iudicii tui
authoritas, quae quidem una tantum apud me potuit, ut simulatque ex iis
litteris quas ad me Tubinga dedisti, haec nostra intellexi tibi et Joachimo
Camerario mirum in modum probari, nihil habuerim antiquius, quam
ut ea in unum velut corpus congererem, ratus nimirum in eo me a sanis
hominibus reprehensum non iri, in quo vestram sententiam atque suasio-
nem secutus essem. Adhibitis igitur in consilium amicis, quorum et inge-
nium et iudicium in huiusmodi rebus singulare saepe iam ante expertus
eram, decerptisque demum his paucis versibus, qui et minus inculti et
paulo velut maturiores visi sunt, hunc tandem libellum confeci. Quem
ego quidem etsi ab initio nemini dedicare constitueram, quod levius
quiddam esse videretur quam ut ullius vel infimi hominis nomen prae-
ferre deberet, mutato tamen consilio, tibi commendare non dubitavi,
partim ut eius rei patrocinium suscipias, cuius tu mihi auctor fuisti prae-
cipuus, partim vero ut, cum uni tibi plus debeam quam caeteris om-
nibus, meam erga te observantiam aut potius pietatem hoc munusculo
testarer. Nec enim deerant permulti, quos vel dignitatis gratia, vel affi-
nitatis, vel amicitiae, possem deligere, quibus etiam hoc qualecumque
officii genus non ingratum videri potuisse scio. Sed ii si cognoscent quae
tua in me constent beneficia, non dubito quin Volmarium quamvis ex-

Théodore de Bèze of Vezelay
sends fondest greetings to his teacher
Melchior Wolmar of Switzerland:

Although it is typical for many important and learned people to find fault with this kind of writing, I was never able to help giving some attention to cultivating it, whether because of some inner drive to do so, or because I never considered this sort of stylistic exercise to be foolish or unproductive. Added to these motivations was the weighty authority of your judgment. It held such great sway over me that, as soon as I realized from those letters that you sent to me from Tubingen that you and Joachim Camerarius surprisingly approved of my poetry, I wanted nothing more than to gather them together, as it were, into one corpus, certain, as I was, that by following your opinion and your encouragement I would not have to fear reproach from reasonable people. Therefore, after consulting friends, on whose exceptional talents and judgment in matters of this sort I have often depended before, and then excerpting the few verses that you see here, which seemed less crude and, as it were, more mature, I produced this little book. Although at first I determined not to dedicate it to anyone, because it seemed to be too frivolous to attach the name of even a lowly man to it, nevertheless I changed my mind, and was happy to dedicate it to you. I did so partly that you might take up the defense of that which you especially inspired, and partly so that I might bear witness to my respect, or rather, devotion toward you by this small token, since I owe more to you than to anyone else. For there was no shortage of people whom I could have chosen, based on their office, or relation, or friendship to me, and to them this kind of a homage, be as it may, would not be displeasing. But I am certain that those who are aware of your constant kindness to me would agree that the honor ought to go to you, Wol-

ternum hominem, sibi praeferri debuisse fateantur. Quod si qui in nobis vel artem requisierint vel naturam, per me id illis vero facere licebit, dummodo id omne quod in me fuit, praestitisse me intelligant, nec tamen ab ingenio vel diligentia tam parum posse, ut istis longe maiora, et studioso homine digniora non audeam polliceri. Vale. Lutetiae, VII. Cal(endas) Jul(ias) qui dies est mihi natalis.

mar, although you are a foreigner. Yet if any will look for skill or natural talent in me, I will allow them to do so, provided that they understand that I have offered all that was in me, and yet that I am not so limited in respect to my talent and diligence, that I do not dare to promise to them greater things by far, and things more worthy of an erudite person. Farewell, from Paris, on 25 June, my birthday.

## 1.

*Descriptio P. Decii Patris, qui se Cos. devovit pro legionum salute, bello cum Latinis ad Veserim gesto: De quo Livius lib. 8. ab urbe cond.*

Iam Romana acies verti, iam cedere laevo
Coeperat in cornu virtus Romana, nec ullum
Subsidium est, retroque omnis spes lapsa referri;
Cum geminas Decius tendens ad sidera palmas,
Quo ruitis? dixit, quo virtus prisca recessit?                    5
Unde fuga haec? unde iste timor? vos cedere notis
Hostibus, et toties victis dare terga Latinis?
At moveat iurata fides, sanctique senatus
Imperium, moveantque foci, moveantque penates.
    Dixerat. interea premit undique fervidus hostis:             10
Deserta fugiunt trepidi statione Quirites.
Ille autem intrepidus, quos consul sistere voce
Non potui, dixit, revocabo morte: sacrati
Me dudum hoc vates monuere, iecurque recisum.
Ergo age sacrorum o custos concepta profare                      15
Carmina, Romanis consul sit victima, nostro
Sanguine quaeratur victoria, sanguine nostro

---

3–4  Subsidium est: patriae Decius cum totus amore | Fervidus et geminas tendens
      ad sidera palmas *1569, 1576, 1597*
10–11 Dixerat, interea victor fugientibus hostis | Imminet, et trepidi nutant hinc
      inde Quirites *1569, 1576, 1597*

# SYLVAE

### 1.

*A Description of P. Decius Pater, Who Offered Himself Up As a Sacrifice for the Safety of His Legions During a Battle with the Latins at Veseris. Livy Tells the Story in the Eighth Book of his History.*

The Roman line had begun to falter, and the soldiers on the left wing began to lose their courage; no reinforcements come to their aid, and all hope dissolves into retreat. At that moment Decius, extending his open hands to the stars, exclaimed, "Whither are you rushing, whither has your ancient virtue gone? Why this flight? Whence comes this fear? Are you yielding to enemies that we know well, and retreating from the Latins whom we've conquered so many times? But let the trusty oath you swore inspire you, as well as the power of the holy senate, your hearths, and the household gods."

(10) Thus he spoke. Meanwhile the raging enemy presses the attack on every side, while the fearful Quirites flee from their deserted posts. But fearlessly he said, "Those whom I, the consul, could not restrain with my words, I will rally with my death. Recently the sacred priests warned me about this, and so too the inspection of the entrails. Therefore, come, guardian of the holy rites; proclaim the prophetic songs you have received, let the consul be a sacrifice for the Romans, let victory be

Placentur saevi Manes, placetur Erynnis.
Mox igitur praetextam armis imponere iussus,
Velatusque caput, mentoque innixus, et imis                            20
Subiecto pedibus telo, imperterritus heros
His se devovit verbis praefante ministro:
    Iane, et tu custos Capitoli Iuppiter, audi,
Et gemini Romae auctores, Mavorsque, Quirineque,
Et reliqua in nostris notissima numina fastis;                         25
Vos etiam, o Manes! Decium haec audite precantem:
Si qua premit patriam invidia, et nunc vincere Romam
Crimina si qua vetant, tandem deponite, quaeso,
Invidiam o divi! Decius luat omnia solus;
Servetur patria incolumis, pulsoque Latino,                            30
Sublimes ducant Romani ex hoste triumphos.
Interea, collega, aciem, patriamque tuere:
Ominor ecce fugam moriens mortemque Latinis.
    Desierat, faciem lux protinus occupat ingens,
Qualis post noctis tenebras cum Thetide Phoebus                        35
Deserta illustrat splendenti lumine terras:
Talis hic insiliens in equum sublimis, habenas
Laxat, et in medios volat imperterritus hostes.
Illum fulgentemque armis, cinctuque Gabino
Ipse admiratur Veseris, miratur, et ipse                               40
Iuppiter, et laevum tonat: audito omine laeti
Prospiciunt Romani omnes, oculisque sequuntur,
Atque hominem esse negant Decium; iam terga Latinus
Vertit, et adventu unius mutata repente
Sors omnis, redeunt acies, animisque receptis                          45
Instant victori victi, tandemque feroces
Romanus pellit, Decio moriente, Latinos.

---

21    fortissimus *1597*

27    Nemesis *pro* invidia *1569, 1576, 1597*

28    *a* tandem *usque ad* divi *om. in 1569, 1576, 1597 edd.*

33    Ominor ecce fugam moriens mortemque Latinis *1569, 1576, 1597* Indubiam
        ipse fero mortemque fugamque Latinis *1548, 1713, 1779*

35–37 Qualis post noctis tenebras fulgore corusco | Emicat et totum illustrat sol
        aureus orbem | Talis equo insiliens Decius sublimis habenas *1569, 1576, 1597*

43    Consulis attoniti facto. Iam terga Latinus *1569, 1576, 1597*

46    victus *1597: post 46 add. in 1597 ed. hi versus duo:* Vana superstitio, quanto
        nos iustius omnes | Vere deus, tibi nos et nostra sacrabimus uni

won from my blood; my blood will placate the fierce Manes and the Furies."

Directly the priest orders him to place a bordered toga on his arms, (20) and with veiled head, resting on his chin, with arrows cast beneath his feet, the undaunted hero consecrates himself with these words as the priest utters a prayer: "Janus, and you, Jupiter, guardian of the Capitol! Listen! And you, twin founders of Rome, Mars and Quirinus, and the rest of the divinities honored at our festivals; you too, Manes! Hear Decius's prayer. If some resentment is causing you to crush our country, and if any crimes keep Rome from prevailing, I beg you, put aside your grudge, gods! Let Decius alone atone for everything. (30) Keep our country safe from harm, and let the Romans repel the Latins and lead glorious triumphs at their expense. Meanwhile, watch over my colleague, the army, and the country. By dying, I myself portend flight and death to the Latins."

He ceased praying, and immediately an extraordinary glow spread across his face, like when Phoebus leaves Thetis after the darkness of night and fills the earth with his radiant light. Ennobled in this way he leaps upon his horse, loosens the reins, and flies undaunted into the midst of the enemy. (40) Veseris herself admires him, glistening in his arms and his girded toga; even Jupiter himself admires him, and thunders approval on the left. The Romans hear the omen and rejoice as they all turn their gaze and follow him with their eyes; they imagine Decius is somehow superhuman.

At that point the Latins turn tail and run, and with the arrival of one man suddenly Rome's fortune is completely changed. The battle line reforms, and the conquered recoup their courage and press hard on the victor, until finally the Roman army repels the ferocious Latins, as Decius lies dying.

## 2.

*Mors Ciceronis. Ex T. Livii Historiarum libro CXX et Vitis Plutarchi, et Valer. Max.*

Ergo ut ventorum rabiem, pelagique furorem
Indomitum aspexit, fatis heu! poscitur, inquit,
Poscitur infelix Cicero: convertite vela,
Et me vicinae moriturum reddite ripae;
Scilicet has grates gladiis erepta tuorum                                5
Patria persolves? moriar, sic numina Divum,
Sic voluere Dei, servata ut Consul in urbe
Tullius intereat. Nec plura effatus, ab imo
Corde trahens gemitus memoratae ad nomina Romae,
Imbre oculos, lachrymisque genas implevit obortis.                      10
At licet assiduis exercita turba periclis,
Inviti lachrymas nautae tenuere diuque
Obnixi saevos pelagi transcendere fluctus,
Omnia laxarunt iratis carbasa ventis,
Et tandem incolumem statuerunt littore proram.                          15
    Descendit moestus Cicero, multoque labore
Membra trahit consecta senex; simul undique magna
Circumstabat herum servorum turba, periclis
Nec nimium stupefacta suis, nec tempore duro
Pollicitam fractura fidem: pars apparat enses,                          20
Pars domino assistit, caecaque ambage viarum
Lecticae impositum ducunt, si fallere saevos
Antoni possint gladio; turbaeque sequentis
Evitare minas. Sic ibat Tullius ille,

---

2    Tullius indomitum aspexit, convertite vela *1569, 1576*

3-13  (Dixit) et huic tandem moriturum reddite ripae. | Scilicet has grates gladiis
      erepta tuorum | Patria persolves? Nec plura effatus, ab imo | Corde trahens
      gemitus memoratae ad nomina Romae, | Imbre oculos lacrymisque genas
      implevit abortis. | Ac licet assiduis exercita turba periclis, | Inviti lacrymas
      nautae tenuere, diuque | Obnixi frustra saevos transcendere fluctus *1569,
      1576, 1597*

23-24 *hi versus reduc. ad hoc unum:* Carnificum possint gladios. Sic Tullius ibat
      *1569, 1576, 1597*

## 2.

*The Death of Cicero, Taken from Livy 120 and the Lives of Plutarch
and Valerius Maximus*

As he saw the raging of the winds, the uncontrollable fury of the sea,
Cicero said, "Alas! I am ill-starred; the Fates are after me; they demand
the death of hapless Cicero. Change the sails, and return me to the near-
est bank so I can die. Rome, will you no longer be grateful now that
you have escaped civil unrest? I will die; the gods resolve and decree the
consul Tullius to die in the city he saved."

He said nothing more, but drawing a deep sigh from the depths of
his heart at the thought of Rome, (10) he filled his eyes and cheeks with
a torrent of tears. Although the sailors were experienced in constant
perils, they held back their tears reluctantly, and after struggling against
the violent waves for a long time, they at length loosened all the sails to
the irate winds, and finally set their prow unharmed on the shore.
Cicero disembarked gloomily, and with much effort the old man
dragged along his weary limbs. Immediately a great multitude of slaves
surrounded their master on every side, not confounded by the risks they
ran for themselves, (20) and not about to break their promises they had
pledged just because times were hard. Some obtained swords, while
others attended their master, putting him on a litter and carrying him
off by a secret and circuitous route, in the hope that they could avoid
the cruel swords of Antony and the threats of the pursuing mob.

Tullius ille togae princeps, magnique Senatus,                           25
Cum procul adventare viros, inimicaque signa
Conspicit, et stricto mortem procul ense minantem
Poppilium, cuius quondam servaverat ipse
Fortunas vitamque rei, cum libera Roma
Olim illum audiret, mirareturque tonantem.                               30
Iam quoque saevus adest, et poscit Herennius hostem.
Quid faciat? num forte manus protendat inermes,
Aut mercede petat veniam? num flectere verbis
Defensi quondam conetur militis iras?
Haec aetas virtusque vetant, et pectore in alto                          35
Fixus amor patriae, Romaeque cadentis imago.
Vertite, ait, currus, plenis curratur habenis
Immeritam in mortem: me pridem nuntia Phoebi
Poscit avis, caeloque novum coniungere civem
Iuppiter exoptat. Bruti Cassique beatae                                  40
Vivite vos animae; quod si non omnia nobis
Fata nocent, forsan nec nos moriemur inulti.
Iam vixi mihi, Roma, fatis, me vita vereri
Acta vetat nigrae damnosa oblivia mortis.
Occidite, at noscent venturi cuncta nepotes,                             45
Aeternamque dabunt morienti haec funera vitam.
Immo (aut fallor ego, et frustra tibi, Roma, creatus
Augur eram quondam) non semper amica favebit,
Antoni, Fortuna tibi, civesque peremptos
Tempus erit victrix a te quo Roma reposcat.                              50
Me iuvet interea speratum invisere caelum.
Desierat, iugulumque parans, immota tenebat
Ora senex; illum properantem in fata nec ipsi
Aspiciunt equites laeti, positoque furore,
Ut nudum videre caput canamque senectam,                                 55

---

31    poscitque *1569, 1576*
35    Hoc virtus aetasque *1569, 1576, 1597*
38-40 me . . . exoptat *om. in 1569, 1576, 1597*
45    Occide *1569, 1576, 1597*
51    meliores quaerere sedes *1569, 1576, 1597*
55    Ut glabrum *1569, 1576, 1597*

So went Tullius, the first man of Rome and of the senate, when from afar he could see men were coming and holding the hostile standards, as well as Popillius threatening death from a distance with his blade drawn. This very man's fortunes and life Cicero had saved when he had been charged with a crime, back when Rome was free (30) and listened to Cicero, and marveled at his thundering rhetoric. Herennius is there also, mad, and looking for the enemy. What should he do? Should he maybe stretch out his hands unarmed? Or should he offer money in exchange for mercy? Should he try to appease the anger of the soldier he once defended? His age and his virtue refuse, as do the love of his country that is fixed deep in his heart, and the image of falling Rome. "Turn about the wagons," he said, "let's go full speed ahead into this undeserved death. Apollo's messenger bird bids me come, (40) and Jupiter is expecting a new citizen to join him in heaven. I want you, Cassius and Brutus, to live; for if not all the Fates are against me, then perhaps I will not die unavenged. My beloved Rome, I have already run the destined course of my life, and the very way I have lived forbids me to fear the cursed oblivion of black death. Kill me, but my descendants to come will know what happened, so that this murder will give eternal life to me even as I die. No (else I am mistaken, and it was all for naught that I was once made an augur for you, Rome), Fortune will not favor you forever, Antony, (50) and the time will come when Rome will demand back from you the citizens whom you have killed. In the meantime, I will find peace in visiting long-awaited heaven."

He stopped speaking, and readying his neck, the old man held his face motionless. The knights themselves were not happy to see him

Vix tandem inviti lachrymas tenuere cadentes,
Et pene e manibus gladii cecidere cruentis.
Unus torva gerens truculentus Herennius ora,
Degeneres, quid statis? ait. simul ense superbo
Colla secat, nec adhuc satiatur caede: scelestum      60
Adiunxisse scelus sceleri iuvat, ergo disertis
Ausas Antoni vitam signare tabellis
Caedit et ipse manus. morientem vidit ab alto
Invitus caelo Phoebus, piceaque refertur
Nube caput texisse diu. flevere cadentem,      65
Et flebunt Latiae aeternum Graiaeque Camoenae.
Flexanimis vero Pitho (mirabile dictu)
Sueta illi quondam tum res tum verba loquenti
Suggerere, et suavi conspergere nectare linguam
Ut patuit iugulus, fugiente aufugit amico,      70
Et terras, eheu! nunquam reditura, reliquit.
Poppilius volat interea, truncoque relicto,
Antoni portat saevis spectacula mensis.

---

57    Ipsique *1569, 1576, 1597*
58    ferox torquens *1569, 1576, 1597*
60    satiatum *1597*
61    iuvat sceleri scelus *1597*
70    moriente *1597*

rushing headlong into his fate, and when they saw his head bare, and his hoary old age, they set aside their anger, and could barely hold back their tears; their swords nearly fell from their bloody hands. Only Herennius, who was vicious and vile, with a wild expression on his face, said, "Cowards, why are you just standing there?" And immediately (60) he strikes his neck with his arrogant blade, but still he is not satisfied with murder alone. He is happy to heap one wicked crime upon another; therefore, he also cuts off the hands which in eloquent writing dared to expose the life of Antony.

From on high Phoebus Apollo was displeased to see him dying, and for the longest time kept his head buried in a pitch-black cloud. The Latin and Greek Muses wept for him when he fell, and continued weeping for him forever after. But Persuasion (a marvel to tell), who used to supply him as he was speaking with both the ideas and the words, and to sprinkle his tongue with sweet nectar (70) whenever he opened his mouth, fled when her friend fled, and—alas!—abandoned the earth never to return. Popillius meanwhile flies to Antony, leaving the trunk of the corpse behind, and carried the spectacles to the sadistic tables of Antony.

## 3.

### *Natalia Domini*

Noctem alius laudet, misero quae munus amanti
Optatum attulerit, facilemque ad vota puellam
Praebuerit, veteris fecunda incendia flammae;
Ceteraque obscenis olim cantata poetis.
At vos, pars equidem caeli non infima, vates,	5
Nec divinum animum ad turpes convertite curas,
Nec calamos adeo infami exercete labore.
Intactas Helicona ferunt habitare puellas,
Inque alias ardens Musis est castus Apollo,
Innupta est Pallas: vestris quae numina sacris	10
Sola placent. procul ergo Venus, procul esse scelesti
Deliciae pueri, castis tu casta Camoenis
Materies, O Nox! esto, quae Virginis olim
Vidisti in sacros aperiri viscera partus,
Viscera quae caeli tempestatumque potentem	15
Gestavere Deum, tandemque illaesa dedere
Humanis cernendum oculis: tu conscia partus
Prima novi, tu nascentis primordia lucis,
Luce prior nox vidisti, te caeca vetustas
Ah nimis! immerito caecamque atramque vocabat,	20
Illius primos solis quae senseris ortus,
Ipse accepta refert clarus cui lumina Titan,
Et quaecunque micant splendenti sidera caelo.
Tu teneri primos vagitus prima puelli,
Tu primos caeli plausus, tu gaudia mundi	25

1-4	Obscaenas alius noctes turpesque tenebras | Infami celebret captans ex cri-
mine nomen | At tu casta meis potius sacrata camoenis | Materies ... *1569*
1-14	*in loco illorum versorum 1597 habet hos:* Pervigiles alius longa in convivia
noctes, | Gaudia consumptas aut in furtiva tenebras, | Infami celebret cap-
tans ex carmine nomen: | At tu sancta meis potius sacrata camoenis | Mate-
ries, o nox, esto, qua virginis olim | Clausa licet sacro patuerunt viscera partu;
18	*ad init.* Una *1597*
19	*ad finem* dignissima lucis *1597*
20	certe *pro* nimis *1569, 1576* quae caeca et nigra vocatur *1597*
21	senserit 1597

## 3.

*Birth of the Lord*

Let another poet praise the night, which brought a long-awaited gift to a poor lover, and offered an easy girl in exchange for vows, ever-renewing passions of an old flame, and the other things once sung by secular poets. But you, poet-priests, who surely belong in not the lowest regions of heaven, do not turn your divine mind to unseemly cares, do not busy your pens with such scandalous toils. They say that virgin girls live on Helicon, and although Apollo burns for other girls, he is chaste with the Muses. (10) Athena is unwed. These divinities alone are pleasing to your sacred songs.

Let Venus stay away, along with that boy who delights in mischief. Night, be the chaste subject for the chaste Muses! You once saw the womb of a Virgin issue forth a sacred child, a womb which bore a God who has power over the skies and the tempests, and finally without blemish offered him for all to see.

You, Night, were aware of the new birth first, and even before daybreak you saw the first glimmers of the emerging light. The blind ancients (20) were very wrong to call you dark and gloomy, since it was you who perceived the first risings of the new sun. To you the famous Titan himself returns the lights he has received, as do all the stars that sparkle in the bright sky.

Audisti, nox o foelix! cum laeta volantum
Ad Domini cunas resonarent agmina fratrum,
Et Domino totus nascenti applauderet orbis.
Tu vili impositum feno, stabuloque iacentem
Es mirata simul, simul es miserata puellum:                    30
Tu quoque pastorum pietatem, et nescia fraudis
Pectora mirata es, cum Tityrus inde relictis
Accurens gregibus, Christi natalia laetus
Viseret, hinc caderet Damoetas, surgeret Aegon,
Dum caeli monitis et clara voce Deorum                        35
Attoniti, properant nascentem invisere regem.
Quid castae matris curas, immixtaque curis
Gaudia commemorem? dum tanto pignore, caeli
Consortem agnoscit sese, natumque tuetur
Ante pedes, nasci quem vix dum senserat ipsa                  40
Parturiens pariensque simul, virgoque parensque.
     At vos interea spatiosa per atria reges,
Aut medios inter lusus turpique luparum
Immixti turbae infelix traducitis aevum,
Aut saturo efflatis pigros e pectore somnos,                  45
Progenies indigna polo, quibus ipse recusat
Committi Dominus nascens, et natus abhorret.
Felices tenebrae, quantumvis clara diei
Lux collata quibus, non lux, sed opaca videtur
Nox potius. nam certa diem sua tempora claudunt,              50
Et vicibus certis Phoebus surgitque caditque.
Est quoque cum ingratae vicinus ab orbe sororis
Sic premitur, nigra ut tectus ferrugine vultum
Quod reliquis praebet, lumenque iubarque requirat.
At vobis tenebrae qui praebet lumina Titan                    55
Phosphorus ipse sibi est, et non finitur horizon.

---

35   claro numinis ore *1569, 1576, 1597*
36   puerum properant invisere regem *1569, 1576, 1597*
40   In gremio *1597*
43   turpesque *1569, 1576*
44   Forte greges miseri *1569, 1576, 1597*
46–47 Gens invisa Deo, magni quam rector olympi | Et quondam sprevit nascens
      *1569, 1576, 1597*

O blessed Night, you heard the first wailings of the tender little child, the first claps from the sky, the rejoicing of the world, when happy throngs of angels were resounding over the cradle of the Lord, and the whole world extolled the Lord's birth.

(30) You both marveled at and pitied the little boy placed on the simple straw, lying in a stable. You also marveled at the piety of the shepherds, whose hearts knew no deception, when Tityrus rushed from over there, leaving behind his flocks, and happily came to see the birth of Christ; Damoetas was falling prostrate over here, Aegon was standing above, while the heavens, astonished by the admonitions and clear voice of the gods, hastened to look upon the king being born. What shall I relate of the cares of the chaste mother, the joys mixed with care? While with such a great pledge, she recognizes that she is the consort of heaven, and stares at the child (40) before her feet. While even she had scarcely yet felt his birth, laboring and giving birth together, virgin and parent.

But meanwhile you kings lead your unhappy lives in your spacious halls, playing games or mingling with disgraceful prostitutes, or snoring loudly from your sated breasts: You are offspring unworthy of heaven. The Lord himself refuses to be entrusted to you at his birth, and even as a baby abhors you.

Happy darkness, to whom howsoever much the clear light of day is compared, seems not light, (50) but rather murky night, for the day ends when evening comes, and Phoebus rises and falls in predictable ways. And also when he is near his ungrateful sister, he is eclipsed when her path crosses his, in such a way that, with his face covered with black dusk, he seeks the light and rays which he offers to others. But to you, darkness, this Titan offers his lights, you have Phosphorus the morning star, and an unlimited horizon. But why, Night, did the Fathers place

Sed cur postremo patres te mense locarunt,
O Nox, quam nostrae testem appellare salutis
Et decet et fas est? cur non haec inchoat annum
Nox, quae felicis spem nobis reddidit aevi?　　　　　　　60
Scilicet exactos quae nox finire labores
Spondet, et aeternae promittit munera pacis:
Iure etiam exactum finire haec debuit annum.
Adde quod hoc primum redituri tempore Phoebi
Spem capimus, ductore capro; iure ergo revectos　　　　65
Uno mense duos olim memorare vetustas
Instituit soles! iure o nox fausta! piorum
Relligione patrum, toto vigilaris in orbe,
Applausuque sonas, sed non tamen orgia qualem
Edere consuerant, ebrio cum sacra Lyaeo　　　　　　　70
Insanae facerent matres, atque aera sonarent
Semiviri quondam ad Cybeles altaria Galli:
Sed qualem decet esse virum, quis pectore in alto
Mens habitat, caeli patrium quae spirat amorem.
Ipse equidem tibi sacra feram, nox sacra, quotannis,　　　75
Solennesque preces addam, o nox optima! nostris
Materies nimium felix inventa Camoenis.

---

58　　　quam nostrae testem appellare salutis *1569, 1576, 1597* cui primae acceptam
　　　　refferre salutem *1548, 1580, 1779*
69　　　quatere *pro* tamen *1597*
70　　　molli *pro* ebrio *1569, 1576* Consuerant madido fierent cum sacra Lyaeo *1597*
71-72 *om. in 1597*

you in the last month, whom it was right and meet to call the witness of our salvation? Why does this Night not begin the year, (60) who granted us the hope of a happy life? I think because Night, who promises to make an end to these works, and promises the rewards of eternal peace, rightly ought to end the year too. Furthermore, it's during this time that we take hope in the return of Phoebus, with Capricorn leading the way. Therefore the ancients rightly decided to commemorate two suns returning in one month! Rightly, lucky Night, you are awake with the religion of our pious fathers in the whole world, and you resound with clapping, (70) but not the orgiastic kind that crazed matrons performed to Lyaeus, or not in the way the half-men Galli once beat bronze instruments before the altars of Cybele, but as befits men of a high mind that breathes the paternal love of heaven. I myself will honor you, sacred Night, every year, and I will add festivals and prayers, best Night, most blessed subject found for our Muses.

## 4.

*Praefatio Poetica in Davidicos Psalmos, quos poenitentiales vocant*

Forte pererratis caelo terraque marique,
Ales amor sacras Iudaea callidus urbes
Visebat, pharetraque minax, flammataque gestans
Tela manu: iamque hospitium, sedemque petebat
Venturae nocti: dumque acres undique versat                    5
Saepe oculos, dubitatque etiam qua sede moretur,
Tandem ad Bersabes convertit lumina formam,
Et mox tam raras mortali in corpore dotes
Miratus, viridesque oculos, frontemque patentem,
Purpureasque genas, pulchri et discrimina nasi,               10
Os roseum, et flavos per eburnea colla capillos,
Marmoreumque sinum, porrectaque brachia longe,
Et teretes digitos: haec dum notat omnia, fertur
Attonitus tacita secum sic voce loquutus:
Quid vos caelorum formam, celeresque rotatus,                 15
Sydereosque ignes adeo, matrisque Diones
Laudatis, Superi, vultus! cum barbara caeli
Luminibus Virgo officiat: me ludere in istis
Fas oculis: iuvet hinc acres vibrare sagittas:
Haec est digna deo sedes; procul ergo pharetrae              20
Este graves: sint arma procul; namque ista ministrant
Lumina tela mihi, lunataque porrigit arcum
Umbra supercilii; hinc regum Mavortia corda,
Fallor ego, aut infans olim vicisse Cupido
Credar, et haec varias spargetur fama per urbes.             25
    Dixerat: et subito pharetraque arcuque relictis
Aereum sumit corpus (mirabile dictu!)

---

*Totum poema post primum versum in posterioribus edd. magnopere commutatum est;*
    *v. notas infra*
9–19  viridesque ... oculis *om. in 1597*
19    (inquit) *pro* acres *1569, 1576, 1597*
20 *om. in 1569, 1576, 1597*
21    Este procul tela et pharetrae *1569, 1576, 1597*
26    Sic ait *1569, 1576, 1597*
27    indutus *1569, 1576, 1597*

### 4.

*A Poetic Preface to David's Penitential Psalms*

By chance winged Cupid, that mischievous boy, was roaming through the sky, over land, and over sea, when he paid a visit to the sacred cities of Judea, menacing them with his quiver as he carried his blazing darts in his hand. At some point, he was seeking hospitable lodging for the coming night. Now as he flashes his keen eyes here and there, he's not sure where he'll stay. Finally, he casts his eyes on the beautiful figure of Bathsheba. At once he marvels at such rare endowments in a human body: the green eyes, broad forehead, (10) blushing cheeks, a beautifully shaped nose, red lips, and tawny hair along an ivory neck, flat belly, long slender arms, and delicate fingers. While he observes all these things, he whispers in astonishment, "Why, gods above, do you praise the beauty of the heavens, the swift rotations, the starry fires, the features of mother Hera? When the wild virgin obstructs the lights of heaven, I should play in those eyes; from there I'll have fun brandishing sharp arrows. (20) This is an abode worthy of a god. Therefore, let the heavy quiver be far off, away with the arms. For these eyes provide weapons for me, and the curved shadow of her brow stretches my bow. And if I am not mistaken, people will know that from there I, Cupid, a mere boy, conquered once the martial hearts of kings, and this report will spread through cities far and wide."

Thus he spoke, and quickly leaving his bow and arrow behind, he assumed an ethereal body (a marvel to tell), so unusual to human eyes that

Corporeis tam rarum oculis, ut cernere nemo
Mortalis possit, quantumvis cernat acute.
Sic indutus amor formosam hinc inde puellam                    30
Observat tacitus furtim, tandemque repertis
Sese oculis infert, claroque in lumine condit.
    Illa deum sensit venientem, et laeta recepto
Hospite, nil praeter Veneris iam cogitat artes:
Omnibus arridet pulchrae sibi conscia formae:                 35
Nunc sinit impexos extrema in fronte capillos
Ludere, nunc varia discriminat arte vagantes:
Iam celare sinum simulat, mammasque coercet,
Et super obiectat tenuis velamina telae:
Iam cunctas ostentat opes, colloque superba                   40
Nudato, pulchra mentitur imagine divam.
Interdum excultis illi qui stabat in hortis
Marmoreo insignis labro, se fontis in unda
Nuda lavat, celeresque oculis iaculatur amores.
    Hanc igitur casu, vitreo cum fonte lavaret,              45
Iudaeis David qui tum regnabat in oris
Aspexit, vir nec cuiquam pietate secundus,
Nec quoquam inferior vates, seu fundere dulce
Ore melos, digitis seu tangere plectra iuvaret.
Quid non audet amor? Regis doctique piique                    50
Protinus excusso violavit lumina telo.
At pavidus tanto caligat lumine David,
Ecce irrumpit amor dominus, sparsisque veneno
Sensibus, humenti iam calfacit offa calore,
Et victor tandem infligit sub pectore vulnus:                 55
Mens quoque victa labat, flammisque oppressa fatiscit.
Ipse sui oblitus caecas sub pectore flammas
David alit, nec iam studiis incumbit honestis,
Nec sibi iam quaerit sese quibus artibus ipse

---

28-29 *om. in 1569, 1576, 1597*
30    Callidus affectans formosam hinc inde puellam *1569, 1576, 1597*
36    extrema crispantes fronte capillos *1569, 1576*
40-123 *text. in 1597 multo differtur*
43    atque perennibus undis *1569, 1576*
44    fonte lavat *1569, 1576*
46-123 text. in *1569, 1576 multo differtur*

no mortal could see it, even while looking intently at it. (30) Clothed in this way, Cupid quietly and stealthily watches the lovely girl strolling about, and, finally, he brings himself into those eyes that he discovered, and buries himself in pure light.

She sensed the god coming and, happy to receive the guest, now thinks on nothing but the arts of Venus. Aware of her beautiful figure she smiles at it all; now she permits her uncombed locks of hair to play down over her forehead, then she tries on various hairstyles. Now she pretends to hide her belly, she pushes up her breasts, and above she throws a finely woven veil. (40) Now she shows off all the wealth of her beauty; proud of her bare neck, she feigns a goddess with her lovely image. Sometimes she bathes her nude body in the water of a fountain, a show for the one standing in his well-kept garden with the marble trim, and her eyes dart flirtatiously at him. So David, who was ruling over those Judean regions, caught sight of her by chance as she bathed in her clear fountain; he was a man second to none in piety, the best of all poets, who poured forth honey from his sweet mouth as he strummed the lyre with his fingers.

(50) What does Cupid not venture? Straightaway and without his weapons he struck the eyes of the skilled and pious king. David, trembling, is bedazzled by such a great light—behold, Lord Cupid bursts in—and the king's senses are sprinkled with the poison, causing him to blaze with a sweaty heat down to his bones. And the victor at length inflicts a wound in his heart. The mind also falls conquered, and, overcome by flames, it falters. David, no longer aware of who he is, nourishes the hidden flames in his heart. No longer does he concentrate on noble pur-

Asserat: hoc unum noctuque dieque labore                          60
Sollicitus volvit magno, qua callidus arte
Efficiat, forma ut tandem potiatur amata.
Quid faciat? blandis adiungit munera dictis.
Paret Bersabe, tantoque authore peracta
Culpa placet: favet inceptis Fortuna nefandis.                    65
Nec mora longa fuit: tumido mox addita ventri
Sarcina, sed nondum David sua gaudia credit
Plena satis: res ipsa placet, crimenque probatur,
At metuit famam, dicique recusat adulter.
Adde onus ignaro conceptum coniuge, quippe                        70
Forte aberat longe Urias, et tempore in illo
Pro patriae afflictae rebus, publicaque salute
Tractabat gladios miles: revocatur in urbem,
Principis imperio, paret, castrisque relictis,
Iussus adest. Illum nec formosissima coniux,                      75
Nec nati traxere domum, sed principis aulam
Ingreditur properans: simulato plurima vultu
Inquirit David: quam tandem exercitus urbem
Obsideat, quibus inclusus sit moenibus hostis,
Eventu quonam pugnatum. singula pandit                            80
Ille, nec infelix novit quam dira parentur.
Quippe, licet mensa exceptum, vinoque madentem,    2 Sam. 11.10-11
Coniugis ut sprevisse thoros, aulaque manere
Assiduum vidit David, iam censet apertum
Omne scelus, iam facta palam sua crimina credit.                 85
Vis igitur, sed tecta placet, capitique parantur
Coniugis insidiae. Tam magnum est numen Amoris,
Scilicet ignorat leges cum matre Cupido.
Iam nil iura valent, nil magni iussa Tonantis,
Expertusque favor divum: iam victus amore                         90
Ipse odit sese; o semper nocitura voluptas,
ut transversa rapis mortalia pectora tecum!
Nox erat, et late carpebant omnia somnos,
At vigil insano fraudes in pectore David
Mille parat, calamum tandem poscitque tabellas.                   95
Et se de patriae rebus dum scribere multa
Versutus simulat, versa in contraria mente,
Imperat ut pugnae statuatur in ordine primus
Urias, primusque ruat moriturus in hostes.

suits, nor does he look for a way to guard himself. (60) He anxiously mulls over in his head night and day, with great effort, how he can devise it so that he can possess that beloved beauty. What should he do? He offers her presents along with beguiling words. Bathsheba gives in, and is pleased to commit the sin at this great man's instigation.

Fortune favors their wicked undertaking, nor was there a long delay. Soon her belly begins to swell and grow. But David does not feel completely satisfied yet. He enjoys the affair, he excuses the sin, but he feared rumor, and he refuses to be called an adulterer. (70) Moreover, there is the unborn child, conceived without her husband's knowledge: For by chance Uriah was far away, busy with affairs on behalf of his country, fighting as a soldier for the public safety. He was called back into the city by the command of the leader. He obeys, leaving behind the camp, and comes as ordered. And it is not his extremely beautiful wife that draws him home, nor his children, but he hastens into the hall of the king. Pretending, David asks him many things, such as what city the army is besieging, or what kind of walls the enemy's city has, (80) what was the outcome of the battle. Uriah answers them one by one, nor does the unhappy fellow know how grave are the things being prepared for him.

But because David sees him eating and drinking wine in his palace, never leaving, ignoring the bed of his wife, now he feels his wickedness is exposed, he believes that his crimes have been committed openly. He plots a secret murder, therefore, laying a treacherous trap for the life of his woman's husband. So great is the power of Cupid! Cupid, along with his mother, simply ignores right and wrong. Oaths no longer prevail, nor do the commands of the great Thunderer, (90) or the tested patience of the gods. Now the king hates himself because he has succumbed to love. O pleasure, always intent on harm, as you seize mortal hearts that cross your path!

It was night, and everything was fast asleep. But David is awake and preparing a thousand evil plans in his mad heart. At last he demands pen and paper, and while he deceitfully pretends to write many things about the affairs of his country, yet all the while having ulterior motives, he commands that Uriah be stationed on the front lines during battle, so

Ergo ut prima dedit venientis signa diei                           100
Lucifer, Uriam mox in sua castra reverti
Rex iubet, inscriptasque duci perferre tabellas.
Laetus at ille volat, nec se sua fata tenere
Clausa manu novit: tandemque in fronte locatus,
Immeritam infelix petiit per vulnera mortem.                       105
Haec pater omnipotens ex alto singula caelo
Cernebat, iam tum iratus, cum cedere foedi
Imperio insanum regem spectaret amoris.
Ut vero insontem cecidisse agnovit amicum,
Et fuso hostiles gladios tinxisse cruore:                          110
Tum demum infremuit totus, vultumque serenum
Iratus posuit: tremuerunt omnia late,
Terribilique procul sonuerunt astra fragore,
Protinus exorto compleri murmure caelum
Turbato cepit Domino, veniuntque frequentes                        115
Aligeri fratres, quae tanti causa tumultus?
Inter se rogitant trepidi, quae litis origo,
Quos haec ira notet? num totas fulmine terras
Perdere forte paret? num caeli extrudere cives,
Aut priscum revocare chaos? quippe affore tempus                   120
Audierant, et ipsos olim quod verteret orbes
Caelorum, et totum flammis misceret Olympum.
    Caelorum in medio, qua se super omnia tollit
Sublimis moles mundum complexa rotundum,
Stat thronus, et gemmis totus conflatus et auro.                   125
Hic divum residet princeps, hinc singula cernens
Temperat, aeterno componitque omnia nutu.
Hunc geminae circum dicuntur stare sorores,
Iustitia, et placido lenis Clementia vultu.
Altera districto cunctis velut ense minatur,                       130
Turbatisque oculis testatur pectoris iras.
Altera blanditurque oculis, similisque precanti
Vertere commoti memoratur numinis iras,
Huc igitur postquam convenere undique divi,
Tum pater iratus: Quaenam haec dementia? quaenam                   135
Improbitas, inquit, nostrum contemnere numen

---

126   superum *1569, 1576, 1597*

that rushing against the enemy first he might die. (100) Therefore, when Lucifer gave the first signs of the coming day, the king orders Uriah to return to his camp immediately, and to relay the papers he had just written to his general. He flies back in haste, happy to do so, unaware that he holds his fate literally in his own hands. Finally, placed in the front line, the unfortunate man is wounded and finds his undeserved death.

The omnipotent Father was watching these events unfold one by one from high heaven, and already He was angered to see the king foolishly giving into his lust. But when He realized that his guiltless friend has fallen, (110) and that his spilt blood stained the enemies' swords, He was finally deeply enraged, and angrily set aside his serene countenance. Far and wide everything trembled, and the stars resounded from afar with a terrible loud noise. The Lord's anger caused heaven immediately to be abuzz, and the angels came crowding in. With dread they ask among themselves what is the cause of so much uproar, what is the source of the charge, at whom is this anger directed? Surely He is not preparing to destroy the world with lightning, or to cast out the citizens of heaven, (120) or recall the old chaos. Yet they had heard that a time would come that would overturn the spheres of heaven, and envelop all Olympus with flames.

In the middle of the sky, where the sublime structure raises itself above all things, surrounding the globe of the world, a throne stands, decorated all over with gemstones and gold. Here resides the King of the gods; from here He sees everything, and He controls and orchestrates everything with a nod of his head. Around Him stand twin sisters, so they say, Justice, and gentle Mercy with peaceful visage. (130) The one threatens all with a drawn sword, as it were, and with her angry eyes bears witness to the wrath in her heart. The other blandishes with her eyes, and as if supplicating is said to avert the wrath of the Divine when He is upset.

Then the irate Father said, "What madness is this, what level of wickedness? Do mortals dare to hold My power in contempt, and with

Mortales audere viros, et pectore ferri
Indomito auctorem contra? quid plurima fando
Commemorem? terraeque datas totius habenas?     Gen. 1
Et maris imperium, liquidoque volantia caelo?        140
Mentem ego divinam tribui, quae libera mortem
Despiceret, quae me, quae caeli edisceret orbes.     Ps. 8
Hoc cunctis commune bonum. quid propria natis
Commoda nunc referam toties concessa Iacobi?
Vos meministis enim regis contusa superbi          145
Pectora, vos medio incedentes aequore turmas,    Ex. 14
Deletasque acies scitis, partosque triumphos:
Scitis ut in terras spreto descendere caelo
Ausus ego, ut leges illis et iura tuendae       Ex. 19ff.
Tradiderim vitae, nostri quoque testis amoris      150
Phoebus erit, sueto vetitus descendere cursu:     Jos. 10
Et scissae Iordanis aquae, sonituque turbarum
Captae urbes, pulsique sua ditione tyranni.      Jos. 3 & 6
Haec illis igitur tribui. quid maxima vero
Tot bona commemorem Iessaeo praestita vati?    1 Sam. 16    155
Illi ego pastori memini tribuisse coronam,
Ereptoque pedo sceptrum donasse ferendum,    1 Sam. 16
Mox etiam manibus vasti eripuisse gigantis     1 Sam. 17
Cumque graves urgere minas, odiumque Saulis
Sensissem, tutum ipse dedi (miseratis egentis)      160
Exilium, et placida florentia regna quiete.     1 Sam. 27
Nunc tamen antiquos mores imitatus avorum,
Oblitusque mei, nec caeli spernere leges,
Nec crudele scelus sceleri iunxisse veretur.
Hinc leges, hinc iura tacent violata sacrati        165
Coniugii, hinc noster non digna morte peremptus
Vindictam petit Urias; nunc ergo superbum
Ulciscar regis pectus, populumque ferocem
Delebo iratus, nostri monumenta doloris.

---

146    gradientes *1597*
148    summo *pro* spreto *1569, 1576, 1597*
149    Sustinui ut *1569, 1576, 1597*
150    Sancirem *1569, 1576, 1597*
151    Sol erit assueto *1569, 1576, 1597*
158    Quinetiam vasto memini eripuisse giganti *1569, 1576, 1597*

an unrestrained heart of iron to despise their creator? Why should I say anything more? Why should I mention that I've given him reign over the whole earth? (140) And power over the creatures in the sea, and the birds that fly in the cloudy sky? I placed in him a divine mind so that he may live carefree and impervious to death, and that he may comprehend both Me and the universe. This was meant to be a gift common to all. Why should I now relate all the benefits I granted to the children of Jacob? For you remember that I subdued the heart of the haughty king, and that they walked en masse through the waters; you know how I wiped out their enemy's army, and you know the victories I won for them. You know how I deigned to descend to earth, forsaking heaven, (150) so that I might deliver to them laws and a covenant to live by. And the sun will be a witness to My love, when I refused to let it descend in its usual course; and so will the parting of the Jordan, the cities captured by the sound of the trumpet, and the tyrants expelled from their kingdoms. I granted them all these things. But why should I recount the many excellent blessings granted to Jesse's offspring through My prophet? I remember that I gave to that shepherd a crown, and exchanged his shepherd's staff for a king's scepter; then I rescued him from the hands of a huge giant who was bellowing forth terrible threats. (160) And when I sensed the hatred of Saul, taking pity on his needs, I gave him a safe exile and kingdoms flourishing in peace. Now, however, he is imitating the ancient habits of his ancestors, forgetting who I am, and fearing neither to spurn the laws of heaven nor to heap cruel wickedness upon wickedness. Hence the laws and the broken bonds of holy matrimony are silent; hence my dear Uriah, who was cut down in an unworthy death, seeks revenge. So, now I will take vengeance on the haughty heart of the king, and I will wipe out an undisciplined people in My anger, as a token of My wrath."

　　　Desierat, toto exoritur cum murmur Olympo:　　　　　　170
Sunt qui dicta probent, scelerumque exposcere poenas
Fas, aequumque putant: pars quamvis ultima regem
Commeruisse sciant, blandis tamen omnia dictis
Emollire parant, iustumque arcere furorem.
Praecipue blando lenis Clementia vultu　　　　　　　　　175
Conqueritur lachrymans: nec enim si plectere dignis
Suppliciis homines placeat, iam fulmina posse
Sufficere, aut animas deinceps captura nocentes
Tartara, desertum fore mox sine civibus orbem:　　Ps. 129.3
Frustra igitur toties miseris mortalibus olim　　　　　　180
Est promissa salus, nec crescere virga sinetur　　　2 Sam. 2
Expectata piis? sua sunt stata tempora poenae,
Integra cum mundi peritura est machina flammis.
Ne, Genitor, ne te crudelem nomine dici
Quaeso sinas, tua nota satis sunt numina mundo.　　　185
At si poena placet, si res tam saeva probatur,
Hoc unum rogito supplex, hoc pectore toto
Flagito, fas ut sit sceleris monuisse peracti
Davidem: feret ille preces, tandemque furore　　　Eccl. 2
Deposito, scelus hoc illi, noxamque remittes.　　　　190
　　　Vix bene desierat mitis Clementia blandas
Ferre preces, cum deposita Pater optimus ira
Conceptum penitus dilabi corde calorem
Sensit, et haec tandem sedato pectore fatur:
Ergone nata meis conatibus obvia semper　　　　　　195
Non sinet irati res tandem ut verba sequatur?
Sed miseros servare iuvat. Sic fatus, abire
Imperat aligero divorum ex ordine lectum
Caesarie insigni iuvenem, cui candida circum
Ludebat stola longa pedes, variaeque micabant　　　200
Distinctae veluti gemmis rutilantibus alae:
Qualis ab Eoo vehitur qui psittacus orbe,

---

164　Nec scelus infandum *1597*
171-74 *om. in 1569, 1576, 1597*
175　Protinus at moesto assurgens Clementia vultu *1569, 1576, 1597*
195-96 *om. in 1569, 1576, 1597*
197　At *1569, 1576, 1597*
198　Aligerum mandat selectum ex ordine fratrum *1569, 1576, 1597*

(170) When He ceased a murmur arose from all over Olympus. There are some who approve His words, thinking that it is right and just to punish the wicked deed. But some, although they know that the king deserves the worst, move to soften everything with soothing words and bend His righteous anger. Especially gentle Mercy, with charming countenance and tears, protests: "If you do not decide to temper your punishments, that your thunderbolts can suffice for now or that eventually Tartarus imprison guilty souls, the world will soon be bereft of citizens. (180) Was it in vain, then, that salvation was promised to poor mortals so many times in the past, and will the longed-for shoot not be allowed to grow for the pious? The time for punishment has been established, a time when the whole structure of the world will perish in flames. Don't allow yourself to be called 'The Cruel', Sire. Your powers are sufficiently known in the world. But if it is punishment you want, and if so fierce a judgment meets your approval, I beg you as a suppliant this one thing, and I plead this with all my heart, that you see fit to warn David of the evil he has committed. He will offer prayers and (190) at last you will set aside your wrath and forgive his crime and his guilt."

Gentle Mercy had scarcely ceased to offer soothing entreaties, when the Good Father set aside His wrath. The deep-felt anger slipped from His heart, and He said this with calm heart: "Will my children always stand in the way of my undertakings, so I may not follow up My angry words with angry deeds? But it is good to protect the helpless." Thus He spoke, and He commanded a lovely-headed youth, chosen from among the angelic hosts, to depart; (200) his long white garb played

Aut nubes inter qualis nitet Iris aquosas.
Hunc igitur propere Solymorum invisere terras
Imperat Omnipotens, culpaeque monere peractae 205
Davidem, simul et poenas mortem minari.
Ille abit, et liquidum variis secat aethera pennis.
Forte et tempus erat, tacito cum victa sopore
Cuncta silent, claroque micant nitidissima caelo
Sidera, conspecta tunc nuntius arce quievit: 210
Et mox humanam (dictu mirabile) formam
Induitur, vatisque latet sub imagine Nathan
Iratis ardens oculis, vultuque minaci
Sic medios inter somnos reprehendere crimen
Visus, et ingratae scelus exprobrare senectae:     2 Sam. 12   215
Tene, ait, o regum rex pessime! tene quietem
Ducere, quem ad poenam poscunt, pro immanibus ausis,
Tartara? sic igitur turpem traducere vitam
Amplexus medios inter? geminone nocentem
Crimine, caelorum fas est convexa tueri? 220
Qui divos, qui te, patriamque, tuosque scelestus
Prodideris: nec tu somnum, lectique superbi
Delicias linques divum venturus ad aras?
Atqui tempus erit, moneo, cum caede tuorum
Ipse oculos pasces, bellique domestica surgent 225
Semina: et incestus, et fratrum vulnera cernes.
Tu modo flecte deos lachrymis. Sic ille locutus,
Protinus in tenues fugiens evanuit auras.
At David monitis, et clara voce deorum
Attonitus, nunc invisos accusat amores, 230
Nunc iussae meminit mortis, crimenque fatetur
Conscius. Ergo thoro vigil exilit, et sua pugnis
Pectora contundens, sceptrumque aulamque coronamque
Abiicit, et partes animum convertit in omnes:
Ut Libyae si quis sitientia rura viator 235
Dum petit, in mediis saevam conspexit arenis

---

202    (mortalia rebus nefas aethereis componere) *post* vehitur *inser. in 1569, 1576:*
       *om. in 1597*
203    Ceu tricolor nubes inter *1597*
205    vatique aperire Nathani *1569, 1576, 1597*
205–50 et 253–60 *text. in posterioribus edd. multo differtur*

around his feet, and his colorful, fantastic wings were flashing as if with gems glowing red, like a parrot brought from eastern lands, or like a rainbow glistening among the watery clouds. It was him, then, that the Almighty ordered to visit the lands of Jerusalem quickly, to warn David of the guilt he incurred, and at the same time to threaten death and punishment. So he departs, cutting through the watery air with his colorful wings.

By chance, it was also the time when all living things were resting in quiet sleep and (210) the shiny stars were twinkling against a clear sky. Then the messenger spotted the citadel and stood still. Soon he clothes himself in human form (a marvel to tell) and disguises himself as Nathan the prophet. And aflame with angry eyes and threatening countenance, he appears in David's dreams to rebuke him for his sin, denouncing the wickedness of his graceless middle age. "How can you sleep, evil king of kings? How, when Tartarus demands that you be punished for the terrible deed you dared venture upon? How can you lead your foul life like this amid embraces? And is it right for you, guilty of a double crime, (220) to look upon the heavens, you, who in wickedness betrayed the gods, yourself, your country, your family? Won't you abandon your sleep and the pleasures of your haughty bed to go to the altars of the gods? But the time will come, I warn you, when you will feast your eyes with the slaughter of your family, and spawn the seeds of civil war. You will see incest, and brother harming brother. Your only choice is to turn to the gods with tears." Thus he spoke, and straightaway he vanished into thin air.

But David, struck by the warnings and the unmistakable word of the gods, (230) now regrets his despicable affair, now he remembers the death he caused, and he knowingly admits his sin. So, he awakes and leaps from his bed, and, striking his chest with his own fists, casts aside his scepter, his court, his crown, and turns his mind this way and that. He is like some traveler who sojourns in the thirsty land of Libya, and

Tygrida, vel maculis distinctum terga draconem,
Horret ad aspectum trepidus, coeptumque relinquit
Cautus iter, latebrasque petit tremebundus opacas.
Talis erat David, pulchra quem uxore potitum,     240
Nilque minus caelo metuentem clara deorum
Numina terruerant, et cognita vatis imago.
Multa est ante oculos Bersabe et nulla calores
Intus flamma parit: victus cum Matre Cupido
et pavor in vacuo solus iam pectore regnat.     245
Quid faciat? num vel miserum se ex arce suprema
Praecipitet, vel visceribus crudum induat ensem?
Num veniam exposcat, iustasque avertere divum
Conetur lachrymis iras? Palatia pone
Antrum erat horrendum, fracti qua culmina montis     250
Exesas vasta claudebant mole cavernas,
Horrebant rubis late omnia, et undique sentes
Dumique, tribulique et soli ignota vorago.
Haec igitur pavidus sublimi David ab arce
Singula spectabat, dubius vitamne, necemne     255
Eligeret, nunc caelum oculis atque astra petebat
Attonitus, largo nunc turgida lumina fletu
Fixa tenebat humi: tandem circumspicit antrum,
Et mox: Tu nostri domus, inquit, conscia luctus,
Tu mihi testis eris iustorum sola dolorum:     260
Sic faveas nostro rubicunda ex crimine Luna:
(Forte erat, aut visa est Phoebe rubicundior), at vos
Sidera, quae invisos toties vidistis amores,
Mutatum spectare virum. Sic fatus, eburnam
Suspendit zona citharam, qua suetus ad omnes     265
Mentis erat curas uti, qua saepe sonante
Depulerat saevos inimico a rege furores.     1 Sam. 16.23
    Ergo abit, atque sago velatus membra cucullo,
Praecipitis tandem evadit super ardua montis
Culmina, mox antrum ingreditur, largo madentes     270
Imbre oculos caelo attollit, tandemque recepta
Mente, miser tales tremebundo pectore fletus
Orditur, moestas cithara resonante querelas.

---

268    et pullo circumvelatus amictu *1597*
269    *om. in 1597*
270    Speluncam ingreditur tacitus, largoque madentes *1597*

encounters a fierce tiger in the heart of the desert, or a spotted snake: He shudders at the sight, full of fear, and warily abandons the well-worn path, and looks for dark hiding places, trembling all the while. (240) So did David feel as he gazed upon Bathsheba. For although he possessed a beautiful wife, and feared nothing less than heaven, the clear power of the gods and the familiar face of the prophet had shaken him. Bathsheba fills his eyes, and yet no flame of passion ignites the lust within; Cupid along with his mother are conquered, and shameful fear alone rules now in his empty heart. What should he do? Should he leap headlong from the top of the citadel, or stab himself in the gut with a bloody sword? Should he ask for forgiveness, should he try to avert the righteous anger of the gods with his tears? Behind the palace (250) there was a dreadful cave, where the peaks of the jagged mountain shut in the hollowed caverns with its huge mass, and where everything, far and wide, bristled with brambles and thorns, barbs and thistles, and an abyss unknown even to the sun.

From his high vantage point, therefore, David was fearfully meditating on the course of events, uncertain whether to choose life or death. Now dumbstruck he looked to heaven and the stars, now he fixed his tear-swollen eyes toward the ground. Finally, he noticed the cave, and immediately he said, "You will be my home, a confidant of my grief, (260) and alone a witness of my righteous sorrow. Thus may you grant favor from our reproach, red moon" (perhaps it was red, or maybe Diana was blushing a bit). "But you stars, who so often saw our hated intimacies, look at a changed man." Thus he spoke, and hung from his belt his ivory lyre, by which he usually soothed the cares of his mind, and with the music of which he had driven the savage madness from the hostile king. So he withdrew himself, and covering his limbs with a prophet's hooded cloak, at length went up the arduous peaks of the steep mountain; (270) soon he entered the cave. His eyes filled with a flood of tears, and he raised them to heaven. Finally, he recovers himself, and such pitiful wailing arises from his trembling breast, while the lyre echoes with sad laments.

# Commentary on the Sylvae

*S*ylvae or *Silvae* was a fairly popular generic term during the Renaissance. It should properly mean "woodland," but because it has the extended meaning of "raw material," it came to be used as a title for poetic collections of varied content, what in English we might term "poetical miscellanies" or "occasional poems." Just as forests contain a wide variety of materials that come to be used to construct our finished products, so too the sylvan collections exhibit a wide variety of subjects and styles that have been polished and composed to make finished poems. J. C. Scaliger, in his *Poëtices* (3.100), explains the origin of the term in this way:

> Materiam ὕλην dixerunt Graeci, inde sylva nobis: innumeris enim pene vel operibus vel officiis suppeditatur a lignis materia. Grammatici recentiores, quod invenissent in libris vetustioribus alia vocali quam Graeca scriptum, a silendo deductum maluere. sane ridicule. Nusquam enim minus quam in sylvis silentium, minima namque aura maximi strepitus excitantur. Poematia ergo quaedam, ut docet Quintilianus, subito excussa calore sylvas nominarunt veteres, vel a multiplici materia, vel a frequentia rerum inculcatarum, vel ab ipsis rudimentis: rudia namque poemata, et sane effusa, postea castigabant.

> [The Greeks called raw material ὕλη, and so we call it *sylva*: for wood supplies to us material for an almost countless number of crafts and tasks. More recent grammarians prefer to derive the word from *silendo* ("being silent"), because they claim they found it written in older books with a vowel different than that

in the Greek. That is obviously ridiculous. For nowhere is there less silence than in the woods, where a slight breeze can make a loud rustling sound. Therefore, as Quintilian says, the ancients termed certain poetic collections *sylvae*, either from the fact that forests can blaze up quickly, or from the variety of material it contains, or from its density, or from its very rusticity. For at first poems are crude and uncultivated, then poets polish them.[1]]

The popularity of the term in the Renaissance must be inspired by Statius's use of it, but Bèze explicitly states in the preface to his 1569 edition that in writing *sylvae* he intended to imitate Vergil. Even so, these are not eclogues, since we find a number of poems under that heading in the Orléans manuscript of Bèze's early poems. Those poems are written in the dialogic, pastoral form one would expect, with stock characters drawn right out of Vergil. In the case of the *sylvae*, however, Bèze likely means that he found in Vergil a vocabulary and idiom, not to mention meter, with which to treat a variety of subjects. The subject matter is always serious in tone, and, as I have noted throughout the commentary on the individual poems, it can easily be related to biblical stories and precepts.[2] Clearly Bèze means the *sylvae* to be didactic and moralizing, just as he does the *icones*. In fact, in the Orléans manuscript the *icones* themselves appear as a unit introduced with the title, *Heroes, ad Macutum Pomponium, Sylva 3.* It is not surprising, then, that the *sylvae*, though reworked, are not expunged from later editions.

---

[1] Much of the argument here comes from Isidore, *Etym.* 13.3 (W. M. Lindsay, *Hispalensis Episcopi Etymologiarum sive originum libri xx*, 2 vol. [Oxford, 1911]): ὕλην Graeci rerum quandam primam materiam dicunt, nullo prorsus modo formatam, sed omnium corporalium formarum capacem, ex qua visibilia haec elementa formata sunt; unde et ex eius derivatione vocabulum acceperunt. Hanc ὕλην Latini materiam appellaverunt, ideo quia omne informe, unde aliquid faciendum est, semper materia nuncupatur. Proinde et eam poetae silvam nominaverunt, nec incongrue, quia materiae silvarum sunt. Cf. Aulus Gellius *Noct. Att.* praef. 6 ("alii [sc. inscripserunt] silvarum"); Quint. 10.3.17 ("diversum est huic eorum vitium, qui primo decurrere per materiam stilo quam velocissimo volunt et sequentes calorem atque impetum ex tempore scribunt; hanc silvam vocant").

[2] This appears to have been a common characteristic of the genre, at least during the sixteenth century. One need only compare the *Sacrae Sylvae* (1594) of Johannes Sadeler, the Flemish writer, who uses the genre to expound upon religious and philosophical doctrines. Among the French, Guillaume de La Mare published his *Sylvarum libri quattuor* in 1513, which include sacred elegies and poems addressed to ecclesiastics. Scévole de Sainte-Marthe, writing in the latter part of the century, includes among his *sylvae* long epitaphs and eulogies, letters, birthday wishes, *epithalamia,* and even the Hippocratic Oath turned into Latin.

## 1.

ABM relate that this piece can be found printed on fol. 14 of a plaquette entitled *Chant XXVIII du Roland furieux d'Arioste. Traduict en francois à la rigueur des Stanzes et de la Rime, par N[icolas] R[apin] P[arisien]* (Paris, 1572).

This is the story of the heroic self-immolation of Publius Decius Mus, a patriotic Roman consul who fell during a battle against the Latins in an effort to save his country.[3] The battle took place near ancient Veseris in Campania, at the foot of Vesuvius, as one episode of the Latin War that lasted from 340 to 338 B.C., and that brought about final Roman domination over Latin and Volscan cities to the south of Rome. Seeing his comrades retreating from the fight, Decius charged headlong against the enemy after "devoting" himself and the enemy to the *di manes*, the gods of the underworld. His actions exemplify the ritual *devotio* that Macrobius describes at *Sat.* 3.9.9–16. It involved prayers and invocations of the type found here, although it was unusual for the commander of the Roman army to include himself in the act of devotion. The sacrifice of the enemy was seen as a sort of indemnity or compensation paid to the gods in a fair exchange for the victory, while the sacrifice of the leader was seen as a formal *consecratio* or dedication of his person to the gods; on this see the following two articles by H. S. Versnel, who discusses the specific case of Decius: "Two Types of Roman *devotio*," *Mnemosyne* 29 (1976): 365–410; and "Self-sacrifice, Compensation, and the Anonymous Gods," in *Le sacrifice dans l'antiquité*, ed. J.-P. Vernant, O. Reverdin, and J. Rudhardt (Geneva, 1980), 135–94.

Bèze may have been interested in this story as a type for the vicarious death of Christ on the cross. Just as Decius exchanged his life to secure the defeat of the enemy and the salvation of his otherwise doomed people, so Jesus offered himself as a substitute to atone for his people and to bring about the destruction of Satan and his legions.

**1. Iam Romana acies verti, iam cedere laevo:** Livy, 8.6, describes how the consuls, forewarned in a dream and by the inspection of entrails that one of them must sacrifice his life, decided that the consul

---

[3] As told in Livy 8.6–11. The story was often repeated and used as an *exemplum* of behavior. For a complete list of passages, see T. R. S. Broughton, *The Magistrates of the Roman Republic*, 3 vols. (Chico, CA, 1984–86), 1: 135.

whose flank yielded first to the enemy during the battle must be the one to carry out the ritual act. The charge then fell to Decius, since he was leading the left flank when it retreated.

2. **virtus Romana**: The common soldiers' lack of *bellica virtus* provides a foil for Decius's extreme display of it. The fullest definition of *virtus* in a Roman context appears in a passage of Lucilius (E. H. Warmington, *Remains of Old Latin*, 4 vols. [Cambridge, MA, 1957], 3: 391–92), who defines it, among other things, as "thinking our country's interests to be foremost of all." Its connection to the Latin word *vir* evinces its origins in notions of "manly courage," especially as that applies to warfare (and therefore appearing frequently in this sense in Vergil, Livy, and Tacitus). Publilius Syrus (402 and 647) speaks of the virtuous man as having "a victor's face" that is unwilling to give in to calamity. For a study of the history of the word, see L. R. Lind, "The Idea of the Republic and the Foundations of Roman Morality, Second Part," in *Studies in Latin Literature and Roman History*, vol. 6, ed. C. Deroux (Brussels, 1992), 5–40, esp. 25–40.

4. **cum geminas . . . palmas**: a sign of petition; cf. Verg. *Aen.* 1.93: "duplicis tendens ad sidera palmas," also 10.844.

11. **Quirites**: an old name for the Romans, used often in poetry to add gravity; see note on *epig.* 17.5.

14. **Me dudum hoc vates monuere, iecurque recisum**: On the omens of the event, see the note on verse 1 (from Livy 8.6); also, according to Livy 8.9, immediately before battle a soothsayer pointed out to Decius that the liver of the sacrificed animal was damaged *a familiari parte*. The Romans learned from the Etruscans the art of foretelling the future through the inspection of the entrails of sacrificial animals. The diviner who presided over the ritual was known as a *haruspex*.

15. **sacrorum o custos**: It was customary for priests to accompany the army in order to perform the necessary rites.

18. **saevi Manes**: or Lares, spirits of the forebearers, whom the Romans believed were immortal like the gods. The Romans often sacrificed to them in private ritual and in the public festival *Parentalia*.

20. **velatus**: the Romans worshiped with veiled heads to prevent themselves from seeing any ill omens during the rite (Plaut. *Amph.* 1091–94; Lucr. 5.1198–99; Livy 8.9.6–7, 10.7.9–10; Varro *Ling.* 5.15.84, 5.29.130; Cic. *Dom.* 124; Val. Flac. *Arg.* 5.95–97; Plutarch, *Quaest. Rom.* 10).

21. **imperterritus**: undaunted, as one would expect of the most heroic Romans. Used of Aeneas at Verg. *Aen.* 10.770.

23. **Iane**: On this important deity, see note on *eleg.* 11.19.

24. **Et gemini ... Quirineque**: a hypermetric line, with synapheia of the final syllable and the first syllable of the next line.

     **Quirineque**: When the Sabines migrated to Rome, they brought with them a god named Quirinus (from Sabine *curis* = lance), roughly equivalent to Mars, but who received distinct worship on the Quirinal Hill. Later, the Romans identified him with the deified Romulus.

32. **collega**: namely, Titus Manlius Lucius, often called Torquatus; he gained infamy at the outset of this same battle for putting his own son to death for disobeying an order not to engage in single combat. Eventually defeating the Latins and their allies, he led the triumphs mentioned in the previous verse.

33. **Ominor ... Latinis**: Macrin considered the *indubiam* of the 1548 version to be inelegant.

35. **Thetide**: As often in poetry, Thetis stands for the sea; see note on *eleg.* 11.22.

39. **cinctuque Gabino**: In early times the Romans wore togas in battle, but in the Gabian manner, after the town of Gabii. The end of the toga that was normally thrown over the left shoulder was instead drawn tightly around the waist to leave both arms free; see Giulio Cressedi, "Caput velatum e Cinctus Gabinus," *Rend. Linc.* 5 (1950): 450–56.

40. **Veseris**: It may have been a river or a town, but at any rate near the volcanic complex known today as Roccamonfina (for this location of the battle, see M. W. Frederiksen, *Campania*, ed. N. Purcell [London, 1984], 185). G. Radke, in his *RE* article, points to related coin legends from Campania as strengthening the case for a town, but the evidence is inconclusive either way. Livy, 8.8, only provides the following information: "Pugnatum est haud procul radicibus Vesuvii montis, qua via ad Veserim ferebat." Veseris is also mentioned at Cic. *Fin.* 1.23, *Off.* 3.112; Val. Max. 6.4.1; and Aurel. Vict. *Vir. ill.* 26.28.

## 2.

*Tottel's Miscellany*, 1: 118–20; 2: 253–54 (= Merrill, *Grimald*, 406–8, 450–52).

Bèze reveals in the title that he draws this account of Cicero's death from Plutarch *Cic.* 47–48, Livy 120 (= frg. 150) ap. Elder Seneca *Suas.*

6.17, and Valerius Maximus 5.3.4. Yet while agreeing on the general course of events, those authors disagree widely in details. Still other variations are given by Appian and Dio Cassius. The story can, however, be reconstructed as follows. After the assassination of Julius Caesar in 44 B.C., Cicero returned from his long absence from politics to make his voice heard again on behalf of the now doomed Republic. Appalled by the tyrannical gestures of Marc Antony, Cicero decided to throw his support behind Antony's rival, the young Octavianus (later Augustus Caesar). It was at this time that Cicero wrote, and in some cases delivered, his patriotic *Philippics*, by which he unleashed scathing and detailed attacks on Antony. Cicero's gamble did not pay off. Soon Antony and Octavianus, together with another senator, Lepidus, formed an alliance known as the Second Triumvirate. As part of the deal, Octavianus betrayed Cicero by allowing Antony to proscribe him as an enemy of the State, thereby making the former consul a marked man. Cicero withdrew then to Formiae, where he had a country home, and then to the coast at Caieta in a rather reluctant effort to make an escape. After embarking on a ship and heading out to sea, contrary winds and stormy weather drove him back, despite the sailors' best efforts, forcing him to disembark to meet his fate. At this point the ancient biographers disagree as to what happened. In the simplest terms, Cicero decided to return to his house at Formiae (about a mile from shore) to await Antony's henchmen, but was overtaken while being carried there on a litter (or perhaps while leaving the house in a second, half-hearted attempt to escape). On seeing his assassins, he groaned, saying that he was prepared to die in the country that he had saved so often. Cicero's slaves, who were very loyal to their master, were ready to defend him with their very lives, but Cicero himself preferred to spare them by calmly extending his neck to the sword. Popillius, whom Cicero had once defended in the courts, and who by the custom of Roman patron-client relationships should have favored Cicero, by most accounts delivered the final blow.[4] But here Bèze follows Plutarch, who says that it was delivered by Herennius, a centurion. Antony then ordered that Cicero's hands and head be cut off and placed on the rostra in the forum, as a warning to those who would dare write and speak against him in the future.

---

[4] For a review of the evidence that suggests Popillius killed Cicero, see M. Gelzer, *Cicero* (Wiesbaden, 1969), 408.

The focus of Bèze's interest in the death of Cicero appears to be the Stoic resignation and bravery with which he faced the inevitable decision of Fate, the irony of the saved murdering the savior, and the expectation for vindication from posterity. As in the previous *sylva*, the parallels with the passion and death of Christ are striking. Not only was Cicero "led like sheep to the slaughter," despite attempts by some of his followers to seize swords in his defense, but also nature itself reacts to the execution, as the sky becomes dark at his death.

5. **gladiis erepta tuorum**: cf. Livy 120: "Moriar, inquit, in patria saepe servata." During his consulship, Cicero exposed what has come to be known as the Catiline Conspiracy, an attempt of certain disenfranchised and disgruntled individuals to lay their hands on the reins of government at Rome around 63 B.C. Thereafter, Cicero boasted of his achievement *ad nauseam*, particularly in the vain and self-propagandizing *De consulatu suo*, for which he was much derided (e.g., Juvenal 10.122). Plutarch sums up Cicero's attitude in this way:

> After this time, then, Cicero was the most powerful man in Rome. However, he made himself obnoxious to a number of people, not because of anything which he did wrong but because people grew tired of hearing him continually praising himself and magnifying his achievements. One could attend neither the senate nor a public meeting nor a session of the law courts without having to listen to endless repetitions of the story of Catiline and Lentulus. He went on to fill his books and writings with these praises of himself and made his style of speaking, which was in itself so very pleasant and so exceedingly charming, boring and tedious to listen to, since this unpleasing habit of his clung to him like fate. (trans. Rex Warner [London, 1972], 334)

It is difficult from our standpoint to judge just how dangerous to the foundations of Rome the conspiracy was, and to what degree Cicero exaggerated the gravity of the events for the sake of his own glory. His boasting has received a rather sympathetic assessment from E. Rawson, *Cicero: A Portrait* (Ithaca, NY, 1983), 90–92. His fellow citizens, however, "thanked" him with exile.

25. **Tullius ille togae princeps, magnique Senatus**: a reference to his consulship of 63 B.C.

28. **Poppilium**: C. Popil(l)ius Laenas from Picenum (= *RE*, s.v. "Popilius 10"), whom Plutarch describes as "an officer in the army" and

Livy (*epit.* 120) as *legionarius miles*, probably meaning a military tribune. Cicero defended him from charges of parricide, of which he was acquitted (or perhaps it was only a private suit; see Elder Seneca *Contr.* 7.2); the speech is lost. Bèze's choice of spelling, *Poppilium*, is unattested.

31. **Herennius:** a centurion who answered to Popillius, and mentioned in all accounts of Cicero's death, but otherwise unknown (= *RE*, s.v. "Ierennius 2").

36. **amor patriae:** reminiscent of Verg. *Aen.* 6.823, "vincet amor patriae ladumque immensa cupido." The subject is Lucius Iunius Brutus, who put to death his sons for trying to restore the Tarquins.

38–39. **me pridem nuntia Phoebi | Poscit avis:** Plutarch reports that ravens from Apollo's nearby temple fluttered around Cicero during his final hours.

40. **Bruti Cassique:** Because they were courageous enough to assassinate Julius Caesar, Cicero now hopes they will be equally willing to assassinate Antony.

48. **Augur:** Cicero joined the priestly college of augurs in 53 B.C. after being nominated by Hortensius and Pompey. Although at the outset augury meant the art of foretelling the future by watching the flight of birds, in Cicero's day it had become relegated to an office that gave guidance and interpretation to the senate. Augurs could be obstructive, nonetheless, since it was their duty to declare whether the gods found satisfactory or not motions that were under consideration (Cic. *Leg.* 3.27).

55. **canamque senectam:** For the collocation, see Ov. *Her.* 14.109.

64. **Phoebus:** i.e., Apollo as the sun.

73. **Antoni ... mensis:** perhaps "sacrificial tables," i.e., tables on which offerings for the gods were placed; cf. Verg. *Aen.* 2.764: *mensaeque deorum.* Elsewhere, Antony's "tables" are used as a metaphor for his excesses; see note on *eleg.* 2.19.

## 3.

Bèze begins by establishing the proper sacred tone for this poem about Christmas Eve with a dismissal of the amatory elegiac genre along with its exploitation of night as a time for sexual intrigue and indulgence. In Bèze's hands, night becomes, not a negation of all that is light and good, and not a cover for debauchery, but a holy, quiet time that saw the birth of the Christ child. The poet is aware, of course, that he is turning the tables on the elegists, whose convention it is to excuse themselves from any sort of serious writing. Bèze himself uses the conceit in his own elegies and epigrams. Now, however, he is most interested in undertaking the priestly duties of the poet to elevate the minds of people to heavenly matters and to provide hope for the downcast. The poem itself develops primarily on the interplay of images of light and darkness. The Christ child is a sun, whose arrival at night symbolizes his own conquest of the dark forces of the world. The lights in the nighttime sky never fade, reminding us that with the coming of the child dawned a new era that will last forever. Night, then, is transformed; no longer foreboding, no longer a source of fear for God's people; night, like all creation, has been redeemed and recovered for Christians as their own.

**8. intactas ... puellas**: anticipating the virgin birth.

**9. Inque alias ... castus Apollo**: The line could be taken two different ways, depending on whether "alias" is an adverb or an adjective. It could mean, "among the Muses Apollo is chaste at times."

**14. in sacros aperiri viscera partus**: cf. Hor. *Carm. Saec.* 13.

**26. Audisti, nox o foelix!**: Cf. Sedulius *Carm. pasch.* (and transposing "O vere beata nox, quae sola meruit scire tempus et horam in qua Christus ab inferis resurrexit" as sung by the Exultet of the the Easter Vigil).

**41. Parturiens ... parensque**: Cf. Avitus 6.200–25 (PL 59: 373 AB),[5] especially the paradoxical assertion, "virginis et matris gemina gaudere corona."

**58. refferre**: Macrin objected to the doubling of the consonant in the 1548 version, saying one cannot create a long syllable in this way except in the case of *rettulit*.

**68. relligione**: indicates the lengthening of the first syllable necessary for hexameter verse; cf. Verg. *Aen.* 8.598: "religione patrum late sacer: undique colles."
**vigilata nox**: cf. Ovid *Fasti* 4.167.

**70–72: Lyaeo ... Cybeles**: The rites of Dionysus and Cybele were especially raucous (Lucr. 2.600ff.). Cf. Dolet's description of Paris:

---

[5] Also, George W. Shea, ed., *The Poems of Alcimus Ecdicius Avitus* (Tempe, AZ, 1997).

Non sua huic urbi Lyaeus, non Cybelle munera,
Non Napeae floridos campos negarunt ...
(*Delitiae*, 1: 870)

73. quīs: = *quibus*, here an ethical dative, or perhaps a dative of reference. The 1713 and 1779 editions both have *virûm queis*.

4.

This lengthy *sylva* provides the historical background to what are known as the seven penitential Psalms (6, 31, 37, 50, 101, 129, 142 Vulg.), which arise out of David's shameful affair with Bathsheba and the murder of her husband Uriah the Hittite. The biblical references given in the margins come from the early editions of his poetry, and follow the conventions of the Vulgate editions. The story itself, which Bèze does not refer to, is told in 2 Sam. 11–12.

There are far too many alterations in later editions to note them all in the apparatus; all the changes reveal Bèze's desire to purge the poem of pagan undertones, with qualified allowance for poetic allegory. He completely reworked the poem after the first line, making an almost absurd effort to place the pagan Cupid into a Christian frame of reference, specifically by turning him into a demon who insinuates himself into the minds of his victims. I reproduce here only the first twenty-nine lines of the 1569 edition along with line 15, added in the 1597 edition:

Forte pererratis caelo terraque marique,
Ales Amor (daemon quo non est certior ullus
Mortales pulchri falsa sub imagine mentes
Fallere, letalique animos afflare veneno)
Invisa sacras Iudaeae callidus urbes                                    5
Venerat: et iam tum magno molimine regem
Fundantem intuitus Solymas feliciter arces,
Progeniemque memor Iessaeo ex sanguine duci,
Venturam Satanae excidio, Satanaeque ministris,
Mene (ait) a prima qui victor origine mundi                           10
His homines domui telis, horrendaque seclo
Diluvia invexi (laus est haec nostra) priori:
Cui Ninon, ingentemque incesta Semiramis urbem
Sacravit, nostras testantia moenia vires:
Cui Sodome versa in cineres, ambustaque longe                      15
In tenues abiit regio vicina favillas:

Quo duce mille furens armavit Graecia naves,
Et nunc Troia novem iacet oppugnata per annos:
Quis prius indomitum (quid non mihi femina praestat?)
Sampsonem insano fregi meretricis amore:                    20
Iessiadae unius non posse abrumpere coepta,
Divinisque procul curis avertere mentem?
    Dixerat iratus, pharetraque accinctus et arcu
Tandem ad Bersabes convertit lumina vultus:
Bersabes, qua non formosior altera cunctas                  25
Isacidum populis inter numerata puellas,
Sed coniuncta viro, et mater iam digna videri.
Et mox tam raras mortali in corpore dotes
Miratus . . .

After this introduction, the later editions pick up at line 19 of the 1548 edition (beginning with *iuvet hinc*) and begin to follow the text somewhat more closely. For the rest of the text I have noted any major alterations in the apparatus, when the general correspondence of texts allowed.

Though he rejected the practice later on, Bèze was interested in poetry that could mix pagan and Christian images into one seamless whole, according to precedents set as early as Ausonius and Juvencus,[6] and as recently as Vida, whose Vergilian-style *Christiad* includes a description of a Hell filled with gorgons, centaurs, chimaeras and the like (1.136–46).[7] Bèze has another, unpublished poem on the Last Judgment where the same blending of pagan and Christian occurs. It would be an oversimplification to say that this is syncretism, a vain attempt to harmonize paganism and Christianity. Lucretius had shown long before that myth could be employed as a honey-coating for austere subjects, so long as the content of the myth is rejected or exposed for the falsehood that it really is. That would explain why Bèze is at pains to note that Cupid is expelled and vanquished in the end by the holiness of the one true God. But it also reveals a desire on the part of some humanists to marry their

---

[6] A complete discussion of the development of the Biblical epic and its basis in the paraphrasis of the rhetorical schools as well as early Christian commentary and exegesis, see Carl Springer, *The Gospel as Epic in Late Antiquity: the* Paschale carmen *of Sedulius* (Leiden, 1988), 9–16.

[7] First published in 1535 at Cremona under the title *Christiados libri sex.* For a more accessible copy, see Marco Girolamo Vida, *The Christiad,* ed. and transl. G. Drake and C. Forbes (Carbondale, IL, 1978).

two great world views, and to find some balance between classical literature and Christian theology.

Other writers during the Renaissance found the practice of creating a poetic vignette of some biblical story to be a worthwhile pursuit as well. Most notably, Bèze's friend Jacques Lect (1560–1611) published his *Ionah, seu Poetica paraphrasis ad eum vatem* as a supplement to Bèze's 1599 edition, and later repeated in the posthumous 1614 edition (fols. 190ʳ–200ʳ in both editions). There, not only do mythic images play a part, albeit small, but also many passages and conceits are borrowed wholesale from Vergil's *Aeneid*.[8] In England, however, Latin versifiers of the Bible explicitly rejected this marriage of secular and sacred content, even at the expense of style. It should be noted, too, that in general Anglo-Latin paraphrasers strove to adhere as closely as possible to the original Biblical version.[9] In contrast, Bèze's story of David and Bathsheba contains at least one conspicuous deviation from the Hebrew text, the odd detail that has an angel disguise himself as Nathan in order to rebuke David for his affair (esp. lines 211–12).[10]

9. **frontemque patentem**: a mark of beauty according to the tastes of Bèze's day; cf. note on *eleg.* 4.31.

18. **officiat**: used often of obstructing the light or sight of something (cf. Cicero, *ND* 2.49, *Tusc.* 5.92, *Div.* 1.93, *Off.* 3.66). The constellation Virgo contains one of the brightest stars in the heavens (see Cicero, *ND* 2.110), but the addition of *barbara* suggests Artemis (Diana), and so by extension the moon.

21. **arma procul**: For the collocation, see Verg. *Aen.* 6.651.

22. **arcum**: The eyebrow recalls the shape of the bow; note the use of *iaculatur* at line 44, a word normally reserved for the hurling of spears or shooting of arrows. Bèze devoted epig. 68 to an analogy between Cupid's bow and Candida's eyebrows (a common conceit).

---

[8] E.g., the verses, *Urbs antiqua fuit, mundi et sub origine prima | Ninive, Assyrii quondam tenuere coloni:*, parallel Vergil's description of Carthage at the beginning of the *Aeneid* (*Aen.* 1.12ff.).

[9] See J. W. Binns, "Biblical Latin Poetry in Renaissance England," *Papers of the Liverpool Latin Seminar* 3 (1981): 385–416. Ironically, some authors even mention that they depended on Bèze's exegesis of Biblical texts as a guide for their understanding of the Hebrew or Greek text.

[10] Bèze was not alone in incorporating non-Scriptural details into his Biblical epic. For example, Sedulius, *Paschale carmen* 4.300–2, includes a description of a donkey who "recognized that the baby lying in the manger was God," even though no Gospel reports this particular fact.

**33. laeta**: Bathsheba receives some of the blame for complicity in the sin committed by David, much as Helen does in ancient discussions about her rape by Paris. Although Cupid is an outside force who exercised his designs on Bathsheba, she receives him happily and is pleased to obey him (lines 64–65).

**43–44: unda | nuda**: note the word play.

**53. dominus**: Bèze lays stress on the power of Cupid (= sin) throughout the poem so that all the more he can highlight God's grace and omnipotence: sin is a master (*dominus*) that ultimately is expelled by the greater Master (*Dominus*). See esp. line 244.

**57–58. caecas sub pectore flammas | David aliit**: Renaissance writers often turned to Vergil's description of Dido's passion at the beginning of book IV of the *Aeneid* as the best idiom to convey the effects of the onset of love. Such feelings are in turn unseated by the fear that comes over David upon hearing the commands of God.

**65. favet inceptis Fortuna nefandis**: Cf. Ovid, *Am.* 3.2.56, addressed to Venus: "inceptis adnue, diva, meis." Also a play on the words of Pompey the Great at Lucan *BC* 8.322: "Roma, fave coeptis" (Pompey expresses his hope that the whole of his life will be looked on with favor, not just his defeat at Pharsalus).

**106–97**: These lines are modeled very closely on Ovid's description of the council of the gods at *Met.* 1.163–261. There Jupiter is enraged at the wickedness of Lycaon's sin, and so he summons the gods to Mt. Olympus to vent his anger and threaten mankind's extinction. Part of the gods approve of his plan to destroy the world, while some are silent, yet all are concerned about the implications if the human race is completely wiped out. Jupiter assures them that he will create another race, and is just about to hurl his thunderbolts to earth, when he remembers that the Fates have predicted a general conflagration that includes Heaven. Therefore, he opts instead for a flood. Not every component of Bèze's description can be related to that of Ovid. The querulous recounting of benefits bestowed, for example, which is so skillfuly woven in through preterition ("Why should I relate. . . . For you know . . ."), is more reminiscent of passages from the Old Testament than classical literature. And when Bèze speaks of *divi*, he means the heavenly host in general, i.e., angels and other spiritual beings around the throne, rather than near-equals with God.

**120. aut priscum revocare chaos**: Cf. Ovid *Met.* 2.299, "in chaos antiquum confundimur," spoken by Earth as Phaëthon lost control of his sun-chariot.

129. Justice and Mercy flanking God's throne are a Christianization of Themis and Dike flanking Zeus's (Jupiter's) throne.

141. **Mentem ego divinam tribui:** an affirmation of the dignity of man from the words of David himself.

148. **descendere caelo:** to Mt. Sinai, where he delivered to Moses the Ten Commandments.

151. **sueto vetitus descendere cursu:** The story is that Yahweh made the sun stand still at Gibeon in the battle against the Amorites.

152-53. **sonituque turbarum | Captae urbes:** a reference to the conquest of Jericho, as described in Joshua 6.

155. **vati:** Yahweh sent Samuel his prophet to Bethlehem to announce to Jesse that one of his sons would become king.

180-81: Isaiah 11.1, "et egredietur virga de radice Jesse."

188-89. **fas ut sit sceleris monuisse peracti | Davidem:** The sentiment appears to be drawn from the Ecclesiasticus (i.e., Sirach) 2.15-17, where it says that those who fear God will obey his laws and seek his approval. Also relevant is Ps. 31 Vulg.

205. **Imperat Omnipotens:** This whole section is modeled after the passage in the *Aeneid* (*Aen.* 4.219-37), where Jupiter sends Mercury to Aeneas to remind him of his goals and to threaten him with punishments (esp. 229-31).

223. **Dumique:** The final *-que* scans as a long before the initial stop-liquid combination of *tribulique*.

261. **faveas nostro ... ex crimine:** i.e., "may you make something good come out of something bad." That "something good" would then refer to the penitential psalms.

**rubicunda ... Luna:** the moon, personified as a goddess; cf. the note on *eleg.* 3.1. Pliny, *NH* 18.347, relates that Egyptian astrologers believed that the red moon was a sign of coming winds. Here, Bèze mentions the red moon primarily to make the connection with blushing in the next line, and also to emphasize that David will be living exposed to the elements.

267. **inimico a rege:** Saul.

# 1.

## *Ad Lectorum*

Tu quem naturae nobis consensus amicum
    Fecit, et e simili sidere natus amor,
Quisquis eris, nisi vel locuples te curia totum
    Possidet, et rauci sollicitudo fori:
Aut nisi te Hippocratis retinent, pia cura, medelae        5
    Aut totum asservit pagina sacra sibi:
Vel nisi te Pallas studiis melioribus aptum,
    Et Venerem, et Veneris tangere scripta vetat:
Aspice quam misere insano consumar amore,
    Quam lateat nostro pectore saeva Venus.        10
Si bene te novi, cum legeris omnia, dices,
    Non erat hic tali dignus ab igne coqui.
Attamen hoc frustra: nam talia fata Sorores
    Nondum etiam nato constituere mihi,
Ut quamvis nil ipse habeam quod possit amari,        15
    Experiar Veneris tempus in omne faces.
Quodque magis mirum, cum nos potiamur amica,
    Qua non est flammis dignior ulla meis,
Perpetuae tamen exagitant mea pectora curae,
    Et premit insomnem sollicitudo comes.        20
Sive graves obscura mihi nox clausit ocellos,
    Tunc quoque cum iaceam semisopitus, amo.
Seu vigilo, praeter nostras nil cogito flammas.
    Candida luminibus proxima sola meis.

# ELEGIES

<hr>

## 1.

### *To the Reader*

Those of you who can sympathize with my situation and who suffer a love born under a like star, look at me!—it doesn't matter who you are, unless the noble senate and the hustle and bustle of the marketplace preoccupy you completely; or the medical arts of Hippocrates, a worthy calling, prevent you, or the sacred page has you under lock and key; or Minerva says you are suited for more serious literature, and forbids you to touch Venus and her writings—see how pathetically I am consumed by love, see how cruel Venus lurks in my heart!

If I am right about you, when you read through this, you'll say, "He didn't deserve to be tormented by such a fire." But you're wasting your time: the Fates planned it out before I was born, that although I have nothing in me worth loving, yet will I suffer the torches of Venus for all time. And what is even more amazing, when I have the girl whom I most desire, still Cares constantly gnaw at my heart, and their friend Anxiety weighs on me until I cannot sleep. Or if dark night has closed my eyes, even then when I am lying half asleep, I feel the love. Or if I am awake, I can't think on anything else but the passion I feel. Candida

Hei mihi, quae nuper nobis insomnia misit     25
    Ille puer, quantis lusit imaginibus!
Nec piguit nostrum populo narrare furorem,
    Et Phoebum in somnos sollicitare meos.
Quippe etiam haec nobis nevere incommoda Parcae
    Nequitiae fiam testis ut ipse meae.     30
Id tamen exemplo liceat fecisse Tibulli:
    Sic Nemesis flammas, culte Tibulle, canis.
Cynthia saepe tibi sic est cantata, Properti;
    Sic est Nasoni dicta Corynna suo.
Hi tamen aeternum meruerunt carmine nomen:     35
    Di faciant, possim post mea fata legi.
Scilicet hoc unum nostros solatur amores;
    Hoc facit ut placeat, quae mihi flamma nocet.
Sive autem id nobis veniens concesserit aetas,
    Seu me quae vulgum fata severa manent,     40
Sic saltem vixisse mihi, te teste, placebit,
    Exemplo ut fieres cautior ipse meo.
Quippe, aut fallor ego, aut nostros cum legeris ignes,
    Et mea cum fuerit sors bene nota tibi,
Sedulus hoc deinceps, et tota mente cavebis,     45
    Ne simili mecum sis ratione miser.
Nostra utinam tibi flamma ferat tot commoda, lector,
    Quot dedit auctori maxima damna suo.

is always before my eyes. Ah me! what insomnia that boy sent me re-
cently, how he teased my imagination! I am not ashamed to tell every-
one about my madness and to reveal my dreams. In fact, the Fates spun
these troubles for me, to make me a witness to my own corruption. Yet
allow me to follow the example of Tibullus: you, elegant Tibullus, sing
of your passion for Nemesis in this way. Propertius, you sing about
Cynthia like this. Ovid, you sing of your girl Corinna so. The names of
these deservedly live on forever because of their poetry. May the gods
grant that be able to be read after I am gone.

Yes, this alone calms my desires, and this alone makes the passion's
pain a pleasant one. Whether I reach a ripe old age, or die young like
most people, at least, you see, I'll find pleasure in knowing that my life
can serve as an example for you to be careful. In fact, either I'm wrong,
or when you read about my burning obsession, and when you know my
lot, you will be alert, and give every attention lest you become wretched
for the same reason as I. Would that my passion grant as many benefits
to you as it gave deep heartache to the author.

## 2.

### *In mediocritatis laudem*

Non frustra solita est medium laudare vetustas:
    Nam nil laudari dignius orbis habet.
In medio posita est virtus, hinc indeque fallax
    Tota sinistra via est, totaque dextra via est.
Icare, si patrem esses inter utrumque secutus,     5
    Icarias nullus nomine nosset aquas.
Si medio Phaëton mansisset calle superbus,
    Non esset saeva terra perusta face.
Nec lenis nimium, nec durat saeva potestas:
    Quae medium servat, sola perennis erit.     10
Te nimia, o Juli, clementia perdidit olim:
    Occidit feritas te, truculente Nero.
Augustus felix cur multos mansit in annos?
    Nec facilis nimium, nec truculentus erat.
Nec nimis ipse coli, nec sperni Juppiter optat;     15
    Sed magis una iuvat mens moderata deos.
Largus opum nullus, nullus laudatur avarus:
    Magnus, in his potuit qui tenuisse modum.
Antoni mensas sic vicit cena Catonis,
    Et tenuem melior fama secuta larem.     20
Nec gracilis structura nimis, nec crassa probatur:
    Haec spectatori displicet, illa ruit.
Ut moderata iuvant, sic aegris pharmaca multis,
    Heu nimium multis, saepe petita nocent.
Dicere plura nefas credo: nam laude nequaquam     25
    Efferri immodica sustinet ipse modus.

---

1     Non frustra medium laudavit docta vetustas *1597*
12    Saevitia occidit te *1597*
13    multos cur *1597*
15-16 Vana superstitio non pacat numinis iras | Quod media gaudet simplicitate
      coli *1597*
23    aegros ... multos *1597*
24    multos saepius hausta necant *1597*
25    licet multo sed laude referri *1597*
26    Immodica sese non sinit ipse modus *1597*

## 2.

### *In Praise of Moderation*

For good reason the ancients used to praise moderation, for nothing in the whole world is more worthy of praise. In moderation lies virtue, while here on the left and there on the right the path is full of treachery. Icarus, if you had followed your father at a moderate height, no one would know the name Icarian Sea. If haughty Phaëthon had remained in the middle path, that land would not have been scorched with an intense torch. Neither does excessive leniency or iron-fisted tyranny endure: Only the government that holds the middle way lasts through the years. Julius, your excessive clemency once ruined you, while your savagery, brutal Nero, brought you down. Why did Augustus happily remain in power for many years? He was neither too permissive, nor too brutal. Even Jupiter himself doesn't want to be worshiped too much, but he doesn't want to be spurned either. Only a temperate mind pleases the gods best. Neither the one who squanders his wealth nor he who is too miserly garners any praises. Great was he who was able to hold to moderation in these matters. In this way, the modest dinner of Cato surpassed the lavish spread of Antony, and a better reputation attended his unassuming home. People do not approve of a gaudy and pretentious building, nor a gauche one: the latter is ugly to look at, the former soon crumbles. The very drugs that help the sick when taken in moderation, often hurt them when used excessively. I should not say anything more: for moderation itself won't bear being praised immoderately.

### 3.

Cornua bis posuit, bis cepit cornua Phoebe;
    Nec tamen es tanto tempore visa mihi.
Vivo tamen, si vita potest tibi, Publia, dici,
    Moerorem et lachrymas quae fovet una meas.
Certe dura mihi mors saepe in vota vocatur,          5
    Mors finem lachrymis impositura meis.
Non aliter queritur ventrem durare Prometheus;
    Et posito mallet numine posse mori:
Fallor enim, aut quisquis figmenta haec repperit olim,
    Vulturis est illi nomine dictus amor.          10
Quae non visa mihi platea est? quid in urbe relictum?
    Urbe tamen tota Publia nulla fuit.
Ergo vel miseram cohibent te coniugis irae,
    O non tam saevo foemina digna viro!
Vel populosa tibi sordere Lutetia coepit,          15
    Et placidi ruris dulcior aura placet.
Forsitan in sylvis nostros meditaris amores,
    Et tuto velles omnia ferre loco.
Ibo igitur; nec me quicquam retinebit euntem;
    Donec sis aliquo sola reperta loco.          20
Interea manuum serves, collique colorem,
    Et fieri nigras ne patiare genas.
Tecta incede caput: nam te si cernat Apollo,
    Ardeat in vultus ustus et ipse tuos.
In sylvis lauri vestita est cortice Daphne:          25
    Hei mihi, si de te fabula talis erit!
Callisto in sylvis summo est compressa Tonanti:
    Ne rogo, ne placeat Juppiter iste tibi.
Heu! quid non timeo? latronum hic regna teguntur:
    Quisquis es, hinc aufer, praedo cruente, manus,          30
Actaeon doceat violati numinis iras:
    Dictynna certe non minor ista Dea est.
Quid loquor? o nostrae pars maxima, Publia, mentis,
    Non poterunt aures ista ferire tuas.
O utinam praesens verba observare legentis,          35
    Et frontis possem signa notare tuae!
Optima tunc nostro spes addi posset amori,
    Et possem mecum dicere, lenis erit

## 3.

Twice Diana has put up a crescent moon, and twice she has taken it away, but meanwhile I haven't seen you at all. Oh, I'm alive, if you can call it that, Publia, you who alone foster my sadness and my tears. To be sure, I pray often for death to deal me its blow and put an end to my tears. I'm no different from Prometheus who complains that his liver regenerates spontaneously and who would prefer to give up his divinity so he can die. If you ask me, whoever once upon a time invented this myth is wrong: he meant "love" when he said "vulture."

What city square have I not visited? What place did I miss? Publia is nowhere to be found in the whole city. So either your husband's anger confines you—you don't deserve such a cruel husband!—or you became weary of crowded Paris, and decided that the fresher air of the quiet countryside is for you. Perhaps you are in the forest thinking about our romantic encounters, and imagine that it would be a safe place for liaisons. I will come, then; nothing can hold me back until I find you alone somewhere.

Meanwhile, keep the color of your hands and your neck intact, and don't allow your cheeks to become tan. Cover your head. For if Apollo sees you, he also may burn and be consumed with love for your face. In the forest Daphne is clothed with the bark of a laurel tree. Ah me! what if this happens to you? In the woods the lofty Thunderer held Callisto—no, please, don't carry on an affair with Jupiter! Alas, what doesn't cause me fear? The forest is a secret hideout for thieves. Whoever you are, keep your hands off, you bloody robber; may Actaeon teach you the anger of a violated goddess: she's definitely every bit the goddess Diana is.

What am I saying? O Publia, greatest part of my soul, you will not be able to hear a word I just said. I wish that I could be there to watch you when you read my words, and to observe the expressions of your face! Then the greatest hope would fuel my love, and I would be able to

Perveniam certe quacumque moreris in urbe,
    Sive aliquo potius, Publia, rure lates.         40
Perveniam; et si non mea per se forma loquatur,
    Fortunae fiam nuntius ipse meae.
Quod si surda preces ausis contemnere nostras,
    Nempe meae subito conscia caedis eris.
Attamen hoc media nobis in morte placebit,       45
    Quod tu causa meae, Publia, caedis eris.

## 4.

Si tibi sinceri nomen bene quadrat amici,
    Cur mihi quae tota est candida, nigra tibi est?
Cur quoties caleo dixi, tibi frigus in ore?
    Cur mihi quod gelidus Caucasus, Aetna tibi est?
At saltem si visa prius tibi nostra fuisset,       5
    Si conspecta foret, quam violata, prius,
Vel me fallit amor, vel si tibi visa fuisset,
    Essemus forma captus uterque pari.
Quod si tam pulchris non esses captus ocellis,
    At levius poteras tunc tamen esse malus.       10
Perfide, quis nostros unquam accusavit amores?
    Candida quo tandem iudice facta rea est?
Actor es et iudex idem: succurite iura,
    Laedit Romanum perfidus iste forum.
Parce tamen, verbis uti si cogor acerbis.       15
    Hei mihi, quod sic est imperiosus amor!
Nunc faveo, Lodoice, tibi; nunc urit amica;
    Et fidei memorem me iubet esse meae.
Utrique est iuratus amor, dominaeque, tibique:
    Nunc, Cytheraea Venus, dic mihi, cuius ero?       20
Cur transversus agor? duplici cur uror ab igne?
    Ah! fuerat nobis unica flamma satis!
Rectus amor, Lodoice, tibi me fecit amicum:
    Nescio cur placeat causa pudica minus.
Scilicet insani merito creduntur amantes:       25
    Quisquis amas, iuris non potes esse tui.
Quod tamen est mirum, iusta est insania nobis,
    Et videor demens cum ratione mihi.

say to myself, "She will give in." Of course, I will come to whatever city you reside in, or, preferably, if you are hiding out in the country, I will go there. And if my appearance doesn't speak for itself, I'll tell you myself about the sorry state I'm in. But if you are unwilling to listen and dare to scorn my entreaties, immediately you will be an accessory to my death. But even in death, Publia, the thought will please me that you are the cause of my dying.

## 4.

If I'm right to think of you as my "true friend," why is it that you call pitch-black what I call bright-white? Why is it every time I say I'm hot, you claim you're cold? Why does my chilly Caucasus become your Mt. Aetna? At any rate, if you had seen my girlfriend first, if you had spied her before I put my hands on her, either love deceives me, or had it happened that way, we would both equally be taken by her beauty. But if you are not captivated by such beautiful eyes, you've proven yourself all the more phony.

Liar, who ever found fault with my love? By what judge is Candida found guilty? You are plaintiff and judge all rolled into one. Laws, come to my aid: this perjurer offends the Roman court! Excuse me for becoming cantankerous. Ah me, love has overwhelmed me! Now I favor you, Louis; now my girlfriend is enraged, and she bids me to remember my promise. I swore love both to my mistress and to you. Now, Cytherean Venus, tell me, whose shall I be? Why am I turned crosswise? Why am I consumed by a double fire? Ah, a single flame once was sufficient for me! A brotherly love, Louis, has made me your friend; yet I don't know why now our virtuous relationship takes second place. Clearly lovers deserve to be called insane: You lovers have no say-so over yourselves.

Nam mea, si nescis (sed nescis, arbitror) una est,
    Quam velit ipsa sibi praeposuisse Venus.     30
Sic caput erectum, sic frons exsurgit aperta:
    Sic virides oculos umbra decora tegit;
Sic oculi geminis radiant hinc inde smaragdis:
    Quae fero, sunt huius vulnera prima loci.
Utraque sic pulcher coniungit lumina nasus,     35
    Purpureis sic est conspicienda genis.
Sic geminis roseus color emicat undique labris:
    O labris toties labra petita meis!
Hic habitat quae me tandem servabit, opinor,
    Nunc in perniciem lingua diserta meam.     40
Quid caput auratum memorem? quid eburnea colla?
    Binaque quae niveo pectore mala latent?
Caetera quid referam? quae si non omnia novi,
    Quis tamen esse suo corpore digna neget?
Et tamen hanc audes maculare et dicere nigram.     45
    Desine: habet certe numen et ista suum.
Quae nisi sit precibus nostris lenita, veremur
    Ne discas laesae quam gravis ira Deae.
Nunc revoces quae scripta tibi: sit foedere iuncto,
    Candida quae nobis, candida et illa tibi.     50
Certe digna meis una es, mea Candida, flammis.
    Di faciant possim dicere, tota mea es.
Tunc licet insanus tota designer in urbe,
    Dum mea sis, nihili nomina vana moror.
At tua qui nigra violarit nomina fama,     55
    Hic hostis nobis, hic inimicus erit.
Illius efficiam, faveat modo notus Apollo,
    Crimina deridens vulgus in orbe legat.
Tuque iterum nostrum si laedas forte furorem,
    Haud equidem vanas experiere minas.     60

---

54    nihili *1548, 1779* nihilum *1713*

Yet it's amazing: I really think my insanity is justifiable, and that I'm mad for a good reason. For my girlfriend, in case you don't know (but I think you do), is the only one to whom Venus herself yields first place. Her head is so perfectly straight, her forehead rises so broadly; and such a beautiful brow arches over her green eyes, that in turn gleam like two emeralds. But I have only scratched the surface. A lovely nose bridges the eyes, and the blush of her cheeks makes her conspicuous. Her two lips sparkle with rosy color—O lips so often sought by mine! Here dwells a smooth-talking tongue, which in the end I think will keep me for my ruin. Why should I mention her golden hair? her ivory neck? the two apples that lie hidden in her snow-white bosom? Why should I relate more? Maybe I don't know everything, but who would deny that she has a fine body? And yet you dare to slander her and call her "darky." Lay off: I'm convinced she also has her own divinity. Unless my prayers can soften her, I fear you will learn how heavy is the blow from an injured goddess. Now take back what you have written: let's agree that what is white to me will be white to you.

Assuredly, my Candida, you alone are worthy of my passions. May the gods make it so I can say that you are totally mine. Then, although I'll be deemed crazy in the whole city, as long as you are mine, I'll have no regard for the empty names they call me. But whoever smears your name with a dark reputation will be our foe and our enemy. Should famous Apollo grant it, I'll make it so that his charges will be the laughing stock of the world. And you, if by chance you insult my madness again, you'll find my threats are not at all hollow.

## 5.

Quisquis amas (aiunt cuncti) fuge corpus amatum,
    Vivere si caeco liber ab igne cupis.
Hei mihi, te quoties fugi, mea Candida! fugi:
    Semper at in nostro pectore regnat amor.
Ecce iterum, fateor, fugi te, Candida: verum          5
    Et potui, et possum dicere semper, amo.
Sive abeo in sylvas, nobis succurrit Adonis,
    Et fit tristitiae conscia sylva meae:
Sive placent horti, quot florum hic millia cerno,
    Tot stimulis captum me premit asper amor.         10
Narcissum hinc croceum video, hinc flentes Hiacynthos;
    Hinc miser ante oculos pulcher Adonis adest.
Magna quidem nostrae fateor medicamina flammae:
    Sed me qui vincit, vincit et ille Deos.
At si prata iuvant, o quantas sentio flammas!         15
    Ardeo tunc flammis totus amoris ego.
Hic videor Cereris fugientem cernere natam;
    Hic videor furvi cernere Ditis equos.
Littora si specto, vitreas tunc cogito Nymphas,
    Fervidaque in medio numina saepe mari.         20
Quo magis evado montes sublimis in altos,
    Hoc propior Veneris fit puer ille mihi.
Si placeant urbes (vis ut semel omnia dicam)?
    Illic cum videam plurima, nulla placent.
Illius nunc carpo oculos, nunc illius ora:         25
    Haec capite, haec pedibus displicet, illa genis,
Denique materies si desit, crimina fingo;
    Et quaecunque aliis candida, nigra mihi est.
Quid prodest fugisse igitur, cum Candida praesens,
    Atque adeo lateri sit comes usque meo?         30
Umbrae igitur merito quadret tibi, Candida, nomen:
    Tale tamen nomen non decet iste color.
Humanum potius debes deponere nomen,
    Una simul gemino quae potes esse loco.

---

3     Candida? *pro* Candida! *1548 (errata), 1580*
27    desit *1548* dedit *1779*

## 5.

You who are in love—everybody says so—flee the object of your desire, if you wish to live free from the hidden fire. Ah me! how often I have fled you, my Candida! Yes, I have fled, but love always rules in my heart. Look, I admit it, again I have fled you, Candida, but still I can always say, "I'm in love." If I go off into the forest, Adonis comes to my mind, and the forest becomes aware of my sadness. And if I try to enjoy the gardens, as many thousands of flowers I see here, with so many thorns prickly Love sticks me, as he holds me captive. Over here I see a yellow Narcissus, here a weeping Hyacinth, here the handsome Adonis stands out. They are, I confess, great remedies for my inflamed passion. But the one who subdued me, subdued even the gods.

But if I try to enjoy the meadows—O how many flames I feel!—then I burn complete with the flames of your love. Here I think I see Ceres's daughter fleeing, here I see the horses of gloomy Hades. If I visit the seashore, then I think about the sea nymphs, and the divinities often on fire in the midst of the sea. The higher I try to escape into the high mountains, the nearer I find myself to Venus's boy. If I choose the cities—do you want me to sum this up once and for all?—that feast for the eyes gives no pleasure at all. I find fault now with this one's eyes, now that one's face. She has an ugly head, that one has ugly feet, that one ugly cheeks. Then if the defects aren't real, I imagine them: so the one who is bright-white to others, is pitch-black to me. What did I gain by fleeing, therefore, when Candida is present, and a constant companion by my side? So, it fits to call you my shadow, Candida, though the color doesn't befit such a name as yours. You really ought to set aside your human name anyway, since you have the ability to be in two places at once. Forgive me, please, goddess, whoever you are: even Venus

Parce, rogo, quaecunque Dea es: subiecit et ipsa          35
    Anchisi sese (res bene nota) Venus.
Ecce fugam fateor; veniam ne, Diva, negato:
    Saepe mihi veniam Iuppiter ipse dedit.
Ipse quidem prima mox ad te luce revertar;
    Quasque voles poenas, si patiare, feram.          40

## 6.

Si te, diva Venus, genuerunt aequora quondam,
    Si Veneris surdo numina nota mari:
Ne me, ne pelago iactatum desere, Diva:
    En madidus raucis undique vincor aquis.
Quaeris ubi fluctus, ubi sint saeva aequora? nusquam:          5
    Sed mare, quo vexor, terra dat ipsa mihi.
Me miserum! quamvis liquidis seiunctus ab undis,
    Auferor a ficto naufragus ipse freto!
Hei mihi! quid ficto dixi? verissima nobis
    Unda nocet; fictum res habet ista nihil.          10
Nusquam undas video; circumstant attamen undae:
    Scilicet in sicco curro, natoque mari.
Ecce iterum, sicco cur dixi? Nempe sepulta
    Ingenii vis est quantulacunque mei.
Hinc toties cogor mentem mutare priorem;          15
    Musaque dissidiis ingeniosa mea est.
Vos, oculi flentes, praebetis flumina puppi:
    Hoc volat infelix flumine vecta ratis.
Nec venti desunt; ventos suspiria praebent;
    Haec laceram ducunt in sua damna ratem.          20
Quid tacitos dicam stimulos, caecumque furorem?
    Dant stimuli remos, dat mihi vela furor.
Spes miserae est cymbae clavus, spes optima Divum,
    Spes medicina malis una reperta meis.
Anchora sunt humili deprompta e pectore verba,          25
    Vix tamen iratas haec remorantur aquas.
Firmus amor ratis est malus; sunt dona rudentes:
    Fune carina regi, munere sueta Venus.
Navis es, o anima insano correpta furore:
    Te miseram caecus navita ducit Amor.          30

submitted herself to Anchises (a well-known story). Look, I admit that I am fleeing; don't deny me this favor, goddess. Jupiter himself has often done favors for me. At dawn I will soon return to you; and if you are so gracious, I will endure all the torments you want.

### 6.

If the sea gave birth to you once, divine Venus, if the power of Venus is manifest from the faint-sounding sea, do not, goddess, do not abandon me buffeted on the water. Look! I am soaked and overwhelmed by the loud-roaring waves on all sides. You ask where are the waves, where are the raging waters? Nowhere. The sea tosses me while I stand on dry land! Poor me, although I'm far removed from the watery waves, I am shipwrecked, borne off by an imaginary storm surge.

Ah me! Why did I say "imaginary"? The waves that trouble me are very real; there's nothing imaginary about them. Nowhere do I see waves, but waves are all around: yes, I am running on dry land, and swimming in the sea. But here I go again, why did I say "dry"? I mean, the power of my genius, however small, is engulfed in flood. Hence I'm compelled so often to change my mind: my muse is schizophrenic. You, weeping eyes, are providing waters for the ship. This luckless raft flies along carried by the water. Nor are winds lacking; my sighs cause the winds. They lead the battered raft to its destruction. Why should I mention the silent goads, the hidden furor? The goads provide the oars, the furor gives me sails.

Hope is the rudder for my sorry vessel, hope is the best of the gods. I have discovered that hope alone is the remedy for my ills. The words drawn from my deep breast are the anchors, yet they can barely withstand the angry waves. Steadfast love is the mast of the ship; the gifts are its ropes. The ship is usually steered by a line, Venus by a present. You

Tempestas, scopuli: nempe ira odiumque timentur.
  Di faciant ut sint ira odiumque procul!
Fulmina quae vereor, sunt verba minantia nobis:
  Ah, procul a nostro sitis amore minae!
Si frons laeta minus, si non, velut ante, serena,                    35
  Tunc madidis cedit fessa carina Notis.
Saepe igitur ventis currunt mea vela secundis:
  Saepe mihi forti carbasa pulsa Noto.
Ut tamen est visum littus, portumque subire
  Iam paro, conspecti captus amore soli.                             40
Auferor infelix, quamvis multumque diuque
  Coner in adverso figere vela solo.
Tunc faciem littus mutat, positoque nitore,
  Sidera pallescunt ignibus orba suis.
Clamo tamen, liceat saltem mihi cernere ripas;                       45
  Redde diem misero, Candida, redde diem.
Haec ego dum gemino, referunt mea carbasa venti,
  Et ruit in nostrum multa procella caput.
Spirant cuncta minas, crebrum micat aethere fulmen,
  Mox oculis abeunt littora visa meis.                               50
Quod tamen est mirum, stat recto pondere malus,
  Et nequeunt saevo cedere vela freto.
Quem tot turbae agitant, hunc, o Cytheraea, negabis
  Sentire insani cuncta pericla maris?
Aut igitur totum moveas, Neptune, furorem                            55
  Ut bibat insanas obruta puppis aquas:
Aut facias tensis intrem mea littora venis:
  Ah! volui velis dicere, parce, Venus.
Parce, Venus: mea culpa levis, si culpa vocari
  Mutatae debet litterae syllabulae.                                 60
Si sit culpa tamen, fateor, Venus, haec mihi culpa,
  Haec, inquam, nobis optima culpa placet.

are a ship, O raging spirit. Blind Love, the seaman, navigates poor you. The weather and the rocks, I mean anger and hate, are feared. Gods, may I steer well clear of that anger and hate! The lightning-strikes that I fear are the words that threaten me. Ah, threats, stay far from my love! If her expression is less than happy, if not serene as before, then my tired keel yields to the humid south winds.

Therefore my sails often run with favorable winds; often my boat is struck by a strong south wind. Yet when I see a shoreline, then I attempt to enter the port, captivated with the desire for the sighted land. I am borne away, unhappy, although I try to direct my sails to the land that lies across from me. Then the shore changes its appearance, and the stars, no longer twinkling, become pale and dim. I shout, "At least let me see the shore! Return the light to your poor sailor, Candida, return the light!" While I repeat these things, the winds bear back my vessel, and many gusts of wind rush against my head. Everything breathes threats, frequent lightening flashes in the sky, and soon I lose all sight of the shore. What's amazing is that the mast stands firm and erect, and the sails are not able to give way to the fierce storm surge. Venus, will you deny the one whom so many storms toss about to feel all the dangers of the raging sea? Therefore, either stir up the whole fury, Neptune, so that my overwhelmed ship may drink up the insane waters, or let me reach the shore with my extended mantool. Ah, sorry, Venus, I meant to say "mainsail," not "mantool." Forgive me. It's a small mistake, if it can even be called that, the exchange of a few letters. But if it is a mistake, I confess, Venus, it's my mistake, and one that pleases me very much.

## 7.

Hei mihi, quae terrent pavidum mala somnia pectus!
    Eheu, quae trepido somnia visa mihi!
At tu quisquis amas, nec speres luce quietem,
    Nec tacitas noctes polliceare tibi.
Vespere colla domum referunt leviora iuvenci,         5
    Et tacitae requiem commeditantur aves.
Vespere nunc stertit fusca cum coniuge Pastor;
    Nunc venerem exercet, laetus et ipse, suam.
Sol quoque postremas postquam pervenit ad undas,
    Fertur in ardentis Thetidos ire sinus.         10
At nos perpetuis exercita turba periclis,
    Quos insana trahit post sua terga Venus:
Sive dies praebet magno sua lumina mundo,
    Nostra latent tenebris pectora caeca suis;
Seu nox nigra sua terras amplectitur umbra,         15
    Semper adest noctis sollicitudo comes;
Ingressusque toros, menti se callidus infert
    Pulicis exiguo corpore tectus Amor.
Quisquis es exemplum a nobis qui quaeris, habeto,
    Alterius damno cautus ut esse queas.         20
Nox erat, et variis vexatus pectora curis,
    Credideram molli languida membra toro.
Necdum prima quies oculos bene clauserat, ecce
    Iam parat insidias sanguinolentus Amor.
Agmina cernebam, armatasque instare catervas;         25
    Et, nisi fallor ego, vix puto, somnus erat.
Agnovi procul ipse acies, fulgentiaque arma;
    Denique vera oculis agmina visa meis.
Expecto trepidus, nec enim fugisse licebat:
    Audio clamores, verbera saeva, minas.         30
Aspicio; en mediis mihi Candida cernitur armis,
    Et laniata genas, et laniata comas.
Talis erat Paridi quondam cum rapta Lacaena est:
    Thisbe, te extincto, Pyrame, talis erat.
Ille comam, ille togam flentis frustraque rogantis         35
    Diripit; ille, mea est, clamat, et ille, mea est.
Dirigui, ut solus viso praedone viator,
    Ut stupet aspectis agna relicta lupis.

## 7.

Ah me! what nightmares shake my trembling heart with fear! Alas! What dreams I see full of fear! But you who love, don't expect rest by day, don't promise to yourself quiet nights. In the evening, the oxen bring back home their unburdened necks, and the silent birds think about rest. At vespers, now the shepherd with his tawny wife snores, now he indulges his own love, happy himself. The sun also arrives at the far waters, and is said to go into the bosom of glowing Thetis. But most of us are engaged in constant troubles, which mad Venus carries around like a backpack. Should day shed its light on the world, our unseen hearts lie hid in the shadows; or if dark night embraces the world with its shadow, always anxiety, night's companion, is near. And when we've gone to bed, clever Cupid, disguised as a flea, works his way into our minds.

Whoever you are, who look for an example from us, take note, so by the ruin of another you can be wary. It was night, and tormented by various cares in my heart, I entrusted my weary limbs to a soft couch. Not yet had I closed my eyes well, when suddenly bloody Cupid lays a snare for me. I saw troops and armed bands approaching, and, unless I'm mistaken, I hardly think it was a dream. I myself recognized the battle lines from afar, the flashing arms. Finally, I saw the actual troops. Afraid, I await them, because I couldn't run away. I hear shouts, wild drumming, threats. I peer a little closer, and—look! I see Candida amid the weapons, and her cheeks lacerated, her hair torn. Helen looked like this once when seized by Paris: Thisbe, when she found you dead, Pyramus, looked like this. The one grabbed her hair, the other ripped off her gown as she wept and pleaded in vain; the one shouts, "She's mine!" and the other, "She's mine!" I became stiff, as when a lone traveler spies a robber, or an abandoned lamb a wolf. What should I do? My anger,

Quid facerem? Iubet ira loqui, pietasque, fidesque:
    At monet aspecta morte tacere metus.                40
Ira metum vincit: medios moriturus in hostes
    Tendo, nec cesso dicere et ipse, mea est.
Illa, ut me aspexit: miser, ah miser, inquit, abito;
    Non tua tam misero tempore digna fides.
Ah! fuge; sic levius moriar. Nec plura locuta,          45
    Voce mihi visa est deficiente mori.
Protinus exclamans, incuso hominesque, Deosque,
    Nec cesso vacuas ingeminare minas.
Illi adsunt, strictoque mihi mucrone minantur;
    Nec miserum cessant figere tela caput.           50
Tandem igitur cunctis unus congressus inermis,
    Ipse meae visus proximus esse neci.
Iamque cadens, carae tangebam corpus amicae,
    Esset ut extremo tempore notus amor.
Ecce abit ex oculis tenues hic somnus in auras.       55
    Territus, et vitae vix bene certus eram.
Non aliter saevi si quando dentibus hostis
    Eripuit pavidam pastor amicus ovem:
Illa licet servata, tamen stupefacta periclo,
    Vix tandem posito discit abire metu.          60
Talis eram, sudorque omnes manabat in artus,
    Sensimus et rigidas undique stare comas.
Talem, quisquis amas, tibi polliceare quietem:
    Talia spectabit somnia, quisquis amat.

piety, and conviction bid me speak, but the fear of death warns me to be silent. My anger overcomes my fear: I make my way into the middle of the enemies, bound to die, and I too keep saying, "She is mine!" When she sees me, she says, "Poor boy, ah, poor boy, go away! Your loyalty does not deserve such misery. Ah, flee; so I may die more easily."

She said nothing else. Her voice faded and she seemed to die. Immediately I begin crying out, cursing men and gods, while repeating empty threats. They stand there, and with swords drawn they threaten me. Arrows keep piercing me in my poor head. Finally then, I, but a single unarmed man, engage them all, almost certain to die. And now falling, I was touching the body of my dear sweetheart, that she may know my love to the very end.

Look!—the dream disappears into thin air. Terrified, I could hardly be sure I was alive. It was no different than if a kind shepherd had snatched a trembling sheep from the jaws of an attacker: it is saved, but bewildered by the danger, and can hardly convince itself to put the fear aside and go on. Such were my feelings, and sweat was pouring over my limbs, and I felt my hair standing on end. Promise to yourself such a rest as this, you who love: whoever is in love will see these kinds of dreams.

## 8.

Ut stupet emisso si quis Iovis igne petitus,
    Ut stupet insanis navita raptus aquis:
Sic stupui, postquam dira te febre retentum
    In moesto didici corpus habere toro.
Quid facerem? nec erat nobis ars nota medendi;                    5
    Nec, si tota foret cognita, tuta satis.
Saepe ego, cum vitae medicus spem redderet aegro,
    Vidi inter medicas membra labare manus.
Ergo, quod licuit, caelum superosque precatus,
    Has coepi pavida fundere mente preces:                        10
Humanae si quem tangit miseratio sortis;
    Si qua potest hominum tangere cura deos;
Quisquis ades superum, iustae miserere querelae:
    Crede mihi, venia res bene digna tua est.
Non ego divitas posco, Croesive talenta,                         15
    Non peto formosae coniugis esse virum:
Hoc peto, si qua pii vos cura attingit amoris,
    Reddatur Valido pristina vita meo.
Ille est, qui superum coluit studiosus honores:
    Nunc iacet in tristi pallidus ille toro.                      20
Quid dixi? magnis immo vult saepe querelis,
    Quod meruit nullo crimine, posse mori.
Iuppiter, et tu olim, non est hoc crimen, amasti:
    Si scelus hoc, sceleris sidera plena tui.
Causa tamen nobis melior, quo castior haec est:                  25
    Causa pudicitiae pondere nixa suae.
Quid potuit sceleris Validus patrasse? quis illum
    Audiit ullius criminis esse reum?
Decipit ebrietas humanam sordida mentem:
    Hinc scelerum nata est prodigiosa cohors.                     30
Ergo ut vitaret Validus tua crimina, Bacche,
    Non puduit lymphas praeposuisse tibi.
Captivos hominum ducit Venus improba sensus:
    Hinc scelerum nata est prodigiosa cohors.

---

Tit.    *om. 1548* Ludovico Valido *1779*

## 8.

I'm stunned, like someone just struck by one of Jupiter's lightning bolts, or like a sailor caught up in a terrific storm at sea! I hear that you are lying sick in bed, weakened by a dreadful fever. What should I do? I don't know the art of medicine, and even if I were versed in it, you still would not have been altogether safe. Often I have seen, when a doctor is restoring the hope of life to a sick person, the limbs fail in the doctor's hands.

Therefore, the only course left was to beseech heaven and the gods above, and so I began to pour forth prayers from my trembling heart, to see if pity for the human condition touches them, if any care for human beings can affect gods. Whoever of the gods is here, pity my just complaint. Believe me, it is a matter worthy of your grace. I do not demand riches, the silver talents of Croesus, I do not ask to be the husband of a beautiful wife. I only want this, if you are touched at all by pious love, restore Vaillant's former life to him. He is one who worshiped and performed the rites of the gods diligently. Now he lies pale on his sickbed. What did I say? Yes, he often complained loudly and asked to die, because he did not deserve any punishment. Jupiter, you loved once, this is not a crime. If this is wickedness, the stars are full of your wickedness. Yet our case has firmer grounds for being thought chaste: our case depends on the weight of his chaste virtue. What crime could Vaillant have committed? Who ever heard that he was guilty of some wrongdoing? Depraved drunkenness has corrupted the human mind, and from

Fallor ego, aut si qui Validum tetigistis amores,                    35
    Una laboranti Pallas amata fuit.
Ergo insontem animam ne saevus tollito, neve
    Tela geras tanti sanguine tincta viri.
Ecquid enim prodest rarum tribuisse colorem,
    Tam color iste brevi si periturus erat?                          40
Ingenium infudisse sagax quid profuit illi,
    Si vetet ingenio mors inopina frui?
Quod si certa manet mortis sententia fatis,
    Si petit hoc etiam Parca scelesta caput:
Hoc facite, o Divi, quae nunc mihi vita superstes,                   45
    Ut Valido prosit, prosit et illa mihi.
Non insueta precor: Ledaeos fama gemellos
    Dividua inter se vivere morte refert.
Sic nos attoniti superos, Lodoice, precamur:
    Di votis faciant pondus inesse meis!                             50
Di faciant mox ut nobis reddamur uterque,
    Et posito cantet Musa dolore iocos!

it an extraordinary horde of misdeeds has been born. So, Bacchus, to avoid these evils, Vaillant was not embarrassed to drink simple water instead of wine. Shameless Venus captures the emotions of people and goads them on, and from it an extraordinary horde of misdeeds has been born. I may be wrong, but if any love has touched Vaillant, he loved Athena as he worked hard.

Therefore, don't be cruel and take away an innocent soul. Don't bear arrows tainted with the blood of such a great man. For what is the benefit of giving us a fine color, if that color was going to fade in so short a time? What did a wise god profit to have poured genius into him, if an unexpected death prevents him from making use of it? But if the Fates are unmoved in their sentence of death, if even Fate itself seeks his life, make it so that the life which remains to me benefits Vaillant, and his life benefits me. I am not praying for anything unusual: myth relates that the twin sons of Leda divided up life and death. So I am stunned and pray to the gods, Louis: May the gods treat my vows seriously! May the gods grant that we are returned to each other soon, and our Muse sing her games without grief!

## 9.

At pereat quaecunque meas extinguere flammas,
    Quae te cunque mihi tollere tentat anus!
Improba, lena, procax, moecha, invida, dic age, curnam
    Laedi visa mea est digna puella tibi?
Vel quod tam castam non possis ferre puellam,           5
    Et tibi tam constans non bene quadret amor.
Vel cum nulla meum turbarent iurgia lectum,
    Displicuit placido pax in amore tibi.
Fallor ego, aut virtus potuit tibi neutra probari,
    Dissimilemque tibi ferre scelesta nequis.           10
Sic premitur forti mitis clementia bello,
    Sic lupus in placidas it violentus oves.
At vos, qui nostris vicinas iungitis aedes,
    Sicne decet iusta credulitate rapi?
Scilicet audaces plectit Respublica fures:           15
    Criminibus merito poena reperta sua est.
Non tamen indicta plectuntur crimina causa:
    Hoc Latii prohibent optima iura fori.
Nos vero insontes, iam dicimur exules esse.
    Quis tamen audivit criminis esse reos?           20
Cuius nocturno turbavi somnia cantu?
    Cuius ego inveniar vi petiisse fores?
Anne ego cuiusquam moechus connubia laesi?
    Candida sola mea est, Candida tota mea est.
Nimirum una anus est, quae nos incusat amoris.           25
    O Venus! an scelus est numen amare tuum?
Si scelus hoc, caelum fas sit vocitare scelestum,
    Atque iterum in sanctos bella movere deos.
Hoc, divi, prohibite nefas; moechaeque scelestae
    Ignea in invisum vertite tela caput.           30
Tene ego perpetiar misero mihi, Candida, tolli,
    Aut Veneris dici numen inane feram?
Nec contra obsistam iratus, magnoque furore
    Praecipites istos pulverulentus agam?
Tunc igitur gladios acuam, tunc bella movebo,           35
    Tunc invicta dabit vimque animumque Venus.
Interea peragent vindictae carmina partem:
    Sic ulta est Vates saepe Camoena suos.

## 9.

Let her perish, the old woman who tries to extinguish my passion, who tries to separate you from me. Cur, bawd, wench, tart, spiteful old woman, come on, tell me, why do you think this girl deserves harm? Is it because you can't tolerate such a chaste girl, and such faithful love doesn't sit right with you? Or does it bother you that we don't quarrel in bed, but instead have a peaceful relationship? I may be wrong, but you can't approve the goodness of either circumstance, nor can you bear someone who's not a tramp like you. In this way, soft mercy is downtrodden by mighty war, and the violent wolf stalks the peaceful sheep. But is it proper for you, sitting there in the next apartment, to be possessed with righteous naiveté?

Clearly the State punishes audacious thieves, but the punishment must fit the crime. Yet crimes are not punished without an indictment: Roman law is at its best when it prohibits this. We really are innocent, but now we are sentenced to be exiles. Who ever heard that we were pronounced guilty of a crime? Whose dreams did I disturb with my moonstruck serenading? Who is claiming I violently banged on their doors? Or did I, an adulterer, seduce someone's wife? Candida alone is mine, she is totally mine. One old woman to bitch about our love is one too many. O Venus! Is it a crime to be devoted to your power? If this is a crime, then I have every right to call heaven outrageous, and to renew the war against the holy gods. Prevent this atrocity, gods, turn your fiery darts against the hateful head of that wicked slut. Shall I endure to have you taken from me, Candida, or permit the power of Venus to be slandered? Shall I not indignantly resist, and like a furious and dirty soldier drive them headlong? Then I'll sharpen my swords, and wage the war; unvanquished Venus will give me strength and courage.

Meanwhile, let the poems accomplish part of the revenge: Often the Muse has avenged her poet in such a way. Who doesn't know the swift

Ecquis enim Archilochi rapidos non novit iambos?
    Tu quoque, anus, nostras experiare minas.          40
Tisiphone quamvis tecum collata, videri
    Iure oculos possit pascere digna Iovis:
Macra licet tibi sit facies, licet undique turpes
    Undique deformet pellis arata genas:
Emineat quamvis dens unus et alter ab ore,         45
    Sordeat et canis tempus utrumque comis:
Te precor insani rabies exedat amoris,
    Et turpi inclusum pectore vulnus alas.
Digna tibi tamen interea videaris amari;
    Te tamen immenso nullus in orbe probet.         50
Sint nigro frustra demissa monilia collo;
    Frustra oneret macras instita longa nates.
Displiceas merito cunctis, sis fabula vulgo,
    Nil nisi perversam fama loquatur anum.
Te mater tenerae demonstret saepe puellae,         55
    Et iubeat mores saepe cavere tuos.
Atque ita bis centum cum tandem impleveris annos,
    Tunc cupias frustra, pessima moecha, mori.
Saeviat in macrum nodosa podagra cadaver,
    Atque diu infirmis ludat in articulis.         60
Dira lues passim putres distorqueat artus,
    Foedus ut absentem prodere possit odor.
Teque notet, velut invisum sis omen, Aruspex:
    Horreat ad vultus femina, virque tuos.
Nec tamen haec quisquam medicari vulnera curet;         65
    Nec manus auxilium porrigat ulla tibi.
Te potius ridens hinc indeque turba iacentem
    Oderit, invisum devoveatque caput.
Atque ita ter centum cum tandem impleveris annos,
    Cedat ab infami corpore vita procul.         70
Silva rogum invideat, nec det tibi terra sepulchrum,
    Funeribus desint ultima vota tuis.
Inferias peragant vulpesque, canesque, lupique,
    Et si qua effuso sanguine gaudet avis.
Interea invisos iubeat discedere Manes         75
    Portitor, et Stygias tangere nolit aquas.
At tu deserto studeas in littore moesta
    Infernum precibus sollicitare Iovem.

iambs of Archilochus? You, old woman, will also experience my threats. Compared to you, the Fury Tisiphone could provide a feast for the eyes of Jupiter: Although your face is emaciated and haggard, and your cheeks are gross, like dry leather on both sides; although you've only got two teeth sticking out of your mouth, and matted, gray hair hangs around your temples; I pray that you fall deliriously and madly in love, and feed a wound shut up in your foul heart. At the same time may you seem lovable to yourself, but no one in the whole wide world will be attracted to you. There's no use in hanging necklaces from your swarthy neck. It's pointless to wear a long flounce over that bony butt. I hope everyone finds you a disgusting joke, nothing but a perverted old woman. May mothers often point you out to their tender daughters, and bid them avoid your ways. And when you've finally lived out two hundred years like this, may you wish in vain to die, you revolting slut. May knotty gout rage through your skinny cadaver, and romp in your weak joints for a long time. May acute disease distort your decaying limbs, so that you leave behind yourself a foul odor. May the soothsayers mark you like a hated omen. May men and women shrink back in horror at the sight of your face. And I don't want anyone to try to heal these wounds, no one to extend a helping hand to you. Rather, I hope the people laugh at you and knock you about as a reviled object, cursing and despising you. But when you have reached three hundred years, may your life depart far from your body. May the forest begrudge you a pyre, the earth a tomb. No last rites at your death. May the foxes, dogs, and wolves perform your ceremony, and if any bird exults in your spilt blood. Meanwhile, may the ferryman bid you depart the hated shades, and forbid you touch the Stygian waters. May you anxiously badger Pluto

Atque ita millenos cum tandem impleveris annos,
    Sis tandem Furiis addita quarta tribus.                     80
Hoc facite, o divi, si castae vota puellae,
    Si possunt casti vota valere viri:
Huius ut exemplo venerari discat Amorem,
    Quae iuvenum flammis invida turba nocet.

## 10.

Dic age, cur vanae iuvat indulgere querelae?
    Cur iuvat immites dicere, stulta, deos?
Nempe doles periisse comam, flavosque capillos
    Tam subito glabrum destituisse caput.
Desine, stulta, queri: nam quod periisse videtur,         5
    Tempora reddiderint non ita longa tibi.
Sic tibi saepe thymum, sic et tondetur anethum:
    Mox tamen in frondes surgit utrumque suas.
Sic cum saepe rosas toto collegeris horto,
    Purpureas idem cras dabit hortus opes.                 10
Fer modo, et haec quamvis possit iactura videri
    Magna, feras parvae taedia parva morae.
Nec tamen interea plores periisse capillos:
    Quam periisse putas, credito, salva coma est.
Quippe huius radios nuper miratus Apollo,            15
    Siderea dignam credidit esse domo.
Scilicet hinc ficto Berenices nomine tecta,
    Iunctaque nocturnis ignibus illa micat.

with entreaties. And when at last you have completed a thousand years like this, may you become added as a fourth member to the Furies. Grant this, O gods, if the vows of a chaste girl and a chaste man are able to accomplish anything, so that envious people who spoil the passion of the youth might learn from her example to respect Love.

### 10.

Come, tell me, why do you like to complain so much? Why do you like to call the gods heartless, foolish girl? I realize that you're upset that you have lost your hair, and that your blonde locks have forsaken your bald head so suddenly. Stop complaining, foolish girl: That which seems to have perished will return to you shortly. You often cut your thyme and dill like this, yet soon they both sprout their leaves again. And often when you gather roses from your garden, the next day it unrolls a rich red tapestry again. Just be patient, and although these things could seem a great loss, put up with these annoyances, they won't last long. And in the meantime, don't cry over lost hairs: trust me, the hair that you think is gone is really safe. Apollo was admiring the radiant beams of your hair recently, and thought they deserve a home in the stars. Evidently he gave to your locks the pseudonym "Berenice," and now they twinkle among the evening fires.

## 11.

*T. Livio et P. Ovidio nasoni cenotaphium*

Ecce iterum Iani nobis rediere Calendae.
    Hei mihi! quos luctus, funera quanta ferunt!
Roma Tito quondam celebrata est maxima magno,
    Est quoque Nasonis carmine dicta sui.
Quae te, Naso, tulit, quae te, Tite, sustulit orbi,          5
    Inter funestos est numeranda dies.
Non adeo infelix, quae infames sanguine Cannas
    Lux videt, et Latio tristia cuncta foro.
Nullum igitur munus nunc expectetis, amici,
    Munera temporibus sunt minus apta malis.          10
Fas mihi sit patrum priscos contemnere ritus;
    Fas mihi consuetas mittere iure preces.
Cernite nunc tristi ploretur ut undique caelo,
    Mersaque demisso terra sub imbre natet.
Ecce, Venus pullo vestita incedit amictu,          15
    Dilaceransque genas, dilaceransque comas.
Et pharetrae oblitus, luctuque immersus acerbo,
    Nasonis cantat carmina moestus Amor.
Ipse suas Ianus damnatque, oditque Calendas,
    Et sua de fastis tollere festa parat.         20
Flet quoque Neptunus, flet raucisona Amphitrite,
    Et patrio plorat gurgite mersa Thetis.
Pelignae lachrymis implent rura omnia Nymphae,
    Et querulus Patavi permeat arva Padus.
Tune igitur lachrymas retinebis, Roma, cadentes,      25
    Nec poteris caeli questibus esse comes?
Hei mihi, quid te olim, demens Auguste, coegit
    Nasonis sacrum sic violare caput?
Julius hoc olim non fecit avunculus, ille
    Qui dedit Italiae sceptra secunda tibi.         30

---

Tit.   *modo habent 1569, 1576, 1597*
24     moenia Brenta lavat *1597*
28-29 Tam sacrum vatis sic violare caput? | Talia non non docuit te quondam
       Iulius, ille *1597*

### 11.

*An Epitaph for Livy's and Ovid's Empty Tomb*

Look, January has come around again. Ah me! What grief it brings, how much death! The great Livy once celebrated lofty Rome, and Ovid recited poems for her. The day that took you away, Ovid, and the day that deprived the world of you, Livy, must be considered a day of mourning. Not so unhappy was the day that saw Cannae infamous for the bloodshed, and all the sad events that took place in Rome's forum.

Therefore, don't expect any present, friends: gifts are inappropriate for unpleasant occasions. Allow me to scorn the old practices of our forefathers, and to dispense of the usual prayers. See now how the gloomy sky weeps all around, and the flooded earth swims under the downpour. Look, Venus strides in, clothed with a dusky mantle, and tears her cheeks and hair. Cupid, immersed in devastating grief, has forgotten his quiver, and sadly sings the songs of Ovid. Janus himself curses and despises New Year's Day, and tries to remove his festival from the calendar. Even Neptune weeps, and boisterous Amphitrite, and Thetis, down in her father's watery abyss, sobs. The Pelignian nymphs fill the countryside with their tears, and the river Po floods the fields of Padua with its protests.

Will you, Rome, fight back your falling tears, and not join the sky in its laments? Ah me! What compelled you, mad Augustus, once to profane the sacred person of Ovid? Your uncle Julius, who gave you long-lasting power over Italy, never did this. And who can rightly call

Et te iam merito clementem dicere quisquam,
    Ingeniumve potest dicere mite tibi?
Quae nunquam Augusti potuit lenire furorem,
    Scivit inhumanos flectere Musa Getas.
Namque Tomitanis exul lugetur in oris,                                    35
    Nasonique parat barbara turba rogos.
Lugete, o miseri vates, totumque iubete
    Parnassum alternos ingeminare sonos.
Flentibus en aderit Phoebus, Pallasque favebit,
    Et peraget partes numen utrumque suas.                         40
Vos quoque, quos caeli dignissima cura fatigat,
    Ne, rogo, ne quinta quaerite luce lyram.
Illa etenim lumen caelo, terrisque negabit,
    Laetaque cum caro Tartara vate colet.
At vos, o manes, quorum nec longa vetustas,                               45
    Nobile nec delet nomen avara dies:
Vos, inquam, solos Iani gaudere Calendis,
    Vos, dare laetitiae mutua signa, decet.
Quippe Titum vobis lux addidit ista peremptum;
    Haec quoque Nasonis lux dedit arte frui.                       50
Ergo occurristis, manes, venientibus illis,
    Totaque in amplexus mortua turba ruit.
Ennius inde pater medium complexus utrumque,
    Hic, ait, est Latii gloria tota soli.
Mox Varro et Cicero properant, tersusque Catullus;                       55
    Mox quoque cum Nemesi, culte Tibulle, venis.
Et tu qui dubium fecisti nomen Homeri,
    Cui vitam debent, rus, pecus, arma suam.
Quid reges memorem priscos, fortesque Quirites,
    Quoscunque exoriens Roma, vetusque dedit?                      60
Scilicet ista Titum venerata est undique turba;
    Hannibal aspecto surgit et ipse Tito.
Vos, o vos Manes, aeternos ducite lusus:
    At nos perpetuo cura dolorque prement.

---

34    *ad init.* Crudeles potuit *1597*
53    utrinque *1597*
58    Laudem cui debent *1569, 1576, 1597*

you kind now, or claim that you have a mild nature? The Muse who knew how to sway the uncivilized Thracians could never soften the fury of Augustus. For an exile mourns on the shores of Tomi, and a barbarous people prepare a pyre for Ovid. Weep, poor poets, and bid all Parnassus to echo your cries. Behold, Apollo will stand near to those crying, and Athena will bless them, and each divinity will do their part. You who toil hard to study the heavens, a most worthy task, please do not seek to discern the lyre on the fifth day. For his lyre will refuse to shine in the sky or on the earth, and will happily dwell in Tartarus with its dear poet.

But, shades of the underworld, only for you, whose noble name is effaced neither by prolonged old age nor by greedy daylight, for you alone, I repeat, is it proper to rejoice on New Year's Day and exchange mutual tokens of happiness. For the light of that day stole Livy in death and added him to your company, and also granted you to enjoy the talents of Ovid. You welcomed them, shades, as they came, and the whole population of the deceased rushed to embrace them. Amidst them father Ennius hugged them both and said, "This is the epitome of the glory of Italian soil." Soon Varro and Cicero hastened up, and terse Catullus; soon also, elegant Tibullus, you came with Nemesis, and you who cast doubt on the fame of Homer, to whom they owe their life, namely country, cattle, and arms. Why should I recount the old kings, the brave Quirites, and whomever rising Rome and antiquity produced? Naturally, that crowd honored Livy from all sides. Hannibal himself stands up at the sight of him. Shades, weep through all eternity. But sadness and

Hanc igitur lucem luctu celebrabo quotannis,                    65
    Et ficto iniiciam thura merumque rogo.
Hi tumulo versus deinde inscribentur inani:
    Di faciant illos postera turba legat:
Quisquis ades, vacuum Nasonis cerne sepulchrum:
    Quisquis ades, magni cerne sepulchra Titi.                  70
Orphei quod precibus Plutonia regna dedere,
    Hoc Titus, et magnus Naso dedere sibi.

---

65    Has ego quottannis luctu celebrabo Calendas *1548, 1779*
66    vacuo *pro* ficto *1597*
67    *sic* 1569, 1776 Hi deinde versus tumulo ponentur inane *1548* Deinde isti ver-
      sus tumulo ponentur inani *1580, 1779*
68    Forsan et hos olim postera turba leget *1569, 1576, 1597*

grieving will torment us forever. Every year I will celebrate this day with sorrow, and I will pour incense and wine on an imaginary pyre. Then these verses will be written on a cenotaph; may the gods grant that people read them throughout the ages:

"Whoever you are, approaching stranger, look at the empty tomb of Ovid; whoever you are, as you approach, look at the grave of great Livy. What Pluto's realm granted by the prayers of Orpheus, this Livy and great Ovid secured for themselves."

## 12.

Helis quod speculo multumque diuque retenta,
    Sacratum Veneri sic remoratur opus,
Fallor ego, aut iusta certe ratione movetur;
    Nec levis est tantae causa reperta morae:
Namque nec ornatos componit rite capillos,        5
    Cui non iussa suo stat coma flava loco:
Nec Tyrio fucare genas credenda colore,
    Cui medias intra purpura nata genas.
Aut igitur creta collum mentitur eburnum,
    Aut labris spargit rubra venena suis:        10
At collum natura illi concessit eburnum,
    Ex minio iussit labra rubere suo.
Cur vero tenues oculorum depilet arcus?
    Cur iubeat patula caedere fronte comas?
Cui geminos talis testudo exornat ocellos,        15
    Qualis Apellaea linea ducta manu;
Et cui lunatae tam larga est area fronti,
    Ut sit tam patula fronte nec ipsa Venus?
Scilicet haec emptis implerit dentibus ora,
    Nativum esse probat cui gelasinus ebur.        20
At vero inflatum pectus, mammasque cadentes,
    Et mollem magna colligit arte sinum.
O di, quam tuta est a tali crimine virgo,
    Cui tumet aequalis semper utrinque sinus!
Quid gestus, cultumque loquar, moresque decoros?        25
    Talis erat, malum cum Cythaerea tulit.
Ergo Helis speculum non sic remorata tuetur;
    Helis enim speculi non eget arte regi.
Ipsa sed in facie dominae crystalla morantur,
    Et raras gaudent cernere delicias.        30
Helida cur ergo absentem sic, turba, requiris,
    Nec pergis potius, dum procul Helis abest?
Quippe absens Helis nullum retinebit euntem:
    Si veniat, cunctos quod remoretur, erit.

## 12.

Because Helis lingers in front of the mirror for a very long time, she hinders the work sacred to Venus. I may be wrong, but it happens for a very legitimate reason. Her long delay has a significant cause. For she does not fix her stylish hair in the customary way, since her blonde hair stays in place already without brushing. Nor should you imagine she adds blush to her cheeks with Tyrian color, since for her deep red is natural. Nor does she feign an ivory neck with chalk, or apply red lipstick to her lips: Nature has given her a neck that is already ivory white, and commands her lips to become rosy from their own minium. Why should she pluck her slender eyebrows? Why should she have the bangs cut from her broad forehead? Her eyelids, like lines drawn by the hand of Apelles, adorn her eyes. Her crescent brow is so broad and ample as to surpass even that of Venus herself. You would think that she has filled her mouth with store-bought teeth, though her dimpled-smile passes them off as ivory of her own making. But truly her voluptuous bosom, her sloping breasts, and soft belly come together, as if an artist composed them. O gods, how can a virgin be safe from the worst lust when she has such perfectly proportioned curves! What shall I say about the way she moves, her elegance, her courtly manner? Venus was like this when she won the apple.

Therefore, Helis does not linger over the mirror to primp; she doesn't need the help of a mirror. The glass itself dotes upon the face of the lady, rejoicing to see such rare beauty. Why do you people ask where Helis is, instead of just going about your business while she's away? Truly Helis won't hold anyone back from going so long as she's absent: but if she comes, she'll be the thing that makes everybody late.

# Commentary on the Elegies

O f all the genres employed by Renaissance poets, the elegy has received the most attention among modern scholars. Robert E. Hallowell (*Ronsard and the Conventional Elegy*), Gertrude S. Hanisch (*Love Elegies of the Renaissance*), John E. Clark (*Elégie: The Fortunes of a Classical Genre in Sixteenth-Century France*), and C. M. Scollen (*The Birth of the Elegy in France 1500–1550*) have each traced the history of the genre in France, singled out its most distinguishing characteristics, and brought forth numerous examples from the period. The primary aim of these scholars was to come to an understanding of the developments and conditions that made the elegiac poetry of the Pléiade possible, and for that reason little attention is given to the actual analysis of Neo-Latin examples of the elegy. Even so, Scollen in particular has observed that Bèze was pivotal in bringing the Ovidian elegy, along with its idiom and motifs, into the popular arena, and through his contact with the members of the Pléiade, elegy found a place in the French vernacular poetry of the mid-sixteenth century. One must keep in mind that although Bèze was not the first to publish elegiac "love" poetry, he was among the first to compose in the genre, since much of his literary activity took place in the 1530s. James Hutton, likewise, has argued that the Pléiade benefitted from the fact that Neo-Latin poets, such as Bèze and Dorat, "pre-digested" the Roman elegists and mediated between their sentiments and those of the moderns.[1] One does not want to underestimate the contributions of Joannes Secundus and the Italian elegists to the

---

[1] James Hutton, "The Classics in Sixteenth-Century France," *The Classical Weekly* 43 (1950): 131–38, esp. 133.

development of the genre during the Renaissance, but in fact Bèze's compositions are more genuine and extensive in their imitation of the Roman elegists.

It has become common to term the poetry of Ovid, Tibullus, Propertius, and Gallus "love elegy," but the term itself is unfortunate, because it is so misleading. While it is true that these poets concentrate most of their energies on what may be called "the exploits of Cupid" by chronicling the ups and downs of their love affair with a particular girl, it is much too simplistic to imagine that the description of the love affair was anything less than a peg on which to hang more profound observations on the nature of the human experience. After all, there are too many conventions shared by all the representatives of the genre for them to be taken seriously as autobiography. So while the poet burns in his desire for the girl, and sings of her beauty, her fidelity and infidelity in turn, and all the triumphs and disappointments that come with any love affair, we must look for something more, something that goes beyond the mundane and worthy of that title that the elegists apply to themselves, *vates*, that is, poet-priest. It must be understood that the writings of the Roman elegists are more than just a reflection of a decadent Rome under the rule of the emperors, where people had more idle time to pursue their love interests because women were playing a more important role in society. Nor is it true that they are devoid of all attempts to promote virtue, honesty, and patriotism. The very fact that the threnodic element remains in the elegy, even amid poems with a superficially lighter subject matter, compels us to contemplate some deeper meaning in all the poems. For just as Ovid laments the death of Tibullus, with his digressions on the inexorability of death, so too Bèze mourns the death of Ovid and Tibullus, using the occasion to make a statement about the lofty role poets play in society. And sprinkled throughout all the elegies are certain important themes: the value of friendship, the golden mean, the immortality of poetry, the praise of simple living, the brevity of youth, the complexity of human relations, and countless others. It would seem, then, that there is a certain value in not dismissing these elegies too flippantly; they deserve, instead, to be read with the same subtlety as that in which their ideas are expressed.

1.

Missing in 1569, 1576, 1597.

The argument of this first elegy runs as follows: a) the poet contrasts the aims of the genre with those of the more "serious" professions, such as medicine, law, politics, etc.; b) he claims that love is an emotion that took control of him against his will; c) he admits that he now is obsessed to the point that he cannot sleep or think about anything else; d) the love that he feels inspires him and compels him to write about his passion; e) other poets have immortalized their girls in poems; f) he hopes that his behavior as revealed in these poems can serve as an example of what to avoid.

A certain logical flaw exists in all of this, perhaps intentionally. Although Bèze expects his readers to learn from his own mistakes, he himself repeats the mistakes of the models he names here. The problem that he faces, as he himself lays it out, is not that he has not had sufficient *exempla* to guide him through the pitfalls of male–female romance, but, rather, that love compels its unsuspecting victims to act against their will. At any rate, to demand logical thought is to miss the point. More important is how Bèze cleverly and subtly weaves a number of programmatic statements and reader expectations into this simple introductory narrative that cast a shadow over the whole collection.

At the outset, Bèze places the elegies within their proper framework: quite simply put, these are poems of the heart, not the head. The sober concerns and drudgery of our mundane life, which drive us to the marketplace, the universities, or the law courts, in no way impinge upon the tone or content of these poems. These poems have in view the underside of life, the emotional, less predictable and quantifiable aspects of human existence, which, it would seem, elegiac poets prefer to examine through the lens of the erotic affair. But there is always the chance that the unscholarly tone of the writing, as well as the light and frivolous themes, will be dismissed out of hand. To counter the predictable objections, Bèze follows up with a claim, albeit somewhat obliquely expressed, to vatic authority. Behind his innocent assertions of madness lie the loftier claims of Hesiod, who maintains that in revealing the origins of the cosmos he is but a mouthpiece for the Heliconian sisters, or those of Homer and Vergil, who invoke the muses to inspire them to unfold the heroic tales. Bèze's aspirations are not so grand or noble, he will admit, but he too is possessed and goaded by divine forces beyond his control to reveal certain eternal truths about human nature. Then, as if pulling out his trump card, he places himself within a generic tradition, comprised of such celebrated poets as Propertius, Tibullus, and Ovid, and immortal in its scope. The names of these poets remind the reader that even a topic so commonplace as love has weighty support among ancient authorities, thus providing the poet with a dignified precedence for this kind of undignified writing. And, he adds with one final attempt at justification, all this self-revelation about a psyche spinning out of control is not without its value to the reader: there are lessons to be learned here, benefits to be gained. Here is the emotional side of life, the passions stripped bare of the will and the constraints of reason, and allowed to roam free through the gamut of experience for all to observe. The reader can expect to hear about the heights of joy and the depths of depression, and the entire emotional range in between. Here are the anxieties that come with the uncertainty of love, and the pleasures born out of the tender moments of intimacy and acceptance. This complex web of cause and effect constitutes a kind of moral code of dos and don'ts in human relations and ultimately provides Bèze with a mechanism for offering his own insights into human nature.

1. **naturae ... consensus:** refers to those who have a natural tie to the poet by virtue of their having similar experiences. The phrase itself comes from Stoic philosophy. Thus, Cicero (*Div.* 2.24), speaking of the lack of correspondence between haruspicy and the prophecies derived from it, refers to a missing "consensus of nature," or lining up of events that the Greeks term "sympathy": "qua ex coniunctione naturae et quasi concentu atque consensu, quam συμπάθειαν Graeci appellant, convenire potest aut fissum iecoris cum lucello meo aut meus questiculus cuum caelo, terra rerumque natura?" Also idem, *DND* 3.28.

2. **simili sidere natus amor:** literally, "love born under a similar star," from the belief that the alignment of stars at birth influences a person's character (cf. Cicero, *Div.* 2.91 and Stat., *Sylv.* 3.4.63). Bèze's sympathizers will share a particular kind of love with certain common qualities.

6. **pagina sacra:** the Scriptures, which are the preoccupation of the clergy.

32-34: **Nemesis ... Cynthia ... Corynna:** the fictitious love interests of the Roman elegiac poets. Their "immortality" is enhanced by the efforts to attach them to real personages. Ancient authors identified Corinna as Julia, daughter of Augustus (Sid. Apoll. 23.159) and Cynthia as a courtesan named Hostia (Apuleius, *Apol.* 10). Tibullus's Nemesis replaces his first interest, Delia, in his second book of elegies, and is often identified as the Glycera mentioned in Horace's *Od.* 1.33.2.

**2.**

Missing in 1569, 1576; *Tottel's Miscellany*, 1: 104–5; 2: 235–36
(= Merrill, *Grimald*, 389–90, 429).

The "golden mean" was a popular theme for poets and philosophers.
The most influential treatment appears at Horace, *Od.* 2.10.5–8:

> auream quisquis mediocritatem
> diligit, tutus caret obsoleti
> sordibus tecti, caret invidenda
> sobrius aula.

The Greeks knew the phrase μηδὲν ἄγαν from an inscription on the
temple of Apollo at Delphi, while both Plato and Aristotle advocated
the "middle course" of life.

Among Bèze's contemporaries, one notes especially the treatment by
Girard:

*Mediocria optima*

> Tanta meis olim concessa potentia fatis,
>     Ut me quo cupiant fortiter illa trahant.
> Si bona sunt, pedicis me stringit dia voluptas:
>     Si mala: magnanimus concutit ossa dolor:
> Immo mihi reliquis mediocria quaero diebus:
>     Divitias nolo: Pauperiem fugio. (*Stichostratia*, [1552]: 61)

[*Middling Things are Best*

Such great powers once were granted to my fates, that they
dragged me forcibly wherever they pleased. If they were good, di-
vine pleasure bound me in shackles. If bad, a deep-felt pain shook
my bones. No, I seek middling things for myself in my remain-
ing days: I don't want riches: I flee poverty.]

5. **Icare:** According to myth, Icarus and his father Daedalus tried to
escape from Crete by using wings that they had constructed from
wax. Despite his father's warnings, Icarus flew too close to the sun,
thus melting the wax and falling into the sea. The region of the Aeg-
ean where he drowned, according to ancient etymologists, derives its
name from him.

7. **Phaëton**: Ovid tells the story (*Met.* 1.747–2.400) of how the impetuous and ambitious Phaëthon, son of Helios the sun god, begged his father to drive his chariots across the sky for one day. Helios relented, but Phaëthon lost control of the horses and drove them too close to earth, scorching it in places.

11. **Juli, clementia**: Julius Caesar had granted clemency to some of the very people who later plotted to assassinate him.

12. **truculente Nero**: Tacitus (*Ann.* 15.44) speaks of Nero's extreme cruelty in executing the Christians for allegedly burning the city of Rome. The list of his other exploits and victims is long, including an incident in which he kicked his pregnant wife, causing her death. In 68 A.D. he had an attendant take his life in anticipation of a sentence of death pronounced by the Senate.

19. **Antoni mensas sic vicit cena Catonis**: According to Plutarch's *Life of Antony* 9, Romans were scandalized to see Antony spreading lavish feasts in groves and at the banks of rivers as he visited cities throughout Italy. There is even mention of golden goblets. Cato, on the other hand, exercised his usual frugality when entertaining.

25. **nēquaquam**: As Macrin points out, the first syllable is long, not short.

### 3.

Missing in 1569, 1576, 1597; *Tottel's Miscellany*, 1: 103–4; 2: 223–25 (= Merrill, *Grimald*, 375–77, 416–18).

In typical lover's fashion, Bèze finds solace for his distress about his lover's absence by various rationalizations: if she is not in the city, he concludes, she must be planning a rendevous in the country. These rationalizations reach the height of absurdity when even in death he finds reason to be cheered. Such self-deception in the face of rejection is familiar to us all. It is unexpected to find Publia instead of Candida as the subject, given Candida's status as Bèze's love-interest throughout the rest of the elegies and epigrams. But Bèze wants to introduce a convention of erotic poetry not congruous with the latter's established character: here Publia has a husband, who stands as an obstacle to the poet's amorous aspirations and adds a touch of intrigue to the entire affair.

1. **Cornua bis posuit, bis cepit cornua Phoebe**: properly Selene

(Greek) or Luna (Roman), she drives a wagon pulled by cows, whose *cornua* symbolized the crescent moon. She is later identified with Diana (Artemis), who carries a hunting bow shaped like the crescent moon. As a counterpart to her brother Apollo, the sun god, she is responsible for the waxing and waning of the moon.

7. **Non aliter queritur ventrem durare Prometheus**: Zeus punished Prometheus for helping humans by chaining him to a rock and sending his eagle or a vulture by day to gnaw at his liver. Prometheus, however, because he is immortal, grows a new liver every night.

10. **Vulturis est illi nomine dictus amor**: i.e., the vulture is a fitting allegory for love. Bèze means to compare the bird's gnawing to the excruciating pain of pining for an absent love; cf. Lucr. 3.984, 992–94:

> Nec Tityon volucres ineunt Acherunte iacentem
>
> . . .
>
> sed Tityos nobis hic est, in amore iacentem
> quem volucres lacerant atque exest anxius angor
> aut alia quavis scindunt cuppedine curae.

> [Nor is there a Tityos lying in Acheron (the underworld) being pierced by birds ... but Tityos is here among us, the man lying down in love whom the birds tear, that is to say, morbid pain gnaws at him or misery pecks at him from some other sort of desire.]

Bèze also appears to be making a pun with *vultus* in line 24: the *vultus* of the girl causes *amor*, which is by nature like a *vultur*.

18. **omnia ferre**: The context precludes the translation "to endure everything"; he seems to envision that she wants to "carry away" or "transfer" their affair into a safe place.

23. **te si cernat Apollo**: because he is the sun god, who looks down upon everything. Bèze fears that if Publia does not cover her face, Apollo will burn for her as he once did for Daphne, and just as the latter turned into a laurel tree to avoid his advances, so something disastrous may befall Publia.

26. **si de te fabula talis erit**: Hor. *Serm.* 1.1.69–70, "de te | fabula narratur." Cf. also Ov. *Am.* 3.1.21, "fabula, nec sentis, tota iactaris in urbe"; Hor. *Ep.* 11.8, "fabula quanta fui."

27. **Callisto**: one of the attendants of Artemis/Diana, loved by Zeus. After their brief affair, Callisto attempted to conceal her loss of virgin-

ity, but it was eventually discovered by Artemis, who punished her by turning her into a bear. Later, when she was surrounded by hunters, Zeus rescued her and placed her in the sky as a constellation.

31. **Actaeon**: While hunting with friends, Actaeon accidentally spied the virgin Artemis naked. She took revenge on him by turning him into a stag and letting him be torn apart by his own dogs.

**violati numini iras**: as of the spirit of Orpheus in his wrath against Aristaeus (Verg. *Georg.* 4.453): "Non te nullius exercent numinis irae." Likewise of Juno's anger (Verg. *Aen.* 1.8–11, esp. "Tantaene animis caelestibus irae?").

42. **Fortunae**: here = *condicio*.

4.

Missing in 1569, 1576, 1597.

Having treated the lover's attempts to rationalize rejection, Bèze moves on to examine another interesting aspect of human nature: two people can form differing opinions while looking at the exact same object. Here Bèze is mystified that Louis (perhaps Louis Vaillant, mentioned in *eleg.* 8 and *epig.* 10) does not see the same redeeming qualities in Candida that he himself sees, despite their being good friends. He suspects, or at least he wants to believe, that Louis has a hidden agenda. The fact that Bèze got first dibs on the girl makes her unavailable, and therefore unattractive, to Louis. Meanwhile, Bèze's protestations and exuberant delineation of Candida's positive qualities serve to underscore a theme that Lucretius develops at some length in his treatment of the physics of love (4.1149ff.), namely, that lust compels the lover to overlook the faults of the object of his desire; sometimes emotions get the upper hand over the mind. Such is the gist of the poem: Love is blind, the heart rules the head. Cf. Propertius's maxim (2.14.18), "scilicet insano nemo in amore videt" ("no one can see who is blinded by mad love"). Yet embedded in this whirl of emotions is Bèze's realization that there exists between Louis and himself a more rational, logical love, and one based on shared interests and personality. Nevertheless, ultimately their friendship only serves as a foil to his love for Candida, since the love that is conducted by the intellect typically takes a back seat to that driven by lusts and emotions.

**2. candida:** a play on his girlfriend's name.

**31. sic frons exsurgit aperta:** The broad or open forehead was considered a mark of beauty, so much so that, as the story goes, Queen Elizabeth I used to have her hair plucked to move her hairline back. Bonefon uses *patens* to express the same (*Delitiae* 1: 657): *Ille frontis honos patentis* ... To this can be compared *epig.* 48.11 and 78.9, and often in Bèze and the other Neo-Latin poets.

**45. nigram:** It is ironic to describe Candida, whose name means "fair," as "darky," as if she were dark-complexioned. The Renaissance ideal was blonde (cf. Shakespeare's Sonnet 130). This creates the suspicion in the reader that Bèze is not seeing Candida as she really is.


## 5.

Missing in 1569, 1576, 1597; *Tottel's Miscellany,* 1: 94–95; 2: 225–26 (= Merrill, *Grimald,* 377–78, 418–19).


As in the previous poem, the emotions of the heart rule the mind and the will. The elegists often turn to flight as a remedy for love, but rarely, if ever, does the tactic work (cf. Ov. *Rem. Amor.* 213). No matter how Bèze tries to put Candida out of his mind, and no matter where he retreats, he constantly sees things that remind him of the aching love that he feels for her. The fact is, love is a torture that the lover cannot resist, and a wound that only the beloved can cure (common Renaissance poetic topoi).


**7. Adonis:** an avid hunter who became the love interest of Aphrodite (Venus). She pleaded with him to avoid hunting big game, but he ignored her, and eventually a boar dealt him a deadly blow. From the blood that flowed from his wound sprang the Greek anemone, a sign of fertility.

**11. Narcissum ... Hiacynthos:** Narcissus was the handsome son of the river-god Cephissus. Because he rejected the advances of the nymph Echo, he was cursed to fall in love with his own reflection. According to Ovid (*Met.* 3.341–510), he pined away staring at his reflection in a pond, and the gods turned him into the flower that bears his name. Hyacinthos was a boy that Apollo loved, who was killed during a discus match, perhaps by the treachery of Zephyr, the west wind (Ov. *Met.* 10.162–219). From his blood also sprang the flower that bears his name, along with the woeful exclamation "AI AI" marked on its petals.

17. **Cereris fugientem ... natam**: Persephone, who was raped by Hades and dragged down into the underworld while picking flowers in a meadow.

28. A reverse of *eleg.* 4.2.

32. **Tale ... color**: Cf. *eleg.* 4.45–46.

36. **Anchisi**: should be *Anchisae*. Anchises was of the royal house of Troy, and father of Aeneas by Venus.

37. **Diva**: Candida, whom Bèze has now transformed into a goddess.

38. **Saepe mihi veniam Iuppiter ipse dedit**: A typical tactic of salesmanship is to point to others who have bought the product. The "goddess" Candida should be especially impressed if Jupiter has granted favors to Bèze and thus be more likely to grant her own.

40. **poenas**: a double-entendre. Bèze deserves punishment for fleeing, but in a sadomasochistic way he also will derive pleasure from submitting to Candida's "discipline."

### 6.

Missing in 1569, 1576, 1597.

Bèze plays on the conventional ship-of-state motif from the more serious genres (cf. Tib. 2.4.10). The allegorical details are reminiscent of Medieval interpretations of Noah's ark (that of Isidore of Seville comes to mind),[2] though the ship in this case is buffeted by the storms of erotic love, not enemies of the Church. On love affair as shipwreck see Steele Commager, *The Odes of Horace: A Critical Study* (New Haven, 1961), 66–67.[3] For various nautical images employed to talk about sexual acts and anatomy, see Adams, *Latin Sexual Vocabulary*, 167. Here, most of the allegorical connections are obvious, and need not be ex-

---

[2] Isidore of Seville, *Quaestiones in vet. testam.* 7.3 (= P.L. 83, 229–30): "Arca enim ista Ecclesiam demonstrabat, quae natat in fluctibus mundi huius. Quod autem eadem arca de lignis quadratis fieri iubetur, undique stabilem vitam sanctorum significat ad omne opus bonum paratam. Quocunque enim verteris, quadratum firmiter stat."

[3] Commenting on Horace *Od.* 1.5, Commager remarks, "The storm of love was a well-worn conceit, while the comparison between a woman and the sea had been current at least as early as Semonides ..."

plained. Adams notes that "the sea resembles a woman because it is moist," (167) an observation which may apply to this poem also.

39. **portumque subire:** i.e., the vagina, which Bèze is trying to enter with his "ship."
56. **obruta puppis:** borrowed from a prolepsis of Vergil, *Aen.* 1.69: *submersasque obrue puppis.*
57. **venis:** The word *vena* can stand for "penis"; see Adams, *Latin Sexual Vocabulary*, 35.
60. **syllabulae:** Macrin objected to the diminutive form of this word. He argues that diminutives of words that come from Greek do not form their diminutives with *-ul-*: "We say *epistolium*, not *epistolula; moechilium*, not *moechula.*"
62. **optima culpa:** An obscene play on "O felix culpa" from the Easter vigil liturgy.

7.

Missing in 1569, 1576, 1597.

Elegiac lovers spend many restless nights tormented by thoughts of their sweethearts; the motif and idiom made its way into the poetry of the Pléiade: on this see Hanisch, *Love Elegies of the Renaissance*, 103 (her discussion of Ronsard, 2: 34–35 of "Second discours de Genèvre, en forme d'élégie"). There is also here a subtle mocking of the heroic attitude. We are led to believe that ordinarily Bèze would be too afraid to engage armed men in combat, but as a soldier-lover he finds the courage he needs to rush headlong into certain death.

5ff. A parallel to the bucolic evening topos as in Sappho frg. 95 (T. Bergk, *Poetae Lyrici Graeci*,[4] 3 vols., Leipzig, 1882 [= Lobel-Page, *P.L.F.* 104; Diehl, *A.L.G.* 120]): ἕσπερε πάντα φέρων ὄσα φαίνολις ἐσκέδασ᾽ αὔως, | φέρεις ὄιν, φέρεις αἶγα, φέρεις ἄπυ μάτερι παῖδα.
10. **Thetidos ire sinus:** Thetis often stands by metonymy for the sea; see note on *eleg.* 11.22.
18. **Pulicis:** The poets often remark that though Cupid is tiny he can do great damage. Although that must be what is behind Bèze's comparison, I can find no precedent for Cupid being disguised as a flea.
21. **Nox erat:** A favorite Ovidian line-opening, e.g., *Fast.* 1.421, *Am.* 3.5.1 et alibi.

**38. agna ... lupis**: Below (line 58) Bèze describes himself as a lamb snatched from the jaws of an attacker. Cf. the lamb and wolf as in Luke 10.3 (ironic here).

### 8.

#### Missing in 1569, 1576, 1597.

On Louis Vaillant, who figures in *eleg.* 4 and *epig.* 10, see the note there. Illnesses of friends and lovers constitute the subject of many epigrams and elegies during all periods (on which see the note on *epig.* 71). Bèze expresses his frustration in the face of the apparent arbitrariness of Fate, who brings suffering upon human beings without regard to a person's merit and unaffected by the efforts of friends and family to interfere. The appeals to the gods and the assertions of Louis's innocence add pathos and intensity to the situation.

**13. Quisquis ades superum**: normally "quisquis es," as at Verg. *Aen.* 1.387, 2.148, 4.577, 6.388.
**15. Croesive talenta**: Croesus, the sixth-century B.C. king of the Lydians, was famed for his wealth in gold, silver, and electrum.
**47. Ledaeos fama gemellos**: the Dioscuri brothers, Castor and Pollux. According to the myth, these sons of Leda were inseparable. Some versions of the myth make Pollux the semi-divine child of Zeus, and Castor the mortal child of Tyndareus. When Castor died, Pollux besought Zeus to allow him to change places with Castor. Zeus responded by allowing the pair to live and die on alternate days.

### 9.

#### Missing in 1569, 1576, 1597.

The ancient Greeks used to believe that the dead were especially attracted to weddings, since there amid the dancing and happiness was an affirmation of the vigor of youth and the continuation of life that they envied. Along the same lines, this poem asserts the youthful spirit of the two lovers in contrast to the decay of the spiteful old woman, who tries to separate them. The representation of a feud between the old and the young had become a convention among the elegiac "love" poets and in-

dicative of the aims of their program (for the influence of Medieval lit-
erature in regard to this motif, see Jacques Bailbé, "Le Thème de la
vieille femme dans la poésie satirique du XVIᵉ et du début du XVIIᵉ
siècles," *BHR* 26 [1964]: 98–119). The character type itself appears to
have been drawn from new comedy. Catullus's famous poem 5, begin-
ning "vivamus, mea Lesbia, atque amemus," is about such censorious
old people who attempt to spoil the poet's love affair; Horace warns his
readers about them too (*AP* 174). Likewise, Ovid (*Am.* 1.8) faced an old
hag who sought to undermine his relationship to his lover: "haec sibi
proposuit thalamos temerare pudicos" (v. 19). He responds to her ef-
forts, as Bèze does here, with a string of imprecations and slurs. Fur-
thermore, the use of legal, religious, and commercial language was com-
mon to this motif as well, and had the humorous effect of jumbling the
more serious and sacred spheres with the familiar and profane, thereby
turning the normal order of things on its head: Catullus counts kisses as
if on a ledger; Ovid invokes the gods and utters curses (*di tibi dent nullos
...*); Bèze turns to a mock court to plead his innocence. Cf. also Hor.
*Epod.* 10.

2. **Quae te cumque**: tmesis, visually representing the separation of *te*
   from *mihi* by *quaecumque anus*.
3. **lena**: Not necessarily a literal "madam," since the term appears to be
   used generally as a term of invective (cf. Ovid, *Am.* 1.8.1), as are the
   taunting appellations "tramp" and "slut."
7. **turbarent iurgia lectum**: For the significance of quarreling in bed,
   see the note on *epig.* 91.18.
14. **credulitate**: She is "credulous" or "naive" in that she has miscon-
    ceptions about love, particularly, that it is in some way a bad or
    harmful thing.
15. **fures**: The old woman is like a thief because she tries to steal the
    couple's love away.
39. **Archilochi rapidos ... iambos**: Archilochus's iambic poems are pro-
    verbial for their harsh invective. The ancients relate the legend that
    Archilochus turned his iambs against a certain Lycambes, whose
    daughter the poet loved, and that he executed his abusive poems
    with such venom that he drove Lycambes to commit suicide.
41. **Tisiphone**: The ancient poets describe the Furies as having snaky
    hair, bloodshot eyes, fangs fouled with rotting flesh, and doglike fea-
    tures. Apropos to their features, they relentlessly hounded those who
    had committed murders.

69. **ter centum cum tandem impleveris annos**: Long life with increasing senility and bodily decline was the curse placed upon the Sibyl by Apollo. According to Petronius (frg. 48.8), her body became so shriveled that she used to complain, "I want to die, I want to die." Cf. line 58, where Bèze says that the old hag will wish to die, but in vain.

76. **Portitor, et Stygias tangere nolit aquas**: In Greek and Roman myth, those who were not buried after their death in the world above could not cross the river Styx for a thousand years. The aimless wandering of one's soul was in itself a cursed existence.

## 10.

### Missing in 1569, 1576, 1597.

Candida appears to have had a haircut that was cropped a bit too close, and now she is distraught. Bèze reminds her of the cycle of life, which ensures that her hair will renew itself, while the old hair will receive its proper recognition. As in many of Bèze's elegies, light subjects provide a mechanism for the subtle introduction of profounder themes.

17. **ficto Berenices nomine**: The *Coma Berenices*, or "Lock of Berenice," refers to the cluster of stars at the tail of the constellation Leo. They were placed there by the gods after Berenice (d. 216 B.C.) had fulfilled a vow to Aphrodite for the safe return of her husband, Ptolemy III of Cyrene. Callimachus's poem on the subject is lost, but Catullus did an imitation (c. 66) that does survive.

## 11.

Both Ovid and Livy died ca. 17 A.D. Bèze appears to know a tradition that places their death on the first day of that year. The poem may seem out of place, given the erotic nature of the previous poems, but this application of the meter is not inappropriate. Horace remarks in his *Ars Poetica* (75) that the elegy had its origins in this kind of funeral dirge: "Versibus impariter iunctiis querimonia primum." Bèze has modeled his lament for these two writers' deaths on that of Ovid for Tibullus (*Amores*, 3.9.3). Like Ovid, he includes some elements from literary *epicedia*: an invitation to the gods and nature to join in the mourning; a *laudatio*, which covers their exploits and scolds those who did not honor them properly; and remarks about the good fortune of the shades who welcome them. But instead of the typical prayer that their bones "rest lightly," Bèze assures the reader that Ovid and Livy have entered the underworld, not as shades of their former selves, but as living flesh and blood. Indeed, the central thrust of the poem appears to be the immortality of poetry. To this elegy one can compare Ronsard's "Elégie en forme d'épitaphe d'Antoine Chateignier," 2: 500 (and see Hanisch, *Love Elegies of the Renaissance*, 81).

7. **Cannas**: a small town in Apulia where Hannibal decisively defeated the Romans in 216 B.C. According to Polybius, the Romans lost 70,000 men in the battle.

9. **munus**: referring to New Year's gift customs (cf. line 48).

19-20. **Ipse suas … | … festa parat**: a play on the fact that Ovid himself composed *Fasti*. Among the Romans feast days were held to be sacrosanct, so any attempt to remove them was taken to be an attack on the foundations of the Republic and thus met with great resistance (cf., e.g., Cicero, *Pro Sestio* 33). Janus, the god of beginnings, was responsible for opening the new year (Ovid, *Fasti* 2.51) and for signaling the start and close of war. The Romans depicted him with a double face that looks in opposite directions, representing the fact that, as the portal of time, he looks back to the past and ahead to the future.

21. **raucisona Amphitrite**: Neptune's wife; the epithet appears to be a translation of ἀγάστονος ("loud-wailing"), which is applied to Amphitrite at *Hom. Hymn Apol.* 94, or Homer's epithet of the sea at *Iliad* 1.34, πολύφλοισβος ("loud-roaring").

22. **Thetis**: a sea nymph, daughter of Nereus and Doris. Her union with Peleus produced the hero of the Trojan War, Achilles.

23. **Pelignae lachrymis implent rura omnia Nymphae**: Ovid informs us at *Am* 3.15.3 that he was born in the Pelignian (Sabine) city of Sulmo in central Italy.

24. **querulus Patavi permeat arva Padus**: Livy was born at Patavium (the modern Padua) in 59 B.C.

27. **demens Augustus**: Augustus sent Ovid into exile in 8 B.C. to Tomi (modern Kustindje) on the Black Sea; the exact source of the emperor's irritation is not known. Ovid himself makes reference to some error on his part (*Trist.* 1.3.37), but nothing amounting to a crime. Julius Caesar, in contrast, extended clemency to many of those who had resisted or offended him in some way.

34. **Scivit inhumanos flectere Musa Getas**: Orpheus's music was said to be so enchanting that it calmed even the savage Thracians.
35. **Tomitanis**: cf. Ovid *Pont.* 1.1.1 ("Tomitanae").
38. **Parnassum**: refers to the mountains around Delphi, where supposedly Apollo lived with the nine Muses.
42. **ne quinta quaerite luce lyram**: a reference to Ovid's *Fasti* 1.315–16, which says that the constellation Lyra rises on the nones of January, i.e., on the fifth day of the month.
53. **Ennius ... | hic ... soli**: By *hic* Bèze must mean Livy. Ennius's great work, the *Annales*, which traces Roman history from the time of Aeneas to his own day in hexameters, most closely associates him with Livy.
56. **Nemesi**: The object of Tibullus's interest in his elegiac poetry.
57. **tu qui dubium fecisti nomen Homeri**: i.e., Vergil (with line 58, indicating respectively his *Georgics, Eclogues,* and *Aeneid*).
59. **Quirites**: On this alternate name for Romans, see the note on *epig.* 17.5.
62. **Hannibal aspecto surgit et ipse Tito**: because Livy devoted books 21–30 of his history to Hannibal and the Second Punic War.
65. **quotannis**: Macrin points out to Bèze that his first version, *quottannis*, is unattested, and that the first syllable must be short.
67. **deinde**: with synizesis in the first syllable. The original *deinde versus* of the 1548 edition did not scan correctly.
69. **Quisquis ades**: For the ancient convention of addressing the wayfarer, see R. Lattimore, *Themes in Greek and Latin Epitaphs* (Urbana, IL, 1962), 230–34. On page 233, Lattimore quotes an epitaph that begins, "Quisquis ades celeri gressu ..."
    **vacuum ... sepulchrum**: Cenotaphs, or empty tombs, were common in the ancient world. Ordinarily they honored the deceased whose body could not be found or important people who were buried elsewhere. Cf. Xen. *Anab.* 6.4.9 (for Arcadian soldiers who could not be found) and Verg. *Aen.* 3.304 (for Hector).
71. **Orphei quod precibus Plutonia regna dedere**: When Orpheus's wife died suddenly of a snake bite on their wedding day, Orpheus used his music to enter the underworld and charm Hades and Persephone so that they would let her return to the world above. They granted his request, on the condition that he not look at her before the two exit the underworld, a condition Orpheus failed to meet. Given the context (the empty tombs, the welcoming that the writers received), Bèze must be thinking of the free passage that the living

Orpheus gained through his music. In other words, Livy and Ovid enter the underworld, but they still live, and there they enchant the shades.

## 12.

### Missing in 1569, 1576, 1597.

This elegy is a celebration of ideal beauty, the source and impetus to love among humans. Helis possesses all the qualities that other women achieve with makeup and adornments, and her presence attracts the attention of everyone and everything.

12. **Ex minio iussit labra rubere suo**: Cf. Pliny, *NH* 33.111ff.: "In argentariis metallis invenitur minium quoque, et nunc inter pigmenta magnae auctoritatis et quondam apud Romanos non solum maximae, sed etiam sacrae ..." Many of the Neo-Latin poets speak of minium's use as a makeup. Pasquier (*Epig.* 3.11) mentions cheeks blushed with minium: *Per genas* [sc. *iuro*] *minio colore tinctas*.

34. **cunctos quod remoretur**: She makes them late because they want to stop and stare at her beauty.

## 1.

*Descriptio D. P. Stellae, LL. Doctoris Celeberrimi*

Mundus ut assidua frueretur luce, suoque
    Vivere sol posset liber ab officio,
Lucifer in terras caelo migrare relicto,
    Atque hominis faciem sumere jussus erat.
At mox ut Stellae discessu clara Deorum          5
    Perpetua coepit regia nocte premi,
Poenituit mandasse Jovem, Stellamque vocavit;
    Et solem antiquas jussit obire vices.


## 2.

*D. Jo. Valentis, Regis A Consiliis*

Extincto nuper Res publica moesta Valente,
    Visa mihi secum sic gemebundo queri:
Saepe alios flevi, dum sic raperentur, alumnos:
    Causa tamen nunquam iustior ulla fuit.

---

1.1    assiduus *1713* frueretur *1569, 1576* gauderet *1548, 1779*

# EPITAPHS

## 1.

*Pierre de l'Estoille, Renowned Professor of Literature*

The gods wanted the world to enjoy unending light, and the sun to have a break from its responsibility, so they ordered Lucifer to abandon the sky and make his way to earth in human form. But soon, when perpetual darkness began to envelop the gods' domain because of Estoille's departure, Jupiter regretted his decision. Therefore, he recalled Estoille, and ordered the sun to resume its former course.

## 2.

*Jean Vaillant de Guélis, of the King's Council*

The Republic was sad recently when Vaillant died, and she seemed to me to sigh and complain to herself like this: "Often I have wept for other children who have been snatched from me, but never has the cause of my weeping been so justified."

**3.**

*Causidico cuidam*

O rerum varias vices, et ingens
Fortunae paradigma saevientis!
Clamosissimus omnium virorum,
Qui verborum operam omnibus locabat,
Nunc raptus Rhadamantium ad tribunal,　　　　　5
Conducit miser, ante quae locabat.

**4.**

*Gulielmi Budaei, Viri Nostrae Aetatis Doctissimi, Qui Lutetiae
Obiit Anno M. D. XL, XIII. Cal. Septemb.*

Ὅστις Βουδαῖον γλώσσης ὀνομάσσατο Φοῖβον
　　Ἀμφοτέρας, ὀρθῶς Φοῖβον ἔειπε μάλα.
Ἄξια δ᾿ οὐκ εἶπεν, μείζων γὰρ κ᾿ ἠελίοιο,
　　Ὅς θνητοῖσι φάος καὶ καταδὺς παρέχει

**5.**

*Eiusdem*

Unus Budaeus terramque, polosque, hominesque,
　　Devinxit magna providus arte sibi.
Caelo animum, terrae corpus donavit habendum:
　　At cerebri nobis dona superba dedit.
Sic decessit inops; nam nil sibi liquerat ipse:　　　　5
　　Verum haec paupertas unica vincit opes.

---

3.　　Tit. *sic 1569 (errata) et Wright (1637),* 6 *omn. al. edd. habent* Advocati cuius-
　　　dam
4.3　　Ἄξια δ᾿ οὐκ εἶπεν *1569, 1580 Icones* Οὐκ εἶπεν δ᾿ ἱκανῶς *1548, 1580*

### 3.

### *A Pleader in the Courts*

O vicissitudes of life, a perfect example of how savage fortune is! The most cacophonous of all men, who used to peddle his advocacy services to everyone, now has been taken away to the tribunal of Rhadamanthus. The poor fellow, now he employs the service he used to peddle.

### 4.

### *Guillaume Budé, The Most Learned Man of Our Times, Who Died in Paris, 22 August 1540*

Whoever calls Budé the Phoebus of both tongues, speaks correctly, but he does not say enough. For he outstrips even the sun, since after setting he still shines among mortals.

### 5.

### *The Same*

Only the foresightful Budé subdued earth, sky, and men to himself by his great skill. He bequeathed his mind to heaven, his body to the earth, while to us he gave the brilliant gifts of his intellect. In this way he departed destitute, for he had left nothing for himself. But only this poverty wins riches.

## 6.

### *Eiusdem*

Budaeum flevere homines, ploravit et aer;
    Budaeus gelidis est quoque fletus aquis:
Sic flevere homines, ut plena volumina moestis
    Carminibus quivis bibliopola terat.
Sic aer luxit, consumptis undique nimbis,         5
    Ut jam quas plueret non reperiret aquas.
Flumina sic flerunt, ut qua modo navis abibat,
    Currat inoffensis sicca quadriga rotis.
Restabant caelum et tellus, communis ut omni
    Quamlibet immenso moeror in orbe foret:      10
Sed cum caelum animam Budaei, terra cadaver
    Possideat, quaeso, qua ratione fleant?

## 7.

### *Nicolae Bezae Patrui, Qui Regis A Consiliis Fuit*

Marmore de Pario nullas hic stare columnas,
    Aera nec artificis vivere jussa manu,
Nec tumuli spectas operosam surgere molem,
    Qualia Mausoli fama sepulchra canit.
Scilicet hos titulos, hos quaerere debet honores,    5
    Qui nil, quo melius nobilitetur, habet.
Hic autem magni quondam pars magna senatus,
    Aut nullo, aut solo Beza Catone minor:
Quem sic eripuit virtus ter maxima morti,
    Vivat ut extincto posthumus ipse sibi.      10
Mortuus e tumulo famam cur captet inanem,
    Illi quam vivo vita peracta dedit?
Immo si verum fas nobis dicere: sed fas,
    Dignus, qui tumulo non tegeretur, erat.

---

7.Tit. Ornatiss. viri, Nicolai à Beza, Patrui, in suprema Parisiensi Curia, integerri
    mae vitae et famae, Senatoris *1597*
1     Marmoreas lector nullas *affix. ad sepulchrum ipsum 1543, 1597*
3     cernes *1548, 1580, 1779* spectas *1569, 1576* spectas surgentem ad sidera mo-
    lem, *1597*

## 6.

### *The Same*

The people wept for Budé, and the sky lamented him. Budé was also mourned by the icy waters. The people wept for him so, that every bookseller prints volumes full with sad poems. The sky so lamented and emptied its clouds everywhere, that now it cannot find water for rain. The streams mourned so, that on former shipping routes carriages now run unimpeded across dry land. Heaven and earth were remaining, so there might be a common grief in the whole universe, despite its immensity. But since heaven possesses the mind of Budé, the earth his body, why, I ask you, would they weep?

## 7.

### *My Uncle Nicolas de Bèze, of the King's Council*

Here you see stand no columns of Parian marble, there is no bronze statue wrought by an artisan's hand; here you see no fancy shrine loom, no mausoleum of legend. Someone who has nothing else to ennoble himself should seek those markers, those honors; but this Bèze, once eminent in the great Senate, was less than no one, except perhaps Cato: his extraordinarily great virtue led him to his death in such a manner that he outlived himself. Why would a dead man chase an empty fame from his grave, if his conduct gave it to him while alive? No (if I may speak the truth—but of course I may), he needs no marker at all.

---

7.5    Sic studeat nigrae vitare oblivia mortis *1597*

7       vero *pro* autem *1597* Hic vero magni pars nuper magna Senatus *e manu B. in suo exemplari*

9–10   *om. 1597*

10      Ut fatis vivat posthumus ipse suis *affix. ad sepulchrum ipsum 1543*

11      Cur tandem e tumulo famam nunc captet inanem *affix. ad sepulchrum ipsum 1543* Scilicet e tumulo famam nunc captet inanem *1597* Fas alios esto nomen debere sepulchro *e manu B. in suo exemplare*

12–14 Extincta vivens posthumus ipse sibi, | Fas alios igitur nomen debere sepulchris, | Beza suum contra nobiliat tumulum *1569, 1576, 1597*

## 8.

*Catharinae Texeae Aureliensis*

Isto quis iaceat loco sepultus
Forsan scire cupis, benigne lector:
Atqui id dicere perlibenter optem,
Sed quo nomine debeat vocari
Quicquid hoc tumulo latet sepultum,                    5
Scire iudico quemlibet sagacem
Nullum, et quemlibet omnium peritum.
Nam si ex corpore iudicare sexum
Decet, virgo latet sepulchro in isto.
At quanam ratione nuncupari                            10
Debet femina, quam timore nemo
Turbatam nimio, aut dolore vidit?
Nemo prosperiore sorte abuti?
Loqui nemo, ubi feminae tacendum?
Nemo, cum decuit loqui, tacere?                        15
Choros nemo sequi parum pudicos?
Nemo ornare comam parum pudenter?
Nemo accersere pharmacis colores,
Hinc vibrare oculos et inde nemo?
Nemo verba loqui petulca vidit.                        20
Ergo vir fuit. At virum vocare
Qua decet ratione, cui virilis
Illa corporis est negata forma?
Ergo utrumque fuit. Fuisse vero
Cur utrumque putem, quod esse neutrum               25
Probatum satis est superque nobis?
Diva ergo fuit, altera aut Minerva,
Quae, cum femina sit, tamen virili
Intus est animo, ut ferunt poetae.
Sed est nota satis cruenta Pallas,                     30
Et insana deum libido nota.
Ergo quid superest, nisi ut putemus
Quiddam hoc in tumulo latere, quod sic
Feminisque, virisque, Disque maius?

## 8.

### *Catherine Tessée of Orléans*

Perhaps you would like to know, kind reader, who lies buried in this place; I would gladly tell you, but I believe that no one, however clever or ingenious, knows what name to give to the person that is buried here. If we should judge the sex on the basis of the physical characteristics, a virgin lies buried in this tomb. But by what rationale should she be termed "woman," since no one ever saw her distraught with excessive fear or grief? No one saw her squander her good fortune; no one saw her speak at times when a woman should be silent, or be silent, when it was proper for her to speak; no one saw her engage in lewd dancing, or adorn her hair immodestly, or use too much make-up, or bat her eyes; no one heard her use saucy language. "Therefore, she was a man," you'll say. But how can we call this person a man, since her beauty belied any masculinity? "So, she was both male and female." But why consider her both, since obviously she was neither? "Therefore she was a goddess, or a second Minerva, since, though a woman, she had a manly spirit, as the poets say." But we know that Pallas had her faults: she could be too bloodthirsty, and, like all the gods, she was subject to irrational passions. Therefore, what is left for us, except to conclude that the person who lies in this tomb is greater than women, men, and gods?

---

Tit.   *add.* virgini Aurelensi lectissimae *1597*
1      quid ... sepultum *1597*
6–7   Posse dicere, vix puto sagacem | Ullum, et quamlibet omnium peritum *1597*
8      sexus aestimentur *1597*
9      Certe *pro* Decet *1597*
11     Possit *pro* Debet *1597*
20     sensit *pro* vidit *1597*
31     Fictorumque Deum libido turpis *1597*
34     Femina, atque viro, deaque maius *1597*

## 9.

*Antonio Pratensi Cancellario Galliarum, inter obesos obesissimo*

Amplissimus vir hic iacet.

## 10.

### *Eobani Hessi Poetae Egregii*

Venerat exutus mortali corpore nuper
    Hessus, ut infernis exciperetur aquis:
Quem torve intuitus squalentis portitor Orci,
    Hic (ait), hic gratus Manibus hospes erit.
Tune Syracusii calamos impune poetae,                                          5
    Maeonidaeque tubam, pessime, surpueris?
Dixerat; et media vates iam puppe sedebat,
    Cum vetuit nautam pergere Mercurius:
Ne saevito, senex, inquit: nam vindicat istum
    Juppiter, et superum caetera turba, sibi.                              10
Extinctis aliis potuit qui reddere vitam,
    Ditis in hunc possunt iura severa nihil.

---

9.Tit. *sic 1569* Antonii Pratensis cancellarii Galliae *1548, 1576, 1580 cui add.* omni-
    um obesorum obesissimi *1779* pontificii in Gallia legati, omnium obesorum
    obesissimi *1597*
10.9   sibi vendicat istum *1569, 1576*
10     Istum, inquam, superum turba beata sibi *1569*

## 9.

*Antoine du Prat, Chancellor of the French, Fattest of the Fattest*

Here lies a very ample man.

## 10.

*Eobanus of Hesse, an Outstanding Poet*

Recently stripped of his mortal body, Eobanus had come to cross the infernal waters. The ferryman of filthy Orcus looked at him grimly and said, "This will be a pleasing guest for the Manes: did you think you would plagiarize the reeds of the Syracusan poet, scoundrel, or the war-trumpet of Homer with impunity?" He spoke: and already the poet was sitting in the middle of the ship, when Mercury denied the ship passage. "Don't rant, old man," he said, "for Jupiter and the other gods above are laying claim to him. The harsh laws of Dis have no power whatsoever over one who could restore life to the dead."

## 11.

*Macuti Pomponii, cum falso nuntiaretur in Alpibus occubuisse*

Vos nunc advoco, flebiles Phaleuci,
Vos voco, o numeri severiores:
Adeste, obsecro, dum meum Macutum,
Meas delicias, meamque vitam,
Morte lugeo pessima peremptum.                                    5
Unde, Pierides, loqui auspicabor?
Dicamne ut patria bene instituta
Natus ille meus Macutus, omnes
Vita vicerit integra et pudica?
Dicamne ut patria bene erudita                                    10
Natus ille meus Macutus, omnes
In hac vicerit eruditiores?
Traxit carminibus suis opacas
Silvas, et iuga montium comata;
Undarum et domuit rapacitatem                                     15
Orpheus: sed superavit hunc Macutus,
Mutis non modo doctus imperare,
Sed pacare hominum potens furorem,
Et lenes itidem incitare mentes;
Nec solum digitos movere doctus,                                  20
Sed lingua pariter loqui diserta.
Pericles potuit tonare quondam;
Sed Graecus tonuit suis Athenis.
Lingua Tullius eloquens Latina,
Romanis tonuit suis Latinus.                                      25
Natus sanguine Gallico Macutus,
Et Graece tonuisset et Latine,
Hoc si Roma foret Latina saeclo,
Et nunc Graecia Graeca personaret.
Apelli Cytheraea picta quondam,                                   30
Nec tota attamen, immo inabsoluta:
Mille autem Veneresque Gratiasque
Expressit lepidus meus Macutus,
Aut vicit potius: nec id colore,
Sed docta lepidaque scriptione.                                   35

## 11.

*Maclou Popon, When It Was Falsely Announced That He Had Died*
*in the Alps*

I invoke you now, mournful phalaecians, I call you, more serious me-
ters. Come near, I beseech you, while I mourn my Maclou, my joy, my
life, who was taken by a vile death. Where will I begin, Pierides? Should
I relate how my Maclou was born in a most civil land and surpassed
everyone with his pure and simple life? Shall I tell how he was born in
a very cultured land, and yet surpassed all in culture?

Orpheus attracted the shady forests and tree-lined mountain summits
with his poems, and controlled the raging waters. But Maclou surpassed
even him, having learned not only how to command mute nature, but
also to calm the passions of men, and to awake sluggish minds. He knew
not only how to move his fingers, but he was equally skilled in using his
voice. Pericles was able to thunder once, but as a Greek he thundered
for his fellow Athenians. Eloquent Cicero thundered in his Latin tongue
for his fellow Romans. Maclou was born of Gallic blood, yet he thun-
dered in both Greek and Latin, if Rome is Latin in our time, and Greece
stands for Greek.

Apelles painted Venus once, but not completely, no, imperfectly. But
my skillful Maclou depicted Venuses and Graces a thousandfold, or
rather he surpassed grace and beauty, but not with paint, rather with

Apelles manui, at meus Macutus
Debet ingenio perennitatem.
Aegyptum penetravit usque in imam
Magnus Pythagoras, Platoque magnus;
Et venit, Scythico gelu relicto,                                    40
Athenas Anacharsis eloquentes.
Vidit Italiam meus Macutus:
Visurus pariter mare atque terras,
Doctrinam ut faceret suam auctiorem,
Coepti si bona sors boni fuisset,                                   45
Aut si quid reperisset, absoluta
Vir quod disceret eruditione.
Vos interrogo, quae caput tenetis
Nascentis Rhodani superba saxa,
Cur saevos homines fovetis illos,                                   50
Macutum mihi qui meum abstulere?
Vos, Nymphae, rogo, quotquot hinc vel inde
Lemani vitreas tenetis undas,
Cur pati potuistis hunc cruenta
Scelestaque manu virum interire,                                    55
Cui Nymphae usque adeo fuere cordi?
Dic mihi, Cytheraea, dic, Apollo,
Dic, Hermes, mihi dicite, o Camoenae,
Cur nostrum, rogo, cur meum Macutum
Passi estis perimi? An minus remoto                                60
Ut possetis eo frui, in deorum
Adiuncto numerum et beatitatem?
Tali dignus eras, Olympe, cive,
Tali dignus eras domo, Macute.
Habetis, superi, mei Macuti                                        65
Nunc divinam animam; at relicta terris
Moles corporea, illa quam Macuti
Divinum ingenium incolebat olim.
Vos curate animam, dii, deaeque;
Nobis corporis est habenda cura.                                   70
Hoc dicamus ei sepulchrum inane:
Hei, cur non licet apparare verum!
Audi nunc, ubicumque sis, Macute;
Sive cum Iove nunc iocaris una,
Ut caeli novus incola, et colonus;                                 75

learned and skillful writing. If Apelles gained immortality from his hand, Maclou ought to from his intellect.

Pythagoras travelled deep into Egypt, all the way to the southern-most parts, as did great Plato. And Anacharsis came to eloquent Athens from chilly Scythia. My Maclou saw Italy, intending to visit both land and sea, to increase his learning, if only his undertaking had been blessed, or had there been anything for a man of absolute erudition to learn.

I ask you, you proud rocks who hold the source of the Rhone, why do you nurture those savage people, who stole Maclou from me? And you, nymphs, as many as dwell in the clear waters of Lake Geneva, why did you allow him to die by a vile and wicked hand, when up until then he had cherished you? Tell me, Venus, tell me, Apollo, tell me, Hermes, tell me, Muses, why, I ask you, why did you allow Maclou to perish? So that you might have him by your side, sharing in the company of the blessed gods? Olympus, you were worthy of such a citizen, Maclou, you were worthy of such a home. Now you have the divine soul of my friend Maclou, gods, but on earth is left his bodily hull, where once dwelt his divine intellect. Take care of his soul, gods and goddesses, we must take care of his body. We will say that this empty tomb is his—alas! why could it not be his real tomb!

Listen, Maclou, wherever you are, whether you play with Jupiter

Sive te potius novem Sorores,
Parnassusque tenet bicornis, audi.
Te vivum mihi sustulere fata,
Extinctum quoque sustulere fata.
Quod unum licet, his tuo quotannis                                    80
Pares inferias dabo sepulchro,
Ut meo Pyladi, meoque Achati.
Sic qui finis erit mihi loquendi,
Deflendi mihi finis est futurus
Te, meum Pyladem, meumque Achatem.                                    85


## 12.

### *Simonis Grynaei, viri longe eruditissimi*

Ecquid ad extincti Grinaei funera, Nymphae,
Tingitis imbre genas largo, Rhenumque per omnem
Turbatae, magno repletis littora planctu?
Ecquid ad extincti Grinaei funera, Phoebe,
Sublatum esse genus, quem par tibi cura sodalem                       5
Fecerat, et simile adiunctum cognomen utrique?
Ecquid nunc iaculatur aquas nimbosus Orion,
Et madidam fundit lachrymosus Aquarius urnam;
Caeteraque obscuro radiantia sidera caelo,
Illustres tingunt nigra ferrugine vultus?                            10
Ecquid ad extincti Grinaei funera, Vates,
Deiecti moerore oculos, lachrymantia verba,
Et moesto alternos trahitis de pectore versus?
O rerum sortes variae, properataque doctis
Semper fata viris! I nunc, et cura latentes                          15
Sit tibi, quisquis eris, naturae inquirere causas.
Scilicet haec stultos mortales fallit inanis
Spes vitae: doctis eadem indoctisque minatur
Mors tamen, et magno finem impositura labori,

---

12.Tit. *add.* Bonarum Artium in Academia Basileensis Professoris *1779*
5        gemis *pro* genus *1597*
15       *ad finem* interruptique labores! *1597*
16–30 *om. 1597*

now, as a new inhabitant and occupant in heaven, or instead you dwell on twin-peaked Parnassus with the nine sisters: the Fates took you away from me while you were alive, now they take you from me when you are dead also. All I can do is pay homage to your tomb every year, as if you were my Pylades and my Achates. Thus here I will stop speaking, and here I will stop weeping for you, my Pylades and my Achates.

## 12.

### *Simon Grüner, by Far the Most Erudite of Men*

Nymphs, are you wetting your cheeks at all with a deluge of tears at the death of Grüner, and distraught along the whole Rhine, are you filling the shores with great wailing? Phoebus Apollo, do you mourn at all that your child has been buried, who enjoyed the same pursuits, and shared a similar surname with you? Now does cloud-bringing Orion buffet the waters at all, and does tearful Aquarius pour forth his water-laden urn, or do the rest of the radiant stars in the black sky wash their bright faces with murky gloom? And do you, sacred poets, cast down your eyes in despair at the death of Grüner and draw your couplets from your saddened hearts? O fickle fortune! O fates always quick to take learned men. Go now, whoever you are, and inquire after the hidden causes of nature. Clearly this vain hope for life deceives foolish mortals, since the same death threatens to put an end to the great effort of the

Desidiae et magnae. Nunc, si sapis, ergo, viator,                    20
Vive tibi: namque ipse tibi moriere, nec unum
Progrediere diem, lethi cum advenerit hora.
Non tamen usque adeo pietatis nescia corda
Sunt, Grinaee, mihi, quin doctos carmine Manes
Prosequar, et cura memet consoler inani.                             25
Ergo agite, o Manes, o mens super aethera pridem
Vecta, pium, quaeso, a nobis hoc accipe carmen:
At tu, summe deum, vasti qui pondera caeli
Dirigis, et vastus cui sese accommodat orbis,
Grinaeum insontem dilectis orbibus infer.                            30


## 13.

### *In Ceratinum, pseudomonachum*

Flete cucullati fratres: iacet ille sepultus,
    Ille cucullatae religionis honos.
Ridite, o reliqui; risu dignissima res est:
    Haec sunt perpetuis funera digna iocis.
Quippe huius quondam mendacibus omnia fucis                           5
    Perdere, sola diu cura laborque fuit.
At dum cuncta tegit, dum fraudibus omnia velat,
    Mors simulatorem non simulata rapit.

---

13.Tit. *add.* qui vulgo dictus fuit De-cornibus *1576* qui vulgo dictus fuit, Frater de
    Cornibus, detestandae, nec tamen obliterandae memoriae ut Deus sicut mise-
    ricors laudatur, ita quoque ut iustus iudex timeatur *1597*
1      Flete agedum, flete, o frates: extinctus abivit *1548, 1580, 1779*
2      cucullatae *1597* unus vestrae *omn. al.*
4      Perpetuis haec sunt funera digna iocis *1597*
6      cura laborque *1597* curaque mensque *1548, 1580, 1779* sollicitudo *1569, 1576*

learned and also to the sloth of the unlearned. Now, if you are wise, then, traveler, live for yourself, for you yourself will die for yourself, nor will you continue one day more, when the hour of death has arrived. Grüner, my heart has not been so unaware of piety, that I do not honor the learned Manes with a poem, and console myself from vain care. Therefore come, Manes! O mind that formerly soared high in the sky, please, receive this our pious song. But you, Supreme God, who directs the massive bodies of the vast heavens, and whom the immense obeys, transport guiltless Grüner into the beloved spheres.

## 13.

### *Cératin, a Pseudomonk*

Come weep, hooded brothers; the glory of your hooded religion has died and gone away. The rest of you, laugh; oh yes, it is a very laughable matter. This is a death worthy of endless jokes. You see, once he gave all his effort and attention to wrecking everything by his crooked guile. But though he feigned everything, though he concealed everything in deception, the death that took that faker was no fake.

## 14.

### *J. O. Quelini, sodalis charissimi*

Ille, Calliope, Quelinus ille,
Et tuus simul, et meus Quelinus,
Ille, inquam, in media senex iuventa
Aquis interiit miser sub illis,
Non quas fonte tuo hauserat, nec illis                    5
Quas secum fluvii trahunt sonantes:
Sed quas, dum vigiles terit lucernas,
Collectas aluit scelestus hydrops.
Sic tuus periit tibi Quelinus
Sic meus periit mihi Quelinus                             10
Ergo hunc, Calliope, fleamus ambo,
Ut illum propriis aquis peremptum
Servemus lachrymis, aquisque nostris,
Ut vincantur aquis aquae, et putetur
Ille, qui periit mihi, tibique,                           15
Servatus studio tuo, meoque.

## 15.

### *Iacobi Belnensis*

Hunc sibi Belnensis tumulum, quem cernis inanem,
    Struxerat; invidit cui laqueus tumulum.
Debuerat certe, sors ut foret omnibus aequa,
    Tardius hic fieri, vel prius ille mori.

---

**14.**9–10 *ad initium utriusque* Ergo sic *1597*
11      Immo hunc *1597* ambo lugeamus *1569, 1576 1597*
12      Sic illum ut sub aquis malis peremptum *1597*
14–16 *om. 1569, 1576, 1597*
**15.**Tit. *add.* summi trium Galliae regum thesaurarii κενοτάφιον *1597* summi trium
        Galliae Regum Thesaurarii. 1527. Augusti XII *1779*
3       potius *pro* certe *1597*: si *pro* ut *1548, 1580, 1779*

## 14.

*Jean O. Quelin, a Dear Friend*

Calliope, that Quelin, both your friend and mine, mature in his youth, died miserably under the water. He did not die in your fountain, where he had drunk, nor in some rushing river. No, he drowned in those waters that a baneful dropsy gathered and retained, while exhausting the night-lamps. And so both you and I lost Quelin. Therefore, Calliope, let us both weep for him, so that the flood of our tears may save him who died by his own flood. Then we may overcome water by water, and save with our devotion the man we lost.

## 15.

*Jacques de Blois*

De Blois constructed for himself this tomb, which you see empty; but the noose begrudged him that tomb. Obviously, for things to have worked out right, either he should have built the tomb later, or died sooner.

## 16.

### *Renati Gentilis*

Fracto gutture stare quem revinctum,
Impellique vides et huc et illuc,
Quondam purpureo sedens Senatu,
Primas Parhisio in foro tenebat.
Verum (Proh facinus, scelusque grande!)　　　　　5
Dum lucri studio impotente captus,
Bonos non minus ac malos coercet,
Iusto numine sic iubente divum,
Vivus qui male sederat tot annos,
Stare nunc male mortuus iubetur.　　　　　10


## 17.

### *Gulielmi Langaei insubriae proregis*

Langaeus ille magnus hic iacet, lector,
Unus Minervam colere doctus, et Martem;
Quo nemo melior pace vixit aut bello.
Vitae genus habes: mortis en genus disce.
Aetate consumpta laboribus multis,　　　　　5
Suis suorumque omnium fere exhaustis
Bonis in usus Galliae suae, tandem,
Cum plus Milone et Curione deberet,
Interiit. Ergo pauper occidit, dices:
Immo locuples, cui patria debuit tantum.　　　　　10

---

**16.**Tit. *add.* Itali Torronensis, in suprema curia Praesidis illaudatiss. *1597* summi in
　　　suprema Galliarum Curia Praesidis illaudatissimi 1538 *1779*
3　　　　sedem *1713*
5　　　　*om. 1569, 1576, 1597*
6　　　　sed *pro* dum 1597: victus *1569, 1576*
7　　　　*om. 1569, 1576, 1597*
8　　　　vivus *pro* divum *1569, 1576, 1597*
9　　　　Qui iudex *1569, 1576 1597*
**17.**Tit. *add.* belli et pacis artibus clarissimi *1597, 1779*
2　　　　*om. 1569, 1576, sed non 1597*
8　　　　*om. 1569, 1576, 1597*

## 16.

*Renatus Gentilis*

The one whom you see standing with broken gullet, and mutilated all over, once sat in the royal senate and held the highest office of Parisian government. But (what a shame! what a scandal!) he was seized by an intense drive for gain, and he bullied both the good and the bad alike. Thus the one who ruled for so long with such abuses, now, under just orders from the gods, stands badly abused.

## 17.

*Guillaume of Langey, Viceroy of Lombardy*

Reader, here lies that great man Langey, who knew how to worship Minerva, as well as Mars; no one lived their life better than he, whether in times of peace or war. Now that you know how he lived, hear how he died: after he spent his whole life working hard, and after he exhausted both his own resources and those of his family for the sake of his beloved France, he died in the end owing more than Milo and Curio together. "Therefore," you will say, "he died a pauper." No, rather, he died rich, since his country owed to him so much.

## 18.

*Stephani Doleti Aurelii*

Ardentem medio rogo Doletum
Cernens Aonidum chorus sororum,
Carus ille diu chorus Doleto,
Totus ingemuit; nec ulla prorsus
E Sororibus est reperta cunctis,                                    5
Naias nulla, Driasve, Nereisve,
Quae non vel lachrymis suis, vel hausta
Fontis Pegasei studeret unda,
Crudeles adeo domare flammas.
Et iam totus erat sepultus ignis;                                  10
Iam largo madidus Doletus imbre
Exemptus poterat neci videri:
Cum caelo intonuit severus alto
Divorum pater; et velut peraegre
Hoc tantum studium ferens sororum:                                 15
At cessate, ait, et novum colonum
Ne diutius invidete caelo:
Caelum sic meus Hercules petivit.

## 18.

*Etienne Dolet of Orléans*

The chorus of the Aonian sisters, so dear to Dolet for so long, spied him being consumed in the midst of his pyre, and they groaned in unison. And there was no sister anywhere, no Naiad, no Dryad, no Nereid, who was not eager to douse such cruel flames with their own tears, or with water drawn from Pegasus's fountain. And when the whole fire was quenched, and Dolet was soaked by a hard rain, it would seem that he was being snatched from death, as the austere father of the gods thundered from high heaven. Although he was deeply stirred by this show of affection on the part of the sisters, still he said, "Cease, and no longer begrudge heaven a new citizen; even my dear Hercules made his way to heaven in the same way."

## 19.

### *Io. Dampetri*

Clausus coenobio latebat olim
Ille Dampetrus, optimus virorum,
Princepsque Hendecasyllabôn poeta.
Et clausus pariter latebat idem
Mole corporea, haud quidem, fatemur,  5
Obesa nimis aut tenebricosa,
Verum corporea, et proinde tali,
Ut divinum animum velut quibusdam
Nexum compedibus tenere posset.
At nunc coenobiique, corporisque  10
Vinclis Dampetrus exolutus exit,
Doctorumque volat per ora liber:
Qui tamen moriens, suis amicis
Heu quot millia lachrymationum,
Heu quot attulit anxios dolores!  15
Ergo haud occidit ipse, quod putaram,
Occidit potius suos amicos.

---

Tit. *add.* Monialium apud Magdalenam Aureliae Rectoris, Poetarum in scribendis
  Hendecasyllabis facile Principis *1779*
9  teneret arctis *1597*
16  Non ergo *1597*
17  suis amicis *1713*

### 19.

*Jean Dampierre*

Once Dampierre, best of men, prince of the hendecasyllabics, was cloistered and hidden away in a monastery. And there he had a body, admittedly, not one that was overweight or sickly, but a body nonetheless, and one with which he could hold his divine mind bound with fetters, as it were. But now Dampierre is free from the chains of the monastery and the body, and he has gone away. He flies free through the mouths of the learned. But when he died he brought to his friends so many thousands of tears and so much torturous sorrow! So he himself did not really die, as I had imagined, rather, he brought death to his friends.

## 20.

*Nobilissimi Principis, Françoisci Borbonii, ducis Anguiennensis, in ludicro certamine interfecto*

Cum nuper gladios, et fortem evaseris hostem,
   Hic, Francisce, iaces; nec tamen ense iaces.
Sed nec in hostili potuisti occumbere campo;
   Nec fortis forti victus ab hoste cadis.
Sedibus at patriis, belli simulacra cientem           5
   Missa infoelici sustulit arca manu:
Arca olim Stygia (credo) compacta cupressu,
   Arca, eheu, quanta nobilitata nece!
Arca, in qua Parcam Mavors absconderat ipse,
   Audiit ut factis aemula facta suis.           10
Sic igitur, miserande, cadis: nec cernere longum
   Illa tua licuit parta trophaea manu.
At si nobiscum vis, o Fortuna, iocari,
   Cur istis mors est seria mixta iocis?

---

Tit.    *add.* post insignem adversus Marchionem Vasti in Pedemonte victoriam in lu-
      dis aulicis infelicissime caesi *1779* in ludicro certamine interfecto, *1569*
4      caesus ab hoste cadis *1597*
7      Stygia (credo) *1569* (*errata*), *1576* ut credo Stygia *1548, 1580, 1779*
13–14 Ite o mortales et tempus fallite ludis | En ipsis ... *1569, 1576*: sors adversa
      *1597*

## 20.

*Our Most Noble Prince, François Bourbon, Duke of Enghien, Killed during a Game*

Although recently you escaped the swords and the brave enemy, you are lying here, François, yet you are not lying here by the sword. You were not able to meet your death in the enemies' camp, nor fall a brave man at the hands of a brave enemy. Rather it was at home, when you were engaged in a mock battle, that an arrow shot from an unlucky hand took your life—an arrow once fashioned, as I believe, from the Stygian cypress, an arrow, alas, ennobled by such a great slaying! an arrow, in which Mars himself had hidden Fate, when he had heard that your deeds rivaled his own. And so you fell, poor prince, and you were not long permitted to witness the trophies that your hand obtained. O Fortune, if you wish to toy with us, why mix grave death in with those games of yours?

### 21.

*Françoisci Valesii, I., Christianissimi Francorum Regis, P. P. et bo-*
*narum litterarum assertoris, vindicisque*

Nobile, quisquis ades, Regis venerare sepulchrum,
    Regis sepulchrum nobilis.
Nec pigeat mecum Francorum incommoda flere,
    Dum multa paucis explico.
Corporis ac animi florentem dotibus, atque        5
    Re facile primum, ut nomine,
Franciscum hunc regem vidit Fortuna, simulque
    Invidit, ut bonis solet.
Illum igitur ficto interdum demulsit amore,
    Et inclytis victoriis:        10
Reppulit irata interdum, vultuque minaci
    Tradidit in hostium manus.
Sed neque sors illum melior sic extulit unquam,
    Ut esset immemor sui;
Nec Fortuna animos illi sic fregit acerba,        15
    Quin victus illam vinceret.
Ergo suos cernens vanos Fortuna labores,
    Et irritos omnes dolos,
Auxilium poscit supplex a Morte: roganti
    Mors paret illi protinus,        20
Et regis primum e natis truculenta peremit,
    Cui tertium mox addidit,
Heu! iuvenes ambos, ambos nil tale timentes,
    Et non mori dignissimos.
Tandem etiam, o facinus! parta iam pace fruentem        25
    Aggressa patrem sustulit.
Sublatum ingemuere omnes, sed prae omnibus, illae,
    Illae Camoenae nobiles,
Hebraeae, Graecae et Latiae, quas ille fovebat,
    Ut filias caras pater.        30
Quae nunc, ut referant illi quae praemia possunt,
    Fovent vicissim mortuum,
Et quantum in sese est, a caeca mortis opacae
    Oblivione vindicant.

## 21.

*François I de Valois, Most Christian King of the French, Father of the People and Patron and Judge of Literature*

Whoever approaches, venerate the noble tomb of the king, the tomb of a noble king; and do not be ashamed to weep with me for the troubles of the French, as I explain many things in a few words. Fortune saw this king François, abounding in the gifts of body and soul, and easily first in the Republic, as he was also by name the first, and she envied him at once, as the good are often envied. Therefore, she softened him from time to time with false love, and with famous victories. At other times she irately rejected him, and delivered him with threatening countenance into the hands of the enemy. But his better luck never made him so haughty as to forget his own people, nor did bitter Fortune ever break his spirit so, that he would want to do anything but conquer and subdue her. Therefore, when Fortune saw that her work was in vain, and all her deceits made void, she fell on her knees and asked Death for help; Death was quick to oblige her, and cold-heartedly killed the first of the king's children, to which he soon added the third. Woe! two youths, unsuspecting of such a thing, and unworthy to die! And then—evil deed!— Death came and took the father at the moment he was enjoying the peace he had won. Everyone wailed at his burial, but especially those noble Muses, the Hebrew, the Greek, and the Latin, whom he cherished, like a father cherishing his dear daughters. They now cherish him in turn as he lies dead, so as to offer what rewards they can, and to the best of their abilities they deliver him from the deep oblivion of dark death.

---

Tit.  Francisci I. Francorum Regis. P.P. bonarum literarum excitatoris sacrae memoriae *1597*

1  venerere *1547 Tumuli*

7  sors olim vidit *1569, 1576* sors falsa *1597*

13  nec *1547 Tumuli, 1548, 1779, 1579*

15  Nec sors illi animos unquam sic fregit acerba *1569, 1576* Nec sors unquam animos illi sic fregit acerba *1597*

17  sors ista *1597*

21  trucidat *pro* peremit

24  Spem patria ambos et decus *1597*

30  caras *1597 omn. al.* solet

33  opaca *1597*

## 22.

*Françoisci Valesii, Françoisci Regis filii et Galliarum Delphini, vene-*
*ficio interfecto*

Hunc etiam iuvenem extinctum, rogo, cerne, viator.
    Hei mihi, cur vivum dicere fata vetant?
Hic est, quo niti regnum debebat avitum,
    Spes patriae nuper, spes quoque prima patris:
Pro quibus intrepidus fortem dum fertur in hostem,        5
    Ipse illum Mavors vidit, et obstupuit;
Aggressusque dolo, et crudelis fraude veneni,
    Sustulit. Heu magnis fraus bene nota viris!
Macte tamen, Princeps: nam te mors ipsa fatetur
    Non aliter vinci quam potuisse dolo.        10
Nempe erat hoc reliquum, Pellaei ut principis acta
    Aequares, simili te quoque fraude mori.

## 23.

*Caroli Valesii, Françoisci Regis filii et Aureliorum Ducis*

Gallia felici felix mihi patria nuper,
    Idem etiam nuper rexque paterque fuit.
Ingenium (nisi me assentatrix turba fefellit)
    Caeleste, et summis aemula forma deis.
Iamque mihi externos Fortuna parabat honores;        5
    Iam poteram magni Caesaris esse gener:
Quando ferox blanda pro coniuge Parca reperta est,
    Quae mihi pro thalamo sterneret hunc tumulum.
Nec tam erepta movent tamen haec me commoda vitae,
    Quam doleo abruptum nobile pacis opus.        10
Sed quanquam haud potui pacem componere vivus,
    Quis scit ab interitu surget an ipsa meo?

---

22.Tit. veneficio interfecto *1569, 1576 add.* propinato apud Avenionem veneno,
    proditiore sublati *1597, 1779*
11-12 *om. 1569, 1576* Nimirum fieres princeps Pellaeus ut alter | Consimili decuit
    te quoque fraude mori *1597*

## 22.

*François de Valois, the Dauphin, Son of King François, killed by poison*

Traveler, please, look on this youth who has died. Ah! why do the fates not permit me to say, "who is alive!" He is the one on whom the ancestral kingdom ought to have relied, recently the hope of our country, the first hope of the father also. Once when for their behalf he hurled himself fearlessly against a strong enemy, Mars saw him, and was dumbstruck. Sneaking up on him, he took his life deceptively with a cruel poison. A trick well-known to great men! It's to your credit, prince, for Death itself admits that he could not defeat you except by deception. At any rate, that alone was left to make you equal the deeds of the king of Pella, to die also by some deception.

## 23.

*Charles de Valois, Son of King François, and Duke of Orléans*

Blessed France was my country of late, and I was blessed, and the king was also my father. I had a heavenly nature (unless the people have deceived me with their approval), and looks to make the gods jealous. And just as Fortune was preparing foreign honors for me, and I was to become the son-in-law of great Caesar, savage Fate was found in place of a charming wife; she prepared for me this tomb in place of a marriage bed. I do not grieve so much that I am deprived of the pleasure of life, as that the work of peace has been disrupted. But even though I could not arrange peace while I was living, who knows whether by my death it may also rise?

## 24.

*In mortem Françoisci Valesii, I. Francorum Regis, et duorum eius li-*
*berorum, Françoisci Carolique, Alterius Galliarum Delphini, Alte-*
*rius Aureliorum Ducis.*

Aspicis infelix tres regum, Gallia, mortes,
    Heu vicina nimis funera funeribus!
Aspicis efferri, quantaque potes pietate
    Prosequeris facibus, prosequeris lachrymis.
Nec mirum: digni siquidem natique paterque,         5
    Quorum elementa necem muta vel ipsa gemant.
Crudeles superi, ut sit mors matura parentis
    (Debuerat princeps si tamen iste mori):
At cur tam subito ternis ex fratribus, unum
    Servastis, rapuit Mors violenta duos?         10
Nam potius, digna ut virtutis praemia ferrent,
    Condendus triplex fratribus orbis erat.

## 24.

*The Death of François I de Valois, King of France, and of His Two Sons, François and Charles, the One Dauphin of France, the Other Duke of Orléans*

Unhappy France, you see the deaths of three kings, death following death in quick succession. You see them taken away for burial, and with all the piety you can muster you escort them with torches and tears. And it is no wonder: the children and the father are certainly worthy; even nature herself bewails their deaths. Cruel gods above, if the king had to die at all, admittedly his death was not premature. But why did you save one of the three brothers, while violent Death took two so unexpectedly? Instead, so they may enjoy rewards worthy of their virtue, you should have fashioned a threefold world for the brothers.

# Commentary on the Epitaphs

During the Renaissance the generic label *epitaphia* normally was applied to poems written on the occasion of someone's death. The person being celebrated need not be famous, though that is usually the case. Many of Bèze's poems treat members of the royal court or humanists with an international reputation, but sometimes the deceased is someone who neither wrote or achieved anything noteworthy, and is known only by virtue of being close to the poet. In the case of Bèze's *epitaphia*, we know that some of the poems were inscribed and placed over the graves themselves, though in most cases, particularly when the individual was important, the poems pay homage only from afar. As to the general character of the *epitaphia* and their range, McFarlane (*Literary History of France*, 109) gives the following sketch:

> ... as a genre it is already common currency with the *rhétoriqueurs,* but is richly exploited by the contemporary Neo-latins, not only at the more exalted level of court ceremonial (though here the *déploration* or eclogue may be the most appropriate form), but as a peg on which the author may hang his virtuosity and wit. There are variations in the form of address, the author speaking in his own voice, or using the *débat* form, or the *prosopopoeia* in which the deceased may deliver a posthumous speech either to the traveler passing by or to a beloved relative still on earth, a mode which allows for the development of some edifying *topos*. The epitaph may concern imaginary characters, usually of comic quality, and it may be the occasion for word-play—and here the influence of Ausonius, Martial, and the *Greek Anthology* is evident. In the hands of some authors, the genre can virtually

merge with the emblem or the *icon* (by way of the *exemplum*).

McFarlane goes on to give examples from Marot that exhibit elevated and solemn tones as well as others that are imaginary and humorous. All of Bèze's *epitaphia*, however, pertain to real people.

While the primary purpose of the poems may have been to pay respect to, or at times to ridicule, the dead, they did carry with them secondary objectives. It has been noted that the Renaissance collective tributes, called *tumuli* or *tombeaux*, that is, booklets devoted to the remembrance of one individual, served a political purpose beyond the homage *per se*. They were used as propaganda, as a means for attracting the notice of influential people, and as way of positioning oneself in the world of humanists.[1] Bèze himself published such a collection in 1547 (entitled *Tumuli*), and most of those poems make their way into his 1548 edition. It would be surprising, then, if Bèze wrote his *epitaphia* without a thought for these broader implications.

## 1.

Missing in 1597.

Pierre de l'Etoille (born 1480, d. 28 October 1537) was professor of law at Orléans, where in 1529 he taught several of Bèze's friends and acquaintances, including Jean Calvin (though l'Etoille himself was an anti-reform zealot), Maclou Pompon, Pierre Daniel, and Lambert Danneau. Bèze, however, never had him as a teacher, but seems to have known his niece well, whom some have connected with the "Candida" of the elegies and epigrams.[2] During his years at Orléans he carried on a lit-

---

[1] See esp. I. D. McFarlane, "La poésie néo-latine et l'engagement à l'époque des guerres de religion," in *Culture et politique en France à l'époque de l'humanisme et de la Renaissance* (Turin, 1974), 387–411; and V.-L. Saulnier, "La mort du dauphin François et son tombeau poétique," *BHR* 6 (1945): 50–97.

[2] F. le Maire, *Histoire et antiquitez*, 2: 123, makes this remark: "A present par le mesnage et vigilence de Messierus les Proviseurs, l'on le rebastit, avec autant d'ornement et beauté, qu'il pouvoit estre, dans iceluy il s'y voit plusieurs Epitaphes elegans comme celuy du Sieur Audebert, celuy de Marie de l'Estoille fait par maistre Theodore Beze lors escolier à Orléans en 1525. Qu'il n'a rapporté en son livre des Epitaphes, parce qu'il est en prose, mais bien celuy de Catherine Texier d'Orléans, et de Mre. Pierre de l'Estoille, Docteur en l'Université d'Orléans, et depuis President au Parlement de Paris." But Bèze was not a student at Orléans in 1525; perhaps 1535 is meant? At any rate, Brainne et al. (*Hommes illustres*, 2: 64) confirm the existence of a Latin and French epitaph that Bèze had engraved on the tomb of this niece, and then identify her as the Candida of Bèze's poems: "Marie de l'Etoile, connue par ses liaisons avec Théodore de Bèze, qui, dans ses Juvenilia, l'a célébrée

erary debate with Udalricus Zasius over his commentary on the *Pandects*; he was greatly influenced by Guillaume Budé. After his wife died, he served in several ecclesiastical posts, and eventually caught the attention of François I, who appointed him clergyman for the Parlement of Paris in 1530. See Moreri, *Grand dictionnaire historique* (hereafter *GDH*) 4.3.253 (first Pierre entry); Bimbenet, *Université d'Orléans*, 354–57 (which records an epitaph in French); Brainne et al., *Hommes illustres* 64–65;[3] J. Boussard, "Ms. 1674," 209–30, esp. 222ff.; Ridderikhoff, *Les livres des procurateurs*, 1: 170, n. 1. Michael Monheit, "Guillaume Budé, Andrea Alciato, Pierre de l'Estoille: Renaissance Interpreters of Roman Law," *Journal of the History of Ideas* 58.1 (1997): 21–40. Here Bèze makes a play on the meaning of his name, "star," as one would expect. Visagier also addresses an epitaph to him that makes a similar play:

*Stellae Aurelii Epitaphium*

Lucem legibus ut darem, reliqui
Caelum, reddita lux meo labore est.
Feci quod volui. Ad locum recurro,
A quo me poterit vocare nemo.
(*Liber hendec.*, 1538, 21v)

The Orléans ms. contains another epitaph to l'Etoille in Greek, where again Bèze turns to the imagery of "light" for material:

Εἰς τὸν αὐτόν

Φεῦ Κῆρας ὀλοῆς. θνῆσκεν δικαιώτατος ἀνδρῶν,
   Καὶ μερόπεσσι φάος ὢν ποτε ἱμερόεν.
Κεῖν' ἀρετὴν δῆθα ποθέων νεφεληγέρετα Ζεύς
   Ἥρπασεν ἀθανάτ' ἄξιον ἀμβροσίης.

---

sous le nom de Candide, était nièce du savant professeur; elle mourut jeune et fut inhumée dans le Grand-Cimetière, où l'on voyait encore au commencement du XVIIIᵉ siècle une épitaphe latine et française que Théodore de Bèze avait fait graver sur son tombeau." Geisendorf, *Bèze*, 14, also believes that Marie lurks throughout the collection, though he stops short of identifying her as Candida: "Et puis, à côté, en dehors de ce groupe amical, voici une silhouette féminine qui traverse furtivement les poèmes les plus chastes et les plus attendris des *Juvenilia*: Marie de L'Estoile, nièce d'un des professeurs de droit d'Orléans, dont la mort en pleine jeunesse interrompra l'idylle à peine ébauchée."

[3] There one finds the following comment: "Théodore de Bèze, qui l'estimait autant qu'il aimait sa nièce, fit en vers latins, deux épitaphes à la mémoire de Pierre de l'Etoile, qu'il appelle *Gallorum jurisconsultorum quondam in Academia Aurelianensi facile princeps*. Gentien Hervet et Vulteius firent aussi son éloge."

The 1597 edition records a poem to l'Etoile where light imagery also figures:

*Ornatiss. viri, Petri Stellae; Gallorum iurisconsultorum quondam in Academia Aureliensi, facile principis, et postea in Parisiensi suprema curia praesidis, meritorum ergo, constituti, memoriae*

> Vero, homines inter, splendore aequique bonique,
> Toto ut regnarent iura sacrata foro,
> Stella haec in terras caelo migrare relicto,
> Atque hominis faciem sumere iussa fuit:
> Sumpsit: sed superas subito remeavit ad oras,
> Nobiscum exiguo tempore visus homo,
> Et nos miramur, sublato lamine Legum,
> Regnare in medio iurgia sola foro?

**3. Lucifer**: also called Phosphoros, the morning star. In reality, "Lucifer" was the name given to the planet Venus when seen in the morning immediately before sunrise. The ancients believed it to be the last star to remain in the sky before daylight.

**6. Perpetua ... nocte**: Catullus's euphemism for death at *c.* 5.6.

## 2.

Missing in 1569, 1576, 1597; cf. Merrill, *Grimald*, 402 and 443.

Jean Vaillant de Guélis, bailiff of Dunois and councillor in the Grand Council, was the father of Bèze's friends at Orléans, the brothers Louis and Germain Vaillant, to whom Bèze addressed several poems (see esp. *epig.* 10 and 53, *eleg.* 4 and 8).

## 3.

Missing in 1597; Wright, *Delitiae delitiarum* (1637), 6–7.
Meter: phalaecian hendecasyllable.

There is no context to help identify this person. *Causidicus* carries a negative connotation in classical literature, and therefore should be preferred here. The joke is that this lawyer who used to plead cases on behalf of so many now is in a position to need someone to plead his case.

2. **paradigma**: The word plays on the meaning of "a rhetorical exam-
ple" such as those learned in law school.
4. **operam ... locabat**: the opposite of *conducit* in line 6, usually with
*suam* added: "to hire oneself out for service."
5. **Rhadamantium**: brother of Minos. By virtue of his just life, the gods
made him a judge in the underworld. His location is variously placed
by classical authors (Pindar, *Ol.* 2.75 places him in the Isles of the
Blessed), but here Bèze must be following Vergil (*Aen.* 6.566), who
assigns him to Tartarus where he oversees the torturing of the worst
criminals and forces their confession of sins.


### 4.

Missing in 1779; this is the only epitaph from the *iuvenilia* to ap-
pear in *Theodori Bezae, theologi et poetae clariss. epitaphia selecta,
cum Anglica versione* (London, 1680).

Guillaume Budé (1467–1540) was a major figure in the early French
Renaissance.[4] He is best known for his passionate devotion to ancient
Greek, his service to Louis XII and François I, and his founding of two
academic institutions which were later to become the Collège de France
and the Bibliothèque Nationale. Among his many works is a treatise en-
titled *Commentarii linguae Graecae* (Paris, 1529), which established him
as the foremost Greek scholar in France. Fittingly, Bèze wrote this trib-
ute to him in his favorite tongue.

Bèze's attraction to this remarkable scholar is further evidence that
he was interested in religious reform even long before his conversion in
1548, as Meylan ("Conversion de Bèze") has argued. Budé maintained
close ties throughout Europe with reform-minded scholars, including
Erasmus and Rabelais, and for that reason some suspected him of Cal-
vinist leanings. Indeed, Bèze identifies him as an early reformer in his
*Icones* of 1580. Furthermore, Bèze's teacher, Melchior Wolmar, who was
so instrumental in turning Bèze to the Reformed movement, had him-

---

[4] For a thorough study, see McNeil, *Guillaume Budé and Humanism*.

self studied under Budé (as well as Lefèvre d'Etaples) while at Paris (see Geisendorf, *Bèze*, 10).

The model for this poem is Plato *epigr.* 2 (= *AP 7.670*):

Ἀστὴρ πρὶν μὲν ἔλαμπες ἐνὶ ζωοῖσιν Ἐῷος.
νῦν δὲ θανὼν λάμπεις Ἔσπερρος ἐν φθιμένοις.

[Until now you have shone among the living as the star of morning; now shine among the dead as the star of evening.]

1. **Φοῖβον**: The epithet, properly belonging to Apollo, but here applied to Budé, means "bright shining." It emphasizes Apollo's function as the sun god, thus the pun.
1–2. **γλώσσης ... Ἀμφοτέρας**: i.e., of Greek and Latin.
**ὀρθῶς, ἔειπε**: The 1548 ed. has errors in its accentuation of these words: ὄρθῶς, ἐειπε.


### 5.

Missing in 1569, 1576, 1597; 1779 uses title from previous epitaph; Kendall, *Flowers of Epigrammes*, 156; Canoniero, *Flores illustrium epitaphiorum*, 269, attributed as *Ex quodam*.

Here Bèze draws upon a familiar biblical principle, which states that only by giving away all one's possessions can one obtain the greatest treasures. Budé has given his mind, his body, and his life's work to others, leaving nothing to himself except everyone's admiration. Classical sentiments underlie the poem too, particularly, the notion that intellectual achievements are a monument to their author "more enduring than bronze" (Hor. *Od.* 3.30).

3–4: **Caelo animum ... dedit**: Note similar phrasing in the following poem from Canoniero, *Flores illustrium epitaphiorum*, fol. 4r:

*P. Ronsardi Gallicorum poetarum principis*

Terra tenet corpus, mentem Deus, acta nepotes:
Hospes, defuncto parce, poeta fuit.

6. **vincit opes**: "to win" rather than "to overcome," which would not fit well in the context. Cf. Ovid, *Her.* 16.76: *causam suam*.

## 6.

Missing in 1569, 1576, 1597, 1779; Kendall, *Flowers of Epigrams,*
156-57; Canoniero, *Flores illustrium epitaphiorum,* 434-35, attrib-
uted as *Ex quodam*; cf. Merrill, *Grimald,* 394-95, 436.

The torrents of tears resulting from the death of someone famous is a
common topic in epitaphs during the Renaissance; usually the result is
a dire flood. Here, however, Bèze adds his own twist: instead of a flood,
the weeping of the elements has produced a drought.

**4-5: plena volumina moestis | Carminibus:** i.e., *tumuli,* or *tombeaux,*
a popular genre of the period. On their importance as propaganda,
see McFarlane, "La poésie néo-latine," 387-411.

## 7.

Canoniero, *Flores illustrium epitaphiorum,* 435, unattributed, and
entitled *Cuiusdam*; the name *Beza* in line 8 is replaced with a
string of dots.

This epitaph honors Bèze's uncle, with whom he lived seven years in
Paris, from 1521 to December of 1528. He died late in 1532. During his
life he had enjoyed several ecclesiastical benefices, was "prieur commen-
dataire" of Saint-Eloi de Longjumeau (since 1522), and was a councillor
in the Parlement of Paris. It was his idea to send his nephew to live and
study in the house of Melchior Wolmar, although he had no intention

of thereby exposing Bèze to Lutheran teachings. Nicolas de Bèze was buried in the nave of the church of Saint Cosme and Saint Damien, his parish. On his tomb, at the entrance of the sanctuary, his brothers had fixed a large tableau of black marble, on which appears the family coat of arms, reprised later in the 1597 and 1599 editions under *Insignia Theodorei Bezae.*

After Bèze received his license in law, he moved to Paris in the same area where he had lived with his uncle. He therefore passed frequently in front of the church of Sts. Cosme and Damien, and must have stopped often to mediate on the tomb of his uncle Nicolas (see Droz, "Notes sur Théodore de Bèze," 596–99). In 1543 Bèze affixed to the existing dedication a parchment containing three inscriptions of his own composition, in Greek, Latin, and French, in honor of his uncle, which was still visible in the eighteenth century; see Bernard de La Monnoye, *Menagiana* (Paris, 1730), 4: 227–29, cited by Herminjard, *Correspondance des réformateurs*, 6: 139n. The texts of the poems are reproduced in E. Raunié, *Epitaphier du Vieux Paris* (Paris, 1890), 3: 1101 (French inscription on the marble tablet), 1102 (Latin poem inscribed in the middle of the tablet), 1103 (Latin poem by Théodore de Bèze beginning *Marmoreas, lector, nullas hic stare columnas*), 1104 (Greek poem by Bèze as follows:

*ΕΙΣ Τ' ΑΥΤΟΝ*

ΤΟΝ Δ' ΑΡΕΤΗ ΕΠΙΛΑΜΠΟΜΕΝΟΝ ΕΠΙΒΛΕΨΑΣ ΑΙΔΗΣ,
   ΤΙ ΠΟΛ' ΕΦΗ ΚΟΣΜΩ ΗΛΙΟΣ ΑΛΛΟΣ ΕΦΥ.
ΩΣ ΦΑΤΟ, ΚΑΙ ΔΟΛΙΟΙΣΙ ΦΡΕΣΙΝ ΚΑΚΑ ΜΗΧΑΝΟΩΣΑΣ,
   ΤΟΝ Δ' ΕΚΕΛΕΥΣΕ ΝΕΚΡΟΙΣ ΝΥΝ ΕΠΙΛΑΜΠΟΜΕΝΑΙ.),

1105 (French poem by Bèze beginning, "Amy passant, si tu as le loisir . . ."). The parchment on which these poems are written is dedicated in this way: *Nicolao a Beza, patruo carissimo, Theodorus Beza, moerens ponebat MDXLIII.*

The version of the 1569 edition (followed by the 1576 edition) is significantly different from line 5 to the end:

> Sic studeat nigrae vitare oblivia mortis,
>    Qui nil quo melius nobilitetur habet.
> Hic autem magni quondam pars magna senatus,
>    Et nullo, aut solo Beza Catone minor,
> Scilicet e tumulo famam nunc captet inanem,
>    Extincto vivens posthumus ipse sibi.

Fas alios igitur nomen debere sepulchris,
Beza suum contra nobilitat tumulum.

1. **marmore ... Pario**: white marble from the Greek island of Paros,
which the ancients had used extensively for their sculptures in prefer-
ence to all others.
4. **Mausoli**: a tomb erected to king Mausolus of Caria, who died 353
B.C. The ancients considered it one of the seven wonders of the
world (Pliny, *NH* 36.30–31). The Romans used the term *mausoleum*
to refer to any magnificent sepulcher.
8. **Catone**: Cato the Younger, often called Cato Uticensis (95–46 B.C.).
The *minor* (normally, "Younger") that follows his name here is a
nice touch. Although it does not properly modify *Catone*, by its
very position it does allude to the younger Cato while syntactically
introducing the comparative. He was the great-grandson of Cato the
Censor, and legendary for his austerity of character and strict adher-
ence to Stoic principles, which earned for him the admiration and re-
spect of the Roman people. During the civil wars, when he failed in
his resistance to the ambitions of Julius Caesar, he committed suicide
at Utica in North Africa, after helping his defeated army escape.
14. **Dignus, qui tumulo non tegeretur, erat**: The idea is that Nicolas
de Bèze's life was so virtuous that no monument is needed to re-
mind people of it. To this one can compare the statement of Pliny
the Younger, *Epist.* 9.19.3: "Impensa monumenti supervacua est; me-
moria nostri durabit, si vita meruimus" ("It is superfluous to erect a
monument, since our memory will endure if our life deserved it").
Cato the Elder had made a similar point when asked by his friends
why many insignificant men had statues while he had none: μᾶλλον
γὰρ βούλομαι ζητεῖσθαι, διὰ τί μου ἀνδριὰς οὐ κεῖται ἢ διὰ τί
κεῖται ["I would much rather people ask why I have no statue than
why I have one"] (Plutarch, *Life of Cato*, 19.6).

## 8.

Missing in 1569, 1576; Kendall, *Flowers of Epigrammes*, 157–59.
Meter: phalaecian hendecasyllable.

No information exists on this Catherine, except for the mention of her
grave in le Maire's description of Orléans (in *Histoire et antiquitez*).
ABM speculate that she may have been the sister of Bèze's friend Jean

Texier, who had obtained a chair of doctor-regent in 1519, and was rector of the university at Orléans in 1530 and 1545.

The sources for Bèze's stereotyping of women here are so extensive that I have deemed it fruitless to repeat them all here. Suffice it to say that Bèze was a product of his age.

**20. petulca:** properly of animals who butt with their horns, thus "butting" or "frisky." Cf. Colum. 7.3, Lucr. 2.267, and Verg. *Georg* 4.10. Servius (ad Verg. *Georg.* 4.10) notes that the term can also be applied to prostitutes: "Haedi petulci dicti ab appendo: unde et meretrices petulcas vocamus." So also Isidore, *Orig.* 10.231. Bèze must mean that Catherine did not employ the aggressive or frisky language of prostitutes.

**25–26. quod esse neutrum | probatum ... nobis:** literally, "because it was more than sufficiently proven to me that she was neither," meaning that she did not have the negative traits of either male or female, and therefore could not be merely a combination of both. Although she has both feminine and manly qualities, Bèze shies away from calling her "androgynous," since such people are socially shunned and ridiculed (cf. *epig.* 21).

## 9.

Wright, *Delitiae delitiarum* (1637) 7;
Kendall, *Flowers of Epigrammes*, 159.
Meter: iambic quaternarius.

Antoine Duprat was born 17 January 1463 at Issoire, the son of Antoine and Jacqueline Bohier. He married Françoise Veiny d'Arbouze in 1493, then entered the Parlement in 1505. He became first president in 1508, then chancellor under François I. He was governing France during the captivity of the king in 1525, and in the same year was named archbishop of Sens. On 21 November 1527, he was appointed cardinal by Clement VII. He resisted Lutheranism and the reform of the Church. He crowned Eleanor of Austria at S.-Denis on 5 March 1531. He died 9 July 1535 at the château of Nantouillet, which he had constructed, and was buried in the cathedral of Sens. He became extremely wealthy due to his influence and shrewdness, leaving behind a huge fortune; by all accounts he was rather stout of build. The authoritarianism with which he conducted himself and enacted his policies, together with his love of titles and money, earned him many enemies.

A. Buisson (*Le chancelier Antoine Duprat* [Paris, 1935], 345–52 [a picture of his tomb appears on p. 344]) reports that his sepulcher in the cathedral of Sens was magnificent. He relays the following information from a report done in 1793 about the monuments in the cathedral:

> Il est composé d'un large socle qui en porte un second, orné de différentes marques de dignités pontificales et autres. Aux quatre coins de celui-ci, sont placées des statues en marbre blanc représentant des Vertus. Derrière ces statues, s'élèvent des colonnes de marbre noir, qui portent une table de marbre semblable. Sous cette table est un cénotaphe, sur lequel est couché le cardinal, nu et le ventre ouvert, signe de la dernière maladie. Le cénotaphe est porté par une base ornée de quatre bas-reliefs très beaux. Au-dessus de la table est le même cardinal, à genouil et revêtu de ses habits. Cet ouvrage, le plus beau de cette église et parfaitement entier, mérite d'être conservé.

Bèze's *amplissimus*, then, must be manifold in meaning, recalling the grandeur of the tomb, the rotundness of Duprat himself, and the eminence of his career. The joke is a one-line epitaph on someone so large in every way. For the comic uses of the iambic quaternarius, see the commentary on *epitaph*. 21, below.

## 10.

Helius Eobanus Hessus (1488–1540) was a native, as his name implies, of Hesse. He was born at Halgehausen near Frankenberg. He was professor of Latin and rhetoric at both Erfurt and Nuremberg, where he befriended Joachim Camerarius, and was a supporter of Lutheran reforms (again, a sign of Bèze's leanings during this period). He published numerous editions of eclogues and sylvae, as well as a book entitled *Heroides Christianae* (Leipzig, 1514). See H. Vredeveld, *Helius Eobanus Hessus, Dichtung der Jahre 1528–1587* (Bern, 1991).

The 1597 version of this epitaph is significantly different:

> *Eobani Hessi, clariss. Germaniae poetae, Homeri Iliada et Theocriti idyllia Latinis versibus feliciter interpretati, memoriae*

Nuper Lethaeas Eobanum venerat Hessum
   Transvecturus aquas portitor ille Charon,
Multa minans, Siculi calamos impune poetae,
   Maeonidaeque auso surripuisse tubam:
Quin etiam media vates iam puppe sedebat,
   Cum prohibens nautam pergere Mercurius,
Ne saevito, senex, inquit, sibi vindicat istum,
   Istum, inquam, superum turba beata, sibi.
Nam qui aliis potuit vitam producere, certe
   Infera iuris in hunc obtinet aula nihil.

**3. squalentis portitor Orci**: Charon, the boatman, who ferries the souls of the dead across the Styx into the Underworld. The adjective *squalentis* comes from Verg. *Aen.* 6.298–99, where it is applied to Charon himself: "portitor has horrendus aquas et flumina servat | *terribili squalore Charon* ..." Cf. also Verg. *Georg.* 4.502.

**4. Manibus**: spirits of the dead, whom the Romans were careful to appease, lest they become envious. Charon is speaking ironically, since the *manes* will not be happy that Hessus imitated them so well.

**5. Syracusii calamos ... poetae**: He is referring to the idyllic poet, Theocritus (fl. c. 270 B.C.), who was a native of Syracuse, and whom Hessus both imitated and translated. See esp. *Theocritus ... idyllia triginta sex, Latino carmine reddita, Helio Eobano Hesso interprete* (Haguenau, 1530). The "reed" or "pan flute" was the instrument most symbolic of idyllic poetry (see esp. Lucr. 4.586–89 and Verg. *Ecl.* 1.10; 2.31–34).

**6. tubam**: specifically of the trumpet that signals war; often of epic poetry; cf. Martial 8.3.22; 8.56.4; 10.64.4; 11.3.8.

**8. Mercurius**: here in his role as psychopompos, escort of dead souls, and messenger from Jupiter.

**12. Ditis**: The underworld was variously called Orcus, Dis, and Hades.

### 11.

Missing in 1569, 1576, 1597.
Meter: phalaecian hendecasyllable.

Cf. *epig.* 69 on the same incident. Popon went to Italy during the years 1541–1542. There are several references to this trip in the poetry and correspondence of Bèze. A letter, dated May 1541 (*Corr.* 1: 39), is addressed,

> Amicorum optimo Maclovio Pomponio.
> Paduae aut Patavii.

At the outset of the letter, Bèze expresses his burning desire to hear news from Popon about his trip and health:

> Ego vero vellem, mi Pomponi, ut quanto videndi tui, aut certe literarum tuarum desiderio flagrem intelligeres. Itane procul es dissitus, ita procul seiunctus, ut ne audire quidem possim quo sis loco, qua valetudine?

The Orléans ms. (ABM, p. 169, no. 4) contains a poem addressed to Popon that apparently refers to the same trip to Italy:

> *De profectione Macuti Pomponii*
>
> Quod peregrina suum retineret terra Macutum,
>    Invida non poterat patria ferre diu.
> Sed tamen illa suo retinebat in orbe Macutum
>    Nec velle hunc a se longius ire virum.
> Consultus tandem respondit Iuppiter, orbi,
>    Non urbi, tantum se peperisse iubar.

> [*On the departure of Maclou Popon*
>
> His homeland was jealous, and could not bear it any longer that a foreign land possessed her Maclou. Yet that foreign country was also clinging to Maclou, and did not want him to go away. Jupiter was consulted and he responded, "I produced such a great ray of light for the world, not for a single city."[5]]

Vindry (*Parlementaires* 1: 166) gives the following information on the career of Popon: he was born in 1514 in the town of Bourgogne, but studied in Dijon, where eventually he was received into the Parlement in 1554 as a councillor. He also studied law in Orléans, where Bèze would have met him, and then in Italy. In 1542 he became advocate of the king, and must have been married around the same time, since a let-

---

[5] A play on the papal "urbi et orbi."

ter of Bèze, dated 7 May 1542, mentions his recent marriage. After having a very distinguished career as a magistrate, he died in 1577. There was published a collection entitled *Macutii Pomponii monumentum* (Paris, 1580), a kind of *tumulus* in his honor, which included a poem of Bèze For more information on his career one may consult Vindry, *Parlementaires*, 1: 166 and Herminjard, *Correspondance des réformateurs*, 6: 139n.

The following two poems of Girard (*Poemata nova* ⌊1584⌋, *Epitaphia*, 108r) mention this premature epitaph of Bèze:

> *D. M. Pomponio Reg. in Senatu D. consil*
>
> Olim mentitus, Pomponi, Beza licenter,
>   Te te defunctum dixerat esse semel.
> Vivebas etenim repletus sanguine venis
>   Invita fama, forsan et invidia.
> Urna tuum tandem corpus sine sanguine coepit:
>   Quid si te nobis vivere Beza neget?
> Mentitur mihi bis, mihi bis mentitur: et errat:
>   Te mea Pomponi vivere Musa iubet.
> Pompa mea Aonides aeterno ab Apolline Musae,
>   Te Pomponi inquam vivere vive iubet.

[Once, Popon, Bèze shamelessly lied and said that you had died. But you were alive, with blood pumping through your veins, with reluctant fame, perhaps even with envy. Then finally your body began to be an urn without blood. What if Bèze denies to us that you live? To me he lies twice, twice he lies; and he is wrong. My muse commands that you live, Popon. Yes, my procession of the Heliconian Muses from eternal Apollo, commands that you live to the fullest, Popon.]

> *Eidem*
>
> Qui mortuum Pomponium
> Putant: et hoc reconditum
> Putri sepulchro, errant male:
> Toto orbe vivus ambulat
> Ut Phoebus inter sidera.

[Those who think that Popon is dead, and buried in this foul tomb, are badly mistaken: He lives and strides about the whole world, like Phoebus among the stars.]

**1-3. Vos ... obsecro**: Remarkably, Bèze reused these lines again for the epitaph of his sister (Maigron, *De Theodori Bezae poematis*, 12):

*Magdalenae a Beza sorori charissimae et mulieri lectissimae*

Eheu hendecasyllabi miselli,
Vos (inquam) miserabiles phaleuci,
Vos eheu numeri severiores,
Quaeso ...

**flebiles Phaleuci**: not normally a meter of mourning (it has its origins in Attic drinking songs and the choral odes of tragedy), but Catullus's *c.* 3 ("Lugete, o Veneres Cupidinesque ...") may have suggested its function as such.

**4ff.**: The language is reminiscent of Catullus *c.* 2.

**16. Orpheus** Orpheus, the great musician of Greek mythology, was said to be able to charm even the rocks and trees with the beauty of his tunes.

**22: Pericles**: Athenian statesman who died in 429 B.C., and saw that city through some tumultuous times. None of his oratory survives (unless one includes the speech in Thucydides), but Quintilian (10.1.82) describes his speech as equivalent to thunder and lightning, and adds that he carried the weapons of Jupiter on his tongue. Here Bèze is acknowledging his prowess in oratory, but notes that his mastery was limited to the Greek tongue only.

**24. Tullius**: Cicero (d. 43 B.C.) was the greatest of all Roman orators. Despite what Bèze says here, Cicero was well capable of delivering speeches in Greek, as he did once in Syracuse.

**28-29. Hoc si Roma ... | ... Graeca personaret**: He seems to be indicating that Popon has given speeches in both Athens and Rome, which by metonymy is equivalent to giving speeches in Greek and Latin.

**30. Apelli**: On Apelles see note on *epig.* 28.

**39. Magnus Pythagoras, Platoque magnus**: According to tradition, Pythagoras had traveled in Africa where he learned many of his doctrines; no reliable information has come down on the matter, however. It is known that Plato went to Egypt as part of his early education, and that there he learned much about mathematics and astronomy, though in his case also legend is mixed with fact.

41. **Anacharsis**: a Scythian prince who came to Athens in 594 B.C. to further his studies. He was well-received there, and even befriended Solon.

49. **Rhodani**: On the Rhone river, see note on *epig.* 49.8. Here it is mentioned because of its proximity to the Alps and Northern Italy.

53. **Lemani**: modern-day Lake Geneva, which is formed by the Rhone river.

82. **Pyladi**: Pylades's friendship with Orestes, son of Agamemnon, had become proverbial. He plays a minor role in several Greek tragedies (*Choephoroi, Iphigenia at Tauris*).

   **Achati**: should be *Achatae*. Achates was the loyal friend of Aeneas and was often called *fidus Achates* (Verg. *Aen.* 1.188, etc.).

## 12.

### Missing in 1569, 1576.

Simon Grüner (c. 1494–1541) was born at Vehringen (Zollern). He became professor of Greek at the University of Basel, then was charged in 1535 with the reorganization of the university at Tübingen. He died of the plague at Basel in 1541. Bèze must have had connections with Grüner through Wolmar. In the 1597 edition, the poem completely changes after line 15:

> Nunc vero cum te plangant infraque supraque
> Omnia, tu Bezae, Grynae, indictus abibis?
> Sancti, immo, o Manes, o mens super aethera pridem
> Vecta, pium, quaeso, a nobis hoc accipe carmen,
> Sic sibi Grynaeum exceptum gratetur Olympus.

The 1597 edition also includes the following poem with an added explanation of the occasion (219):

> Obiit Basileae ex peste, Anno Domini 1541.
> Anno aetatis xlviii. Calendis Augusti.

> *Simon Grynaeus*

> Te quicunque, Simon Grynae, aspexit, amavit,
>    Splenduit in vultu gratia tanta tuo:
> Te quicunque, Simon Grynaee, audivit, amavit,

Facundo fluxit tantus ab ore lepos.
Amplius at cur non audire et cernere fas est?
Scilicet hoc fati vis inopina vetat.
Immo fallor ego. Nam sint paucissima quamvis:
Ingenii nobis scripta relicta tui,
Te spectamus adhuc, te nos miramur in illis,
Aeternoque manes dignus honore, Simon.

6. **simile cognomen**: Presumably he means "Phoebus" ("bright shining").

7. **nimbosus Orion**: here, *Oriōn* (normally, *Orīon*), as at Verg. *Aen.* 1.535, where the noun with this epithet appears in the same position in the line. The constellation Orion rises and sets in the rainy season.

8. **lachrymosus Aquarius**: The zodiac sign of Aquarius is used as a metaphor for winter rains; cf. Verg. *Georg.* 3.303–4: "cum frigidus olim iam cadit extremoque inrorat Aquarius anno." Fittingly, the "Water-bearer" pours tears from his urn.

10. **nigra ferrugine**: cf. Verg. *Georg.* 1.467 (concerning the year 44 B.C.): "cum caput obscura nitiduum ferrugine texit [sc. sol]." The word "ferrugine" adds a touch of the gloomy (cf. Verg. *Aen.* 6.303, of Charon's boat).

16. **naturae inquirere causas**: recalls Vergil's statement concerning Lucretius (*Georg.* 2.490; cf. Lucr. 3.1072 and 5.1185): "felix, qui potuit rerum cognoscere causas."

18. **doctis eadem indoctisque**: recalling Ecclesiastes 2.15–16, esp. 16: "moritur doctus similiter et indoctus."

19–20. **Mors tamen ... | Desidiae et magnae**: from Homer, *Iliad* 9.320 (possibly an interpolation): κάτθαν᾽ ὁμῶς ὅ τ᾽ ἀεργὸς ἀνὴρ ὅ τε πολλὰ ἐοργώς ["death comes alike to the idle man and the worker"].
**magno finem impositura labori**: cf. Verg. *Aen.* 2.619, "finemque impone labori."

29. **vastus ... orbis**: In Vergil's so-called messianic eclogue, the world is said to teeter in response to the birth of the child who ushers in the golden age (*Ecl.* 4.50): "aspice convexo nutantem pondere mundum."

### 13.

This poem addresses Pierre de Corne or Cornu (see Moreri, *GDH*, 4.1: 148; not to be confused with the Cornu of the same name who pub-

lished his *Œuvres poétiques* in 1583), a Parisian Franciscan preacher of
great renown who vehemently opposed the Lutheran heresies, and thus
drew the ire of those interested in the so-called new learning. Rabelais in
particular railed against him and Erasmus refers to his "confused bab-
bling." Even so, he was appointed on 2 January 1534 as an advisor of
the Parisian Parlement on matters of faith and served as spokesman in
many disputes and colloquies. At his funeral François le Picart pro-
nounced his eulogy amid great pomp; a collection of verse in Greek and
Latin was published in his honor. Yet the precise date of his death has
become a source of confusion. ABM (289) assign his death to 22 May
1542, a date arrived at undoubtedly on the basis of the date of the epi-
taph in the Orléans ms., which one would assume post-dates the death
itself. Bietenholz (*Contemporaries of Erasmus*, 1: 341–42) places his death
at 21 May 1549, and refers to Bèze's epitaph in this way: "Most authors
have accepted Théodore de Bèze's citation of a spurious epitaph to con-
clude that Petrus died in 1542, but he appeared in the registry of the fac-
ulty of theology on April 1, 1546. He died in 1549 and was buried in the
Franciscan convent chapel in Paris." That date is supported by Raunié,
*Epitaphier du vieux Paris*, 3: 1152 and James Farge, *Bibliographical Regis-
ter of Paris Doctors of Theology, 1500–1536* (Toronto, 1590), no. 115.
Bèze may have wanted to follow in the footsteps of the satirical and
spurious *Epitaphia honorandi magistri nostri Petri a Cornibus . . . edita a
compluribus orthodoxis et catholicis . . . quibus eius tumulum adornarunt in
ecclesia Fratrum Minorum Parisiensium* (Paris, 1542); indeed, the last line
of the poem hints that the veracity of Cornu's death is an issue. An even
later date is given by Ristelhueber (editor of Henri Etienne's *Apologie
pour Hérodote* [Paris, 1879], 2: 345), who assigns his death to 1555, fol-
lowing, one supposes, Moreri, who gives the same date.

ABM note that the humanists could not forgive him for his attitude
in the censuring of Marguerite d'Angoulême's rather evangelical *Miroir
de l'âme pécheresse* in 1533, and dragged his name in the mud; e.g., Henri
Etienne, in *Apologie pour Hérodote*, cap. 39, labels him a villain who died
from a horrible case of syphilis. Bèze attacked him again fifty years
later: "detestandae, nec tamen obliterandae memoriae" (*Poemata* [1597],
142). Note, too, the epigram with the same theme on p. 179 (part of
*Cato Censorius Christianus*) of the same edition: *In pseudomonachos.*


1. **cucullati**: From the fourth century onward *cucullus* refers to the
monk's cowl.

## 14.

Meter: phalaecian hendecasyllable.

ABM (289) offer the following information (my translation): "The poem must be talking about Jean Quélain, a comrade of Bèze at Orléans, who died of dropsy, possibly before the end of his studies.[6] He was undoubtedly a brother or cousin of Michel Quélain,[7] a lawyer, who was received into the Parlement of Paris in 1543, and for whom Beza composed several verses on the occasion of his marriage. (Cf. *Catal. des actes*, vol. 4, p. 608). Later, he became councillor of the Parlement of Rennes. (Cf. F. Vindry, vol. I, p. 342)."

The poem develops around the several pairings of *tuus-meus* and *tibi-mihi*, which ultimately build to the immortality won for Quélain both by the poems he wrote (represented by the weeping Calliope, *tuo studio*) and the poem that Bèze is here composing (*meo studio*).

1. **Calliope**: one of the nine Muses, mother of Orpheus. She presided over epic poetry and eloquence.
7. **vigiles terit lucernas**: "night-lamps" (cf. Hor. *Od.* 3.8.14), which become overworked during the bedside vigils of his friends.
8. **hydrops**: generalized edema. Among Bèze's emblems (1597, 13) we find one entitled "Hydropicus potans" ("A man with dropsy taking a drink"), the woodcut of which depicts a man swollen with hydrops and yet drinking water. The inscription reads as follows:

> Iniuste partis opibus si forte beatos
>     Putas avaros, falleris.
> Epotis avide lymphis quis posse beari
>     Hydropicos existemet?

> [If by chance you think that the greedy are happy when they have acquired their wealth unjustly, you are wrong. Who thinks that a man with dropsy can be happy after gulping down water?]

---

[6] But at *Corr.* 1: 27, n. 1, it is noted that Jean qualified for a license in law in 1543, along with Alexis Gaudin.

[7] Michel Quélain receives mention in *epig.* 50.

## 15.

Canoniero, *Flores illustrium epitaphiorum*, 435, unattributed.

The 1779 edition notes that Jacques de Blois was a treasurer who died 12 August 1527. Quite often during this period, those who were hanged were subsequently burned. Such may be the case here, since something about the hanging kept Jacques de Blois from being buried in his undoubtedly noble tomb.

4. **Tardius hic fieri ... prius ille mori:** The parallelism of the two phrases in this line serves to highlight the two alternatives.

## 16.

Canoniero, *Flores illustrium epitaphiorum*, fol. 8v, unattributed,
follows version of 1597.
Meter: phalaecian hendecasyllable.

The 1779 edition adds the following note concerning René Gentil: "summi in suprema Galliarum Curia Praesidis illaudatissimi 1538." ABM, 290, give the following information: He was of Italian origin, councillor, then president, in the Parlement of Paris, one of the judges of Semblançay and Poncher, also himself sent to the gallows in 1542 (cf. F. de Crue, *Anne de Montmorency: grand maître et connétable de France* [Paris, 1885] 4: xxvii).

The tone of this epitaph has much in common with that of the *icones*. The reader is to imagine s/he is looking at a statue of Gentil that stands over his grave site. Note the *vides* of line 2. Because Gentil was so unpopular while he was living, people have slashed and mutilated his image (one is reminded of the mutilation of the Hermae in Thucydides), so that now what was meant to do him honor reveals his shame.

3. **purpureo:** "purple," because the ancient Roman senators wore a purple-bordered toga (*toga praetexta*).
9–10. **Vivus qui male sederat ... | Stare nunc male mortuus:** The chiasmus brings out the irony of his death: alive he sat badly, dead he stands badly. *Sederat* alludes to his seat of honor in the Parlement.

## 17.

Wright, *Delitiae delitiarum* (1637), 7, follows 1569 version;
Nicole, *Epigrammatum delectus*, 375.
Meter: Scazon (also called "choliambus" and "limping iambus").

Guillaume du Bellay, Lord of Langey (and often called simply "Langey"), who died early 1543, was an ardent supporter of François I. He was related to the poet of the Pléiade, Joachim du Bellay (see Charles Besnier, "Sur les rencontres de Ronsard et du Bellay," *IL* 14 [1962]: 79–86). He has received full biographical treatment in V. L. Bourrilly's *Guillaume du Bellay, seigneur de Langey, 1491–1543* (Paris: Société Nouvelle de Librairie et d'Edition, 1905). Bourrilly also published his correspondence in *Revue de la Renaissance* 6 (1905): 45–50, 106–10, 173–76, 243–46, 283–92. Nicole annotates this poem with the following testament to the force and power behind his rhetoric: "Similia de hoc Langaeo omnes historici, de quo haec Caroli V. Imperatoris vox memoriae prodica: 'plura illum Regi suo verbis, quam caeteras duces armis conficere.' Ea erat in eius verbis auctoritas et pondus."

**2. Minervam ... Martem:** Here Minerva stands for cultural arts (probably rhetoric in particular), Mars for military ones.

**8. Milone et Curione:** These comparisons carry with them some degree of irony. C. Scribonius Curio had fallen into deep debt as tribune of the plebs at Rome, and he became obligated to Julius Caesar when the latter paid his bills (Plut. *Pomp.* 58). He was eventually killed during the civil wars while leading an army against Pompey. Titus Annius Milo Papinianus was the notorious Roman nobleman who carried on a feud with a certain Clodius during the same period. When Milo's gang of gladiators met with that of Clodius on the Appian way in 52 B.C., Clodius ended up dead, and Milo went to trial (Cic. *Mil.*).

## 18.

Meter: phalaecian hendecasyllable.

This epitaph strikes one as odd for its sentimentality given the vicious attacks Bèze makes on Dolet in his epigrams (see notes on *epig.* 14) and the fact that he had been denounced by the theology faculty of the Sorbonne as a heretic. Dolet's contemporaries had mixed reactions toward him. On the positive side stood Marot, Charles de Sainte-Marthe, Jean Voulté, Bourbon, and Muret, though some of those became cool to him later on. But Buchanan, Pasquier, and Julius Caesar Scaliger speak of his sour personality and his general poverty of intelligence and wit (Scaliger, *Poëtices* [1594], 791). E.g., Buchanan writes,

> Carmina quod sensu careant mirere Doleti?
> Quando, qui scripsit carmina mente caret.

[Are you amazed that Dolet's poems lack sense? After all, the one who wrote them lacks a brain.]

Pasquier is even more to the point about Dolet:

> Cui placuit nullus, nulli hunc placuisse necesse est. (*Icones* 143)

[The person who liked no one must not have been liked by anybody.]

The mixed reactions stem from the stormy way in which Dolet lived his life and from the many misfortunes into which he fell. Born at Orléans in 1509 to a good family, Dolet eventually studied law at the University of Toulouse in 1532. After a disappointing showing in a composition contest, either in 1532 or 1533, he delivered a scathing oration denouncing the Parlement and magistrates' religious intolerance and disbandment of national societies, and proclaiming their actions as a threat to humanism. That was the beginning of the end for him. Dolet was active in a time rife with charges of heresy, based on any hint of affection for Lutheranism in one's writings along with any visible failure to perform some common Catholic ritual. Rumors began to surface that Dolet denied the immortality of the soul and the personal involvement of God in the life of mankind, and Dolet had to flee to Lyon in 1534, where eventually he set up a printing press.

Even so, his problems only multiplied exponentially on 31 December 1536, when he killed a painter named Compaing who assaulted him on the streets of Lyons. He was to be charged with murder, but escaped to Paris to try to gain a royal pardon. The poet Voulté was an ardent supporter of Dolet during this time, but when Dolet vainly boasted that he had obtained pardon without the help of his "friends," he alienated himself from Voulté. The latter began to attack him under the thinly veiled pseudonym *Ledotus* and with the adjective *ingratus*. Nicolas Bourbon and Hubert Sussanée also cut themselves off from Dolet.

Dolet achieved some success thereafter in printing, especially in the years 1540–1542. But in late 1542 his troubles started again. He was arrested on suspicion of heresy for publishing the Bible in French translation and other books of an evangelical nature, and would have suffered severely had it not been for royal intervention in 1543. In 1544 there was a seizure in Paris of some heretical books that bore his name, forcing him to flee to Piedmont, then Lyons, then finally to Troyes where he was arrested and brought to Paris for trial.

Dolet, who, as mentioned earlier, had always been suspected of heresy in respect to the immortality of the soul, was charged with mistranslating a passage in his volume on the *Dialogues of Plato*. In the *Axiochus* (369c) a dialogue about the soul, Socrates makes the following remark concerning death:

> Ὅτι περὶ μὲν τοὺς ζῶντας οὐκ ἔστιν, οἱ δὲ ἀποθανόντες οὐκ εἰσίν· ὥστε οὔτε περὶ σὲ νῦν ἐστίν, οὐ γὰρ τέθνηκας οὔτε εἴ τι πάθοις, ἔσται περὶ σέ· σὺ γὰρ οὐκ ἔσῃ.

Dolet translated the passage in this way:

> Pour ce qu'il est certain que la mort n'est point aux vivants: et quant aux defuncts, ilz ne sont plus: doncques la mort les attouche encores moins. Parquoy elle ne peult rien sur toi, car tu n'es pas encores prest à deceder; et quand tu seras decedé, elle n'y pourra rien aussi, attendu que tu ne seras plus rien du tout.

It is the last phrase that the faculty of theology at the Sorbonne could not tolerate: *rien du tout*. They felt that it was a mistranslation and a misrepresentation of Plato, making him out to deny the immortality of the soul. Therefore, they said, Dolet had blasphemed and proven himself to be an atheist. Technically, the charges brought before the Parlement were blasphemy, sedition, and trafficking in prohibited and condemned books. He was sentenced on 2 August 1546, after two years of trial and imprisonment, to be tortured, then hanged by the gallows over a fire, where he and his books would ultimately be burned. The execution took place on the Feast of Pope St. Stephen I the next day. He received little sympathy from any of his contemporaries, even years later. In 1561 (Lyon) Julius Caesar Scaliger wrote about him in his *Poetices* (6.4):

> Dum optimi atque maximi regis Francisci fata canit, eius nomen suo malo fato functum est; quodque tum illi, tum illius versibus

debebatur solus passus est Atheos flammae supplicium. Flamma tamen eum puriorem non effecit: ipse flammam potius effecit impuriorem.[8]

Perhaps the dignity with which Dolet faced his eventual execution swayed Bèze's opinion about him, though after he became a Calvinist he became silent on the matter. Biographical and bibliographical information can be gleaned from the following: R. C. Christie, *Etienne Dolet: The Martyr of the Renaissance* (London, 1880); C. Longeon, *Bibliographie des oeuvres d'Etienne Dolet* (Geneva, 1980). See also C. A. Mayer, "The Problem of Dolet's Evangelical Publications," *BHR* 17 (1955): 405–14; Henri Weber, "La pensée d'Etienne Dolet et le combat humaniste," in *Actes du colloque sur l'humanisme lyonnais au 16ᵉ siècle* (Grenoble, 1974), 339–68.

2. **Aonidum chorus sororum:** i.e., the Muses, who live in the area around Mt. Helicon and the fountain Aganippe, in Aonia, a part of Boeotia.

6. **Naias nulla, Driasve, Nereisve:** water, wood, and sea nymphs, representing here all of nature.

8. **Fontis Pegasei:** the fountain sacred to the Muses, called Hippocrene, which Pegasus caused to spring from Mt. Helicon by a blow from his hoof.

12. **Exemptus poterat neci videri:** According to biographies, however, Dolet was dead before his body was burned.

18. **Caelum sic meus Hercules petivit:** a reference to the hero's apotheosis. Hercules was being burned alive on a funeral pyre, after putting on a cloak coated with the Hydra's poison, when Jupiter sent down a storm cloud to transport him to Mt. Olympus.

## 19.

Meter: phalaecian hendecasyllable.

On Dampierre, cf. *epig.* 30 and see esp. J. Boussard, "Un poète Latin, directeur spirituel au XVIᵉ siècle: Jean Dampierre," *Bulletin philologique*

---

[8] See also I. Reineke, *Scaligers Kritik*, 358–60.

*et historique* 1946–47 [1950]: 33–58. During the time Bèze was in Or-
léans as a student, Dampierre was rector of the convent of the Made-
leine-lès-Orléans (see le Maire, *Histoire et antiquitez*, 2: 131–37) and
friend to both an older and younger group of humanists there. He was
widely respected for his piety, and most noted for his work entitled *De
regimine virginum*. Ms. 1674 of the Municipal Library of Orléans pre-
serves the correspondence of Dampierre, Bourdineau, Truchon, Viart,
and Groslot; for a description see J. Boussard, "Le ms. 1674 de la Biblio-
thèque Municipale d'Orléans," *BHR* 5 (1944): 346–60. Other poetic let-
ters of Dampierre appear in mss. 141 and 450 of the Library of Berne,
some of which are treated in Louis Jarry, "Une correspondance litté-
raire au XVIᵉ siècle: Pierre Daniel et les érudits de son temps d'après
les documents inédits de la Bibliothèque de Berne," *Memoires de la Soci-
eté archéologique et historique de l'Orléanais* 15 (1876): 343–430; also ms.
Lat. 8143 of the Bibliothèque Nationale in Paris.

The dates of Dampierre's life are not well documented. Most early
biographical entries place his death around 1550. Such is the case in
what is the fullest biographical sketch, that of Jean Bernier, in his *His-
toire de Blois* (Paris, 1682), 475–80 (he also cites a handwritten note in a
late edition of Bèze's poetry as evidence of his place of burial). Yet the
appearance of our epitaph in ms. 1674 (Orléans) indicates an earlier
date, sometime before 1545. Other valuable biographical information
can be gleaned from Moreri, *GDH*, iv.2: 22; and Brainne et al., *Hommes
illustres*, 1: 185–86.

Bèze considered Dampierre one of his closest companions while in
Orléans, as a poem of the Orléans ms. attests (ABM 171, epig. 11):

*Ad amicos*

In partes quatuor fuit secata
Nuper mens mea. Tu, Truchi, quadrantem,
Duos, Dampetre, possides quadrantes.
Quadrans qui reliquus fuit, secatus
Rursus in quatuor fuit quadrantes.                    5
Unum habes, Lodoice, tu secundum,
Pomponi, reliquos habes, Alexi.
Sic amens ego vivo, sic relictus
Nullus est mihi vel quadrans quadrantis.

[*To my friends*

Recently my mind was cut into four parts. You, Truchy, occupied a quarter of it, Dampierre, two quarters. The quarter which remained was again cut into quarters. Lodoicus, you have one, Popon, you have a second, Alexis, the rest. Thus I live my life dispossessed of mind, not having even a quarter of a quarter left to me.]

We are fortunate that a poem of Dampierre to Bèze survives in Paris ms. Lat. 8143 (transcribed in *Corr.* 1: 191) to record the affections returned. This is surely one of the finer efforts of Dampierre:

*Theodoro Bezae*

Quod tanto studio tibi tuendam
Nostram amicitiam, diserte Beza,
Censes, gaudeo, plurimumque juvit
Erga nos animum tibi esse talem,
Nam confido parem tibi exhibendum                5
A nobis quoque nec minus tenacem.
Sed parum placuit, quod huc videris
Hac motus ratione, quod juvandi
Bezam copia Dampetro sit idque
Non his praesidiis quibus parandis                10
Nostros nunc homines videmus (inquis)
Se totamque operam suam dicare
Quae sunt fluxa, fugacia et caduca,
Verum his, ex quibus illa certa manat
Consolatio, nec fluens voluptas                  15
Quam praestant Sapientiae, et bonarum
Nempe amor studiumque litterarum.
In quo deciperis, viaque tota
Erras, optime Beza, fallerisque,
Dampetrum potius tuum est juvare                 20
His in rebus opem huic tuam tulisse,
Hae cui scilicet affluenter adsunt
Pridem, deinde in ea urbe qua moraris
Horum quam pelagus vocant bonorum,
Cum Dampetrus inanis et sit istis                25
Solitudinis et sit inquilinus.
Qualiscumque tamen sit in tuenda

Bezae amicitia sui nec ipsi
Bezae cesserit, hicque se minorem
Minor caetera non sinet videri.                              30

[*To Théodore de Bèze*

I am glad that you feel that our friendship should be guarded
with great zeal, eloquent Bèze, and I was very pleased that you
have such feelings for me, for I am certain that I should exhibit
feelings to you that are equal and no less resolute. But I was none
too pleased that you seem motivated up to this point by the fact
that, as you claim, "Dampierre has abundant means to benefit
Bèze because," in your opinion, "he consecrates himself and his
every effort, not to those kinds of self-improvements to which
we see our people dedicating themselves nowadays, which are
transitory, fleeting, and fickle, but to those from which that sure
comfort flows; and not elusive pleasure, which the liberal arts
transcend; and, of course, to the love and pursuit of literature."
In this you are deceived, and wander far off track, excellent Bèze,
and you are mistaken. To the contrary, it pleases your friend
Dampierre that in these matters you have brought your wealth to
him, a wealth that was already present in you in abundance from
long ago, and continued in you thereafter, in the city where you
dwell, which they call "sea of the noble." For Dampierre is de-
void of those things and a mere lone hermit. Yet would he go to
any lengths to protect his friendship with Bèze, and not yield to
Bèze himself, and he, though otherwise lesser, will not allow
himself to seem lesser in this.]

1. **coenobio**: a late fourth-century word, related to the Greek κοινόβιος
   ("communal living"): here it means a monastery.
3. **Princepsque Hendecasyllabῶn poeta**: Dampierre never published his
   poetry. The bulk of it exists now only in ms. Lat. 8143 of the B. N.
   of Paris and in Gruter's *Delitiae* (1: 833–61), which includes the
   lengthy *In obitum Erasmi*. Boussard attaches little value to them,
   both in terms of content and the handling of the Catullan meter (see
   "Un poète Latin ...," 53–58). But Bèze consistently has high praise
   for his abilities, particularly in his unpublished poetic epistles. In *ep.*
   7 (ABM 268) Bèze refuses to make annotations on them because
   they are too well composed. Later he places him among the three

best poets at Orléans (*ep.* 9, ABM 270), then advances an even bolder claim in the next epistle, making him out to be a more charming poet than Catullus and Ovid (*ep.* 10, ABM p. 271). Furthermore, in the preface to the 1569 edition, much the same as here, Bèze refers to him as *felicissimus hendecasyllabōn poeta.* Boussard also lists the positive judgments of Salmon Macrin, Visagier, Scaliger,[9] Sainte-Marthe, and Nicolas Bourbon.

5. **Mole corporea**: an unusual collocation, perhaps meant to echo Dampierre's own eulogy of Erasmus, along with the thought that follows it (*Delitiae*, 834):

> Hanc molem nisi corporis caduci,
> Coelestem illum animum quod opprimebat?

Here *coelestem illum animum* is echoed by Bèze's *divinum animum* in line 8. Bèze wrote a poem about Dampierre's eulogy, entitled *De Erasmi tumulo a Dampetro descriptio* which survives in the Orléans ms. (ABM 171). The thought is Platonic.

6. **tenebricosa**: The shades in the underworld are pale and weak.

12. **Doctorumque volat per ora liber**: i.e., he becomes famous (cf. Cic. *TD* 1.15). The verses are reminiscent of Ennius' hope for poetic immortality: "Volito vivus per ora virum" (Ennius, *Epigrams* 9–10, Warmington). So Bonefon (*Delitiae*, 1: 687): *Aeternum volites virum per ora.*

16-17. **occidit ... Occidit**: The hendecasyllabic metrical scheme forces the first of this pair to be intransitive (*occidit*) while allowing the second to be transitive (*occīdit*). The thought again may be a play on lines of Dampierre (*Delitiae*, 834):

> Nam si quis putat interisse, multum
> Errat: vivit enim, idque cum ante, sane
> Multo verius, omnibus solutus
> Curis scilicet, omnibusque morbis:

then, a few lines later, on the top of 835:

> Sed ne forte putes perisse nobis
> Caelo dum fruitur, Deoque vivit:
> Nobis ingenii sui reliquit
> Foetus, in quibus hic quoque est superstes.

---

[9] See also I. Reineke, *Scaligers Kritik*, 352.

## 20.

Nicole, p. 376; Canoniero, *Flores illustrium epitaphiorum*, 435–36,
unattributed and entitled *Ducis Anguiennensis*,
following version of 1548.

Born 23 September 1519, the third son of Charles de Bourbon, duke of
Vendôme, and Françoise d'Alençon. He joined the army of François I
in 1542 and took part in the campaign in Luxemburg. In 1543 he was
named Lieutenant General in charge of the Eastern Mediterranean, and
joined with the Turks in invading Nice. His role at Ceresole, where he
made excellent use of the cavalry, is noted at *epig.* 52. There are two ver-
sions of how he died in February of 1546. One story relates that when
a group of friends besieged his house in a snowball fight, it happened
that one player ran out of snow, and used an arrow to continue the
game. That arrow struck the duke in the head and killed him. Another
version has it that, while he was playing snowballs with his friends, it
happened that a certain Cornelio Bentivoglio inadvertently caused a
heavy chest to fall on the duke's head and killed him. Clearly Bèze is
following the first version. At any rate, the duke was buried at Ven-
dôme in the church of St. Georges.

**2. evaseris hostem**: referring to the victory over the Imperialists at
   Ceresole (see notes on *epig.* 52 for the incident).
**7. Stygia ... compacta cupressu**: an allusion to the story of Cyparissus,
   who inadvertently killed his own stag, and then grieved so much
   that Apollo turned him into a cypress tree. The cypress was sacred
   to Pluto (and therefore called "Stygian" here), and used by the an-
   cients at funerals as a sign of weeping.
**13–14. At si nobiscum vis ... | ... iocis?**: The phrase *istis iocis* refers to
   *iocari* in the previous line. In other words, Bèze wonders why For-
   tune, who enjoys so the vicissitudes of life, spoils her own jokes by
   mixing them with death.

## 21.

Bèze's *Tumuli*, 3–4.
Meter: dactylic hexameter followed by iambic quaternarius.

François I was born at Cognac, 12 September 1494, and succeeded Louis

XII to the throne in 1515. He died at Rambouillet on 31 March 1547. On 18 May 1514, he married Claude de France (1499–1524), daughter of Louis XII and Anne de Bretagne. She bore him the following seven children: 1) Louise, who died at the age of two (1515–1517); 2) Charlotte (1516–1524); 3) François, Viennese Dauphin and Duke of Bretagne, born at Amboise 28 February 1518, and died at Tournon on 10 August 1536; 4) Henri, later Henri II, then Henri of Orléans, born at Saint-Germain-en Laye on 31 March 1519, and married Catherine de Médicis (1533), and then became Dauphin in 1536, later king on 31 March 1547, and died 10 July 1559; 5) Madeleine de France, born 10 August 1520, wed January 1537 at Notre-Dame of Paris to James V, king of Scotland, and died 2 July 1537; 6) Charles, later called Charles d'Angoulême, then Duke of Orléans after Henri became Dauphin; he was born 21 January 1522, died of the plague on 8 September 1545; 7) Marguerite de France, duchess of Berry then of Savoy (1523–1574); in 1559 she wed Emmanuel Philibert of Savoy; she died at Turin on 18 September 1574.

The second marriage of François I to Eleanor of Austria was negotiated by the treaty of Madrid (14 January 1526) and ratified by the treaty of Cambrai (3 August 1529). Eleanor was born at Louvain (1498–1588); she was daughter of Philippe I, archduke of Austria and king of Spain, and of Jeanne de Castille, and was sister of Charles V and widow of king Emmanuel of Portugal, whom she had married in 1519. She came to France in June of 1529 bringing with her the royal children whom Charles had held as hostages in Spain; the marriage took place in July of 1530 in the abbey of Capsjoux (between Bourdeaux and Bayonne), but the union remained sterile. She died in 1558.

In the latter part of 1547, after the death of François I, Bèze published *Tumuli Francisci Primi et duorum eius liberorum: Querela de Caroli morte; Epigrammata in Henricum II et duos eius liberos,* at the press of Conrad Badius at Paris. It contains epitaphs 21–24 of our collection. The pamphlet is extremely rare (only seven examples are known), and several copies do not include Bèze's name. The work was first attributed to Bèze by Droz, "Notes sur Théodore de Bèze," 403–12. Shaw ("Tumuli Francisci Primi") then located seven exemplars and identified two "states" of the edition, some of which have Bèze's name. I have examined the edition in the Newberry Library, Chicago. See also Renouard, *Imprimeurs,* 2: 306–7.

The meter of the poem consists of a dactylic hexameter line followed by an iambic quaternarius, an arrangement that Bèze has chosen for three other poems as well (*epitaph.* 9; *epig.* 44, 48, and 89). The iambic quaternarius was rare in Roman literature, occurring primarily in the dialogues of Roman comedy as single lines in a larger metrical structure.[10] It is used here to round off the thought after the stately dactylic hexameters and to give some balance to the gravity that those introduce (cf. Hor. *Epod.* 14–15). The dactyls remind the reader that the subject matter is sad and serious, the iambs that the tomb itself is speaking.

6. **facile primus**: playing on the tag "facile princeps," as at Cic. *Clu.* 5.11, *Div.* 2.42.87, *Fam.* 6.10.2. But Cicero uses the phrase itself at *Rosc. Am.* 6.15: "Sex. Roscius, pater huiusce, municeps Amerinus fuit, cum genere et nobilitate et pecunia non modo sui municipii, verum etiam eius vicinitatis facile primus …"

9. **ficto interdum demulsit amore**: François had a reputation as a womanizer from the many mistresses he entertained.

12. **Tradidit in hostium manus**: François was defeated and captured by Imperialist forces in the Battle of Pavia in 1525.

29. **Hebraeae, Graecae et Latiae**: Although he had not himself excelled in the study of these ancient languages, he did promote such learning throughout his kingdom. Pasquier's phrase, "liberalium disciplinarum et humaniorum litterarum fautor" (*Epigrammatum libri VI* [1585], fol. 20v), reflects the enthusiasm of the age for the new culture that flourished during François's reign. Among humanists whom he supported with special favors and patronage we find Clément Marot, Rabelais, Salmon Macrin, and Budé. He also introduced many Italians into the court, including Tagliacarne, the teacher of his children (see *epig.* 13). He took numerous other steps to bolster culture within the kingdom, including the collection of manuscripts for the Royal Library (with the help and guidance of Jan Lascaris), the creation of the Royal Readerships, and the appointment of Robert Etienne as the first royal printer. Greek printing was introduced in France during his reign by the efforts of Simon de Colines, while the study of Hebrew began in earnest, despite the resistance of the Sorbonne to anything that encouraged philological research. It should be noted that François's sister, Marguerite de Navarre, protected many of the humanists from the Sorbonne's attacks during the 20s and 30s.

---

[10] For the variations permitted in the iambic quaternarius, see D. S. Raven, *Latin Metre* (London, 1965), 59–60.

On François's contributions to humanism in France see McNeil, *Guillaume Budé and Humanism*; Arthur Tilley, "Humanism under Francis I," *English Historical Review* 15 (1900): 456–78; G. Gadoffre, *La révolution culturelle dans la France des Humanistes. Guillaume Budé et François I*<sup>er</sup> (Geneva, 1997).

## 22.

Bèze's *Tumuli*, 4; Nicole, *Epigrammatum delectus*, 374–75;
Canoniero, *Flores illustrium epitaphiorum*, 436, unattributed,
follows 1548.

When the eldest son of François I died suddenly on 10 August 1536 at the age of eighteen, suspicion fell immediately upon his riding attendant, Sebastien de Montecuculli of Ferrara. The latter had handed to the Dauphin François a glass of icy cold water after a rigorous game of tennis in a meadow near Lyon, and immediately the Dauphin felt ill. After accompanying the court as it traveled toward Provence along the Rhone, the Dauphin turned aside at Tournon, where he passed away, only a few days after drinking the mysterious water. It was generally believed that he had been poisoned, and, since the father of Charles V had died in exactly the same manner, ultimately suspicion was cast on the Emperor. Montecuculli was arrested, tried, and convicted as his agent after a forced confession. A book on poisons was said to have been discovered in his possession and the poison of choice was reckoned to be arsenic. He was drawn and quartered, and subsequently mutilated in grisly fashion by an angry mob of the people. In the end the official version of the cause of death was that Charles V had wanted to weaken French power by poisoning the children. Others suspected the work of Catherine de Médicis, wife of the Dauphin's younger brother Henry, who stood to gain from the murder.

Shortly after the burial of the Dauphin's ashes, Etienne Dolet published a collection of Latin and French poems containing the laments of the most noted poets of the day (cf. Verdun L. Saulnier, "La mort du Dauphin François et son tombeau poétique," *BHR* 6 [1945]: 50–97): *Recueil de vers latins, et vulgaires de plusieurs Poets Francoys, composés sur le trespas de feu Monsieur le Daulphin* (Lyon, 1536). The efforts of twenty-one poets are represented there, including such notables as Dolet himself, Maurice Scève, Gilbert Ducher, Salmon Macrin, Nicolas Bourbon,

Clément Marot, Jean Visagier, and Claude Fournier, to name but a few. The major themes expressed there, namely, the great accomplishments of the young prince; the wickedness of poisoning a great man; and the Dauphin's entry into the company of the gods, to one degree or another all play a part in Bèze's poem.

At the death of the Dauphin François, Bèze, who was only seventeen and not yet known as a poet, composed an epigram that appears in the Orléans ms. (ABM, 169, no. 3):

> *In mortem Francisci Valesii, Gallorum, ut vocant, Delphinis*
>
> Scis bona cur toto (lector) pax exulet orbe?
>     Scis fera cur miles quilibet arma petat?
> Sublatus Delphin divos turbavit, et ista
>     Sic potuit secum Iuppiter ipse queri,
> Hunc humana deum postquam fraus sustulit orbi,
>     Qui poterit tutus Iuppiter esse magis?

It was perhaps immediately after the death of the boy that Bèze also composed an epitaph that should be viewed as an earlier version of the epitaph presently under consideration. That version appeared in the *Tumuli* (see notes on *epitaph.* 21 above) on page 4. The two versions differ greatly, except for the tell-tale first couplet and random words here and there (e.g., *spes*). The text of the earlier version is as follows:

> Hunc etiam iuvenem extinctum, rogo, cerne viator:
>     Hei mihi, cur vivum dicere fata vetant!
> Hic est qui regum censeri debuit albo,
>     Spes patriae quondam, spes quoque prima patris.
> Hic obses patrem captivum ex hoste redemit,
>     Vix puer: insignis sed pietate puer.
> Quid loquar invictos animos, aciesque paratas
>     Itala Gallorum subdere colla iugo?
> Quae dum facta notat nostris Mors rebus iniqua,
>     Et nequit imberbes cernere caeca genas,
> Arbitrata virum matura aetate, peremit.
>     Heu, cur tam certo vulnere caeca feris!

The story of the poisoning appears to have spread after the latter poem was written, thus explaining Bèze's failure to mention it. One wonders, though, what provoked Bèze to rework the poem for the *Poemata* of 1548, but not for the *Tumuli* of 1547. The absence of both epitaphs from the Orléans ms. may indicate that Bèze had not produced either version before 1547.

**11. Pellaei ... principis**: namely, Alexander the Great, from Pella in Macedon. He too died from drinking, though in his case the drink was wine. Many ancient historians, however, report their suspicions that he was poisoned. Bèze seems to have in mind (cf. Bèze's *icon.* 6) one particular version of that story, which included a rather bizarre account of a very cold draught of Stygian water. Plutarch reports it as follows:

At the time, nobody had any suspicion of his being poisoned, but upon some information given six years after, they say Olympias put many to death, and scattered the ashes of Iolaus, then dead, as if he had given it him. But those who affirm that Aristotle counseled Antipater to do it, and that by his means the poison was brought, adduced one Hagnothemis as their authority, who, they say, heard King Antigonus speak of it, and tell us that the poison was water, deadly cold as ice, distilled from a rock in the district of Nonacris, which they gathered like a thin dew, and kept in an ass's hoof;[11] for it was so very cold and penetrating that no other vessel would hold it. However, most are of opinion that all this is a mere made-up story, no slight evidence of which is, that during the dissensions among the commanders, which lasted several days, the body continued clear and fresh, without any sign of such taint or corruption, though it lay neglected in a close sultry place.

---

[11] Pausanias, 8.18.4–6, also knows of this water: "The water trickling down the cliff by the side of Nonacris falls first to a high rock, through which it passes and then descends into the river Crathis. Its water brings death to all, man and beast alike. It is said too that it once brought death even upon goats, which drank of the water first; later on all the wonderful properties of the water were learnt. For glass, crystal, myrrhine vessels, other articles men make of stone, and pottery, are all broken by the water of the Styx, while things of horn or of bone, with iron, bronze, lead, tin, silver and electrum, are all corroded by this water. Gold too suffers just like all the other metals, and yet gold is immune to rust, as the Lesbian poetess bears witness and is shown by the metal itself. So heaven has assigned to the most lowly things the mastery over things far more esteemed than they. For pearls are dissolved by vinegar, while diamonds, the hardest of stones, are melted by the blood of the he-goat. The only thing that can resist the water of the Styx is a horse's hoof. When poured into it the water is retained, and does not break up the hoof. Whether Alexander, the son of Philip, met his end by this poison I do not know for certain, but I do know that there is a story to this effect" (transl. W. H. S. Jones, 1933 [Loeb], vol. 3).

## 23.

Bèze's *Tumuli*, 5;
Canoniero, *Flores illustrium epitaphiorum*, 436–37, unattributed.

This third son of François I died on 8 September 1545. Bèze here refers
to the terms of the Treaty of 18 September 1544 made at Crépy-en-
Artois, a central feature of which was that this Charles would marry a
relative of Charles V (thus Bèze's "a son-in-law of great Caesar") and
become the duke of Milan. That marriage never took place, because
Charles d'Orléans died of a mysterious illness. As Bèze remarks here
("the work of peace has been disrupted"), his death essentially nullified
the peace instituted by the treaty.

## 24.

Missing in 1569, 1576, 1597; Bèze's *Tumuli*, 5–6.

These three deaths, discussed individually in the previous epitaphs, were
a hard blow to the French people. The second son of François I, who
is alluded to here, is Henri II; he took over the throne on 31 March
1547 (see notes to *epig.* 49), then died in 1559. Bèze complains to the
Fates that the world could not have been divided into three parts, with
each of the three sons ruling one of them.

**7. matura:** François I died shortly before turning fifty-three.

## 1.

*Hercules Oeteus*

Certavit mecum Virtus, superataque cessit:
　　Hac volui victa, victor et esse mei.


## 2.

*Dido rogum conscensura*

Funere Didonis sapientes este puellae:
　　Sunt nulla hospitii pondera, nulla tori.


## 3.

*Hector*

Hectoris incolumis mansisti, patria, dextra:
　　Hectore quid mirum si pereunte, peris?


## 4.

*Pythagoras*

Laudent vitam alii suam loquendo:
Virtutem ipse meam probo tacendo.

# ICONS

## 1.

### *Hercules on Oeta*

Virtue struggled with me, and when I conquered her, she yielded. I wish I could conquer myself too.

## 2.

### *Dido about to ascend the funeral pyre*

Girls, learn a lesson from the death of Dido: men take lightly both hospitality and marriage.

## 3.

### *Hector*

You remained safe, fatherland, protected by the right hand of Hector. Why marvel, then, that you perished as soon as Hector died?

## 4.

### *Pythagoras*

Some praise their own life by speaking: I myself prove my virtue by remaining silent.

## 5.

### *Xenophon*

Pallada dilexi, pariter me Pallas amavit:
    Et Pallas artes, et dedit arma mihi.

## 6.

### *Alexander Magnus*

Post Persas fusos, quaesitasque orbis habenas,
    Armis non potui cedere; cedo dolis.

## 7.

### *Democritus*

Omnia Democritus ridebat: tu quoque, lector,
    Democriti ride, si sapias, tumulum.

## 8.

### *Demosthenes*

Magnum opus est, hominum regere et componere mentes:
    Sed tamen hic magnum praestitit illud opus.

## 9.

### *Spartana filium interfectura*

Ergo ubi sunt comites? tun' es Lacedaemone natus?
    At peperit matrem terra Lacaena tibi.

---

5.2    Et Pallas artes *1779* Et literas Pallas *1548, 1580*
6.Tit. *add.* hausto veneno moribundus *1597*

## 5.

### *Xenophon*

I loved Pallas, and Pallas loved me in return: she gave me both letters and weapons.

## 6.

### *Alexander the Great*

After I conquered the Persians, and took the reins of the world, I could not be defeated with arms: instead, I am defeated by deceit.

## 7.

### *Democritus*

Democritus used to laugh at everything: reader, if you're smart, laugh at the tomb of Democritus.

## 8.

### *Demosthenes*

It is a great task to control and subdue people's minds: even so, he accomplished it with distinction.

## 9.

### *A Spartan mother, as she is about to kill her son*

So, where are your companions? Are you a Spartan boy? But Spartan earth has given birth to your mother.

## 10.

### *Sappho*

Auxit Musarum numerum Sappho addita Musis:
　　Felix, si saevus sic voluisset amor.

## 11.

### *Lucretia*

Pollutum est corpus, mansit mens integra nobis:
　　Et non ex isto corpore casta fugis?

## 12.

### *M. Brutus, Caesaris interfector, seipsum interfecturus*

Divitiis uti licuit cum Caesare partis:
　　Ferre necem possum, non potui dominum.

## 13.

### *Cato Uticensis*

Vicisti Magnum, Caesar, sed quidlibet aude:
　　Unus dicetur se superasse Cato.

---

11.1 mihi mens vero integra mansit *1597*
12.Tit. αὐτόχειρ *1569, 1576, 1597*
13.2 te *1779*

## 10.

### *Sappho*

Sappho was added to the Muses and increased their number. She would have been happy, if cruel love had wished it so.

## 11.

### *Lucretia*

My body has been polluted, but my conscience is clear: do you not depart this body chaste?

## 12.

### *M. Brutus, assassin of Caesar, as he is about to kill himself*

I could have enjoyed great wealth under Caesar: I can bear the death, I couldn't bear the master.

## 13.

### *Cato Uticensis*

You conquered Pompey the Great, Caesar, but try as you may, they will still say that only Cato was able to conquer Cato.

## 14.

*Camillus*

Romanam, fateor, construxit Romulus urbem;
  Capta ego restitui moenia. Maior uter?

## 15.

*P. Virgilius Maro*

Et tu, docte Maro, es sublatus orbi,
Mori numina posse quis putasset?

## 16.

*Juppiter Phidiacus*

Ut tali sese cognovit imagine pictum,
  Tandem etiam geminus Juppiter, inquit, ero.

## 17.

*In eundem*

Quantum hic a vero distet Jove Juppiter audi:
  Nempe hic est castus, priscus adulter erat.

## 18.

*Venus*

Me Paris, et natus nuper, Pallasque salutant,
  Haec Venerem, matrem natus, at ille deam.

### 14.

*Camillus*

Romulus built the city of Rome, I admit; I restored the walls after they had been captured. Which of the two is greater?

### 15.

*P. Vergilius Maro*

Even you, learned Maro, were taken from the world. Who would have thought the immortals could die?

### 16.

*Pheidias's Jupiter*

When he saw himself depicted by such a great image, "Finally," Jupiter said, "I'll be a twin too!"

### 17.

*On the same*

Hear how much this Jupiter differs from the real Jupiter: this statue is chaste, whereas the original Jupiter was an adulterer.

### 18.

*Venus*

Paris, my child, and Pallas Athena greet me. The last calls me "Venus," my child "mother," and the first one "goddess."

## 19.

*In eandem*

Nunc demum coepi Venus esse venustior: olim
  Quae fuerant sociae, contineo Charites.

## 20.

*In eandem*

Falluntur, qui me cohiberi posse negarunt:
  En basis haec Venerem sistere parva potest.

## 21.

*Titi Livii*

Tumulum Tito nuper parabam Livio;
Cum sic Apollo iussit ut desisterem:
Haec mortuos, inquit, decent, vivit Titus.

## 19.

*On the same*

Now at long last I, Venus, begin to be more charming: I have assimilated the Graces, who once were my companions.

## 20.

*On the same*

Those who say that I cannot be contained are wrong: look, this small base is able to support Venus.

## 21.

*Titus Livy*

Recently I was preparing a grave for Titus Livius, when Apollo ordered me to stop. These things befit the dead, he said, but Titus lives.

# Commentary on the Icons

While it may be immediately evident that the term *icones* (from Greek εἰκών) has something to do with "images," it is not so apparent how the term functions as a generic label for the elegiac distichs included here. Indeed, few other Neo-Latin poets used the term,[1] though a perusal through the anthologies reveals that many composed in its style. Later editions of Bèze's own poetry characterize the *icones* in this way: "et quae peculiari nomine iconas inscripsit" ("which are inscribed with the distinctive name 'icons' "). In the first edition they come between the *epitaphia* and *epigrammata*, and appear to have affinities with both. On the one hand they deal with the deceased—one poem begins with the word *tumulum*, while collections of epitaphs were often entitled *tumuli* in the Renaissance—and on the other hand they often involve a clever turn, a mark of the epigrams. In the authorized second edition they fall after the epigrams, where the description *alia epigrammata* further characterizes the term *icones*.

More important for understanding the genre is the transferral of the epigram *Descriptio Virtutis*, which in the first edition is associated with the *epigrammata*, to the *icones* in the second edition, though with the new title *Descriptio Religionis*, and slightly altered content. In the 1597

---

[1] The *icones* of Boissard, Pasquier, and Reusner are discussed below. Buchanan's *icones* are discussed briefly in Grant, "Shorter Latin Poems of George Buchanan," 344–45. Others using the term include Nikolaus Gerbelius, *Icones imperatorum, et breves vitae, atque rerum cuiusque gestarum indicationes* (Strasburg, 1544); Giuseppe Silos, *Musa canicularis, sive, Iconum poeticarum libri tres, qui continent icones heroicas, icones gentium, icones varias* (Rome, 1650); and Jacques Moisant de Brieux, *Poemata* (Caen, 1658, 1663) including *Iconica seu de variis picturis et imaginibus*.

edition, this *Descriptio Religionis* appears twice, oddly enough, once with yet another name, *Vera Religio,* with several variations in wording, yet still placed with the *icones* (218), and elsewhere under a new rubric that has a rich tradition in the Renaissance, *emblemata.* Thus the nature of the *icones* must not be far removed from that of the *emblemata.* Indeed, when in 1580 Bèze published a very different kind of *icones*—a work devoted to the lives of famous reformers—he again tied together *emblemata* and *icones* in the title of the work: *Icones, id est, verae imagines virorum doctrina simul et pietate illustrium ... additis eorundem vitae et operae descriptionibus, quibus adiectae sunt nonnullae picturae quas "Emblemata" vocant.* Here *icones* denote the verbal portraits of the subjects as opposed to the visual ones that *emblemata* indicate.

The content of the *icones* in the 1597 edition provides further insights into the nature of the genre. To here, Bèze moves all earlier published poems that have in view some artistic depiction of the person involved, including poems in Greek and Latin about a *picta tabella* representing Erasmus, and another one relating to a painting of the flood. Yet another poem describes the resemblance between the face of Michel L'Hôpital and sculpted images of Aristotle. Here also poems with portraitures of Calvin and Simon Grüner in view appear for the first time. A new poem to Xenophon is inscribed with the title, *Xenophon, laeva calamum, dextra gladium gestans,* presumably alluding to some image of the historian, possibly a woodcut in a book. Thus, on the basis of this later augmentation of the content, we can say with certainty that the generic term *icones* refers to poetry that is inspired, for the most part, by artistic representations of people and objects.

There is more to understand about the genre, though, than just to acknowledge that its poems are inspired by art. It has its roots in ancient literary theory. Both Aristotle and Quintilian originally used the term *icon* to denote a rhetorical device, a kind of comparison or simile. The definition was still current as such during the Renaissance. For example, Henry Peacham, in his *Garden of Eloquence* (London, 1577), defines it as a "forme of speech which painteth out the image of a person or thing by comparing forme with forme, quality with quality, one likeness with another." The idea of "painting the image of a person" is fundamental to the iconic genre. Furthermore, scholars of Renaissance *emblemata* trace that genre's roots to the *ecphrasis* of classical literature. Examples include Homer's detailed description of the shield of Achilles, and Vergil's of the shield of Aeneas. Cups, tapestries, gardens, buildings, all garner the attention of poets. Prudentius wrote a collection of Latin *ecphra-*

*seis* with Christian subject matter.[2] But it is in the *Greek* (or *Palatine*) *Anthology* (hereafter *AP*) that short poetic descriptions of statues, paintings, sepulchers, and other objects (baths are particularly popular) rank as a genre unto themselves. A particularly long collection of them appears at book IX.582–827, and still other examples comprise almost all of book XVI. Sprinkled throughout the *Anthology* we also find poems about famous personages, real or mythological, who sometimes speak for themselves in the first person, and sometimes are merely alluded to without clear reference to a painting or other representation. Mostly these are sepulchral, as often in book VII, and are reflected in Bèze's frequent references to the *tumuli* and *funera* of his subjects. In yet another twist, book IX.583 clearly refers to a book containing Thucydides's histories that speaks to the reader. That from the very beginning Bèze meant to model his *icones* after the various kinds of poems in the *Greek Anthology* is evident from the close correspondence between a poem of Plato about Sappho (IX.506) and Bèze's poem on the same subject: in both cases the authors declare that Sappho increases the number of Muses to ten. Still, Bèze's *icones* do not exactly correspond to the *ecphraseis* in the *Greek Anthology,* nor can they be sufficiently defined as epigrams, emblems, or epitaphs. Clearly, the Renaissance *icones* are inspired generically by Ausonius's commemorative poems in books 4–6 of his collection, particularly in book 6, where fictitious epitaphs of Trojan War heroes figure. Ausonius, it would appear, is himself inspired by the *ecphraseis* in the *Greek Anthology.*

Yet while Ausonius establishes the unmistakable precedent, we must turn to other composers of *icones* in the sixteenth century for an explanation of the aims of the genre. Such is the case with both Etienne Pasquier (1529–1615), who published his *Icones* in 1582, and Jean-Jacques Boissard, who published his *Disticha in iconas diversorum principum, Caesarum, philosophorum, et aliorum illustrium hominum, tam antiqui, quam hodierni temporis* in 1587. The very title of Boissard's work provides some useful information: the *icones* treat the lives of famous people, both from antiquity and recent history. Boissard makes the point again to his reader, which reads in part as follows (4):

> Conatus fueram (neque haec fefellit
> Me cura) exprimere elegantiore

---

[2] See Renate Pillinger, *Die Tituli historiarum, oder, Das sogenannte Dittochaeon des Prudentius* (Vienna, 1980).

Vultus arte Ducumque Principumque,
Priscis qui tenuere sceptra saeclis.
Quorumque historiae celebre nomen
Publicis referunt ubique libris.
At ne tempora nostra cedere unquam
Antiquis videantur, addidi illis
Non paucos, hodierna queis superbit
Aetas: seu pretium quis aestimabit
Virtutisve, scientiaeve; vel qua
Gloria superi polum occuparunt.

Here Boissard limits the subject of the genre strictly to celebrated people, omitting what the emblematic genre most favors, namely, abstract concepts, relatively complex scenarios, animals both real and fantastic, and inanimate objects.

In addition to the subject matter appropriate to the genre, Boissard also defines the immediate inspiration. As Bèze suggested in his 1597 edition, the distichs are based on artistic portraits. We could be tempted to believe that at least some of the portraitures are imagined, but Boissard is very specific about their reality and source in the introduction to his book (2):

Iconas collegit auctor ex museis Pauli Iovii Novocomensis Episcopi, Victoris Mocenigi Veneti, Marci Mantuae Bonaviti Patavini, Fulvii Ursini patricii Romani: ex palatio Cosmi Medices Ducis Florentini; et aliorum nobilium, et doctorum virorum Italiae: Potissimum opera Lentuli Ventidii Nucerini; qui et idem opus aggressus erat, sed morte praeventus imperfectum reliquit. Reliqua ex numismatibus, et marmoribus antiquis excerpta sunt.

One sees then that Boissard depended on sketches of art pieces from collections and museums primarily in Italy, though for the more recent subjects many of his sources must have been in the public domain in France.

Returning to Boissard's introductory poem, we can identify yet another aspect of the genre. Given the emphasis on virtue, glory, and the contribution of wisdom, it would seem that the aim of the *icones* is moral, a presentation of the best of human achievement and character as both a reminder and a model for the reader. Clear examples of this principle can be drawn from Pasquier, who follows up his *icones* with notes on the modern figures presented there. For example,

*Franciscus primus* (no. 24)

Excitor et martis strepitu, sonituque tubarum,
    Mi magis at musas restituisse meis.

[*François I*

I am stirred by the din of war, by the sound of trumpets, but it
is more to me that I have restored the arts to my people.]

This he elucidates as follows (20v):

Franciscus multa bella fortiter et strenue gessit contra Carolum
Quintum Germanorum Imperatorem, et Erricum octavum An-
glorum Regem: sed imprimis commendatur, quod liberalium dis-
ciplinarum et humaniorum litterarum fautor. Baltazar Castalio in
eo, quo Urbanitatem Aulicam effinxit, libro, hoc de eo vaticina-
tus fuerat, antequam Regni fasceis susciperet. Itaque quemadmo-
dum Ludovicus populi, sic et Franciscus litterarum parens,
iudicio Patrum appellatus est.

Pasquier does more than merely extol the deeds of François I here; he
provides a benchmark for measuring achievement: his bravery in war is
to be commended, but the promotion of the arts, both as a practitioner
and a patron, has benefitted France the most.

The importance of this moral slant pervades an elegy of Boissard to
yet another author of *icones*, Nikolaus von Reusner (123).[3] The full text
of the elegy follows:

*In N. Reusneri Leorini I. U. Doctoris Iconas*

Splendidius nihil est fama Virtute parata,
    Aut bello, aut culti dotibus ingenii.
Cui qui contulerit fortunae dona faventis,
    Et quas illa solet tradere divitias:
Vilia componet caris, firmisque caduca:                          5
    Et solidi umbra illi corporis instar erit.
Nec bona sunt vocitanda, quibus sors imperat: aut quae
    Sunt dubia: aut tantùm nomen inane gerunt.

---

[3] The full title is *Icones, sive imagines vivae, literis clarorum virorum Italiae, Graeciae,
Germaniae, Galliae, Angliae, Ungariae, etc. per Nicolaum Reusnerum* (Basel, 1538).

Quaeque suo intereunt cum possessore, nec illi
    Ac verso veniunt tempore in auxilium.      10
Sola suo virtus pro sectatore laborat
    Obscurae Lethes flumina ne subeat.
Marmorei ereptum gravida de mole sepulchri
    Inter honoratos collocat Indigites.
Mortales tantùm exuvias tellure recondit:      15
    Numen at insigni posteritate beat:
Utens scriptorum calamis, qui pondera rebus
    Reddere divino sunt soliti eloquio.
Inter quos primas delegat haec tibi partes,
    Reusnere, et factum dia Minerva probat.      20
Addit se socium Phoebus, facilesque Camoenae:
    Peithoque, et terno numine firma Charis.
His ducibus nullos posthac moriture per annos
    Aeternum scriptis aggredieris opus:
Aoniae immortale decus Reusnere cohortis,      25
    Haec debebantur munia nempe tibi.
Ut nostri caneres illustria nomina saecli,
    Spiranti vulgans vivida signa typo.
Elogiis quae cuncta ornas, et honore decoro:
    Sic facis ut tota haec non Libitina ferat.      30
Defunctis vitam reddis, vitaque fruentes
    Egregia prohibes sedulitate mori.
Sic tibi consultum est, aliis dum prospicis, estque
    Communis quae te gloria nobilitet.
Dum famam sollers alienam condis, eadem      35
    Tuque tuum tollis nomen ad astra tuba.
Te simul et praesens, et postera noverit aetas.
    Et tibi erit pulchra laude perennis honos.

The gist of the poem is that Reusner aids Virtue as it labors not to be overwhelmed by the waters of death and oblivion; his efforts likewise will be immortal. We should then expect the tone of the *icones* to be positive throughout.

One final requirement of the genre should be noted. Boissard suggests it in line 31 of the previous elegy: "Defunctis vitam reddis" ("You restore life to the dead"). Pasquier has a similar sentiment in one of his *icones* addressed to the reader.

*Ad lectorem* (no. 158)

Authores vivos prudens omitto sciensque,
  Viventi vitam nam dare ridiculum est.

[*To the reader*

I have exercised prudence and wisdom by omitting living auth-
ors, for it is ridiculous to give life to the living.]

It appears to have been an accepted stricture of the genre to treat only
personalities who have passed on. Furthermore, the goal was to give
vivid portrayals in as concise a space as possible. Boissard had called it
"breathing life into the dead."

Therefore, the nature of the genre can be summed up in this way:
*icones* celebrate the literary and virtuous accomplishments of historic
persons, both ancient and recent, male and female, real and mythologi-
cal; they can be in the first, second, or third person, whichever brings
the person most to life, but in any case they take their inspiration from
an artistic representation of the person involved.

## 1.

### Missing in 1569, 1597, 1779.

The life of Hercules was full of extreme contradictions, a difficult strug-
gle between the power of his divine nature and the weakness of his hu-
man nature. Though with his strength he accomplished incredible deeds
for the sake of humanity, from the taming of the uncivilized landscape
to the conquest of death, ironically those tasks were imposed upon him
as punishment for his misdeeds. Not only had he killed his music teach-
er Linus at a very young age, when he could not master the lyre, he
later murdered his wife and children in a fit of anger and dared to
wrestle with Apollo over the tripod at Delphi when he did not approve
of an oracle that he had received. Ultimately, his folly lead to his painful
death on Mt. Oeta (and thus the epithet *Oeteus*), the depiction of which
Bèze seems to have in view here.

1. **Virtus**: Hercules's youthful encounter with the two paths of virtue
   and pleasure was a favorite topos among the ancient philosophers,
   and may be the story in Bèze's mind in this line. Cicero, *Off.* 1.118,
   relates the following version drawn from Xenophon:

For we cannot all have the experience of Hercules, as we find it in the words of Prodicus in Xenophon: 'When Hercules was just coming into youth's estate (the time which Nature has appointed unto every man for choosing the path of life on which he would enter), he went out into a desert place. And as he saw two paths, the path of Pleasure and the path of Virtue, he sat down and debated long and earnestly which one it were better for him to take.' This might, perhaps, happen to a Hercules, 'scion of the seed of Jove' ... (Loeb transl. [Walter Miller])

According to Xenophon's version (*Mem.* 2.1.21), Virtue and Pleasure confront the young Heracles in the form of two women, who try to win him over with their arguments. Needless to say, Heracles chooses Virtue, and though he stumbles often during his life, his labors were viewed by ancient writers as an allegory of the triumph of Virtue over the passions. In the Christian interpretation, the two-natured Christ also went out into a desert place before undertaking his active life (cf. the "Christian Herakles" in Basil of Caesarea, *PG* 31.573 AB).

## 2.

The thought is very compressed, but since Dido is directing her advice to girls specifically, she must intend to warn them that men typically do not honor the sacred rules of hospitality nor the holy bonds of matrimony, and if they disregard the first, it follows that they will disregard the second. Such, in her view, was the case with Aeneas.

Bèze completely reworked the poem for the 1597 edition:

*Dido* αὐτόχειρ

Discite Didonis casu vidua, atque puellae,
    Qua solvat stultis praemia stultus amor.
Et quae ipsi quondam vates docuere prophani,
    Ex scriptis pudeat non didicisse sacris.

[*Dido the suicide*

Learn, widows and young girls, from the misfortune of Dido, how foolish love rewards the foolish. And those things that the secular poets once proclaimed, we should be ashamed not to learn them from sacred scriptures.]

The latter is a remarkably succinct expression of Bèze's post-conversion attitude. Although God gave to the pagan writers what Calvin called "common grace insights," even in terms of moral behavior, they were by no means the preferred source for that information.

### 3.

#### Missing in 1569, 1597, 1779.

Troy's fate was sealed when its greatest warrior, Hector, son of King Priam, died at the hands of Achilles. In political terms the thought behind this little vignette was not irrelevant to Bèze's day. Many of the French humanists, including Bèze, embraced the concept of the benevolent, heroic ruler, on whose shoulders alone the entire fate of the nation rests.

### 4.

#### Meter: phalaecian hendecasyllable.

This poem is influenced somewhat by *AP* 16.325:

Εἰς ἀνδριάντα Πυθαγόρου

Οὐ τὸν ἀναπτύσσοντα φύσιν πολύμητιν ἀριθμῶν
    ἤθελεν ὁ πλάστης Πυθαγόραν τελέσαι,
ἀλλὰ τὸν ἐν σιγῇ πινυτόφρονι· καὶ τάχα φωνὴν
    ἔνδον ἀποκρύπτει, καὶ τόδ᾽ ἔχων ὁπάσαι.

[*On a Statue of Pythagoras*

The sculptor wished to portray, not that Pythagoras who explained the versatile nature of numbers, but Pythagoras in discreet silence. Perhaps he has hidden within the statue the voice that he could have rendered if he chose. (Loeb transl. [W. R. Paton])]

Pythagoras did not practice absolute silence, as is evident from many sources, but he did compel new recruits to remain silent for as long as five years while they studied his doctrines. Otherwise, tradition says that he urged caution in speech, and advised his followers to prefer silence to hasty conversation. This is probably related to the Pythagorean maxim found in Diogenes Laertius (8.15), that "not all of Pythagoras's doctrines are for all men to hear." Furthermore, Cicero describes his manner as being *sine ulla hilaritate* (*Off.* 1.108; cf. D.L. 8.20).

Pasquier appears to know the same tradition about Pythagoras in one of his *icones*:

> *Pythagoras*
>
> Pythagoram Samium nuper celebrare volebam,
> Sed me Pythagoras ipse tacere iubet. (*Icones* 69)

> [*Pythagoras*
>
> Recently I wanted to honor Samian Pythagoras, but Pythagoras himself ordered me to keep quiet.]

## 5.

Missing in 1569, 1576 and 1597, but replaced with the following (along with Wright, *Sales epigrammatum* [1663], 44):

> *Xenophon laeva calamum, dextra gladium gestans*
> Quid Marti, et Musis, Xenophon? sic vicimus olim
> Barbariem gladio, barbariem calamo.

> [*Xenophon bearing a reed in his left hand, a sword in his right*
>
> What has Xenophon to do with Mars and the Muses? We once vanquished barbarians with a sword, and barbarians with a pen.]

1. **Pallas**: Athena, the patron of both military strategy and literary activities, would have been pleased with both of Xenophon's main pursuits. Early in his career he made his way as a mercenary soldier and general, first for the younger Cyrus, then for anyone who would hire him and his troops. During the Peloponnesian Wars he supported Sparta, despite the fact that he was born in Athens and educated by Socrates. Later, he settled in Elis, near Olympia, where he wrote, among other things, the *Anabasis* and *Hellenica*.

2. **artes**: I could not find a source for this reading outside of the 1779 edition, but the line will not scan with *li(t)teras*.

## 6.

On the story of Alexander the Great's death through poisoning, see note on *epitaph.* 22.11. It is one of the constant motifs in myth and history that heroes and great individuals tend to meet their end by some sort of treachery. Jesus was betrayed by Judas, Heracles by Nessus, Theseus by the king of Scyros, Julius Caesar by his friend Brutus.

## 7.

### Missing in 1569, 1576, 1597.

Democritus was often called "the laughing philosopher," because he had the habit of laughing at everything he saw when he went out in public. He is often juxtaposed to Heraclitus, "the weeping philosopher," who wept at everything he saw. Seneca, *De tranq. animi* 15.2, says that the latter viewed human activity as misery, the former as folly. Cf. Hor. *Epist.* 2.1.194: "Si foret in terris, rideret Democritus." The story appears first in Cic. *De or.* 2.235, but must have had a long tradition.
So Pasquier writes,

> *In Democritici authorem*
>
> Omnia qui ridet, ridetur ab omnibus ipse. (*Icones* 59)

## 8.

The ability of Demosthenes to sway audiences with compelling arguments and thunderous delivery caused posterity to hold him in the highest esteem. Quintilian ranks him first among orators (10.1.76): "quorum longe princeps Demosthenes ac paene lex orandi fuit ..."

1. **hominum regere**: The phrase seems to play on the etymology of Demosthenes's name (see note on *epig.* 15.11).
2. **Praestitit**: The word has the sense of "accomplishing or discharging one's duty," but always with an added tint of distinction.

## 9.

### Missing in 1597.

The theme of the Spartan mother is suggested by Palladas's epigram at *AP* 9.397, though Bèze has handled it in an original manner. Palladas says that a Spartan mother, upon seeing her son fleeing from a battle, took a sword with which to strike him. Before she delivers the blow, she exclaims that by killing him, she is saving herself and her country from disgrace.

Hutton, 706, mentions three other French authors who imitate the theme, all of them much more true to the original than Bèze: François Beaucaire de Péguillon, Paul Estienne, Jean Commire. One should also note Dulcat's version, in which he drops all mention of the sword and adds his own innovation:

*Mater Spartana*

Viderat e pugna timidum secedere natum,
   Et dare femineae terga Lacaena fugae:
Eminus exclamat, sublatis vestibus; ecquo
   Pergis? an haec repetis viscera, germen iners?
      (*Delitiae*, 1: 878)

[*The Spartan Mother*

She had seen her timid son withdraw from the fight, and turn his Spartan body around in feminine flight. From a distance she shouts, while lifting up her clothes: "Where are you going? Or are you trying to return to the womb, you good-for-nothing son?"]

2. **terra Lacaena**: i.e., "your mother is Spartan too, and will not hesitate to punish her own son." Spartans lived under a harsh warrior code of discipline and self-sacrifice. The individual lived solely for the sake of the State as a whole. Although the youth here has abandoned the principles whereby he was trained, his mother will not.

## 10.

### Missing in 1597.

This poem corresponds to Plato's poem at *AP* 9.506, where it is also stated that Sappho (b. ca. 612 B.C.) increases the number of Muses to ten. Pasquier has a similar poem in his collection:

> *Sapho*
>
> Haec etiam addatur doctis Sapho ultima Musis,
>   A qua mellitus nomina versus habet. (*Icones* 65)

> [Let Sappho, from whom the honeyed verse takes its name, join the learned Muses as their latest member.]

The graceful and passionate style of Sappho's Aeolian strains led many in antiquity to rank her among the best poets of all time. Her name is given to the "Sapphic stanza" four-line verse form.

## 11.

In the 1569 edition (170), Bèze adds another poem on Lucretia with strong moralizing overtones:

> *In eandem*
>
> Si fuit ille tibi Lucretia gratus adulter,
>   Immerito ex merita praemia morte petis,
> Sin potius casto vis est allata pudori,
>   Quis furor est, hostis crimine velle mori?
> Frustra igitur laudem captas, Lucretia: namque
>   Vel furiosa ruis, vel scelerata cadis.[4]

Heywood publishes the following translation in his anthology:

> If to thy bed the adulterer welcome came, | Lucretia, then thy death deserves no fame. | If force were offred, give true reason why, | being cleare thy self thou for his fault wouldst dye? | Therefore in vaine thou seekst thy fame to cherish, | since mad thou fal'st or for thy sinne dost perish.

Death and shame came to Lucretia unexpectedly (Livy 1.57–60). This virtuous wife of Tarquinius Collatinus, nephew of Tarquinius Superbus,

---

[4] The 1597 edition reverses the last line in this way: "Vel scelerata cadis, vel furiosa ruis."

last king of Rome, was forcibly raped by one of the king's sons. She had resisted him as best she could, but when he threatened to kill her and one of her slaves naked and side by side, she succumbed rather than face that shame.[5] When her husband found her overcome by her distress, she revealed what had happened, demanded her honor be avenged, and then stabbed herself with a knife. The Romans portray her virtuous act as the final challenge to the outrageous behavior of their kings.

As a Calvinist, Bèze was induced to doubt the motives of this pagan noblewoman. In the present poem, however, the young poet is willing to give Lucretia the benefit of the doubt by insulating her unblemished mind, over which she retained control, from her polluted body, which was overpowered against her will.

2. **isto**: derogatory, since the body has been defiled.
   **casta**: modifying the implied "tu" (f.).


## 12.

Wright, *Delitiae delitiarum* (1637), 14; Wright, *Sales epigrammatum* (1663), 44.

Plutarch, at the end of his *Life of Brutus*, relates the virtuous final moments of the life of Caesar's assassin. He reassured his friends and slaves that Fate had been kind to him, since it is better for him to die with his reputation for virtue intact rather than live wealthy yet wicked like Caesar's followers. Additionally, he expresses to them his confidence that by his actions mankind will learn that those who execute good and just citizens are unfit to rule.


## 13.

Missing in 1569, 1576, 1597.

On this Cato, see note on *epitaph*. 7.8. Despite his sometimes unwavering attitude and staunch Stoicism, he was respected by his peers and con-

---

[5] Her dilemma was acute: under Roman law, the female victim of a rape was herself guilty of adultery. Therefore, in the end she could retain a measure of her honor only if she committed suicide.

sidered a paragon of virtue by posterity. Here he is said to have escaped personal defeat at the hands of Caesar during the civil wars because he took his own life at Utica before Caesar could capture him.

Cato and his suicide also figure in an *icon* of Pasquier:

### Cato Uticensis

Romula dum felix vixit respublica, vixi,
    Et certum est nobis hac moriente mori:
In nos edantur quantum vix Anticatones,
    Calcabit fastus mors mea Caesareos. (*Icones* 48)

### [Cato Uticensis

So long as the Roman Republic lived secure, I lived, and rest assured that at her death I die too. As much as my detractors may struggle to rail against me, my death will trample Caesar's pride.]

## 14.

### Missing in 1569, 1576, 1597.

The facts of M. Furius Camillus's life are shrouded in legend and fantasy. Traditional accounts make him out to be the savior and second founder of Rome at a critical juncture in that city's history. After many campaigns consolidating Roman power throughout Italy, including a difficult struggle against the city of Veii, he was accused of embezzlement and banished. Later, as Gallic invaders were overrunning the countryside and besieging Rome, Roman refugees begged him to lead them against the enemy in order to rescue the capitol. Magistrates in Rome rescinded the former charges against him and the people voted him dictator for the occasion. In 390 B.C., he returned from his exile, leading 40,000 troops, who drove the Gauls from their siege of the capitol and utterly destroyed their army. According to Livy, Camillus then entered the city in triumph and was hailed a second Romulus. Although the city was in ruins and the people set on abandoning it, he insisted that they stay to rebuild the city's buildings and walls.

**15.**

Missing in 1597.
Meter: phalaecian hendecasyllable.

Vergil, the most famous of the Roman poets, died in 19 B.C., and was buried at Naples. The inscription on his tomb is said to have read as follows:

> Mantua me genuit, Calabri rapuere, tenet nunc
> Parthenope. Cecini pascua, rura, duces.

Pasquier's more elaborate *icon* on Vergil echoes that epitaph, while concluding that "one country is not able to contain such a celebrated man":

> *Virgilius*
>
> Mantua, Roma suo gaudent, Calaberque Marone,
>   Atque in eo male quo digladientur habent.
> Mantua protuleras, invidit romula tellus,
>   Eripuit vobis aemula Parthenope.
> Miraris quorsum tanta haec contentio? ferre
>   Tam celebrem nequiit unica terra virum.
>     (*Icones* 90 [1585])

Ultimately, Bèze's distich is making the same point as that of Pasquier. While it is true that Vergil is dead as if he were a mere mortal, his divine status (*numina*) indicates that he will never truly be detained by death.

**16.**

Not in 1569, 1576, 1597.

Bèze is thinking of Pheidias's renowned sculpture of Zeus at Olympia, which the ancients considered one of the seven wonders of the world.

**17.**

Not in 1569, 1576, 1597.

The immorality of Jupiter always presented a problem for the ancients, leading Plato to denounce them as bad for the ideal city. His misdeeds provided comic excuses for the elegiac poets and fuel for the criticisms of early Christian writers.


### 18.

Not in 1569, 1576, 1597.

This is a concise delineation of three kinds of love, all revolving around the goddess of love herself: erotic love (Paris), a love between parent and child (either Cupid or Aeneas), and the love between friends (Athena).


### 19.

Missing in 1569, 1576, 1597.

The play here is on the name *Venus* and the word *venustior*, which begins with the goddess's name while evoking thoughts of the Graces. Though in antiquity Venus (Aphrodite), the goddess of love, and the Graces (Charites), the goddesses of charm and beauty, were often worshiped together, Bèze seems to have in view an all-encompassing image of Venus that depicts her as the epitome of both love and charm.


### 20.

Missing in 1569, 1576, 1597.

The key to this *icon*, a description of a small statuette that sits on a base, lies in the word *cohiberi*. While most consider love to be an uncontrollable force, which no person can restrain, here the personification of love remarks that in fact she can be contained.


### 21.

Missing in 1569, 1576, 1597; Kendall, *Flowers of Epigrammes*, 159;
cf. *Tottel's Miscellany*, 1: 120; 2: 255 (= Merrill, *Grimald*, 409 and 452
[addressed to Cicero instead of Livy]).
Meter: iambic senarius.

The thought is to be compared to *eleg.* 11.70ff.: "Quisquis ades, magni cerne sepulchra Titi..." The expectation to live on through one's writings is a well-known literary convention. Ovid has one of the finest examples:

> ergo etiam cum me supremus adederit ignis,
>     vivam, parsque mei multa superstes erit.
>         (*Amor.* 1.15.41–42)

Therefore, when the last fires have consumed me, I will live on, and a great part of me will survive.

2. **Apollo**: here in his function as patron of the arts.

**1.**

*Ad lectorem*

Sunt qui lectori longo fastidia libro
    Longa ferant: fas sit scribere pauca mihi.
Iste tamen poterat, lector, liber esse, libellus:
    Pendere sed versus, non numerare decet.

**2.**

*Ad eundem*

Non convitia, nec latrationes,
Nec ronchos timeo, calumniasve,
Nec ullos obelos severiores.
Non quod iudicio meo poeta
Sim tantus, nihil ut queat reprendi:           5
Sed quod iudicio meo poeta
Sim tam ridiculus, parumque doctus,
Ut nullum fore iudicem eruditum,
Meos carpere qui velit labores:
Nam quis Aethiopem velit lavare?          10

---

1.3    et tamen hic potuit *1597*

# EPIGRAMS

## 1.

*To the Reader*

There are those who wear down their readers with a wearisome book; so permit me to be brief. Although the *booklet* you have in your hands, reader, could have been a *book*, I thought it best to weigh verses, not count them.

## 2.

*To the Same*

I am not afraid of insults, yelps, snorts, slurs, or hyper-pedantic obeli— not because I reckon myself such a great poet that no one can find fault with what I have written, but because I am such a ridiculous poet, and so lacking in learning, that I believe no scholar will bother to take my efforts to task. For who would want to wash an Ethiopian?

### 3.

*De geminis solibus visis Lutetiae Parisiorum, Anno 1539*

Aspiceres nuper geminos cum, Gallia, soles,
    Mirata es soles, Gallia tota, duos.
At nunc mirari potius tua commoda disce,
    Quae spondere tibi sidera bina vides.
Sol est Franciscus, sol est quoque Carolus, istos         5
    Nimirum soles astra benigna notant.
Quod si concordes foedus coniunxerit ictum,
    Eclipsis fuerit nulla timenda tibi.

### 4.

*In Claudium*

Non cessas veteres, Claudi, incusare poetas
    Claudo ausos Venerem iungere Mulcibero.
At divos ego non cesso vocitare furentes,
    Uxor quod claudo sit data bella tibi.
Attamen hoc nostrum coepit lenire dolorem,         5
    Quod tua nunc Martem coepit habere Venus.

---

3.Tit. anno MDXXXIX finiente, Carolo Caesare, Calendis Ianuarii anno MDXL
    urbem ingressuro *add. 1597*
3-4    Desine mirari, nihil his protenditur atrox | At potius dantur commoda multa
    tibi *ABM, p. 183*
5-6    illis | Quatenus Europa dat Deus imperium *1597*

### 3.

*The Twin Suns Seen at Paris, 1539*

Recently, France, as you gazed at the twin suns, you were surprised that there were two. But now learn to marvel more at the blessings that you see twin stars promising to you. François I is a sun, Charles V is also a sun; surely the stars are shining favorably on them. But if the treaty that they have struck unites them in harmony, you will never have to fear an eclipse.

### 4.

*Claudius*

Claudius, you constantly berate the ancient poets for daring to wed Venus and the crippled Vulcan. Now I cannot help calling the gods crazy, because to you, a lame man, they have given a beautiful wife. Still, I'm finding some solace for my disappointment, since your Venus has started up a romance with a Mars.

### 5.

*De commentariis D. Melchioris Volmarii, praeceptoris charissimi, in Homeri poesim*

Maeonidem ingrati privarant lumine divi,
  Nec vati quicquam proderat esse sacro.
Hoc scelus advertens noster Volmarius illi
  Restituit, divi quos tulerant oculos.
Parcite mi, superi, vobis est maior habendus,                    5
  Irrita qui superum reddere iussa potest.

### 6.

*In quendam asinorum encomiasten*

Dum laudas asinos, toties cur, Pontice, peccas?
  Nempe tibi ignotum γνῶθι σεαυτόν erat.

### 7.

*In Amorem*

Esse hominum curam superis si credere fas est,
  Et quae sentimus commoda ferre deos,
Cur, rogo, felici divum numeratur in albo
  Fraudibus ille suis nobilitatus Amor?
Sane illum quisquis supremo adscripsit Olympo,                    5
  Hunc nimius, credo, cepit Amoris amor.

## 5.

*The Commentaries of My Dear Teacher Melchior Wolmar on the Homeric epics*

The ungrateful gods deprived Homer of sight, and the poet gained no benefit from being pious. Noticing this injustice my friend Wolmar restored to him the eyes which the gods had taken away. Forgive me, gods, but if a man can nullify your commands, then he must be considered greater than you.

## 6.

*A Man Fond of Asses*

Why do you make so many mistakes every time you sing the praises of asses, Ponticus? Obviously you do not know the maxim: "Know thyself."

## 7.

*Cupid*

If it is right to believe that the heavenly gods care about mankind, and grant to us the blessings we enjoy, why, pray tell, is Cupid, who is infamous for his misdeeds, counted among the blessed roll of the gods? I'm convinced that whoever assigned him to lofty Olympus loved the god of Love too much.

### 8.

*De Venere marmorea regi donata a Renzo equite*

Quae tibi missa fuit nuper, rex maxime regum,
    Non est ficta Venus, vera sed ipsa Venus.
Scilicet illa polum, Martemque, Iovemque reliquit,
    Quod te his maiorem crederet esse tribus.

### 9.

*Ad Carolum Quintum, cum Lutetiam ingressus esset*

Te praesente sua est facies quod reddita coelo,
    Et sensit numen Iuppiter ipse tuum,
Miratur vulgus: sed cui est tua cognita virtus,
    Virtus, perspectum, quid tua possit, habet.
Scilicet hoc aequum est, ut qui moderamine tanto          5
    Iura dat in terris, iura det ille polo.

### 10.

*Ad Lodoicum Validum*

An est credibile, hunc meum libellum,
Hunc, inquam, illepidum meum libellum
Perlectum esse tibi, et molestiarum
A te taedia tanta devorata?
Esto, legeris, et molestiarum                             5
Semel taedia tanta devoraris:
Dic mihi, Lodoice, amabo, tune
Ullum unquam insipidum magis poetam
Legisti? An retices? nec id fateri
Vis? personam igitur tuam ipse sumam,                    10
Et satisfaciam mihi roganti,
Et quanta potero intonabo voce:
Non vidi insipidum magis poetam.

## 8.

*A Marble Venus Given to the King by the Knight Renzo*

The Venus that was recently sent to you, greatest king of kings, was not artificial, but the real Venus herself. Obviously she left her home in the sky, as well as Mars and Jupiter, because she considers you greater than all three of them together.

## 9.

*Charles V's Entrance into Paris*

The crowd is amazed that at your presence the sky became clear, and Jupiter himself felt the power of your will. But he who knows your virtue, understands well what your virtue can do. Surely this is just, that the same person who dispenses laws on earth with such great skill should also dispense them in the sky.

## 10.

*Louis Vaillant*

Am I to believe that you read through and through this little book of mine, yes, this repugnant little book, and devoured such nauseating stuff? Let's assume for a moment that you have read it and devoured such nauseating stuff. Tell me, Louis, please, have you ever read another poet more bland than this? Are you silent? You don't want to admit it? Therefore, I myself will assume your persona, and I will give an answer to myself, and proclaim as loudly as I can: "I have never seen a more bland poet."

## 11.

### *De Amicitia cum Truchio inita*

Heu, vos advoco, vos malos sophistas,
Fallaces, querulosque homunciones,
Qui noctes teritis diesque totos,
Quaerendo insidias locutionum.
Vos, inquam, advoco, vos malos sophistas,          5
Qui posse hoc fieri simul negatis,
Ut quis victitet in locis duobus.
Tandem vera loqui, o tenebriones,
Discite, et fieri videte posse,
Posse quod fieri simul negatis,          10
Cum sim unus, tamen in locis duobus
Vitam vivo simul, velutque nostra
In partes geminas secata mens est:
Apud me altera vivit, altera autem
Vivit in Truchio meo. Ergo nobis          15
Palmam ceditis, o tenebriones?

---

1    Heus *ABM 170*: malos *1569, 1576* acres *1548, 1580, 1779*
5    acres *1548, 1580, 1779* malos *1569, 1576*

## 11.

*A Friendship Struck Up with Truchon*

Hey there! You, the unscrupulous sophists, the deceivers, the quibbling little men, you who spend day and night trying to trap people with your way of talking, come be my witnesses. You unscrupulous sophists, you who say it is impossible for someone to live in two places at the same time, come be my witnesses. Learn finally to speak the truth, swindlers, and see that what you say cannot happen simultaneously, actually can: Although I am but one, still I live my life in two places, with my mind cut into two parts, as it were. One part dwells here with me, another part dwells in my Truchon. Now do you forfeit the prize to me, you swindlers?

### 12.

#### *In Sapidum*

Dum sese egregium Sapidus putat esse poetam,
    Desipit, et Sapido nil magis insipidum.


### 13.

#### *De Theocreni libello*

Arva Maro laudare docet spatiosa colonos,
    Idem parva docet rura colenda Maro.
Qui volet, hic terram centenis vertat aratris:
    Plus iuvat hic parvus, sed bene cultus ager.


### 14.

#### *In Philaenum*

Nil non egregie facit Philaenus.
Tersus, integer, elegans Philaenus.
Testem si petis, en tibi, Philaeno
Teste, haec omnia perficit Philaenus.

---

13.Tit. De beati Theocreni, regiorum sub Francisco primo liberorum praeceptoris,
    epigrammatum libello *add in 1597 ed.*
1     arma *1580, 1713*

## 12.

### *Sapidus*

Sapidus thinks he is an outstanding poet, but in fact he is stupid, and nothing is more insipid than Sapidus.

## 13.

### *Tagliocarno's Booklet of Poems*

Vergil teaches farmers to praise spacious fields, while also teaching that they should cultivate small farms. Whoever wants, let him dig the earth with one hundred plows; this small but well-cultivated field brings more joy.

## 14.

### *Philaenus*

There is nothing that Philaenus does not do exceptionally well. He is pithy, irreproachable, sophisticated. If you're looking for a witness, here he is, Philaenus will testify on his own behalf: "Philaenus does all of the above perfectly."

## 15.

### *Ad bibliothecam*

Salvete incolumes mei libelli,
Meae deliciae, meae salutes,
Salve, mi Cicero, Catulle, salve,
Salve, mi Maro, Pliniusque uterque,
Mi Cato, Columella, Varro, Livi,                                    5
Salve mi quoque Plaute, tu Terenti,
Et tu salve Ovidi, Fabi, Properti,
Vos salvete etiam disertiores
Graeci, ponere quos loco priore
Decebat, Sophocles, Isocratesque.                                  10
Et tu cui popularis aura nomen
Dedit: tu quoque, magne Homere, salve,
Salve Aristoteles, Plato, Timaee.
Et vos o reliqui, quibus negatum est
Includi numeris Phaleuciorum.                                      15
Cuncti denique vos mei libelli,
Salvetote, iterumque tertiumque,
Atque audite meam precationem:
Hoc ergo precor, o mei libelli,
Ut ne longa mihi mora illa (senis                                  20
Nam a vobis procul abfui diebus)
Obsit quominus undiquaque tali
Sitis in me animo et favore deinceps,
Quali, dum proficiscerer, fuistis,
Nimirum facilique candidoque.                                      25
Quod si istam mihi supplicationem
Vos concesseritis, mei libelli,
Id vobis quoque pollicebor ipse,
Non me unam hebdomadam procul, quid? immo
Non diem procul unicum abfuturum.                                  30
Quid diem? immo nec horulam, immo nullum
Punctum temporis, ut libet pusillum.

---

2     mei lepores pro meae salutes *1569, 1576*
10    Decebat quibus est gravis cothurnus *1569, 1576*
29    Non me unam procul hercle septimanam *1569, 1576*

### 15.

*My Library*

Hello! my books, safe and sound, my precious sweethearts, my very life! Hello, my friend Cicero! Catullus, hello! Greetings to you, Vergil, and you two Plinys! My friend Cato, Columella, Varro, Livy, and you also, Plautus and Terence, hello! And hello to you, Ovid, Quintilian, and Propertius! Greetings to you too, eloquent Greeks, whom I should have put first, Sophocles and Isocrates! And greetings to you, whom popular favor gave a name. And you, great Homer, hello! Hello, Aristotle, Plato, and Timaeus! And greetings to the rest of you, who aren't permitted to be included in the measures of my Phalaecean verses. Finally, I greet all of you, my dear books, a second and a third time, hello! Now hear my prayer, for I'm hoping and praying, my books, that my long delay (for I was away far from you for six days) might not prevent you from being so well-disposed to me, from here on out, with mind and heart, as you were when I was leaving. As it was, you were compliant and good-natured. But if you grant this wish to me, my books, I myself will make a promise to you, that I won't go away for a week at a time. What am I saying? a week? No, not even one single day. A day, I say? No, not even a little hour; in fact, not for an instant, however short.

## 16.

*Ad Sodales, de Melchioris Volmarii, praeceptoris charissimi, adventu in Galliam*

Audite, o lepidi mei sodales,
Ter suavem atque hilarem locutionem.
Ille Volmarius, mei o sodales,
Integerrimus omnium virorum,
Ille Volmarius modo est reversus.                          5
Hunc ergo, o lepidi mei sodales,
Diem cantibus, oro, transigamus.
Procul moestitiae, molestiaeque,
Procul tristitia, atque solitudo,
Procul sint gemitus, procul dolores.                       10
At tu, laetitia, adveni; tuumque
Adducas comitem, optimum deorum
Lyaeum, et Cererem optimam dearum.
Io, mi bone Bacche, mi Lyaee,
O Ceres mea; ne mihi negetis,                              15
Quaeso, istam exiguam petitionem:
Advolate, rogo, deis relictis.
Hic nulli tetrici deambulones,
Hic rixosus erit sophista nullus;
Sed convivae aliquot boni poetae,                          20
Nempe Rillerius, Iobertiusque:
Tertius quoque Claudius futurus,
Locum post alios tenebo quartum.
At tu, Melchior, in loco supremo
Sedens, Mercuriique Apollinisque,                          25
Et vices Charitum supplebis unus.
Quod si forte tua eruditione
Audita (quis enim tuam negarit
In caelum quoque transiisse famam?)
Facundus veniat nepos Atlantis,                            30
Aut Phoebus, Charitesve: tunc manebis
Suprema nihilominus cathedra,
Et tacentibus omnibus loqueris.
Nam quis (ni penitus caret cerebro)
Phoebo, Mercurioque, Gratiisque,                           35
Neget Volmarium eruditiorem?

## 16.

*The Arrival of Melchior Wolmar, My Very Dear Teacher, in France:*
*An Announcement to My Friends*

Listen, dear friends, to my sweet and joyous announcement: Wolmar, the most virtuous of all men, has just returned. So, please, dear friends, let's sing this day away. Away with gloom, anxiety, sadness, loneliness, away with grief and pain. But you, Happiness, come; bring your companion Lyaeus, best of the gods, and Ceres, best of the goddesses, with you. Yo, my good Bacchus, my Lyaeus, my Ceres; I beg you, do not deny me this one small favor: fly from the other gods, please. Here there will be no sour-faced peripatetics, here there will be no quarrelsome sophists; rather, several good poet buddies of mine, Rillerius and Jobertius, will be here, and Claudius as a third, and I'll take up the fourth spot after the others. But you, Melchior, sitting in the top spot, you alone will take the place of Mercury, Apollo, and the Graces. But if, after hearing of your erudition (for who could deny that your fame has crossed over into heaven also?), let the eloquent grandson of Atlas come, or Apollo, or the Graces: even then you will remain in the top spot. For who but a madman would deny that Wolmar is more eloquent than Apollo, Mercury, and the Graces?

## 17.

### *In Laudem Columellae*

Orphea mirata est Rhodope sua fata canentem,
  Si modo Virgilii carmina pondus habent.
Tu vero, Iuni, sylvestria rura canendo,
  Post te urbes ipsas in tua rura trahis.
O dii, quos olim nutrivit Roma Quirites,                    5
  Quae tam facundum viderit agricolam!

## 18.

### *De Aldo Manutio, omnium quidem authorum, praecipue vero poetarum excellentissimo typographo*

Didonis cecinit rogum disertus
Maro: Pompeii rogum Lucanus:
Et diserte adeo hoc uterque fecit,
Ut nunc vivere iudicetur illa,
Nec iam mortuus hic putetur esse:                           5
Immo sint redivivi et hic et illa.
Ergo credere fas erit poetas
Divos, ut pote qui loquendo possint
Vitam reddere mortuis: quod ipsis
Est divis proprium et peculiare.                           10
Quod si credere fas Deos poetas,
Vitam reddere quod queant sublatam:
Quanto est iustius, aequiusque, quaeso,
Aldum Manutium deum vocare,
Ipsis qui potuit suo labore                                15
Vitam reddere mortuis poetis.

---

17.4  ipsas urbes *1569, 1576, 1597*
5     O superi, quales habuit tunc Roma Quirites *1569, 1576* Vah, quales, quantos-
      que habuit tunc *1597*
6     Cum tam facundum cerneret *1569, 1576, 1597*

## 17.

### *In Praise of Columella*

Thrace marveled as Orpheus sang of his own lot, at least if we believe
the poems of Vergil. But you, Columella, by singing of the idyllic farms,
you entice the very cities into the countryside. O gods, what Quirites
Rome once nurtured! What an eloquent farmer she saw!

## 18.

### *Aldus Manutius, Most Excellent Printer of All Roman Authors, and Especially the Poets*

Vergil eloquently sang the death of Dido; Lucan the death of Pompey.
And each did this so skillfully that we imagine Dido is still living, and
Pompey is not dead; no, both are brought back to life. Therefore we
have every right to believe these poets are divine, since they are able
through their words to give back life to those who are dead: that ability
belongs to the gods alone. But if we are justified in believing that the
poets are gods because they can restore life to the deceased, how much
more warranted are we in calling Aldus Manutius a god, since at his
press he revives the dead poets themselves.

## 19.

### *De Candida*

Defessus medio thoro iacebam,
Et somno grave iam caput cadebat,
Sui Candida cum miserta Bezae,
Praesens est mihi visa dormienti,
Iocos, deliciasque factitare,                                   5
Et tractare manu, et notare ocellis,
Et blaesa velut increpare voce.
Contra sic ego somnians loquebar:
    Ni sis me mihi carior, puella,
Dissolvi cupio, et perire totus.                               10
Vix haec edideram, repente nostrum
Cum lux invida somnium diremit,
Et meam mihi sustulit puellam.
    At tu, quisquis es, o tenebricosae
Praeses optime cogitationis,                                   15
Seu te Morphea, seu vocare Somnum
Fas est, fac vigil ut queam videre
Quod somno potui videre captus.
Aut, si non aliter potes mederi
Huic desiderio meo, perennem                                   20
Inducas mihi somniationem!

## 20.

### *In Sextum*

Caecus es, et cunctos reprendis, Sexte, poetas:
    Sanum reprensor debet habere caput.

---

20.1   et Bezam reprendis, Sexte, Quid ergo? *1569, 1576, 1597*

## 19.

### *Candida*

I was lying exhausted on my couch, and already my head was nodding into a deep sleep, when Candida, feeling sorry for her Bèze, appeared standing next to me in my sleep and was teasing and flirting with me, massaging me with her hands and batting her eyes, and seemed to be slurring childish babble. In my sleep I was replying to her, "Unless you are dearer to me than myself, dear girl, I want to die, and to perish completely." But hardly had I gotten out those words when suddenly the jealous light snatched away my dream and took my girl from me. But you, whoever you are, great guardian of shadowy perception, whether we should call you Morpheus or Somnus, grant that I can see in waking hours what I could see when I was deep in sleep. Or, if you cannot relieve my desire in any other way, put me into a perpetual sleep.

## 20.

### *Sextus*

You are blind, and you criticize all the poets, Sextus: a critic ought not to be sick in the head.

## 21.

### *In Thaida Caecam, et Ponticum Claudum*

Thaida cras duces caecam, pede claudus utroque;
  Convenis uxori, convenit illa tibi.
Integrum e duplici surget sic corpore corpus,
  Si praestes oculos, praestet at illa pedes.
Ergo rem faciunt te dignam, Pontice, divi,                    5
  Semiviro qui dent ἡμιγυναῖκα tibi.


## 22.

### *In Lupum*

Ieiunus mihi sobrium Platonem
Laudabas, Sophiamque praedicabas:
Mox vero ut tibi cena sumpta mecum,
Mutasti faciem atque opinionem.
Qui factum hoc, Lupe, tam cito ut iuberes                     5
A cena sophiam valere? nempe
Cenatus, Lupe, non eras apud te.


## 23.

### *De Francisco Rabelaeso*

Qui sic nugatur, tractantem ut seria vincat,
  Seria cum faciet, dic, rogo, quantus erit?

---

22.1   mihi sobrium *1597* sobrium mihi *1548*

## 21.

*Thais the Blind Girl, and Ponticus the Club-footed Boy*

Tomorrow you will marry blind Thais, you with your two clubbed feet. You are a help to your wife, she is a help to you. So a whole body will emerge from this union of two, if you provide the eyes, and she the feet. Therefore, Ponticus, the gods are doing something that suits you just right, since they are giving a half-woman to a half-man.

## 22.

*Mr. Wolf*

You used to fast and praise Plato's ideas on self-control, and you were always preaching about philosophy. But when you came to eat at my house, you did an about-face and changed your opinion quickly. How did it happen so fast, Mr. Wolf, that you bade philosophy farewell from the table? Ah, because you weren't eating at your house.

## 23.

*François Rabelais*

When the fellow who writes comic satires so well that he outdoes those who treat serious subjects, himself composes serious works, tell me, please, how impressive will he be?

## 24.

### *De Helionora Francorum regina*

Nil Helena vidit Phoebus formosius una;
    Te, Regina, nihil pulchrius orbis habet.
Utraque formosa est, sed re tamen altera maior;
    Illa ferit lites, Helionora fugit.


## 25.

### *In Asinium*

Seu domi mihi, seu foris repertus,
Promissi et fidei datae admoneris,
Tu contra velut admodum occupatus,
Has facis nihili petitiones,
Sed horam tamen inquis adfuturam,           5
Qua me ex paupere divitem et beatum
Reddas. En igitur tibi ipse dono
Horas quod tibi nuntiabit omnes.
Tandem nunc, Asini, potes iubere,
Haec ut hora sonet diu expetita.           10


## 26.

### *De Francisci et Caroli induciis*

Roma olim cessit soceri generique furori:
    Et cecidit gladiis inclyta Roma suis.
Quod si illi placidas iunxissent foedere dextras,
    Robore staret adhuc Martia Roma suo.
Sic fratrum immitis nuper discordia, pene       5
    Funditus Europae verterat imperium:
At quoniam iungunt, concordia pectora fratres,
    Servatum Europae dicitur imperium.

---

2    Et cecidit gladiis Martia *1569, 1576* Et gladiis cecidit Martia *1597*

## 24.

### *Eleanor, Queen of the French*

Phoebus never saw anything more beautiful than Helen. The world, O queen Eleanor, has nothing more beautiful than you. Both are beautiful, but one surpasses the other in one respect: Helen sows discord, Eleanor avoids it.

## 25.

### *Asinius*

Whether I catch you at home or out on the street, I remind you of the promise and pledge that you made. You, on the other hand, act as if your are very busy and brush off my pleas; but still you claim the hour will come, when you will transform me from a poor man into a rich and happy one. Look, I give you this clock that will bong every hour on the hour. Now, Asinius, you can set it so that this long-awaited hour will finally bong.

## 26.

### *The Treaty between François and Charles*

Rome once yielded to the madness of father-in-law and son-in-law, and renowned Rome fell by its own swords. But if they had joined their hands in peaceful covenant, Mars's Rome would still stand by its own might. Likewise, recently the hateful quarrel of brothers almost completely overturned the power of Europe. But since the royal brothers join their hearts in harmony, we can say the power of Europe is preserved.

## 27.

*De morbo Francisci Gallorum Regis, saluteque mox illi reddita*

Aegroto Pallas Francisco aegrota iacebat,
    Optabat Mavors aeger et ipse mori.
Illa, quod hoc tutam solo se credat alumno:
    Hic, quod sit studio natus uterque pari.
Quod si Franciscum mors eripuisset, eodem          5
    Funere Mars functus functa Minerva foret
Atropos hoc mirata nefas, feritate reposta,
    Tres una vetuit morte perire deos.

## 28.

*Ad Cl. Marotum*

Tam docte Venerem divinus pinxit Apelles
    Illi ut credatur visa fuisse Venus.
At tantam sapiunt Venerem tua scripta, Marote,
    Ut tibi credatur cognita tota Venus.

## 29.

*Ad Candidam, de ipsius facie in tabella expressa*

Quanto pulchrius elegantiusque
Picta haec est tabula omnibus tabellis:
Tanto pulchrior elegantiorque
Hac ipsa mihi crederis tabella.

---

27.Tit. valetudine *1597*
7      Atropos hoc *1597* Hoc Atropos *1548*
8      Servavit salvo numina Rege duo *1597.*

### 27.

*The Ailment of King François of the French, and His Quick Recovery*

Athena was sick when François lay ill, and Mars himself was ailing and hoping to die. She is sick, because she believes that she is safe by this child alone; he because both of them were born to the same pursuits. But if death had beaten François, then Mars and Athena would have died together with him. Atropos marveled at this scandal, set aside her cruelty, and refused to let three gods perish together.

### 28.

*Clément Marot*

Godlike Apelles painted Venus so skillfully that people believed he had actually seen Venus. But your writings, Marot, smack of so much Venus, that we have to believe that you saw *all* of Venus.

### 29.

*Candida's Portrait*

By how much more beautiful and more elegant this painting is than all paintings, by so much you seem to me more beautiful and elegant than the painting itself.

## 30.

### *Xenium Truchio et Dampetro*

Sinceris mos est nunquam neglectus amicis,
    Anni sub primos mittere dona dies.
Nempe quod ut veteris renovatur circulus anni,
    Fas sit ut antiquus sic renovetur amor.
Ergo cum Bezam Truchius fateatur amicum,     5
    Nec me Dampetrus deneget esse suum:
Non temere, priscos homines imitatus, utrique
    Parva quidem mitto dona, sed apta tamen.
Ambo estis vates, ambobus carmina dono,
    Carmina quae nostri pignus amoris erunt.     10
Vos pridem sincerus amor coniunxit in unum:
    Unum igitur decuit munus habere duos.

## 31.

### *Descriptio Virtutis*

Quaenam tam lacero vestita incedis amictu?
    Virtus antiquis nobilitata sophis.
Cur vestis tam vilis? Opes contemno caducas.
    Cur gemina est facies? Tempus utrumque noto.
Quid docet hoc frenum? Mentis cohibere furores.     5
    Rastros cur gestas? Res mihi grata labor.
Cur volucris? Doceo tandem super astra volare.
    Cur tibi mors premitur? Nescio sola mori.

## 30.

### *A Gift to Truchon and Dampierre*

True friends never fail to send gifts on New Year's Day. Why, because as the circle of the old year is renewed, it is right that old affections be renewed likewise. Therefore, since Truchon admits that Bèze is his friend, and Dampierre does not deny that I am his friend too, I am not rash to send, like men of old, small but appropriate gifts to each. You are both poets, so I give poems to both of you, poems that will be a token of our love. Long ago true love joined the two of you into one: therefore it seemed good that the two of you share one present.

## 31.

### *Description of Virtue*

Who are you who walk with tattered garb? "I am Virtue, whom the ancient wise men made famous." Why do you wear poor man's clothes? "I scorn fleeting riches." Why do you have a double face? "I signify both good and bad fortune." What does this bridle represent? "It indicates that I tame the mind's passions." Why do you carry a hoe? "I like to work." Why the wings? "I teach people to soar above the stars." Why are you crushing death under your feet? "I alone never die."

## 32.

### *In Fori Mancipia*

Cum sit hoc proprium fere poetis,
Rebus omnibus ut peculiarem
Divum constituant, suumque numen:
Cur lucrum, forum, et elocutionem,
Uni Mercurio tamen sacrarunt?                                    5
Prisci scilicet hoc modo indicarunt,
Futurum ut rabiosa quisquis arma
Tractaret fori, haberet ille curam
Lucri, non minus ac locutionis.

## 33.

### *Ad Marianum*

Augustas, Mariane, Deum venturus ad aras,
    Nulla cremas magno thura Sabaea Iovi.
Nec capis externos cultum qui spargat odores,
    Nec diti tractas aspera signa manu.
Gemmatae nunquam sudas sub pondere vestis,              5
    Nec digitos onerat res peregrina tuos.
Sed placidam et nullo pollutam crimine mentem,
    Atque sua notas a pietate manus,
Caeteraque integros domini testantia mores,
    Haec, inquam, magnis das, Mariane, deis.              10
Quod si rara solent merito pretiosa videri
    Nemo dedit, nemo plus, Mariane, dabit.

---

32.1  Prisci cum fere sueverint poetae *1597*
2     *om. 1597*
3     Rebus quodque suis sacrare numen *1597*
6     Vates scilicet hoc modo indicarunt *1597*

## 32.

### *The Slaves of the Forum*

Although it is generally within the purview of the poets to assign every individual thing its own god and its own guardian spirit, still why did they imagine that money, the marketplace, and eloquence are sacred only to Mercury? Obviously the ancients were trying to show that whoever enters into the rat race of the business world will concern himself no less with money than with smooth talking.

## 33.

### *Marianus*

Marianus, as you approach the august altars of the gods, you do not burn Arabian incense to great Jupiter, nor do you put on attire which reeks of foreign perfumes, nor do you handle the carved icons with a rich hand. You never sweat under the weight of a studded garment, nor does anything exotic load down your fingers. Rather, you offer to the gods, Marianus, a peaceful mind unstained by any evil deed, and hands known for their piety, and other things that testify to a person's pure character. For if it is customary to view rare things as precious, as is proper, then no one has given more, Marianus, and no one ever will.

## 34.

### *Ad Erasmi Imaginem*

Illum, quo totus nunc personat orbis, Erasmum
  Haec tibi dimidium picta tabella refert.
At cur non totum? mirari desine, lector:
  Integra nam totum terra nec ipsa capit.

## 35.

### *Ad Musas*

Si rogat Cereremque, Liberumque
Vitae sollicitus suae colonus,
Si Mavortis opem petit cruentus
Miles, sollicitus suae salutis:
Quid ni, Calliope, tibi, tuisque                                5
Iure sacra feram, quibus placere
Est unum studium mihi, omnibusque
Qui vatum e numero volunt haberi?
Vobis ergo ferenda sacra, Musae.
Sed quae victima grata? quae Camoenis                          10
Dicata hostia? parcite, o Camoenae,
Nova haec victima sed tamen suavis
Futura arbitror, admodumque grata.
Accede, o tinea, illa quae pusillo
Ventrem corpore tam geris voracem:                             15
Tene Pieridum aggredi ministros?
Tene arrodere tam sacros labores?
Nec factum mihi denega: ecce furti
Tui exempla, tuae et voracitatis.
Tu fere mihi passerem Catulli,                                 20

---

34.1   *ad init.* Ingens ingentem quem *1569, 1580 Icones*
35.Tit. Ad musas iocus *1569, 1576* Ad musas, tineae sacrificium ludicrum *1597, 1779*
12     *ad fin.* futura vobis *1597*
13     *ad init.* Suavis *1597*
14     pupillo *1597*
20     Pene tu *1569, 1576, 1597*

## 34.

### *A Portrait of Erasmus*

This painting of Erasmus, with whom the whole world now resounds, depicts for you only half of him. But why not the whole? Wonder no more, reader. For not even the entire world can contain the whole of Erasmus.

## 35.

### *To the Muses*

If a farmer who is anxious for his own livelihood pleads with Ceres and Liber, and a bloodthirsty soldier concerned for his own safety seeks the help of Mars, why, Calliope, should I not bring sacred gifts to you and your sisters, since pleasing you is my only desire, as it is for all who wish to be counted among the vatic poets? Well then, I have to bring you sacrifices, Muses. But what kind of victim is appropriate? What sacrifice should be dedicated to the Camenae? Be patient, O Camenae, this is an unusual victim, but still I think it will be gratifying and very welcome. Come, bookworm, you who carry such a voracious belly in so small a body. Are you assaulting the ministers of the Pierides? Are you gnawing at such sacred labors? Do not deny to me what you have done. Behold, evidence of your thievery and of your voracity. You almost took away from me the sparrow of Catullus, and Lesbia too. Now cer-

Tu fere mihi Lesbiam abstulisti.
Nunc certe meus ille Martialis
Ima ad viscera rosus usque languet,
Et quaerit medicum suum Triphonem.
Immo et ipse Maro, cui pepercit                                    25
Olim flamma, tuum tamen cerebrum
Nuper, o fera ter scelesta, sensit.
Quid dicam innumeros bene eruditos,
Quorum tu monimenta, tu labores
Isto, pessima, ventre devorasti?                                   30
Prodi, iam tunicam relinque, prodi.
Vah, ut callida stringit ipsa sese!
Ut mortem simulat scelesta! prodi,
Pro tot criminibus datura poenas.
Age, istum iugulo tuo cruento,                                     35
Mucronem, excipe, et istum, et istum, et istum.
Vide ut palpitet, ut cruore largo
Aras polluerit prophana sacras!
At vos, Pierides, bonaeque Musae,
Nunc gaudete, iacet fera interempta,                               40
Iacet sacrilega illa, quae solebat
Sacros Pieridum vorare servos.
Hanc vobis tunicam, has dico, Camoenae,
Vobis exuvias, ut hinc trophaeum
Parnasso in medio locetis, et sit                                  45
Haec inscriptio. De fera interempta,
Bezaeus spolia haec opima Musis.

---

21    Pene tu *1569, 1576, 1597*
24    *om. 1597*
26-27 Iusto Caesare sic iubente, flamma | Laesus dente tuo, scelesta, moeret *1597*
35    *ad fin.* mucronem *1548*
36    Cruenta *1548*
37    palpitat *1597*
38    polluat haec *1597*
47    Beza dat *1569, 1576, 1597*

tainly my Martial book lies heavy, consumed, in the very depths of your guts, and pleads for his doctor Triphon. Yes, even Vergil himself, once rescued from the fire, recently felt your drill, you dastardly monster. What will I tell these countless learned men whose monuments and labors you, rotten scum, have devoured with that belly? Come forth, give up your hide. Oh, how the clever little fellow draws himself up tight! How the wicked thing feigns death! Come forth, you who are about to pay the penalty for so many crimes. Come on, fellow, take that blade on your bloody neck, and that, and that, and that! See how the profane thing convulses, how he has polluted the sacred altars with his profuse blood! But you, Pierides and good Muses, now rejoice, here lies a slaughtered beast, here lies that sacrilegious monster, who used to devour the sacred servants of the Pierides. I dedicate this hide to you, these spoils to you, Camenae, so you can set them up there in the middle of Parnassus as a trophy, and let this be the inscription: "Beza gave these spoils of victory of a slaughtered beast to the Muses."

## 36.

### *In Philaenum*

Aurelias vocare vespas suevimus,
Ut dicere olim mos erat nasum Atticum:
At te, Philaene, Aurelium vocabimus
Fucum, quod omnes adeo pungas frigide,
Aculeum ut interim relinquas nemini.

## 37.

### *Ad Triputium Aurelium Iurisc.*

Doctum illum et lepidum tuum libellum,
Quo mysteria iuris explicasti,
Fertur Mercurius tulisse nuper
Ima ad Tartara, protinusque doctis
Illis Manibus, ut Papiniano,                    5
Paulo, Scaevolae, et Ulpiano, et illi,
Iuris quem merito vocant lucernam,
Legendum exhibuisse: deinde lecto
Sic coepisse loqui tuo libello:
Ecquid ceditis? At Papinianus,                 10
Cuncti cedimus, inquit, haud gravate.

## 38.

### *In Philopatrum*

Damnabis (fateor) nostros, Philopatre, libellos,
    Et tibi non lectum despicietur opus.
Quid tum? Si nostros carpas, Philopatre, libellos,
    Debebunt tanto nostra placere magis.

## 36.

### *Philaenus*

We have come accustomed to speak of "the wasps of Orléans," like once it was common to speak of an "Attic nose"; but you, Philaenus, we will call "the drone of Orléans," because you sting everyone so feebly, that you end up not leaving a barb in anyone.

## 37.

### *Tripault of Orléans, Jurisconsult*

They say that recently Mercury carried down to the depths of Tartarus that learned and charming little book of yours, in which you explain the mysteries of law, and straightaway offered it to the learned shades there to read, to Papinianus, Paulus, Scaevola, and Ulpianus, and to him, whom they deservedly call "the lamp of the law." Then, when they had read the book, Mercury began, "Do you yield?" "Yes," Papinianus replied, "we all yield, and without any hesitation."

## 38.

### *Philopater*

You will condemn my little books (I admit it), Philopater, and you will despise my work even though you have not read it. What then? If you censure my little books, Philopater, then they are bound to be all the more pleasing.

## 39.

### *In eundem*

Sive palatina Philopatrus inambulet aula,
    Et fatuo incessu marmor utrumque terat:
Sive fames illum locupletum quaerere mensas,
    Et procul e vacua iussit abire domo:
Seu ieiunus eat, seu pleno ventre vacillet,          5
    Seu lateat solus, seu comitatus eat:
Semper habet quiddam turpi quod garriat ore
    Quod merito possit carpere, semper habet.
Semper hiat, semper colloque humerisque laborat,
    Et simulat magnum voce, manuque sophos.       10
Sed cum te audierint multi bene multa loquentem,
    Nemo bene audivit te, Philopatre, loqui.

## 40.

### *Xenium Candidae*

Vestes divitiis graves et arte,
Aptandumve tuo monile collo,
Aut quos India mittit uniones
Iani nec queo, nec volo Calendis
Ad te mittere, Candida, una Bezae          5
Dilectissima Candida. At quid ergo?
Ipsam nempe animam tibi dicatam,
Amorisque tui ignibus perustam,
Quae, pridem tua sit licet, suamque
Te pridem dominam vocetque ametque,      10
Se rursus tibi datque dedicatque,
Inclusa his numeris Phaleuciorum.
Quod si munera raritate censes:
O dii! quam tibi grande mitto munus!

---

39.1      hora *pro* aula, *1548, 1580, 1779, Machard tamen transl.* 'cour'

## 39.

### *The Same*

Whether Philopater strolls around the palace courtyard, and rambles back and forth along the marble with his clumsy gait, or hunger forces him to prowl the tables of the rich, and go far from his empty home; whether he goes hungry, or waddles with a full belly, whether he skulks alone, or goes with company, his foul mouth is always blabbing about something, and he always finds something he can justly criticize. His mouth is always open, and cocking his neck and shoulders ostentatiously, he feigns great wisdom with his voice and gestures. But though many have heard you saying many things nicely, Philopater, no one has heard you speak nicely.

## 40.

### *A Gift to Candida*

Candida, Beza's only joy, I cannot nor do I want to send to you clothes laden with finery and wrought with skill for New Year's Day, or a necklace to adorn your neck, or large pearls from India. But what then? My heart itself, dedicated to you, consumed with the fires of love, which, though long since yours, and long since loving you and calling you its mistress, again dedicates itself and gives itself to you, wrapped up in these Phalaecean verses. But if you value gifts for their rarity—my goodness!—how grand a gift I send to you!

### 41.

*De Truchio et Valido*

Vos ego, divini Manes appello Platonis,
   Integer est cuius munere notus Amor.
Dicite, non cur nam in sese moriantur amantes,
   Curve anima vivant alter in alterius:
Aut quales merito nobis dicamus amicos,                    5
   Aut solidi verum quod sit amoris opus.
Haec ego non quaero, nec quae retulisse Platonis
   Sobrius ad casti prandia fertur Amor.
Sit satis haec dixisse semel: nunc dicite, Manes,
   Quaedam animo nondum sat bene nota meo.        10
Mens simplex atque una mihi est, hanc attamen unam
   Pridem Amor in partes iussit abire duas:
Atque ait, hanc animam divisam trado duobus,
   Dimidiam Truchio, dimidiam Valido:
Salva tamen mens est, vivo, scriboque, loquorque,         15
   Et tamen haec Validi est, et tamen haec Truchii est.
Quodque magis mirum, quum sit divisa duobus,
   Utrumque integra diligo amoque anima.

---

41.Tit. Amicissimis duobus, Ioanni Truchio, et Lodoico Valido *1597*
2     Est cuius castus *1597*
8     casti *1597* sobrii *1548*
18   integram ... animam *1548, 1580, 1779*

## 41.

### *Truchon and Vaillant*

I invoke you, shades of divine Plato, who taught us in your book about unbroken love. Tell us, not why lovers die in each other's arms, or why they live with mingled hearts; or what sort deserve to be called friends, or what is the essential ingredient of lasting love. I do not ask these things, nor those things that sober Love is said to have related at the dinner party described by blameless Plato. Let it suffice that you have already addressed those matters. Now tell me, shades, things I do not already know well enough. My mind is simple and one: but even so Love bid it long ago to divide into two parts; "And," he said, "I am giving this heart that I have divided to two people: half to Truchon, half to Vaillant." Yet my mind feels fine: I live, I write, I speak, and still this part belongs to Vaillant, this to Truchon. And what is more amazing, although it is divided into two parts, I love and cherish both with my whole heart.

## 42.

### *In Hubertum*

Norunt Hubertum ganeones prodigi;
Norunt magistri cocta quos crambe necat:
In urbe tota nullus histrio latet,
Nec moechus ullus, leno scurrave impudens,
Nec chiromantis ullus, aut cadaverum                    5
Molestus excitator, aut vates malus,
Cui non Hubertus iste sit notus bene.
Sed scire vis ignotus hic cui sit? sibi.

## 43.

### *In Ollum*

Quamvis illa mihi forensis esset
Pridem perfidia usque et usque nota;
Nec donis ego, nec pecuniarum
Peperci cumulo, ut mihi innocenti
Praesto iudicis ad Tribunal esses.                      5
At tu muneribus meis receptis,
Me, nec id semel, Olle, prodidisti.
Sane es integer et bonus patronus,
Spem qui fallere non velis clientis.

---

42.Tit. *add.* perditissimum nebulonem *1597*
2      *om. 1569, 1576, 1597*
6–7    *om. 1597*

## 42.

### *Hubert*

The gluttons with their enormous appetites know Hubert, the teachers too, whom he kills with his boiled cabbage. In the city no actor lurks, no slut, no pimp or shameless clown, no palm reader or pesky necromancer, no shoddy poet, who does not know Hubert's reputation. But do you know who does not know Hubert's reputation? Hubert.

## 43.

### *Ollus*

Although I have long known about your constant legal trickery, still I kept right on loading you up with gifts and money in the hope you would show up in court as my advocate. You took all my gifts, but then you betrayed me, Ollus, and not just once. Obviously, you are a decent and honorable patron, the sort not wanting to dash the expectations of his client!

## 44.

*De Ioanne Secundo, Hagiensi, poeta eximio*

Excelsum seu condit opus, magnique Maronis
    Luminibus officere studet:
Sive leves elegos, alternaque carmina, raptus
    Nasonis impetu canit:
Sive lyram variis sic aptat cantibus, ut se          5
    Victum erubescat Pindarus:
Sive iocos, blandosque sales epigrammate miscet,
    Clara invidente Bilbili:
Unus quattuor haec sic praestitit ille Secundus,
    Secundus ut sit nemini.          10

## 45.

*Ad Fabullum*

Si cenare voles, Fabulle, mecum,
(Sed cenare voles, Fabulle, mecum)
Audi quae tibi cena sit parata:
Perdices gemini duas edemus:
Turtur mox aderit, nec ille solus,          5
Sed quem casta etiam sequetur uxor.
Haec nos frigidulo mero, Fabulle,
Et fame haec quoque condiemus ipsa.
Sed scis qualia vina comparavi?
Quae si non vocites Opimiana,          10
At certe Optimiana iure dicas.

---

44.10 Ut antecellat plurimos *1597*
45.Tit. Ad Labullum *1597*
4     aderunt duo duobus *1597*
8     Fame vel *1597*
11–12 Quod si grammatici pati recusent | Oblato sibi poculo tacebunt *1597*

### 44.

*John Secundus of the Hague, an Excellent Poet*

Whether he creates a lofty work, and strives to outshine the great Vergil; or sings light elegies and couplets, seized with the inspiration of Ovid; or adapts his lyre to the various odes, making Pindar blush from being vanquished; or mingles jokes and charming wit, enough to make Martial envious: Secundus alone so excels these four that he is second to no one.

### 45.

*Fabullus*

If you want to dine with me, Fabullus, and certainly you do, listen to what kind of dinner you would get: we both will eat two partridges. Soon after a turtledove will be served, not just a male by itself, but his faithful mate too. These things, Fabullus, we will make savory with strong chilled wine as well as with our very appetite. But do you know what kind of wine I have obtained? If you would not call it *Opimian*, certainly you would rightly call it *Optimian*.

## 46.

### *In Philaenum*

Erasmus ille, quo fatentur plurimi
Nihil fuisse, vel futurum doctius:
Tibi, Philaene, stupidus est et plumbeus?
Et quicquid uspiam ab omnibus fingi potest
Calumniarum, stulte in illum congeris.                              5
Latra, Philaene, quamdiu et quantum voles:
Hunc scire constat plura, quam tu nescias.


## 47.

### *Genethliacon Francisci Valesii, Henrici Valesii Galliarum olim Delphini, et illustrissimae principis Catharinae Medices, filii*

Fertur in Alcmenes venturus Iuppiter olim
    Brachia, ter noctis continuasse vices.
Nempe quod in magni divinos Herculis ortus,
    Nox hiberna licet, non foret una satis:
Sic, princeps Henrice, tuo cum e semine vellent              5
    Alcidem Gallis gignere fata suum,
Unius in prolis conceptum currere messes
    Iusserunt, magna cum ratione, decem.
Scilicet haud aliter prorsus, quam pluribus annis
    Formari tantus debuit iste puer.                              10
Et (si fas homini res est aperire futuras,
    Nec dici vatum numen inane decet)
Quo deni plures ternis sunt noctibus anni,
    Hoc tuus hic infans Hercule maior erit.

---

47.Tit. primogeniti *add.* 1569, 1576 Carmen genethliacon Francisco Henrici II. Galliarum regis F. primogenito, decem demum annis nato, post coniugium cum Catharina Medicea initum *1597*
11    si res homini fas *1547 Tumuli*
12    vanum *1597*

## 46.

### *Philaenus*

The famous Erasmus, who most agree was and will be the most learned scholar, is nothing to you, Philaenus, but a stupid lead-head, and any abuse imaginable anywhere in the world you foolishly heap against him. Bark, Philaenus, as long and as much as you wish: clearly he knows more things than you don't know.

## 47.

### *On the Occasion of the Birth of Francois Valois, Son of Henri Valois of France, Formerly the Dauphin, and Catherine de Medici*

The story goes that when Jupiter intended to come to Alcmene's arms, he strung together three nights in a row. This was mainly because one night, even a winter one, would not be sufficient for the divine birth of the great Hercules. And so, prince Henri, when the Fates were wanting to produce for the French their own Hercules, they bid ten harvests to pass for the conception of a single infant, and with good reason. Naturally, such a great boy ought to be formed in no other way than by many years. And (if it is right for man to reveal the future, and proper to claim that the poets' gift is effective), by how much more ten years are than three nights, by that much will the newborn boy be greater than Hercules.

### 48.

*Genethliacon Isabellae a Francia, Henrici Valesii, Galliarum olim*
*Delphini, et illustrissimae principis Catharinae Medices, filiae*

Ecce novos peperit Gallis Catharina triumphos,
    Iam prole dives altera:
Natorumque loco felicem crescere turbam
    Avus nepotum conspicit.
En vixdum nata in cunis Isabella videtur     5
    Vagire quiddam regium,
Moxque iocos blandae tenero cum fratre sororis
    Spectabit Henricus pater:
At Gallus primis iam nunc miratur in annis
    Suos futuros principes.     10
Et quamvis tenerae magnum iam frontis honorem,
    Notasque regias colit:
Donec paulatim, illorum crescentibus annis,
    Spes patriae adolescat simul:
Francisco ut domitos forti victosque pudico     15
    Isabellae amore blandulae,
Gallica conspiciat venerari lilia pronos
    Orbis superbos principes.
Illi etenim nullus poterit par viribus esse,
    Odisse nullus hanc volet.     20

Tit.    olim *om. in 1569 et 1576 edd.*
16    Gallia *1597*

## 48.

*On the Occasion of the Birth of Elizabeth of France, Daughter of Henri of France, Formerly the Dauphin, and Catherine de Médicis*

Look! Catherine bore new triumphs for the French, now she is blessed with another child. The grandfather eyes, instead of sons, a happy flock of grandchildren grow. Lo, but scarcely born, Elizabeth seems to wail royally. And soon her father Henri will see his sweet girl playing with her tender brother. But already now France marvels at its future rulers in their early years. And even though her forehead is tender, she wears there a large crown and the marks of royalty. Then, little by little, as they grow older, the hope of the country will swell to see the bravery of François and the chaste love of precious Elizabeth subdue and disarm the proud rulers of the world, so that they prostrate themselves and venerate the French lilies. For no one will be able to equal his power, and no one will want to hate her.

## 49.

*De felici inauguratione Henrici II. Christianissimi Francorum Regis*

Francisco postquam sublato, Gallia sensit
    Cuius lene foret mox subitura iugum,
Finiit, ut potuit, gemitus, animisque receptis,
    Istaec fassa fuit damna lucrosa sibi.
Ergo age, quam primum fac huius, Sequana, regis     5
    Ad gelidas Arctos nuntia fama volet:
Haec, Liger, Hesperiis Rheni, Mosa, dicito ripae,
    Haec, Rhodane, ambustos perfer ad Aethiopas,
Gallorum Henricum felicia sceptra tenere,
    Ingentem ingenti de genitore satum.     10
Nec regem esse tamen, dubium quia fecerit ipse,
    Rex Gallis dici debeat, anne pater.

## 50.

*D. Quelino Senatori*

Seu dea, seu deus est, qui te tam laeta parantem
    Coniugia, e tristi vix sinit ire toro,
Illa deae, iste dei privari numine dignus,
    Dignus qui superum cedat ab arce procul.
Nam tua vel virtus, vel castae vota puellae,     5
    Materies iusti plena favoris erat.
Perge, Queline, tamen, nec tam bene coepta morare:
    Finem etiam morbis Di statuere suum.
Perge, puella, simul; namque aegrotante Quelino
    Vix alius toto sanior orbe vir est.     10

---

49.Tit. De felici coronatione Henrici II Francorum regis, *1597*
4      commoda damna sibi *1569, 1576*
5      Henrici fac *1569, 1576*

### 49.

*The Happy Inauguration of Henri II, Most Christian King of the French*

After François had been buried, France realized whose soft yoke she was soon to undergo. She collected herself and stopped her mourning, as much as she could, and acknowledged that her loss had been a gain. So come, Seine, make the news of this king fly to the cold arctic regions as soon as possible. Loire, tell this news to the West, Meuse, to the banks of the Rhine. And you, Rhone, bear these tidings to sweltering Ethiopia, that Henri holds the blessed sceptre of the French, great child of a great father. And do not say that he is king, however, since he makes us doubt whether France ought to call him king, or father.

### 50.

*To the Honorable Quélain, the Senator*

You are making preparations for a happy marriage, but some god or goddess prevents you from leaving your sickbed except with great difficulty. He or she deserves to be stripped of power and sent into exile far from heaven. For either your virtue or the vows of your faithful fiancée earned the utmost compassion from the gods. Carry on, Quélain, do not delay what you have begun so well: the gods have set their own end to your illness. You too carry on, girl: for truly there is scarcely a healthier man in the whole world than Quélain even when he is sick.

50.Tit. Mich. Quelino, qui cum esset uxorem ducturus, aegrotare coepit *1569, 1576*
     D. Quelino senatori Parisiensi, cum uxorem ducturus aegrotare coepisset *1779*
1     Te, Michael, quodumque malum tam laeta parantem *1569, 1546*
3-4   Seu febris, seu rheuma hoc est, me iudice dignum est, | Altera quod febris, rheuma quod interimat *1569, 1576*
7     morere *1548, 1580, 1779*
8     tempora laeta dabunt *1569, 1576*

## 51.

### *Ad Ponticum*

Nostras, Pontice, somniationes
Narro cum tibi, tunc moves cachinnos,
Et haec plena putas ineptiarum.
Atque, Pontice, somniare nuper
Sic mi contigit, ut mihi viderer                              5
Omnes divitias, opes, talenta,
Pactolique, Tagique, possidere.
Esse haec somnia vera tunc negabis?

## 52.

### *De Victoria parta adversus Marchionem Vasti, Anno 1544*

Francorum victas acies Insubria vidit,
    Vidit, sed Franci robore freta ducis.
Namque velut quondam Romam oppressere Quirites,
    Sic est pene sua Francia versa manu.
At nunc eversas aquilas Insubria cernit,                     5
    Et colubris rursus lilia iuncta suis.
Ergo seu vincat, seu cedat Francus, utrinque,
    Virtutis laudem, quod mereatur, habet.

---

**52.**Tit. Gallorum *add.* 1569, 1576 apud Pedemontem *add.* 1597, 1779

## 51.

*Ponticus*

When I tell you my dreams, Ponticus, you laugh at them and think they are really stupid. But recently I had a dream in which I thought I possessed all the gold and wealth and treasures of the Pactolus and the Tagus. Will you deny, then, that these dreams are true?

## 52.

*The Victory Won against Le Marquis del Vasto in 1544*

Once the Lombards saw the French armies conquered, but for their victory they relied on the strength of a French general. For just as once the Quirites overwhelmed Rome, so was France overturned almost by its own hand. But now the Lombards see the Imperial eagles overturned, and again the lilies are joined to their serpents. Therefore, whether the French win or lose, in either case, they deserve to be praised for their courage.

## 53.

### *Ad Germanum Valentem*

Ergo Germani vultus violabit amoenos
    Barba, licet lenis, flavaque, dura tamen?
Dura equidem, nobis quae tam cito praeripit illas,
    Illas quas Phoebus vellet habere genas.
Et mediam nobis faciem quae surripit illam,        5
    Quam lepos incoluit, cumque lepore iocus.
Istos barba decet, quibus est sic acta iuventus,
    Ut canae tuti sint sub honore comae.
At quid non didicit primis Germanus ab annis,
    Quem vicena videt bruma peracta senem?        10
Cede igitur, lanugo, procul: nisi cesseris, ecce,
    Quod queat invitam cogere, tonsor habet.


## 54.

### *De Francisco Galliarum Rege*

Vidimus, heu, fratres in mutua bella paratos,
    Vidimus accensas Martis ubique faces.
Nunc tamen, o superi, placidis allabitur alis
    Aurea perpetuos pax habitura dies.
Quis porro tanti tibi, Gallia, muneris author?        5
    Gallia, quo tandem vindice facta tua es?
Scilicet hic superum favor est, haec munera divum,
    Non sunt haec caeli munera tota tamen:
Quippe etiam partem doni sibi vindicat huius,
    Et rex, et regis natus uterque tui.        10
Roma igitur patriae patres numeraverit olim:
    Nos patriae patres et numeremus avum.

---

54.Tit. De pace inter Franciscum I. Galliarum regem, et Carolum V. Caesarem,
    inita *1569, 1576, 1597, 1779*
7    caeli *1569, 1576*

## 53.

### *Germain Vaillant*

So will a beard, though soft and blond, yet scraggly, ruin the handsome features of Germain? You heard me, I said "scraggly," and it steals from us too soon those cheeks that enamor Phoebus, and robs us of a clear view of his face, where resides his boyish charm together with a mischievious smile. A beard befits those whose youth has passed, as they try to garner respect from their hoary hair. But what has Germain, whom twenty winters past has found an old man, not learned while growing up? Go far away, then, wool; if you do not go away, look, the barber has something to remove you whether you like it or not.

## 54.

### *François, King of France*

We saw brothers prepared to join battle, we saw the firebrands of Mars inflamed on all sides. Now, however, heavenly gods, a golden peace that will last forever glides down on peaceful wings. Who gave you such a great gift, France? By what liberator were you finally set free? To be sure, this is the kindness of the heavenly gods and these are their gifts, yet these are not completely gifts from heaven: both the king and the sons of the king lay claim to at least part of this gift. Thus, as Rome once enumerated its founding fathers, let us enumerate our founding fathers, and let's include a grandfather too.

## 55.

*In Paulinum*

Paulino quoties condixi, Testile, cenam,
    Nunquam, cum taceat caetera turba, tacet.
Nec nisi depositis dapibusque, meroque, quiescit.
    Ergo satur, dices, non abit: immo venit.

## 56.

*In Caecilium*

Quandocumque sibi parare amicos
Optat Caecilius fideliores,
Hos solo probat aestimatque censu,
Nec quemquam colit ut suum libenter
Virtus unica quem facit beatum,               5
Sed cuius titulos superbiores
Triplex linea vix notare possit:
Hunc suum vocat, hunc colit libenter,
Sic servitur, avare, non amatur.

## 57.

*In Posthumum*

Saepe quidem verbo solvis, re, Posthume, numquam.
    Quod toties solvis, iam rogo, solve semel.

## 55.

### *Paulinus*

Testilus, everytime I invite Paulinus for dinner, he's never quiet, not even when the rest of the guests are quiet. He doesn't shut up, not until the dinner and the wine are removed. "So," you will say, "he goes home hungry." No, he comes already full of it.

## 56.

### *Caecilius*

Whenever Caecilius hopes to acquire more devoted friends, he chooses and values them according to their wealth alone. He doesn't willingly cultivate a friendship with anyone who is merely blessed with virtue; no, he chooses those whose lofty titles three lines of text can barely contain. He calls such people his friends, and spends time on them. But this is the way to get patrons, greedy fellow, not friends.

## 57.

### *Posthumus*

You often give lip-service to paying, Posthumus, but you never pay. Now I ask you, pay at least once what you pay so often.

### 58.

#### *In Bergedum*

Audes (o facinus!) censoris sumere normam,
    Et semper moesti verba sonare senis.
Audes, o mores, o tempora! dicere, cum sis
    Socraticos inter gloria prima canes.
Sic tamen, o demens, sic inquam, Bergede, ploras,         5
    Sileni vector qualia nempe rudit,
Quale gemunt calami crasso tractante bubulco,
    Quale gemit viridi fulta quadriga rota.
Denique sic ploras, ut qui tua carmina ridens
    Non legat, inventus sit, puto, nullus adhuc.          10

### 59.

#### *Ad Ianum*

Aureolos Paulo vicenos, Iane, dedisti:
    Credita nam qui non reppetit, ille dedit.
Sed quamvis dederis, quamvis nil inde reposcas,
    Aureolos reddet bis tibi, Iane, decem:
At quando? dices, Graecorum nempe Calendis:              5
    Cum dederis nummos, credere verba potes.

---

58.Tit. In M. Scaevolam *1569, 1576*
5      Tale tamen demens, tale *1597*
6      Sileni vector qualia nempe rudit *1597* Quale rudit vector, pande Silene, tuus
       *1548*

## 58.

*Bergedus*

You dare (what a scandal!) to act like a censor, and you always talk like a glum old man. You dare to say, "What times! what manners!" although you rank first among the Socratic dogs. Yes, so it is, you madman, yes, Bergedus, you complain, like the mount of Silenus brays, like reeds moan when played by a boorish ox-plougher, like a fresh wheel creaks under the weight of a chariot. In short, you complain in such a way that I don't think that anyone can be found still who does not read your poems and laugh.

## 59.

*Jean*

Jean, you gave twenty gold coins to Paul: we have to call it "giving" when you do not demand payment on a loan. Yet, though you gave it, and ask for nothing in return, he will repay you the twenty gold coins. But when? You will say, "On the Greek calends." Since you lent the coins, you can credit the words.

## 60.

### *In Daedalum*

Seu te seria, seu ioci morantur,
Seu lites medio foro tueris,
Seu vicos teris otiosus urbis,
Seu potes, recitesve, redeasve,
Cuncta accepta tuo refers parenti:                              5
Quid si, Daedale, Posthumus fuisses?

## 61.

### *De Francisco Valesio Galliarum Rege*

Quod, Francisce, tibi iam dudum spondet Olympus,
    Id sors obtulerat nuper amica tibi.
Scilicet ut posset victorem agnoscere Francum,
    Excusso alterius terra beata iugo.
Tu tamen haec (quamvis et magna et certa) tuorum         5
    Non es dilecto sanguine passus emi.
Ergo quod illaesos, o rex, servaveris hostes,
    Nemo metum credat, sed pietatis opus.
Pugnabas etenim nolens pugnare, tuique,
    Tunc cum hostem nolles vincere, victor eras.         10

---

61.Tit. e Picardia, soluta Landrisii obsidione, reverso *add. 1569, 1576*
4        hostili Gallia tuta *1569, 1576* hostili Gallia tota *1597*
7        Illaesos igitur quod tu servaveris hostes *1569, 1576, 1597*

## 60.

### *Daedalus*

Whether you spend your time on serious matters or trivial ones; whether you watch trials at the courthouse, or in leisurely fashion stroll around the streets of the city; whether you are drinking or reciting or laughing, you relate everything you've heard to your father. What if, Daedulus, you were Posthumus?

## 61.

### *François Valois, King of France*

François, what Olympus long ago promised to you, Luck (only recently a friend to you) had prevented. Obviously, she did so that the region could rejoice shaking off the yoke of another and knowing François as her conqueror. But you did not want to pay for these things (however great and secure) to be bought by the precious blood of your people. Therefore, because you spared your enemies unharmed, let no one put their trust in fear, but in the work of piety. For you were fighting unwillingly, and at that moment when you were unwilling to vanquish the enemy, you were conqueror of yourself.

### 62.

### *In Zoilum*

Brevem, Zoile, dicis hunc libellum:
O si possit idem omnibus videri!

### 63.

### *Ad amicos*

Hunc quamquam illepidum, et malum libellum,
Vos o perlepidi mei sodales,
Quaeso sumite blandiore vultu,
Deinde perlegite usque ad umbilicum.
Nam vos id rogat ille Beza vester,       5
Cuius vos animamque, corculumque,
Idque, mehercule, iure possidetis.
Sed sic perlegite, o boni sodales,
Ut nec falsa aliqua eruditionis
Nostrae opinio, nec mei tuendi       10
Cura nominis ulla vos moretur.
Figatis potius vel hinc, vel illinc,
Stellulisque obelisque virgulisque,
Cultu splendidus ut decentiore
Testetur titulo tenus parentem.       15
Id vero mala turba Zoilorum
Damnabit, fateor, nihilque dicet
Hic, praeter titulum, meum videri:
Sed clamet licet usque, et usque, et usque,
Sit totus volo vester hic libellus,       20
Cum vester quoque sit poeta totus.

---

**63.**6–7 *om.* 1597

## 62.

### *Zoilus*

You call this book "short," Zoilus: if only it could seem that way to everybody!

## 63.

### *To My Friends*

Take up this little book, my sophisticated and gracious friends, regardless of how unsophisticated and graceless it is, with a somewhat agreeable mien, then read it through cover to cover. For your friend Beza asks this of you, who rightly own, I swear, his heart and soul. But read through it, good friends, disregarding any false impressions about my learning, and without any worry about my reputation. Rather pierce it here and there with asterisks, obelisks, and spits, so that magnificent in its more noble garb it may bear witness (at least in name) to its father. Undoubtedly Zoilus and his ilk will condemn it, I'm sure of that, and they will claim that nothing here is mine except the title. But let him shout over and over and over again; I want this little book to be all yours, since the poet is all yours.

## 64.

### *In Philenem*

Parvus ille deus minutulusque,
Cui vates tribuunt et arcum et alas,
Nuper Gallica permeabat arva,
Illam cum subito aspicit Philenem,
Quae nostras toties precationes                    5
Contempsit rigido superba vultu,
Quae Cupidinis et faces, et arcum
Sprevit hactenus, et sibi negoti
Cum Cupidine nil fore asserebat:
Atque perfidae suae invocabat               10
Testem Castora, fratre cum gemello.
Sed postquam ille deus, Cupido parvus
E gravi pharetra unicam sagittam
Deprompsit, subito suam Philene
Mutavit tetricam severitatem.                     15
O potens Amor, o levis Philene!

## 65.

### *In Poardum*

Illam Dorida, bellum illud amabile
Scortillum, et totius lupanaris decus,
Illam Dorida Poardus ille deperit,
Senex, vietus, edentulus, calvus, putris.
Hinc urbis omnes visit angulos miser,             5
Uno Poardus nec potest stare in loco.
Rem scilicet curat Poardus publicam.

### 64.

*Philene*

That small and puny god, to whom the poets ascribe a bow and wings, recently was wandering through the fields of France, when suddenly he caught sight of Philene, the haughty girl with the stiff upper lip who resisted my overtures and 'til now spurned the bow and firebrands of Cupid, insisting that she would never have anything to do with Cupid. She invoked Castor and Pollux as witnesses of her own perfidy. But after that tiny god drew a single arrow from his heavy quiver, suddenly Philene changed her sour and unyielding attitude. O Love, how powerful you are! How fickle, Philene!

### 65.

*Poardus*

Doris—you know her, that beautiful, lovable slut, glory of every whorehouse—well, Poardus is desperate for her. He's old, wrinkled, toothless, bald, and disgusting. So the poor guy visits all the street corners of the city, unable to stay in one place. Obviously, Poardus cares a great deal for the commonwealth.

## 66.

*Ad Candidam*

Es quoties vicina mihi, tunc aestuo totus,
    Ut cum sulphureis ignibus Aetna fremit.
A te discessi quoties, tunc frigeo totus,
    Ut cum Caucaseus sub nive anhelat apex.
Ergo fas alium te, Candida, dicere solem,         5
    Utpote quae facias aestum, hyememque mihi.

## 67.

*De eadem*

Nuper Candidulam meam salutans,
Salve, inquam, mea mens, mei et lepores,
Corculumque meum. Illa tunc disertam
Cum sese cuperet mihi probare,
Salve, inquit, mea mentula. o disertam         5
Et docto bene feminam cerebro!
Nam si dicere corculum solemus,
Cur non dicere mentulam licebit?

## 68.

*De eadem*

Dicite cur arcum, vates, tribuistis Amori,
    Exiguus non est aptus ad arma puer.
Nempe supercilii nobis sic forma notata est,
    Saepe quod hinc primus concilietur amor.
Ergo mirari nunc desino, Candida, cur te         5
    Depeream, sensi tela supercilii.
Dii facite, ut postquam laesit nil tale merentem,
    Tandem etiam telum sentiat esse mihi.

## 66.

### *Candida*

As often as you are near me, I become hot all over, as hot as Aetna when it rumbles with its sulfuric fires. As often as I am away from you, I shiver with cold, like Caucasus's peak when it is choked with snow. Therefore, I should call you another sun, Candida, since you bring summer and winter to me.

## 67.

### *The Same*

Recently, when greeting my little Candida, I said, "Hello, my pet, my joy, my pussy cat." She, then, trying to show how clever she is, said, "Hello, my wiener dog!" What a witty woman! She really has a sharp head on her shoulders! If we men can say "pussy cat," why can't the girls say "wiener dog"?

## 68.

### *The Same*

Tell us why, poets, you make the bow an attribute of Cupid, a tiny child not suited to weapons. I've noticed that the eyebrow has a similar shape, because, I suppose, this often ignites the first spark of love. So I no longer wonder, Candida, why I am desperate for you—I felt the shafts of your eyebrow. Gods, make it so that, after wounding an innocent man, she will come to realize that I have a shaft too.

## 69.

*Ad Cloridem, quum falso nunciatum esset, Macutum Pomponium in Alpibus occubuisse*

Amabo Chloris, o Chloris Macuto
Sic dilecta meo, velut Catullo
Quondam Lesbia, sic Macuto amata,
Nasoni veluti fuit Corinna,
Si demas animum parum pudicum.            5
Amabo Chloris, o Chloris Macuti
Magnae delitiae, attamen pudicae.
Iube ad te veniam ipse lacrymatum,
Adferam tibi quicquid undiquaque
Latet tristiae atque taediorum,            10
Moerorisque, molestiaeque, curae,
Aegritudinis, infacetiarum:
Nam noster periit Macutus ille,
Amatus pariter mihi, tibique.
Fleatur pariter mihi, tibique.            15
Fleamus Chloris, o Chloris fleamus,
Tam dure graviterque, ut et nepotum
Audire has lacrymas queant nepotes:
Tam largumque oculis pluamus imbrem,
Ut communibus obruamus undis            20
Alpes, Italiamque ter scelestam,
Quae meum mihi sustulit Macutum,
Et tuum tibi sustulit Macutum.

## 69.

*To Cloris, When We Heard a False Rumor that Macutus Pomponius
Died in the Alps*

Please, Cloris, O Cloris, get rid of that mock-modest attitude: my friend
Macutus cherished you as Catullus once cherished Lesbia, and loved you
as Ovid loved Corinna. Please, Cloris, O Cloris, great, though modest,
delight of Macutus. Bid me come to you to weep, to bring to you any
gloom and disgust from wherever it lurks, sadness and trouble, care and
sickness, even coarse jokes. For our friend Macutus has perished, whom
we both loved and now weep together. Let us weep, Cloris, O Cloris,
let us weep, so long and hard that even our children's children can hear.
Let us produce such a torrent of rain from our eyes that together we
flood the Alps and Italy, three times accursed, that took away my Macu-
tus from me, and yours from you.

## 70.

*Ad Fibulam Candidae*

Quaeso fibulula illa, fibula illa,
Quae pectus dominae meae coerces,
Quae sinum niveum, measque flammas,
Illos quae globulos duos rubentes
Intra caeca iubes manere claustra,                    5
Quaeso fibula, ne mihi misello,
Istis ne miseris meis ocellis
Thesaurum hunc niveum invidere pergas:
Nam quid commeruisse, quid patrasse
Pectus hoc niveum, sinusque candens,                 10
Dignum carcere, vinculisque possit?
Non cernis, rogo, non vides, ut illae
Mammae, isti globuli duo laborent
Luctantes avide, suoque pulsu
Testentur, sibi non placere claustra?                15
Non times, rogo, fibula ista, ne nix
Liquatur, nimio calore cocta?
Pergis, fibula? pergis innocentes
Intra vincula continere mammas?
Meas divitias, opes, talenta                          20
Non vis reddere, fibula? at iubebit
Hoc tandem Venus ipsa: quippe et illam
Ausa es, pessima, vulnerare nuper,
Cum Martem cuperet suaviari.
Haec illa est Cytheraea, quae iubebit                 25
Thesaurum hunc oculis meis patere,
Thesaurum hunc manibus meis patere,
Quem nunc invidia premente, celas:
Tunc tu, fibulula illa, fibula illa,
Quae pectus dominae meae negabis,                    30
Ipsis sordida sordibus tegeris.

## 70.

### *Candida's Button*

Please, button, dear little button, that fastens up my lady's bosom, her snowy-white breasts, the flames of my desire; that bids her two red nipples to stay within their hidden confines; please, button, don't continue to begrudge wretched me and my pitiful eyes a glimpse of this snowy-white treasure. For what crime could this snowy-white bosom have committed, or what have these fair breasts done to merit prison and chains? Tell me now, don't you realize, don't you see that these breasts and those two nipples are struggling to free themselves and declaring by their own heaving that they despise these confines? Tell me, button, don't you fear that the snow might melt from the excessive heat? Are you standing your ground, button? Are you continuing to confine these innocent breasts in chains? Don't you want to return my gold and wealth and treasures, button? But in the end Venus herself will demand this. In fact, you dared to wound even her recently, wicked button, when she wanted to kiss Mars. Yes, Venus herself will bid you to expose this treasure to my eyes, to expose it to my hands, though your envy compels you to conceal it. Then you, button, puny little button, you filthy fellow, who used to deny me my lady's bosom, you will end up in the filthy garbage.

# 71.

## *Ad Candidam*

Ergo desinitis micare ocelli?
Ergo desinitis tumere, mammae?
Ista quis vetuit rubere labra?
Quis istas vetuit genas rubere?
Ubi illae faculae duae micantes?                                5
Ille ubi tumor est papillularum?
Ubi purpura, quae genis sedebat?
Illa ubi rosa, quae labris nitebat?
Febris pessima, sanguisuga febris
Tibi haec, Candida, sustulit, mihique:                          10
Sic ut, Candida quae prius fuisti,
Iure Pallida debeas vocari.
    At vos, o Medici! quibus tuendos
Nos dat Iuppiter, otiosus ut sit,
Ferte pharmaca, quotquot undiquaque                             15
Mos est transvehere ultimis ab oris:
Ferte pixidas omnium universas,
Ferte emplastica, ferte potiones,
Clysteresque, bolosque, cum trochiscis,
Butyrumque, oleumque, mella, fungos,                            20
Gummi, lac, adipesque, cassiamque:
Nec desit crocus, et fragrans amomum:
Adsint thura, rosaeque, cinnamomumque,
Adsit denique quicquid aut colorem
Amissum dabit, aut dabit cruorem.                               25
Quod si quaeritis istius laboris
Vobis praemia quae futura, dicam:
Primum haec gloria, lausque magna vobis
Erit, pharmaca dum admovetis uni,
Conservasse duos, medendo et uni,                               30
Vitam restituisse sic duobus.
Mille praeterea dabo phaleucos,
Dabo mille elegosque iambicosque:
Ut vos, qui miseros duos amantes
Mortis eripuistis e barathro,                                   35
Vivatis pariter labore amantum.

### 71.

*Candida*

So, do you cease to sparkle, eyes? Do you cease to swell, breasts? Who told those lips no longer to be red? Who told those cheeks to stop blushing? Where are those two sparkling eyes? Where is that swelling of the breasts, the blushing in the cheeks? Where is the rose that was glistening on the lips? A cruel fever, a blood-sucking fever, has stolen these from you and me, Candida. As it stands, you, who were once Candida, now ought to be called Pallida.

But you, doctors, to whom Jupiter has entrusted our care (lest he be bothered with such details), bring drugs, as many as are usually brought from all the ends of the earth. Bring all the medicine chests available, bring plasters, bring drinks, and lotions, pills, butter, oil, honey, mushrooms, gums, milk, grease, and cassia. And don't neglect to bring saffron and fragrant amomon, or incense, roses, cinnamon, or whatever will restore her lost color or strengthen her blood.

But if you want to know what will be your reward for your effort, I will tell you. First, you will have great glory and praise, that while you apply drugs to one, you save two, and by curing one, you restore two to life. Besides, I will dedicate to you a thousand phalaecians, a thousand elegies and as many iambs, so you, who snatched two lovers from the jaws of death, might live in return by the lovers' toil. Each one of you

Rubris basia Candidae a labellis,
Genis basia Candidae a rubellis,
Ferent singula singuli, ut ruboris
Arte vestra operaque restituti                              40
Ipsi commoda prima sentiatis.
Vos primi tumidis manus papillis
Admovebitis, huius ut tumoris
Arte vestra, operaque restituti.
Ipsi commoda prima sentiatis.                              45
Quod si forte oculis frui velitis,
Permitto id quoque: Sed cavete, quaeso,
Ne vos flammea lumina ista fallant:
Namque in his habitant Venusque, Amorque,
Et tela hinc iaciunt Venusque, Amorque:                    50
Nonne praemia digna, digna merces?
    Ergo, Candida, nunc relinque luctus,
Et missas face lacrymationes.
Namque haec omnia, quae perisse credis,
Certe non periere, sed peregre                             55
Profecta, incipient brevi reverti.
Certe restitui cito videbis
Labellis, oculis, genis, papillis,
Rosas, lumina, purpuram, tumorem.

## 72.

### *In Ligurinum*

Aedilis ille, Ligurine, qui tua
Repertus a te nudus est cum coniuge,
Nil hercle fecit praeter officium suum,
Qui evincere a te rem voluerit publicam.

will receive a single kiss from the red lips of Candida, a single kiss from her little red cheeks, so you yourselves may reap the first fruits of the redness restored by your skill and work. You first will put your hands on her swollen nipples, so you yourselves may reap the first fruits of the swelling restored by your skill and work. But if you wish by chance to enjoy her eyes, I allow that also. But be careful, please, do not let those burning eyes deceive you, for there live Venus and Cupid, whence they shoot their arrows. Isn't this payment a worthy reward?

Therefore, Candida, stop your grieving now, and dry the flow of tears from your eyes. For all these things, which you believe have perished, surely have not, but having gone abroad, will begin to return shortly. Surely you will see restored quickly the rose to your lips, the lights to your eyes, the redness to your cheeks, and the swelling to your breasts.

## 72.

### *Ligurinus*

That official, Ligurinus, whom you discovered naked with your wife, wasn't doing anything, I swear, except his civic duty: He wanted to evict you from public property.

## 73.

### *Ad Pedem Candidae*

O pes, quem geminae premunt columnae,
Illae, inquam, geminae premunt columnae,
Quarum ex arbitrio quiescit illa,
Quarum ex arbitrio movetur illa,
Illa Candida, cuius intra ocellos,                                      5
Illa Candida, cuius in papillis
Omnes delitiae latent Bezaei.
   O pes candide Candidae, o tenelle
Mi pes, dic mihi, o tenelle mi pes,
Qui meam mihi Candidam adferebas,                                       10
Cur meam mihi Candidam abstulisti?
At saltem decuit profectionem
Nunciare mihi, ut velut experirer
An possem precibus fugam morari,
Vel tibi comes esset hic meus pes.                                      15
O fur pessime, quid tibi imprecabor?
An nodosa tibi ut podagra cunctos
Vexet articulos? an ut molestus
Sic scrupus premat, ut libido nunquam
Ulla te capiat profectionis?                                            20
At dolere nequis, sceleste, solus:
Nullos ergo tibi imprecor dolores,
Non peto quadruplum, (licet teneri,
Ut fur, hac merito actione possis)
Hoc unum peto, quod mihi abstulisti.                                    25
Redde me mihi, quaeso, redde, mi pes:
Mi pes, redde mihi meos amores.
Emam mille tibi, hercle, margaritas,
Smaragdos totidem, ut superbus istis
Eas divitiis: dabo phaleucos                                            30
Qui te in astra ferant, ubi sublimis
Inter sidereos micabis ignes.
Sin minus, (nec enim genus relictum
Vindictae est aliud) tibi nec unum
Pedem, o pes, dederint meae Camoenae.                                   35

## 73.

*Candida's Foot*

Listen, foot, yes, you, the one who supports my girlfriend's legs, and decides her comings and goings, foot of my girl Candida, within whose eyes and breasts lie all Bèze's secret delights. O candid-white foot of Candida, O my tender foot, speak to me, you who used to carry my Candida to me; why have you taken her away from me? But you should have at least announced your departure to me, so I could try to delay your flight by begging, or see whether my own foot might be your companion. O wretched thief, what shall I invoke upon you? That a knotty gout should vex all your joints? Or that a sharp stone should annoy you so much, that you will loathe the thought of leaving? But, accursed foot, you are unable to suffer alone; therefore, I will invoke no hardships upon you, nor do I seek fourfold compensation from you (although you could, as a thief, be held bound by such a claim). I only want what you took away from me. Please, please, dear foot, restore my life to me, I beg of you, return my sweetheart to me. I will buy a thousand pearls for you, I swear, and just as many emeralds, so you can sashay in style. I will give you hendecasyllabics, which will carry you up to the stars, where you will twinkle sublime among the starry fires. But if you don't bring my Candida back to me (for there is no other kind of vindication left), my Muses will not give one foot to you, O foot.

## 74.

### *Ad quandam*

Qualis pruna sinus contingit saepe gemella,
    Qualis Apellaea linea ducta manu,
Tale tibi quiddam levem discriminat alvum,
    Tale tibi quiddam iungit utrumque femur.
Immo, fallor ego: nam nulla hic linea prorsus,        5
    Inque utero pars est nulla pudenda tuo.
Aurea quanam igitur descendunt parte fluenta?
    Languidulus quanam parte quiescit amor?
Haereo, si qua tamen tibi rimula, rimula si qua est,
    Rimula (dispeream) ni monogramma tua est.        10

## 75.

### *In Gelliam*

Moechos dicere quos solemus, illos
Mavult Gellia filios vocare:
Nec id iudicio meo imperite.
Nam si dicere filios suerunt
Matres, quos aliquot tulere menses:        5
Quos decem minimum tulit per annos,
Quidni Gellia filios vocabit?

## 74.

### To a Certain Girl

Something like the fold twin plums often make, something like the lines drawn by Apelles's hand, some such thing divides your smooth lower belly and joins each thigh. No, excuse me, there's no line at all here, and on your lower belly there is no privy part. Where then descend the golden streams? Wherein does languid love take its rest? I am perplexed: yet if you have some little crack, any little crack at all, I'll be damned, if your little crack is more than a trace.

## 75.

### Gellia

Those whom we usually call adulterers, Gellia prefers to call "sons." In my opinion, that makes good sense. For if mothers have gotten in the habit of calling those whom they have borne several months "sons," why shouldn't Gellia call those whom she has borne for at least ten years "sons"?

### 76.

#### *Ad Candidam*

Cum nos, Candida, mutuis favillis,
Communique velut calore cocti,
Vitam una peragamus innocentem,
Ut cum turture turturilla casto:
Qui fit innocuos ut hos amores                              5
Tot doli exagitent calumniarum?
Haec est scilicet omnibus statuta
Lex mortalibus, ut perenne nil sit
Quod gratum: et vicibus suis recurrant
Voluptasque, dolorque, pax, et ira.                        10
Ergo haec, Candida, fortiter feramus,
Nos, inquam, quibus haec statuta lex est.
Ille autem deus, ille qui favillas
Nostro in pectore primus excitavit,
Nec perire potest, nec hos fovere                          15
Ullo tempore desinet calores.
Premetur, scio, flamma nostra, quid tum?
Tanto fervidior futurus ignis.


### 77.

#### *In Aulam*

Quid saevum damnare Iovem, magnaeque Dianae
    Numina tot precibus sollicitare iuvat?
Scilicet incusas sterilis commercia lecti,
    Et tumidi velles cernere ventris onus.
Erras si sterilem te credis: quippe tulisse               5
    Ut pueros nequeas, at potes, Aula, viros.

## 76.

### *Candida*

When we, warmed with our mutual embers, as it were, and by our common flame, spend our innocent life together, like a little turtledove with her faithful mate, how does it happen that so many deceitful slanders harass our harmless love? Doubtless this law has been established for all mortals, that nothing good lasts forever: pleasure or grief, calmness or anger all take their turns with us. So let us bear these things bravely, Candida, since this is the established law. But that god, the one who first stirred up these embers in our heart, cannot perish, nor can he ever stop stoking the fires of love. Our flame will be quenched, I know: what then? That much hotter will the fire burn in the future.

## 77.

### *Aula*

What good does it do to curse Jupiter for being cruel and vex great Diana's divine spirit with so many prayers? I realize that you blame them for your infertile sexual unions, and you would like to see your womb pregnant with a baby. You are wrong, though, if you think that you are sterile: Even though you cannot bear boys, Aula, you can bear men.

### 78.

*Ad Candidam ex ictero convalescentem*

Vidit te nuper Venus, o mea Candida, vidit,
    Inviditque tibi mox inimica Venus.
Et se questa Deam mortali a corpore vinci,
    Binas vicisset quae tamen una deas,
Crudelis tandem nati crudelia poscit                                    5
    Tela; neget matri tela rogatus Amor?
Arma parat, cornu stridens volat acta sagitta,
    Nec tamen haec iussum missa cucurrit iter.
Nam simul ac frontis divinum aspexit honorem,
    Cuspis in obliquum coepit abire latus.                          10
Ergo servata es, sed non tamen unica, quippe
    Est iaculatori sic quoque parta salus:
Quem simul ac vultu spectasses laesa minaci,
    Aut nimis, aut esses acriter ulta satis.

### 79.

*Ad Gillium*

Hoc te nomine praedicas beatum,
Gilli, quod facili fruare amica
Et benigna adeo, ut rogata nondum,
Mox supina cadat, pedesque tollat:
Sed erras nimium, miselle Gilli:                                        5
Nam quae nil penitus negare nescit,
Opus, non homines, amat puella:
Et quaecunque nimis cadit libenter,
Surgit ista nimis quoque illibenter.

## 78.

### *Candida, Recovering from Jaundice*

Venus recently saw you, my Candida, she saw you and that spiteful goddess immediately envied you. And she complained that she, a goddess, is surpassed in beauty by a mortal, although she had surpassed two goddesses in beauty herself. In her cruelty then she asked for the cruel arrows of her son. Will Cupid deny his arrows to his mother when asked? She takes aim, and a screeching arrow hurls forth from the bow, but does not fly the intended path. For as soon as it spied the divine beauty of your face, the point began to swerve off to the side. Thus, you were saved, but you were not the only one; she who shot the arrow in the first place was also saved. Had you been wounded and glared at her with a mean look, you would have avenged yourself enough or, better yet, more than enough.

## 79.

### *Gillius*

You proclaim that you are happy, Gillius, because you enjoy an easy girl, who is so kind that, before she is even asked, she lies on her back and spreads her legs. But you are very wrong, poor Gillius: for the girl who can't say "no" to anything loves the act, not the individual; and she who is too eager to lie down, will be very reluctant to get up.

### 80.

#### *Ad Candidam*

Formosas videam cum, Candida, saepe puellas,
  Saepe mea est, fateor, sollicitata Venus.
Sed tua, vel peream, castum me reddit imago,
  Et quamvis cupiam, Candida, nolo tamen.

### 81.

#### *Ad eandem*

Cum te nunc dicat populosa Lutetia civem,
  Inter me numeres, Hedua terra, tuos,
Cum nos tam longum disiunxerit intervallum,
  (O Martis semper damna timenda feri!)
Quaeris an absentem te, Candida, saepe requiram:                5
  Non ego te quaero, Candida, sed video.
Ipse licet terris involvat Iuppiter astra,
  Absit ut unquam absit, Candida, quisquis amat.

### 82.

#### *Ad eandem*

Attonitos inter populos cum Caesaris esset
  Absentis praesens nuper ubique metus,
Saturnique sequens propius vestigia Mavors,
  Iras in toto promeret orbe suas,
Concordes soli, mea Candida, viximus ambo,                     5
  Nec fuit hic ulla lite diremptus amor.
Fallor, an idcirco Martis tibi saeva pepercit
  Ira, quod es Marti, Candida, visa Venus?

## 80.

### Candida

Whenever I see beautiful girls, Candida, often—I admit it—I am turned on. But the thought of your beauty keeps me faithful, on my life I swear it. And although I desire them, Candida, I don't want them.

## 81.

### The Same

Since bustling Paris calls you a citizen now, since you count me among your citizens, Burgundy; since so long a distance separates us (we always have to fear the treachery of ruthless Mars!), you ask whether I often miss you in your absence. I do not miss you, Candida, I see you. Although Jupiter himself should envelop the stars with the earth, away with the thought, Candida, that those who love might ever be absent!

## 82.

### The Same

Recently, when chaos and panic were sweeping over the people in the city with Caesar outside the walls, and Mars, following closely the course of Saturn, was unleashing his wrath on the whole world, only the two of us lived in peaceful harmony, my Candida, and no quarrel disturbed our love. Am I wrong, or did the cruel wrath of Mars spare you, Candida, because Mars took you for Venus?

### 83.

*Ad eandem*

Esse quid hoc dicam, quoties sum, Candida, tecum,
    Cur faveat pigro nullus Apollo mihi?
Discessi quoties, caleam tunc pectore toto,
    Et numeris currant singula verba suis.
Nimirum totos exposcis, Phoebe, poetas:        5
    Sed totum praesens me mea flamma tenet.

### 84.

*Ad Sequanam, de eadem Candida*

Ecce iterum navem praegnans conscendit amica!
    Et dominam, et dominae, Sequana, perfer onus:
Perfer, ut incolumes ambo sua littora tangant,
    Sive utero lateat femina, sive puer.
Sic et Yona tibi, et concedat Matrona nomen,        5
    Et victis Isarae sic dominere vadis.
Fallor, an in dominam video saevire procellas?
    O res plena malae suspicionis amor!
Mergas, si libeat, nostras, o Sequana, flammas,
    Mersa tamen mediis flamma resurget aquis.        10

## 83.

### *The Same*

How can I explain it, Candida, why, as often as I am with you, I feel sluggish and Apollo gives me no inspiration? Yet, whenever we are separated, my whole heart is inflamed, and each word hastens to its right place in the verse. Without a doubt, you demand poets whole, Phoebus, but when my flame is present it is she who possesses the whole of me.

## 84.

### *To the Seine, on the Same Candida*

Look! Again my pregnant girlfriend boards a ship! Convey her, Seine, along with the unborn child. Convey them, so that both may reach their destination, be it a girl or a boy hidden in her womb. So, let the Yonne and Marne yield their name to you, and may you rule victoriously on the shores of Isara. Am I wrong, or do I see gale winds raging against my lady? O love—a thing full of evil suspicion! You may drown my flames, Seine, if that is what you want, but the flame you drown will rise again from the midst of the water.

## 85.

*Ad eandem Candidam*

Ex quo diiuncti, mea Candida, viximus ambo,
    Nec tua luminibus sidera visa meis,
Hora diem, mensemque dies, annumque moratus
    Mensis, iam canos pene dedere mihi.
At simul ac nobis iterum reddemur uterque,                    5
    Teque mea potiar, meque fruere tuo:
Hora die, Lunaque dies numerabitur una,
    Quique aliis annus, vix mihi mensis erit.
Sic tempus praerepta mihi mea tempora reddat,
    Haec eadem ut reddam, Candida cara, tibi.                 10

## 86.

*In Andraeam Tiraquellum, Senatorem Parisium, alterum nostri secli*
*Varronem*

Est tibi natorum quae computat agmina coniux,
    Est tibi quae natos bibliotheca parit.
Fortunate senex! te nulla oblivia mortis,
    Te nunquam totum tollet avara dies.
Namque alia ex illis mox est ventura propago,                5
    Ex his est pridem gloria nata tibi.
Ut vero pereant illi, illorumque nepotes,
    Haec tamen incolumis cum patre neptis erit.

---

3     oblivia *1569, 1576* oblivio *1548*

## 85.

### *To the Same Candida*

Since we have lived separately from each other, my Candida, and my eyes no longer see your stars, the hour has lingered for a day, the day for a month, the month for a year, and already time has given me white hairs. But as soon as we are restored to each other, I will possess you as mine, and you will enjoy me as yours. Then the hour will be reckoned by the day, the day by the cycles of the moon, and what is a year to others, will hardly seem a month to me. Thus let time return to me what it stole, so that I may return the same to you, my dear Candida.

## 86.

### *Andreas Tiraqueau, Senator of Paris, a Second Varro of Our Time*

You have a wife who can count an army of children for you, and you have a library that bears you children. Lucky old man! No oblivion of death nor greedy time will ever erase your memory completely. For your children will soon have children, and your books have long since provided you with glory. But although one day your children will perish, and then your grandchildren, still this glory will be an offspring safe with his father.

## 87.

### *In Spurinnam*

Tollendae cupidus Spurinna prolis
Altae dum superat iugum Pyrenes,
Divo porrigat ut preces Iacobo,
Inde Alpes quoque praeterit nivosas,
Petri ut limina visat atque Pauli:                    5
Et mox Hadriacum in sinum reflexus
Laureti attonitus deam precatur:
Inde per medii maris pericla
Sacram perveniens ad usque Idumen,
Sacratum Domini petit sepulchrum.                    10
Nec contentus adhuc, latrocinantum
Arenas Arabum siticulosas
Gibbo permeat insidens cameli,
Sublimem properans ad usque Sinam,
Et divae iuga sacra Catharinae.                      15
Quid profecerit hoc labore quaeris?
Tres natos reperit domum reversus.

---

Tit.    In Tolenonem *1597*
1      Toleno *1597*
4      transilit *1597*
7      Laureti attonitus deam precatur *1569, 1576, 1597* Divae offert sua vota Lauretanae *1548*

## 87.

*Spurinna*

Since Spurinna desires to rear children, he climbs the summit of the high Pyrenees to offer his prayers to Saint James, then from there passes over the snowy Alps to visit the shrines of Peter and Paul: and soon having doubled back into the Adriatic Sea, with fear and trembling he prays to the lady of Loreto. Then passing through dangers on the deep sea, and arriving at holy Palestine, he heads for the holy sepulchre of our Lord. Still not satisfied, he traverses the dry sands of Arabia, land of thieves, on the hump of a camel, hastening his way to the lofty Sinai, and the sacred summit of Saint Catherine. What was the result of all this effort and determination, you ask? He found three children when he returned home.

## 88.

### *Callartio Iurisconsulto*

En senos tibi mitto pippiones,
Ruris munera rusticana nostri:
Nostri non penitus tamen, sed olim
Futuri, nisi forte me fefellit
Patronus, mea iura qui tuetur,       5
Iura tanta quidem, ut nec his ferendis
Terga sufficiant onusta muli:
Hos ergo tibi mitto pippiones,
Obtestorque simul deos deasque,
Ut senis tibi messibus peractis,       10
Fas sit ex lepida tua puella
Tot natos numerare vagientes,
Quot foetus tibi mitto pippientes.

---

9      Obtestorque Deum simul beato *1597*
11     coniuge de tua pudica *1597*

## 88.

### *Callartius, the Jurisconsult*

Look, I am sending to you six piping squabs, simple presents from my country estate: well, not really from my country estate, but from my future country estate, unless perhaps my advocate has misled me. He is defending my rights, you see, such considerable rights in fact that not even the loaded back of a mule would suffice to carry them. Therefore, I send to you these little chirpers, and at the same time I implore the gods and goddesses to grant to you in six years six wailing infants from your tender girl to match the number of these piping squabs.

## 89.

*In basium Candidae*

Vos, teneri rores, calathos quibus aurea gaudet
    Venus rosarum aspergere:
Te cannis incluse liquor, qui dulcia condis
    Mensis secundis fercula:
Et vos, deliciae patrum, coelestia mella,           5
    Testes apum solertiae:
Vos ego, vel vobis quicquam si dulcius usquam est,
    Et suxi, et hausi, et imbibi,
Hesterna felix nuper cum nocte putarem
    Me basiare Candidam.           10
Vos etenim pariter spretis cannisque, rosisque,
    Et alvearium favis,
Intra verna meae constat sedisse labella
    Tenellulae puellulae.
Hei mihi! quis nobis hos somnos interrupit?       15
    Quis gaudii tantum abstulit?
Ah! Venus, haec postquam prohibes me carpere vera,
    At somniare me sinas!

## 89.

### *Candida's Kiss*

With you, tender dewdrops, golden Venus fancies sprinkling her baskets of roses; you, sugarcane, provide us with sweet dishes for dessert; you, divine honey, our fathers relished, a testament to the industry of the bees; I sucked, quaffed, imbibed you (or whatever may be sweeter than you), while last night I smiled and dreamt I was kissing Candida. Everyone knows that you've spurned the roses, canes, and honeycombs and have found a new home within the tiny lip-blossoms of my tender little girl. Oh no! Who interrupted my dream? Who stole away this splendid fantasy? Ah Venus! Since you prevent me from enjoying these pleasures for real, at least let me dream them.

## 90.

*Theodorus Beza, de sua in Candidam et Audebertum benevolentia*

Abest Candida, Beza, quid moraris?
Audebertus abest, quid hic moraris?
Tenent Parisii tuos amores,
Habent Aurelii tuos lepores,
Et tu Vezeliis manere pergis,                                    5
Procul Candidulaque, amoribusque,
Aut leporibus, Audebertuloque?
    Immo, Vezelii, procul valete,
Et vale, pater, et valete, fratres:
Namque Vezeliis carere possum,                                  10
Et carere parente, et his, et illis,
At non Candidula, Audebertuloque.
Sed utrum, rogo, praeferam duorum?
Utrum invisere me decet priorem?
An quenquam tibi, Candida, anteponam?                           15
An quenquam anteferam tibi, Audeberte?
Quid si me in geminas secem ipse partes,
Harum ut altera Candidam revisat,
Currat altera versus Audebertum?
    At est Candida sic avara, novi,                           20
Ut totum cupiat tenere Bezam:
Sic Bezae est cupidus sui Audebertus,
Beza ut gestiat integro potiri:
Amplector quoque sic et hunc et illam,
Ut totus cupiam videre utrumque,                               25
Integrisque frui integer duobus.
Praeferre attamen alterum necesse est.
O duram nimium necessitatem!
    Sed postquam tamen alterum necesse est,
Priores tibi defero, Audeberte:                                30
Quod si Candida forte conqueratur:
Quid tum? basiolo tacebit imo.

## 90.

*Théodore de Bèze's Two Favorites, Candida and Audebert*

Candida is gone, Bèze, why do you tarry? Audebert is gone, why do you stay here? Paris holds your love, Orléans your darling, and you continue to hang around Vézelay, far from your little Candida, your love, and your darling boy, little Audebert?

Well, farewell, Vézelay, and so long, father, goodbye, brothers, for I can do without Vézelay, without my father, or these sundry people, but not without my little Candida or Audebert. But which of the two do I prefer? Whom should I visit first? Shall I favor anyone above you, Candida? Or shall I choose anyone before you, Audebert? What if I were cut in two, so one part could visit Candida, while the other runs off to see Audebert?

But Candida is so possessive, I know, and would want to hold all of Bèze. And Audebert is so fond of Bèze, that he would insist on possessing all of him. And I cherish both of them so much that I would want to be whole when I see them, and complete to enjoy them completely. But I have to choose—what a hard decision this is!

But since I have to choose one or the other, I pick you, Audebert, because should Candida complain, I can always quiet her with a deep kiss.

### 91.

*Ponticus Cornelio, de uxore non ducenda*

Cum velis uxorem, Corneli, ducere: quaero
    Coniugium placeat qua ratione tibi?
Scilicet ut deinceps vivas foelicior: atqui
    Fallor ego, aut non hac lege beatus eris.
Uxor enim aut deformis erit, (tune, obsecro, talis          5
    Si tibi sit coniunx iuncta, beatus eris?)
Aut forma mediocris erit: modus iste, fatemur,
    Optimus, at subito deperit iste modus.
Aut formosa, ideoque viris obnoxia mille,
    Et de qua nequeas dicere, tota mea est.          10
Ut sit casta tamen, (nemo si forte rogarit),
    Mille feret natos, taedia mille feret.
Aut sterilis tecum tardos sic exiget annos,
    Nullus ut e multis sit sine lite dies.
His addas caput indomitum, mentemque tenacem,          15
    Caeteraque a multis quae didicisse potes.
Desine sic igitur vitam sperare beatam,
    Sic potius celebs et sine lite torus
Hic etenim si qua est felicis semita vitae,
    Femineas iuxta non latet illa nates.          20

## 91.

*Ponticus to Cornelius: Avoid Marriage!*

Since you want to marry a wife, Cornelius, I ask you, what is it about marriage that attracts you? You say that it will add happiness to your life. Now, maybe I'm wrong, but I don't think this will bring you happiness. Either your wife will be ugly (be serious, will you ever be happy married to a dog?), or she'll be average-looking: moderate beauty is best, I admit, but it fades quickly. Or she'll be beautiful, bound to a thousand men, and you could never say that she is wholly yours. But even if she's faithful to you (let's suppose for a moment no one flirts with her), she will bear a thousand children, and with them a thousand ills. Or infertile she will wind out the slow days with you, quarreling all the way. Be assured that on top of all this she'll be stubborn-headed, dogged in her intents, and other things—just ask anybody who's married. So, stop hoping for a happy life; instead, let your bed stay celibate and free from rancor. The path to happiness, if it exists at all, does not lie between a woman's legs.

## 92.

### *Cornelius Pontico, de uxore ducenda*

Uxorem cupiam quum ducere, Pontice, quaeris
    Coniugium placeat qua ratione mihi?
Deformem nolo, formosam exopto: placebit,
    Si nequeo pulchram, quae mediocris erit.
Formosam, dices, alii mox mille rogabunt,           5
    At nulli, quamvis saepe rogata, dabit.
Forma perit subito mediocris: id ille queratur,
    Qui praeter formam nil muliebre probat.
Si dederit natos, natos spectare iuvabit:
    Si sterilis, quid tum? sarcina nostra levis.         10
Caetera, quae narras, certe sunt magna, fatemur,
    Est animusque tenax, indomitumque caput.
Sed sua sunt cunctis connata incommoda rebus,
    Ipsa etiam damnis commoda plena vides.
Et me miraris vitam sperare beatam,           15
    Si mihi sit deinceps femina facta comes?
Semita virtutis stricta est, si vera loquuntur.
    Haec quoque quam quaero, Pontice, stricta via est.

## 93.

### *De Phillide et Damone*

Bis senas hyemes accensus Phillide Damon
    Pertuleratque faces, pertuleratque gelu.
Quam tamen ut vidit crudeli funere raptam,
    Attonitus fertur conticuisse diu:
Et tandem lingua singultibus interrupta,          5
    Dixisse haec multis paucula cum lacrymis:
Felix, Damon, eras, hac si tibi fata dedissent
    Vivere vel viva, vel moriente mori.
Dixit, semianimisque cadens perfecit, ut ambo
    Corpora sint uno pene cremata rogo.          10

## 92.

*Cornelius to Ponticus: Marrying a Wife*

Since I'm thinking about getting married, Ponticus, you ask what is it about marriage that attracts me. Mind you, I don't want an ugly wife, I'm hoping for a beautiful one: still, I'll be happy to have an average-looking one, if I can't find a good-looking one. But you'll say that soon a thousand other men will proposition her if she's beautiful. Let them; I'm confident she'll remain faithful to me. "Average looks fade quickly," you say. That's the complaint of the guy who focuses only on a woman's looks. If she bears children, they will be a joy to look upon; and so what if she's infertile? That just means our luggage will be lighter. The other things you tell of certainly are worth thinking about, I admit. It's true that a woman can be dogged and stubborn-headed. But everything is born with its defects, and you see that even good things have thorns. So, you're amazed that I expect a happy life by taking on a woman as a companion? "The path of virtue," so the saying goes, "is narrow." Yes, Ponticus, that's the path I'm looking for: the straight and narrow one.

## 93.

*Phillis and Damon*

For a dozen winters Damon was passionate for Phillis, and he had endured scorching heat for her, he had endured bitter cold. But when he learned that cruel death had taken her away, he was dumbstruck, and the story is that he remained silent for a long time. Finally, barely able to talk for the sobbing, he said these few words as tears rolled down: "You would have been happy, Damon, if the fates had allowed you to live while she lived, or to die when she died." With that he fell down unconscious and died. And so it happened that on one pyre—or nearly so—both bodies were cremated.

## 94.

*In Italiam*

Cur Italas urbes Phoebus torrentior urat,
　　Si quaeras fieri qua ratione putem:
Nec, vicina magis quia Phoebi semita, dicam,
　　Dicere nec mendax quae solet astrologus.
Verum aliud dicam, quod si vis teste probari,　　　　　5
　　Hoc tibi vel gemino teste probare licet.
Nulla magis tellus pulchris fecunda puellis,
　　Italia nulla est terra beata magis.
Hi sunt nimirum, quos Phoebus dum videt, ignes,
　　Credibile est ignes multiplicare suos.　　　　　　10

## 94.

*Italy*

If you ask me why I think Phoebus blazes more hotly on Italian cities, I will not say it's because Phoebus's paths are closer, or say anything like a lying astrologer usually says. But I will say something else, and if you want some sort of verification, I can give you two: no land produces more beautiful girls, nor is any land more blessed. When Phoebus sees these flames, then, I believe, he intensifies his own.

## 95.

### *De coma Candidae, ad Zephyrum*

Aura nec nimio aestuans calore,
Aura nec nimio rigore frigens,
Sed verno comes ire sueta Phoebo;
Aura frigidula, aura mollicella,
Quae sic lacteolae meae puellae                                    5
Crines aureolosque, crispulosque,
Audax exagitasque, ventilasque;
Ecquid obsecro, dum per universum
Laeta perstrepis et vagaris orbem,
Cernis candidula mea puella                                       10
Tenellum mage delicatulumque?
Sed, quaeso, mihi dic et istud, Aura,
Dum tu sic temere hanc comam pererras,
Cincinnique agis hinc et inde nodos,
Non times, rogo, ne vel hinc vel illinc                          15
Veloci misera impliceris ala?
Nam qui tam tenues tibi capilli,
Quae molles adeo comae videntur,
Non sunt, crede mihi, comae aut capilli,
Sunt plagae potius, quibus scelestus                             20
Irretit miseros Cupido amantes,
Ut tela tenui sagax Arachne
Incautas solet occupare muscas.
Sic me, sic miserum Cupido cepit,
Sic tu, ni caveas, peribis, Aura:                                25
Sed quam suaviter, o dii, peribis!

## 95.

*To the West Wind: A Warning about Candida's Hair*

A breeze not too hot, a breeze not too cold, but one that usually escorts the vernal sun; cool breeze, soft breeze, you who dare to whisk and flutter the golden curls of my milky girl, please tell me, as you whir and wander through the whole world, do you see anything more tender and delicate than my fair-skinned girl? And another question, breeze: while you pass so rashly through her hair, and drive here and there the ringlets of her curly locks, aren't you afraid that you might accidentally entangle your swift wings in the mesh? You think that her hair is fine and soft, but believe me, it is not; it is actually a trap, with which the scoundrel Cupid ensnares poor lovers, just as a clever spider often catches careless flies with its fragile web. So Cupid caught me, poor me, and so will you perish, breeze, unless you are careful: but, my goodness! how sweetly you will perish!

## 96.

### *In quendam, ad Posthumum*

Cincinnatulus ille, cui undulati
Propexique humeros gravant capilli,
Qui tersa cute, blaesulaque voce,
Qui paetis oculis, graduque molli,
Et pictis simulat labris puellam,                    5
Heri, Posthume, nuptias parabat,
Cum nequissimus omnium sacerdos,
Urbanus tamen et facetus hercle,
Utra sponsus foret rogare coepit.

## 97.

### *Comparatio amantis cum venatore*

Dum leporem nuper nemorosa per avia sector,
    Antiquae in mentem mi rediere faces.
Nec mirum, studio quum delectentur eodem,
    Cui Dictynna placet, cui Cytheraea placet.
Ille etenim leporem sectatur, et iste leporem,      5
    Res fugitiva lepus, res fugitiva lepos.
Venator casses, et casses tendit amator,
    Quos saepe incassum tendit uterque tamen.
Ex aequo pluvias et ventos spernit uterque,
    Damnosos nutrit stultus uterque canes.          10
Attamen hoc distant, quod cum fera sternitur, alter
    Praemia solliciti iusta laboris habet.
Tum demum vero infelix superatur amator,
    Cum similis victae praeda supina iacet.

---

96.Tit. In viros, more turpissimo, γυναικοκομῶντας *1597, 1779*
8     ille *pro* hercle *1597*
9     foret *1569, 1576, 1597* erat *1548, 1580, 1779*

## 96.

*To Posthumus, about a Certain Man*

That guy "Curlylocks," with the wavy hair dangling down on his shoulders, with the smooth skin and the lisping voice, who imitates a girl with his leering eyes, his delicate gait, and his lip gloss, was getting ready yesterday to be married, when the naughtiest priest imaginable (but funny and quick-witted, I have to admit!), started off by asking, "Which one of you girls is going to be the groom?"

## 97.

*The Lover and the Hunter*

I was chasing a hare recently through forest trails, when I was reminded of my old flames. It struck me then that those who admire either Diana or Venus find pleasure in the same pursuit. You see, one pursues his hare, the other his "bunny," the hare runs, the "bunny" does too. The hunter sets his traps, the lover lays his snares, yet both often return home empty-handed. Hunter and lover alike despise winds and rains, and both foolishly feed their ferocious hounds. Still, they do differ in one thing, that when they lay low their prey, only the hunter has just rewards for his trouble; the unhappy lover loses the game precisely at the moment when his booty, like a victim, lies on her back.

## 98.

*In nuptias Iani Garneri, et Margaretae Uraniae*

Redde tu mihi, Margareta, redde,
Redde, inquam, mihi, tu puella, Ianum,
Ianum quem violenta surpuisti.
At istis male sit genis rubellis,
Et istis quoque blandulis ocellis,          5
Et vobis quoque vesculae papillae,
Et vobis quoque crispuli capilli,
Meum quae mihi amiculum abstulistis.
Margaretula, tene, tene deinceps
Ianus delicias suas vocabit,          10
Et hunc delicias tuas vocabis?
Totus ergo tibi, puella, Ianus
Deinceps et vigilabit et quiescet?
Et si quando fores adibo Iani,
Non confestim aderit velut solebat,          15
Sed prodibit anus scelesta tandem,
Herum quae procul hinc abesse iuret,
Intus cum foveat suos amores?
At Ianum interea foris requiret
Frustra tota cohors amiculorum,          20
Cum Ianus tamen aut labella bella
Miretur simul et suavietur,
Aut tractet lepidae salax puellae
Audaci teretes manu papillas,
Et quantum quoque distet haec ab illa          25
Forsan discere curiosus optet.
At Iani interea ad fores sedebit
Frustra tota cohors amiculorum,
Cum fruare tuo, puella, Iano,
Et tanquam iocus hic sit insuavis,          30
Lucteris simul, et suavieris,
Mineris simul, atque blandiaris,
Donec deposito furore tandem,
Ianum suxeris, o puella nequam,
Audacemque tamen tuum esse Ianum          35
Voce deficiente conqueraris.

### 98.

*The Marriage of Jean and Marguerite*

Please, Marguerite, please, give back my Jean to me, yes, Jean whom you stole away by force. I curse those ruddy cheeks of yours, your little batting eyes, your tiny breasts, and your curly hair too, for you took away my friend. Will Jean call you "sweetheart," then, little Marguerite, and will you call him "sweetheart"? Will Jean spend every waking and sleeping moment with you, girl? And whenever I come to the door of Jean's house, will he not answer it immediately as he used to, or will a nasty old woman finally appear and swear that her master is gone far away, although he is inside and cuddling with his girlfriend? This prompts his buddies to make a futile search for Jean in town, while Jean either is admiring and kissing his charming girl's beautiful lips, or lustfully fondling her smooth breasts with his presumptuous hand, trying to find out how far apart the two are. Meanwhile, an ensemble of little friends will sit in vain outside Jean's doors, while you, girl, enjoy him as your lover. And, as if this game displeases you, you act reluctant at the same time that you give kisses, and you make threats while you flirt. Then, when you've finally set aside your fury, you will have exhausted Jean, you wretched girl, and still you will complain with failing voice that your lover Jean is audacious. But at least, wicked Marguerite, let's

At saltem, improba Margareta, foedus
Hac tecum liceat ferire lege,
Ianum fas tibi sit, puella, toto
Possidere die: frui in tenebris                40
Mi saltem liceat, puella, Iano.
Fallor, an tibi plus placent tenebrae?
Immo vis pariter diem atque noctem?
Et dat ille tibi diem atque noctem?
Nocte sit tuus ergo, sitque luce,             45
Dum, Iani unius in locum, quotannis
Des nobis alios, puella, Ianos.

strike a deal whereby you get to possess all of Jean during the day, but I at least get to enjoy Jean during the evening hours. What's that? Do you like the night-time better? Oh, I see, you want him day and night? And he offers you day and night? So, let him be yours at night, and let him be yours during the day, provided that, in place of the one Jean, you give us a new Jean every year.

# Commentary on the Epigrams

The epigram was one of the most popular genres in the time of the Renaissance. Its conciseness and familiar meter made it a manageable way to exercise one's Latinity while allowing for closure of thought in a brief span of time. Such brevity and rapid output were especially desirable since it was the habit of the Renaissance poet to circulate individual poems among a circle of scholarly friends, perhaps in imitation of Catullus, who swapped short epigrams with his *sodales* on a regular basis. Catullus's epigrams, in fact, exerted an enormous influence on the Renaissance epigrammatists. They derived from his poems much of their vocabulary and spirit, and assumed his programmatic aims, as expressed in his first poem. Catullan diminutives, the Lesbia cycle, carnival exaggerations, sexual innuendos, harsh invective and social criticism likewise color the Renaissance epigram. But Catullus was not the only model for the Renaissance epigrammatist: in some ways, Martial had an even greater impact. Martial touches on a range of subjects far wider than that of Catullus, and his penchant for witty and sententious endings, a borrowing from the rhetorical schools, attracted authors who were brought up on such works as Erasmus's *Adagia* and who wanted to exhibit their own cleverness to their friends. In addition, Renaissance poets were drawn to Martial for his extensive use of stock characters. These characters have names, but cannot be identified, and likely represent personality types rather than individuals, though clearly the poet often had in mind an individual who fits the mold. Girard, in the introduction to his own epigrams, explains that the use of stock characters maintains the levity in poems whose purpose it is to make everyone laugh at themselves:

Nec vero is sum qui in alienis oculatus, ullum mihi reprehenden-
dum statuerim: Aliorum vitia non agnovi, et si agnoverim, ig-
novi, ut qui nominibus pepercerim. Si quid tamen inciderit, quod
ad suos mores pertinere taciti existiment, ridiculum est eos a meis
nugis modum exigere, quem suis moribus non imponant. Quin et
multa de me meisque per iocum scripsi, quae is quis serio inter-
pretetur, totus ineptiat. Est ut in segetibus, ita in Epigrammati-
bus, ingenii quaedam luxuries, quam si depascas, perinde facias
(quod ait ille) ac is cum ratione insanias.

[And I have intentionally not paid attention to the business of
others, and do not want anyone to hold a grudge against me. I do
not know the faults of others, and if I do know by chance, I have
spared the use of their name. Yet if anything appears here that se-
cretly they think relates to their own conduct, it is ridiculous for
them to demand caution in my *nugae* that they don't impose on
their own conduct. But note that I have made jokes about myself
too, and if anyone takes them seriously, he is a complete fool. As
it is in fields of grain, so it is in epigrams: There are certain ex-
cesses, which if you consume, you become like a madman.]

Girard also mentions a girl, Sabina, who appears in several poems as a
love interest. He warns his readers not to imagine that there exists an ac-
tual girl whom she represents and by whom he is obsessed: She is
merely a figment of his poetic imagination. As mentioned above, Catul-
lus's Lesbia provided to subsequent epigrammatists the model for how
to conduct a literary affair with a girl. It would be useless, then, to won-
der about the identification of Bèze's literary girlfriend, Candida. He
himself denied that she ever existed, as we have noted in the introduc-
tion. Candida is simply Bèze's way of introducing sexuality and pruri-
ence into his epigrams. She is an image on which he may focus his lens
for some satirical effect. Indeed, judging from a poem of Pasquier, Ren-
aissance epigrammatists understood that their poems were supposed to
combine satire and love in a way that distinguishes them from both
satire and elegy:

*Ad Antonium*

Non ego sum fateor tenerorum scriptor amorum,
   Hos agitet damno Naso poeta suo.
Sed nec ego Antoni Satyrarum scriptor acutus.

Persius has parteis, has Iuvenalis agat.
   At iuvat et Venerem nonnunquam ludere, gestat
      Ut pharetram Phoebus, sic pharetratus Amor.
Vix etiam a satyra possunt epigrammata abesse,
   Sunt sine, ni mordent, carmina nostra sale.
Atque adeo satyrae facili mihi lege colentur,
   Dum tamen in satyris sit venus ulla meis.
                    (*Epigrammatum libri VI* 1.69)

[*To Antony*

I am not, I confess, a writer of tender love poetry; let the poet
Ovid deal with that to his own condemnation. But neither am I
a sarcastic writer of satires; let Perseus and Juvenal handle that
territory. But I like to play with Venus sometimes, since Cupid
carries a quiver just like Phoebus does. And epigrams can hardly
be distanced from satire, for unless they bite, my poems have no
wit. And my satires will be cultivated in an easy way, so long as
there is any love in my satires.]

One cannot help seeing in all of this a degree of vindication for the the-
ories of Bakhtin, particularly as they are set forth in his *Rabelais and His
World*. The epigram truly has its roots in the life and language of the
street. It is filled with laughter and grotesqueness; it aims at shocking
and distorting, it proceeds by turning the world upside down and inside
out. It insults, it stings, it parodies. It does not do these things for their
own sake, but for a more serious purpose. Bakhtin speaks of the regen-
erative power that the festive spirit holds for human beings.[1] It shakes
them from what is humdrum and conventional, and liberates them to a
new outlook on the world. Renaissance writers saw in their epigrammat-
ic models a serious purpose long before Bakhtin noted the same. One
can see this in an icon written by Pasquier on Martial:

*Marcus Valerius Martialis*

In me multa leges et spurca et putida, quae te
   (Ingenue fateor) praeteriisse velim.

---

[1] M. Bakhtin, *Rabelais and His World* (Bloomington, IN, 1984), 21–22.

Hic quoque seria sunt quae tu si legeris, idem
   (Crede mihi lector) legeris et Senecam. (*Icones* 98)

[*Marcus Valerius Martial*

In me you will read many things that are coarse and lewd, which,
with some degree of embarrassment, I ask you please to ignore.
Here there are also serious things, and if you read them, believe
me, it will be as though you are reading Seneca.]

That Bèze took his epigrams to be serious is evident from a number
of factors. It is true that Bèze expresses uneasiness about the frivolous
tone and crass subject matter of many of the poems, but statements to
that effect come only after he was a leader in the Calvinist movement.
One must keep in mind that sprinkled among the epigrams of a lighter
nature are others whose gravity is striking. Some poems, for example,
honor the court with sincerity, while others bring strong criticism to
bear on the materialism and ostentatiousness of the Catholic Church.
These poems, with their serious subject matter, would be completely
out of place in a collection that wallowed in its own immorality. The ar-
rangement, however, is somewhat analogous to what one finds in the
Catullan corpus: polymetric and elegiac poems, many of the most inde-
cent sort, surround a cycle of longer poems that touch on weighty sub-
jects such as marriage and death. The tone of those poems spills over to
the rest of the collection and suggests that a deeper purpose might lie be-
neath its sometimes sordid surface. Bèze himself tells a friend that his
poems arose as he "watched the habits of people as if in a very large
theater" ("Ibi omnium hominum mores velut in amplissimo theatro in-
tueor," *Corr.* 1: 35). A theatrical performance, then, is precisely what we
should expect here in the epigrams. They are poems that parade a series
of characters and situations before our eyes, offering us, not an escape
from ourselves, but a reminder of who we really are.

## 1.

Wright, *Delitiae delitiarum* (1637), 8.

Bèze enters a long-standing debate on the relation between the length of
a poem or a book of poems and its quality. The debate is encapsulized
in Callimachus's maxim (fr. 465 Pfeiffer) that "a great book is a great

evil" (Καλλίμαχος ὁ γραμματικὸς τὸ μέγα βιβλίον ἴσον ἔλεγεν
εἶναι τῷ μεγάλῳ κακῷ). Cf. Pliny, *Ep.* 1.20.4, who claims that the bet-
ter (*melior*) a book is the greater (*maior*) it is. Bèze hopes that his reader
will use the weightiness of the book's content rather than the number
of verses as the sole criterion of its merit. Even Callimachus's rather un-
equivocal censure of the "great book" has as its primary focus, not so
much a book's length (long books are not inherently bad), as its quality.
Callimachus's specific complaint was directed against those writing long
epics aping the Homeric style without taking the time to craft each line
carefully and deliberately. So, although Bèze admits to the brevity of his
book, his principal intent is to stress the fact that his collection of poet-
ry is at least well-crafted, not that it would have necessarily been bad if
it were long, since it "could have been a book."

Likewise, Bèze is assuming one aspect of Catullus's programmatic
poem (*c.* 1), where that poet says that his verses bear the marks of re-
finement and polish (*lepidum* and *arido pumice expolitum*). In fact, this
particular poem of Bèze appears to be a replacement for an earlier poem
to the reader that appears in the Orléans manuscript (*epig.* 41, p. 177),
and which has in it a clear embrace of Catullus's "dry pumice." The
text is as follows:

### Ad Lectorem

Lector, quisquis eris mei libelli,
Seu tibi otia tanta quod supersint
Iacturam facere ut queas diei,
Seu te noster amor iubet vorare
Tediumque molestiasque tantas,                                        5
Te vult admonitum prius poeta
Ne quod ex reliquis soles libellis
(Fructum scilicet atque amenitatem)
Reportare suo arido ex libello,
Speres id tibi posse comparari.                                       10
Aquam e pumice quis petivit unquam?

The ending aphorism comes from Erasmus's *Adagia* (1.4.75, from
Plautus's *Asinaria* 99–100). The conceit of lines 4–5 appears again in *epig.*
10, on a similar theme. The connection of *aridus* to such a word as *libel-
lus* in line 9, though not a Catullan collocation, has precedent in classical
authors. On this see William W. Batstone, "Dry Pumice and the Pro-
grammatic Language of Catullus 1," *Classical Philology* 93 (1998): 125–35,

who argues that the epithet *arida*, long ignored by commentators, is a word drawn from rhetorical theory referring to stylistic restraint. Thus even in the poem that in the end Bèze did not use, the concern is with quality.

Here we must return to the idea of the weighing of verses, because it is a concept that carries with it something more than simply a reference to artistic refinement. While Callimachus's cloistered existence in the library of Alexandria under the domination of the Ptolemies gave rise to an entire movement in poetry, Alexandrianism, it is a poetry that only subtly engages the society in which it is created. On the other hand, some authors are said to have weighed their words for how they would affect their audience's choices and values (see note on *pendere* below). It is likely, then, that the word *pendere* does not look back to Callimachus and his ivory tower alone. Rather, by it Bèze asserts a weightiness for his poems, even amid all the frivolity of them, that his expressed models, Catullus and Martial, also claim for theirs. In that regard the following poem of Martial (11.1) is especially relevant:

> Si nimius videor seraque coronide longus
> esse liber, legito pauca: libellus ero.
> terque quaterque mihi finitur carmine parvo
> pagina: fac tibi me quam cupis esse brevem.

> [If I seem too big a book (*liber*), and if it takes a long time to reach the colophon, just read a few of the poems: then I'll be a booklet (*libellus*). Several of my pages finish off with short poems. Use those to make me as short as you want.]

Immediately we see in line two an affinity to line three of Bèze's first poem, but with what appears at first glance a completely opposite meaning. Martial claims he has written a long book that the reader can shorten by reading only the shorter poems! Martial's eleventh book, however, is only negligibly longer than Bèze's entire collection, and the reader of Martial knows full well that Martial never wrote anything long. But by calling his book "long," and a *liber*, Martial is signaling the same thing Bèze is with *pendere*, as another poem of Martial shows (4.29.7–8):

> saepius in libro numeratur Persius uno
> quam levis in tota Marsus Amazonide.

[Persius counts for more in his one book than light-
weight Marsus does in his whole epic "The Amazons."]

Clearly Martial finds more weight in the social satire of Persius's scanty
volume than he does in the bulky epic of Marsus. Elsewhere, at 10.4,
this same attitude leads him to reject the model of Callimachus with its
erudite ambiguities and mythological allusions. "These pages of mine,"
Martial asserts there, "smack of man *(hominem pagina nostra sapit)*; here
the reader can expect to observe his own *mores*, to know himself ... if
that's not what you're after, go read Callimachus." In the same way,
Bèze's play with the difference between a book and a booklet, and with
the imagery of weighing, hints at his confidence in the epigram's ability
to reveal humanity in its myriad of guises, which has made his verses
weighty.

**1-2. longo (libro) ... longa (fastidia):** That is, "inflict long boredom
on their readers with a long book." The doublet, here emphasized
by the interlocking word order, is reminiscent of Callimachus's μέγα
... μεγάλῳ. The idiom *fastidia longa ... ferant* is rare, but appears at
Verg. *Ecl.* 4.60–61 with the meaning "to wear down":

> incipe, parve puer, risu cognoscere matrem:
> matri longa decem tulerunt fastidia menses.

The meaning of Vergil's passage must be that the "ten long months (of
pregnancy) have worn down your mother," which provided for Bèze a
vivid image for expressing the tediousness of reading long books. The
idea that long books can be burdensome to the reader can be found also
at Ovid, *Amores* 1 (*Epigramma ipsius*):

> Qui modo Nasonis fueramus quinque libelli,
>     tres sumus; hoc illi praetulit auctor opus.
> Ut iam nulla tibi nos sit legisse voluptas,
>     at levior demptis poena duobus erit.

[We used to be "Five Books of Ovid," but now we are "Three."
The author preferred to make us shorter like this. And even
though you still might not enjoy reading us, at least now that it's
shorter you won't suffer as much.]

**3. iste tamen poterat:** *Iste* emphasizes the fact that the book is in the
reader's hands and away from the author more precisely than does

the *hic* that appears in the 1597 edition. Martial's use of *ista* at the beginning of *epig.* 11.16 is analogous:

> Qui gravis es nimium, potes hinc iam, lector, abire
>    quo libet: urbanae scripsimus ista togae ...

Bèze may have later decided that the shift in focus from the writer (introduced in the second line with *mihi*) to the reader (implied in *iste*) was too jolting.

**liber ... libellus**: the contrast is between the diminutive (*libellus*) and the standard form (*liber*).

4. **pendere ... numerare**: Cf. Cicero's *De orat.* 2.309: "When I collect arguments for my cases, my habit is to weigh them rather than simply count them" ("equidem cum colligo argumenta causarum, non tam ea numerare soleo quam expendere"). The idea first appears in *Frogs* 799, where Aristophanes says that phrases of Aeschylus and Euripides will be judged by "rulers and measuring-tapes" (κανόνας ... καὶ πήχεις ἐπῶν). Other instances include Cicero, *Phil.* 2.97 (of coins), *De optimo genere oratorum* 14 (of words), and *Rep.* 6.1 (fr. 4).


## 2.

Missing in 1569 and 1576; greatly altered in 1597 (see below);
Giles Fletcher, in his *Licia* (Cambridge, 1593),
uses this poem without attribution.[2]
Meter: phalaecian hendecasyllable.

Maigron believes that with this poem Bèze now retracts his own self-praise from the previous poem (*De Theodori Bezae poematis*, 92). It is more likely that Bèze is looking to his literary predecessors, Catullus and Martial, who often express an antipathy for all things academic and serious. Martial rebukes the stern Cato for trying to attend his strip show, as it were, while Catullus is careful to differentiate his poetry from Nepos's learned histories.[3] With his mock modesty (*ridiculus ...*

---

[2] Most accessible in the edition published and edited by A. Grosart (London, 1871), in the series *Miscellanies of the Fuller Worthies' Library*, 77–78; also, *Licia, or Poemes of Love, in Honour of the admirable and singular vertues of his Lady, to the imitation of the best Latin Poets, and others; whereunto is added the rising to the crowne of Richard III* (Cambridge, 1593), fol. 1v.

[3] Most of the epigrammatists are at pains to prepare their readers for the unacademic

*parumque doctus*), then, Bèze is urging his readers to lower their expectations and set aside their critical acumen and erudition when they enter the arena of his epigrams. Those who criticize or censure this poetry will be wasting time. No matter how many times they try to clean it up, like the Ethiopian, his epigrammatic poetry will always have its superficially "dirty" appearance, because that is its nature or skin, so to speak.

But it is clear from other poems (esp. *epig.* 63) that Bèze agrees with the recommendation of Horace (*AP* 419–52), that the poet needs to subject his poetry to a candid critic. In the end, the irony of this epigram can only be understood in the spirit of Martial's *epig.* 13.2:

> Nasutus sis usque licet, sis denique nasus,
>     quantum noluerit ferre rogatus Atlans,
> et possis ipsum tu deridere Latinum:
>     non potes in nugas dicere plura meas
> ipse ego quam dixi, quid dentem dente iuvabit          5
>     rodere? carne opus est, si satur esse velis.
> ne perdas operam: qui se mirantur, in illos
>     virus habe, nos haec novimus esse nihil.
> non tamen hoc nimium nihil est, si candidus aure
>     nec matutina si mihi fronte venis.          10

[Although your nose may be as large as can be, in fact you might be all nose, so big Atlas would refuse to hold it up if asked, and you might be able to deride Latinus himself, still you cannot say more against my *nugae* than I have said myself. What satisfaction will it give to grind your teeth against me? If you're hungry, eat some meat, but don't waste your effort here. The self-admirers, keep your venom for them. I know this stuff is nothing. And yet it's not *altogether* nothing, if you come to me with the right attitude: with a friendly ear and a countenance not sober and serious.]

---

tone and content of their work. Bourbon's example of this tactic reveals how close the conceit is to the *recusatio*, as he warns his readers not to expect anything as grand as scientific inquiry or epic battles in his poetry: "Quem iuvat immensi causas inquirere mundi | ... Res gestas regumque ducumque et bella gigantum | ... *abito:* | Ista tibi est alio fonte levanda suis: | Hic nihil est, aut si quid inest, audacior aetas | Musaque colludunt, et puerilis amor" (*Nugae* [1533], fol. 8r–v).

In its own way, Bèze's poetry *does* have something to offer, something important. But first the readers must transport themselves out of the office, away from the business of the courts and the assembly, or wherever the serious, workaday world dulls their perspective and casts a somber shadow on their minds, into the light-hearted world of friends and laughter, love and wine, where human emotions and affections can really play themselves out for the poet's pen. Only with that attitude can these poems be appreciated.

In the 1597 edition Bèze completely reworked the poem, most notably removing the last line:

> Non saevas metuo reprensiones,
> Non ronchos timeo, calumniasve,
> Non ullos obelos severiores,
> Non quod vel placeam mihi ipse stultus,
> Ut nullis stolidus calumniarum       5
> Confixus iaculis queam moveri:
> Sed quod si merito reprendar, adsit
> Quod possim mihi iure gratulari:
> Sin vero immeritum imperitus ullus
> Carpat, invidus aut sophista, quid tum?       10
> Istis maxima displicere laus est.

The emphasis now falls, not on the poems' lasciviousness, but on the invariably cantankerous nature of certain critics.

1. **lātrationes**: Macrin points out that the first syllable should be long, not short, as Bèze would have it here. The poem disappears after the first edition, however, so there is no way to print a better reading, except in the largely reworked form printed above. At any rate, it is a very rare word, occuring only in glosses for ὑλαγμός and *latratus*. See *Corpus glossariorum latinorum a Gustavo Loewe incohatum*, ed. G. Goetz, *Corpus Glossariorum Latinorum* (Leipzig and Berlin, 1888–1923), II.462.38, II.495.7, and II.585.40.

For "barking" as a word applied to critics, cf. also Pasquier ("Zoilus" being a frequent label for a carping critic, as in Eobanus Hessus et al.):

*In Zoilum*

> Adlatras, rapidoque miser nos dente lacessis,
>     Quique aliquid scribunt hos nihil esse putas.

Dentibus authores et cum corroseris omneis,
　　Ipse nihil scribis, num potes esse aliquid?
Invidiam hanc veteres quondam dixere caninam,　　5
　　Cum noceas aliis, nec tibi proficias.
Nil ego sum fateor, tu qui mordesque, latrasque,
　　Esse aliquid iam te dico: quid ergo? canem. (*Epig.* 4.77)

[*Against Zoilus*

You bark at us and annoy us with your slashing teeth, you poor thing, and you count those who actually write something as nothing. Yet when you gnaw at every author with your teeth, while you write nothing, surely you can't be something. The ancients used to call this kind of envy "canine," when you harm another, but don't profit yourself. I admit that I am nothing, and I agree now that you who bite and bark are something. What? a dog.]

Bourbon admits that such "barking" and "canine words" hurt for a time, but soon they disappear into the soft, southerly breezes:

*In Livorem*

Cum mea Cerbereo laedatur fama latratu,
　　Impetat et versus invida lingua meos:
Cum nimium dicar petulans, mordaxque Poeta;
　　Et dicar iuvenes et lacerare senes:
Cur celeber maneo, passimque poeta salutor?　　5
　　Inque leves abeunt verba canina Notos?
　　　　(*Delitiae*, 1: 790)

[*Against Envy*

Although my reputation is attacked by your Cerberus-like barking, and your envious tongue lashes out against my verses; although I am called too lascivious, and a biting poet; and I am said to ruin young and old alike: why do I remain popular, and hailed as a poet everywhere, while your canine words blow away on the soft, southerly breezes?]

2. **ronchos ... obelos severiores**: From the time of the textual critics Zenodotus and Aristarchus (c. 216–145 B.C.), the obelus (†) marked a line as spurious. Here it is used simply as a metaphor for an aca-

demic snobbery that is antithetical to the light-hearted world of the epigram. Bèze's line is reminiscent of Mart. 1.3: *maiores nusquam rhonchi* ("nowhere will you find greater snorts") and *neve notet lusus tristis harundo tuos* ("lest his stern pen keep marking up your playful lines"). At 1.35 Martial asks Cornelius to lay aside his sternness and not castrate his books. Cf. 1.4, where Martial tells Caesar, *pone supercilium*. The same fear of the academic, serious-minded reader is implied in Catullus 5.2, *rumoresque senum severiorum*; 7.10, *vesano Catullo*; and 14.9, *Sulla litterator*. Secundus expresses the sentiment this way:

> *Ad grammaticos, cur scribat lascivius*
>
> Carmina cur spargam cunctis lasciva libellis,
>   Quaeritis? insulsos arceo grammaticos!

[*To the grammarians, why he writes rather playfully*

Why should I scatter sexy poems in all my little books, you ask? I'm fending off insipid grammarians.]
      (Nichols, *Anthology of Neo-Latin Poetry*, 486–87)

The demeanor is typical of most of the epigrammatists of the period, as with the case of Bourbon's *Ad lectorem* (*Delitiae*, 1: 766):

> *Ad doctos*
>
> Ite alio docti; non sunt haec carmina vobis
>   Facta, nec in vestras digna venire manus.
> Hic nihil est prorsus caperata fronte legendum,
>   Vel quod Aristarchi lima severa notet.
> Atque hunc ne tristis vexet censura libellum,                5
>   Pro titulo Nugas ipse libenter habet ...

[Go away, pedants, these poems are not composed for you, nor are they worthy to come into your hands. Here you should not read with crinkled brow, or expect to find something fit for Aristarchus's exacting pen. I gave my little book the name "Nugae" so that no one would trouble it with their cheerless censuring ...]

The antithesis to this fear of strict criticism appears in Horace's precept at *AP* 450, where the candid critic is recommended in this way:

> fiet Aristarchus, nec dicet, "cur ego amicum
> offendam in nugis?" hae nugae seria ducent
> in mala derisum semel exceptumque sinistre.

Despite the epigrammatic posturing, Bèze certainly welcomed the "stern obeli" offered by Macrin, and we have evidence that Bèze's circle of friends depended on one another for amicable criticism (see Dampierre's letter to his friends in Perosa and Sparrow, *Renaissance Latin Verse*, 363–64).

7. **ridiculus**: The self-demeaning tone of the poem is part of the epigrammatic posture. Catullus has a similar judgment of himself in *c.* 49: "Catullus ... pessimus omnium poeta;" likewise, in *c.* 14a: "Si qui forte mearum ineptiarum lectores eritis." But *ridiculus* also carries with it a hint of the ambience of buffoonery, as at Catullus *c.* 56: "O rem ridiculam, Cato, et iocosam ..."

**parumque doctus**: Although Martial (1.61), Lygdamus (6.41) and Ovid (*Am.* 3.9.62) call Catullus *doctus*, he never calls himself that. Instead, he draws a line between his own *nugae* and the *chartae doctae* of Nepos in *c.* 1. For both Catullus and Bèze the denial of the application of the term to their own work further defines the genre against the backdrop of the academic world.

10. **Aethiopem**: the standard word for "Black African" among the Romans. Varro, *De L. L.* 8.38 and 41, 9.42; *Thes.* s.v. 1156.30, 6.599, 8.33; Juvenal 2.23; Pliny *NH* 32.141. The Ethiopian is treated negatively by Martial at 7.87.

**Nam ... lavare**: In other words, an Ethiopian/black cannot change his skin color. Cf. Jer. 13.23: "Can the Ethiopian change his skin, or the leopard his spots?" (KJV) The immediate source of Bèze's phrase about the Ethiopian must be Erasmus *Adagia* 1.4.50, *Aethiopem lavas* (from Lucian, *Adv. indoctum* 28: Αἰθίοπα σμήχειν ἐπιχείρω) and 3.10.88, *Aethiops non albescit* (from Aesop, *Fables, The Ethiopian*: Αἰθίοπα σμήχειν). The latter is the story of a man who bought a black slave, and, not understanding that the color of his skin was natural, but thinking the former master left him dirty, tried to scrub him white until he made the man ill. Cf. Diogenianus of Heraclea 1.45, Zenobius 1.46, Suda AI 125 for the story. Ovid *Met.* 11.315 and Juv. 3.30 do not use the word "Ethiopian" but contain in essence the same idea that black cannot be made white. The phrase was and is proverbial to many European cultures. Thomas Becon, the English Protestant, wrote in 1543 (*Early Works*, 49), "Here, therefore, do ye nothing else than, as the common proverb is, go about to make an Ethiope white." Richard Brathwait (*Omphale* [1625], 275) writes, "The French say, 'À laver la tête d'un More on perd sa lessive' ['In washing the head of a Moor one loses one's soap']." See F. Snowden, *Blacks in Antiquity* (Cambridge, MA, 1970).

## 3.

Bèze would later expand the title of this occasional poem to *De pareliis Lutetiae Parisorum visis, anno MDXXXIX finiente, Carolo Caesare, Calendis Ianuarii anno MDXL urbem ingressuro* ("On the parhelia seen at Paris in 1539, towards the end of the year, when Charles V was about to enter the city on the calends of January, 1540"). ABM (183) report that a note of Bèze in his own copy of the 1597 edition reveals that this poem was recited by university authorities at Charles's arrival. This is an indication of the respect as a poet Bèze was gaining already at the young age of twenty-one.

The phenomenon of the parhelion (or "mock sun") had been noted by the ancients, though the true scientific explanation escaped them. Seneca (*Q. N.* 1.11.2) defines it as "images of the sun on a dense and nearby cloud after the manner of a mirror." He goes on to say that some define a parhelion as "clouds, round and resplendent like the sun." At *id.* 1.13.1 he speaks of twin parhelia (*bina parelia*). In truth, "parhelion" denotes a natural phenomenon in which a bright light appears near the sun, often on a halo or luminous ring, caused by the interplay of sunlight and ice in the earth's upper atmosphere. Here Bèze believes that one particular parhelion heralds the two kings who are like two bright suns illuminating France by their treaty and protecting her from the dark shadows cast by war (no eclipse is possible if the two suns work in tandem). François I and Charles V had been engaged in war off and on since 1521. The treaty in question in this poem was signed in 1538 at Nice,[4] only to be broken already by 1542. Bèze may have been willing to include this poem in his 1548 edition on the basis of another treaty signed by the two monarchs in 1544.

The 1597 edition records another poem on the same episode:

---

[4] Visagier has a series of poems on the hopes spawned by this treaty (*Hendecasyllabi* [1538], fol. 15r-v).

*Oblatum ipsi Carolo Quinto Imperatori, Lutetiam ingredienti, Cal. Ianuarii, anno MDXL*

Te veniente sua est facies quod reddita caelo,
    Perpetuo madidum quod prius imbre fuit,
Miratur vulgus. Sed cui est tua cognita virtus,
    Virtus perspectum quid tua possit habet.
Scilicet ipsius regnantis Caesaris ora                    5
    Gestiit ipsa etiam cernere pura dies.

**1. geminos ... duos**: This phrase, meaning "twin suns," refers to the parhelion, while in the next line the slightly different *soles duos* ("two suns") is applied to the two kings. The practice of connecting kings or emperors to the sun extends back to Egypt, through Greece, Etruria, Rome, and Byzantium. On this see J. K. Newman, "Empire of the Sun: Lelio Guidiccioni and Pope Urban VIII," *IJCT* 1 (1994): 63–70. Other French poets connect their rulers to the sun during this period also; one such example is Dorat's poem entitled *De tribus Galliae solibus*:

Prodigium fuerat tres olim cernere Soles,
    Et nunquam terris sors ea laeta fuit.
Tres quoque iam vidit laeto non omine soles
    Gallia, tres soles noxque secuta triplex.
Nam cum tres pariter praecedens viderit annus         5
    Fratres, qui solis triplicis instar erant;
Mox prior ex oculis abiit sol fulgidus unus
    Henricus, sua quem nunc procul arctos habet,
Illius ex abitu sol postmodo maximus alter
    Carolus, heu, nuper tabidus occubuit.            10
Tertius et qui nunc superest, moerore duorum
    Franciscus faciem deficientis habet.
Nox gravis hinc premeret Gallos; Catharina sed una
    Lux micat ut Lunae dum redit alma dies.
        (*Delitiae*, 1: 266)

The natural point to be made by such a comparison is that the ruler(s) dispels the darkness that formerly brooded over the land.

**5-6. istos | Nimirum ... notant**: The clear meaning of the version of the 1597 edition, "since God gives them the power of Europe," suggests the sense of *astra benigna notant*.

**8. Eclipsis ... tibi**: Presumably he says this because the moon could block out only one sun at a time. It was already well-known from antiquity that the moon caused eclipses, by Empedocles (fr. B42 Diels), Anaxagoras (*Hipp. Ref.* 1.8.9), Lucretius 5.751–61, and Epicurus *Ep. ad Pyth.* 96.

4.

Missing in 1569, 1576, 1597.

The poem appears to be an excuse to make a play on the name Claudius, who like Vulcan, is *claudus*, club-footed. No only does Claudius share Vulcan's disfigurement, but also surprisingly both married beautiful wives. The gods had awarded Venus to Vulcan as part of a bargain to release his mother Hera from the chair to which he had bound her. Venus, however, could not be content with her homely husband, and while he was away during the day at his forge she turned her affections to Mars. The story of how Vulcan snared them in bed is told by Demodocus in Homer's *Odyssey*. Claudius does not recognize that he is a Vulcan-figure himself, and as a result faults the old poets for imagining the very thing he is doing. Bèze takes comfort in the fact that Claudius's Venus-like wife has found for herself a Mars-like lover, confirming, it seems, the principle the old poets recognized long ago.

The whole theme may have been suggested to Bèze by Ovid, *Amores* 2.17.11–24, where the poet tries to convince his beautiful and charming girl Corinna that there is precedent in myth, legend, and even verse composition for incongruous unions. At vv. 19–20 he draws a parallel to the case of Vulcan and Venus:

> Vulcano Venerem, quamvis incude relicta
> turpiter obliquo claudicet ille pede.

As for the name Claudius, we may imagine it disguises Claude Framberge, one of Bèze's friends at Orléans, since the "Claudius" at *Corr.* 1: 35 seems to refer to him; see also Meylan (*D'Erasme à Théodore de Bèze*, 140), who adds the epithet "scelleur," an indication of his profession. The scenario given in the poem, however, must be imaginary, since no one would so distastefully tease a friend about his wife's infidelity.

**1. incusare**: Though not etymologically related with *incudere* (to hammer) or *incus* (anvil), this word nonetheless evokes images of Vulcan's forge.

**3. divos . . . furentes:** By calling the gods crazy Bèze plays one-upmanship with Claudius, who had himself faulted the poets.

### 5.

### Missing in 1569, 1576, 1597.

We know from the title of another poem to Wolmar (1497–1560), appearing in the 1597 edition (p. 150), that Bèze heard him expounding Homer in the Academy of Bourges in 1534, when Bèze was only fifteen. But Wolmar had published a commentary on Homer years before: *Homeri Iliados libri duo una cum annotatiunculis Volmarii, passim suis locis adpositis* (Paris, 1523) at the press of G. de Gourmont.[5]

In what sense can Wolmar be said to have restored Homer's sight? The emphasis of the poem does not hinge so much on the notion of blindness and the restoration of sight as it does on the ingratitude of the gods toward Homer and his poetry contrasted to Wolmar's profound appreciation. The gods had committed a crime (*scelus*) against Homer by not rewarding his service to them as a poetic priest (*vates sacer*), but Wolmar had given Homer his due though his explication of the text. For the importance of Wolmar in fostering the Reformed movement, see J. De Groot, "Melchior Wolmar: Ses relations avec les réformateurs français et suisses," in *Bulletin de la Société de l'histoire du protestantisme français* 83 (1934): 416–39. Bèze pays special tribute to him in *Icones, id est verae imagines* (1580).

The poem of the 1597 edition reads as follows:

> *In Meliorem Volmarum praeceptorem summe observandum, doctissime Homerum in Academia Bituricensi interpretantem, anno Domini MDXXXIV, quum ageret annum Beza XV*

---

[5] A very rare work (B. does not mention it in his short biographical sketch of Wolmar [see appendix 1]: "et ab omni ambitione tam remotus, ut, quamvis Graece et Latine scribendo excelleret, nihil tamen praeter unicam perelegantem praefationem grammaticae Graecae Demetrii Chalcondylae praepositam ediderit . . ."). There is a copy at the Bibliothèque Nationale in Paris, Rés. Yb 169.

Flacce, tibi quandoque bonus dormitat Homerus,        (= Hor. *AP* 359)
Sed num propterea caecus Homerus erat?
Immo oculis captus quinam credatur Homerus,
Quem sequitur vatum caetera turba ducem?
Illius sed enim splendorem longa vetustas.                      5
Obruerat densis, heu, nimirum tenebris.
Tu Melior, donec, fato meliore, renato
Dux ipsi fieres, Volmare magne, duci.
(*Poemata varia*, 150)

1. **Maeonidem**: Literally, "a native of Maeonia or Lydia," used often of Homer. Cf. Ovid *Am*. 3.9.25; Mart. 5.10.8.

2. **vati ... sacro**: Cf. Cic. *Pro Arch*. 8: "Qua re suo iure noster ille Ennius sanctos appellat poetas, quod quasi deorum aliquo dono atque munere commendati nobis esse videantur."

4. **restituit ... oculos**: In modern parlance we would say that sight is restored, but not the eyes. For this wording cf. Suet. *Vesp*. 7; Pliny *NH* 25.8.50. In translating John 9 (*Novum Testamentum* [1582] part 1: 362–66), where the story of the healing of the blind man occurs, Bèze prefers to use forms of *aperire*, explaining in his commentary that the expression "opening the eyes" in reference to the blind is a Hebraism. Cf. Isa. 35.5.

## 6.

Wright, *Delitiae delitiarum* (1637), 8;
Wright, *Sales epigrammatum* (1663), 42.

The phrase "know thyself" from Apollo's temple at Delphi (see Plato *Charmides* 164d; possibly it originated with Thales of Miletus, according to Diog. Laert. 1.36) originally meant "understand your limitations and capacity as a mere human being in the face of the almighty gods," a sentiment expressed neatly in a Greek proverb attributed to the comic poet Antiphanes (fr. 289 Kock): "Friend, if you are mortal, think as mortals should." On this interpretation of the maxim see H. Traenkle, "Γνῶθι σεαυτόν. Zur Ursprung und Deutungsgeschichte des delphischen Spruchs," *WJA* 11 (1985): 19–31. But Ponticus's problem here is not so complex as a misunderstanding of the nature of his humanity, rather, an obliviousness of the fact that he is really less than human, an ass. The theme may have been suggested to Bèze by Aesop's fable, "The Ass in the Lion's Skin."

The saying was so well known that Bèze did not have to borrow it consciously from anywhere, but still it is relevant to note that Erasmus gives both the Greek and the Latinized *Nosce teipsum* at *Adagia* 1.6.95, and, following Cicero *Ad Quint.* 3.5.7, includes a positive interpretation as well, that the maxim "know thyself" recommends we recognize our blessings. For other uses of the maxim note Plato, *Phaedrus* 229e; Ovid, *Ars Amat.* 2.499–500 (with the sense, "Be yourself"); Juvenal 11.27; Cicero *Tusc. Disp.* 1.52 (= "Know your soul"); Plutarch, *Moralia: On Tranquility* 472C (= "Recognize your natural talents and use them"); and countless more. For the entire tradition of the saying, see E. G. Wilkins, "Know Thyself in Greek and Latin Literature" (Chicago, 1917; repr. New York, 1979); Pierre Courcelle, *Connais-toi toi-meme de Socrate à Saint Bernard*, 3 vols. (Paris, 1974–75).

Note the use of "ass" in the following poem from the 1597 edition (175):

> *In Turnonum, indoctum quidem, sed doctorum non paucorum Mecoenatem*
>
> Indoctus doctos pascis, Turnone: beatus,
>   Si tam animo saperes, quam tibi mensa sapit.
> Euge tamen, Musae, vestras alere improbus artes
>   Cum detrectet honos, sic modo pascat ὄνος.

It is remarkable how closely Pasquier appears to imitate Bèze at times, as here:

> *In Aprum*
>
> Omnia novit Aper, verum sic omnia novit,
>   Ut nullus magis hunc omnia nosse sciat,
> Cunctaque qui norit, dum scit se noscere cuncta,
>   Non alium quam se novit et ambit Aper.
> Iam valeat vestrum hoc sapienteis γνῶθι σεαυτόν    5
>   Perdidit hunc nostrum, γνῶθι σεαυτὸν Aprum.
>                         (*Epig.* 1.65)

1. **Pontice:** His identity is unknown; "Ponticus" was a common name for an addressee among the Neo-Latin poets. See several instances in Boissard, *Poemata* (1589), 362–64.

asinos: It hardly needs to be said that calling someone an "ass" or "asinine" is an insult. The vocative *asine* is used often in Latin literature in this way, especially in comedy (e.g., Ter. *Ad.* 935; cf. Cic. *Pis.* 30). Also related is Plaut. *Ps.* 136: "neque ego homines magis asinos umquam vidi." But why would anyone praise asses? Bèze may be using the word as a cover for the Asinier clan, a wealthy Lombard family living in and around Orléans (cf. notes to *epig.* 25).

2. ignotum: To recognize the pun with the Greek γνῶθι it helps to know that *ignotum* is a compressed form of *in-gnotum,* and thus linguistically related to the Greek.

7.

Missing in 1569, 1776, 1597.

Bèze raises the question how humans can include Love (Cupid) in the pantheon when the gods are supposed to be the source of blessings. Cupid, by implication, is a cruel god who brings ills to mankind. While the poem ends with a frivolous play on the word *amor* and its personification as a name of Cupid, by stark contrast it begins with one of the central issues in the philosophical debate between Epicureans and Stoics: Do the gods intervene in the lives of human beings?

1. hominum curam superis: For a similar expression, cf. Ovid *Fast.* 2.64 ("sit superis opto mutua cura tui"), *Epist. ex Ponto* 2.2.108 ("curaque sit superis Caesaribusque tui"), and often in Cicero's *Div.* Contrast the idea expressed in Ennius fr. 353, "Ego deum genus esse semper dixi et dicam caelitum, sed eos non curare opinor quid agat humanum genus," and often among the Epicureans (Lucr. 2.646–51, Diog. Laert. 10.139, Cic. *ND* 1.45, etc.). Dido is indignant and ironic (and perhaps Epicurean) when she confronts Aeneas at *Aen.* 4.379–80: "scilicet is superis labor est, ea cura quietos sollicitat."

3. foelici ... albo: A transferred epithet; strictly speaking, the gods are happy, not the roll. *Album* is a term from Roman political life, referring properly to a white tablet on which the names of senators (or any other officials) were inscribed. For example, Tacit. *A.* 4.42 (sc. Tiberius): "Merulam quod in acta divi Augusti non iuraverat albo senatorio erasit." The word occurs most often in the later Roman legal digests, codices, and corpora, where Bèze, a student of law, probably learned it.

**6. Amoris amor**: This collocation at the end of an elegiac couplet appears twice in Ovid (*Am.* 3.11a.20 and *Her.* 19.104), but in neither case does *amoris* carry the meaning "Cupid" as here. But cf. the close imitating by Pasquier:

*In Amorem*

Quem non ulla quies, quem pax non afficit ulla,
    Quique novo antiquum vulnere vulnus alit.
Qui pharetra gaudet, pando qui gaudet et arcu,
    Pacifici ne meret nomen amoris Amor? (*Epig.* 4.26)

Cf. also Pasquier, *Epig.* 5.79 for a repetition of the closing collocation.

## 8.

### Missing in 1569, 1576.

The lifelike nature of fine statues is a constant conceit of the *Greek Anthology* (see C. Mango, "Antique Statuary and the Byzantine Beholder," *DOP* 17 [1963]: 53–75). The knight Renzo can be identified as Lorenzo de Cere, of the Orsini family, and closely connected to François I (the identification is made by ABM, 174). He played an important role in the campaigns of Italy until his death in 1536. The statue of Venus was placed in the castle of Amboise, and much celebrated by contemporary poets. Germain de Brie dedicated ten poems to it (*Delitiae*, 1: 764–66, "Ad Franciscum Regem de Venere marmorea eidem ab Renzo equite donata") and Marot two (*Oeuvres*, ed. Guiffrey, 5 vols., 2nd ed. [Paris, 1911; repr. Geneva, 1969], 4: 40ff.).

**2. ficta Venus, vera . . . Venus**: Similarly Ovid, *Met.* 14.322–23, says of Pictus, . . . "licet ipse decorem | adspicias fictaque probes ab imagine verum."

## 9.

### Missing in 1569, 1576; greatly altered in 1597.

When Bèze originally composed this poem he addressed it, not to Charles V, but to François I, under the title: *De supplicatione a Rege de-*

*creta ad mutandam aeris intemperiem* (ABM, 175), which clearly points
to the rogation procession "for the weather" decreed on 13 July 1535
(see *Journal d'un bourgeois de Paris sous le règne de François 1ᵉʳ (1515–
1536)*, ed. Victor Louis Bourrilly [Paris, 1910], 391). Paris had suffered
from constant rains since Easter of that year. The act of supplication
must have been effective, and so Bèze supposes that François I dispenses
laws in heaven as well as earth. Apparently, Charles V's entrance into
Paris coincided with good weather there, thus Bèze imagines that Char-
les V has decreed it be so; therefore, he dispenses laws in heaven as he
does on earth.

The whole situation is clarified by the version in the 1597 edition:

*Oblatum ipsi Carolo Quinto Imperatori, Lutetiam
ingredienti, Cal. Ianuarii, anno MDXL*

Te veniente sua est facies quod reddita caelo,
    Perpetuo madidum quod prius imbre fuit,
Miratur vulgus. Sed cui est tua cognita virtus,
    Virtus perspectum quid tua possit habet.
Scilicet ipsius regnantis Caesaris ora                                        5
    Gestiit ipsa etiam cernere pura dies.

Line 2: "[sc. the sky] which was formerly drenched with constant rain."
Lines 5–6: "Obviously even the day is glad to see the clear, bright face
itself of Caesar himself who governs supreme." The play is on *pura,*
which normally would indicate a cloudless day, but instead here modi-
fies *ora.*

## 10.

Missing in 1569, 1576, 1597.
Meter: phalaecian hendecasyllable.

If Louis Vaillant is devouring Bèze's books (he will not admit it him-
self), then he must know that Bèze is a distasteful poet; so goes the joke,
built up through a number of words that can refer to food. Here Bèze
repeats in different guise a number of the *topoi* of other poems: Vaillant
is the stern censor of Bèze's lascivious poems; Bèze exhibits a mock
modesty in the face of academic criticism. Here also are two elements
taken from the stage: dialogue and character portrayal. Bèze can only at-
tempt a dialogue with Vaillant, since his friend prefers to remain silent

(*retices*) to his inquiries (*roganti*), but the masking of the poet for his acting role is clearly signaled by the phrase "personam igitur tuam ipse sumam."

Louis Vaillant de Guélis was one of Bèze's *sodales* at Orléans. For his important family, related to Bèze's own, see Meylan, *D'Erasme à Théodore de Bèze*, 140 and 150; *Corr.* 3: 50 n. 9; see also the notes on *epitaph.* 2.

2. **illepidum . . . libellum**: A collocation surprisingly not used by Catullus or Martial. In fact, the word *illepidum* does not appear in Martial at all. Its three occurrences in Catullus are linked once with *inelegantes* (6.2, referring to *delicias*) and twice with *invenustum* (10.4, *scortillum*; 36.17, *votum*). What Catullus and Martial preferred was to call their books *lepidus,* as in the following: Cat. 1.1, *lepidum libellum*; 6.17, *lepido versu*; Mart. 8.3.19, *lepidos libellos*; 11.20.9, *lepidos libellos.*

5–6. **molestiarum . . . taedia**: The words conjure up images of rancid, disgusting food. Cf. Plin. *NH* 15.7: "vetustas oleo taedium adfert, non item ut vino."

10. **personam . . . sumam**: i.e., "I will assume your character and play your part." An indication of the histrionic nature of Bèze's epigrams. For the phrasing see Cic. *Planc.* 41.100: "abjecta quaestoria persona comitisque assumpta;" and, Pliny *Epist.* 8.7.2: "Sumam tamen personam magistri."

13. **insipidum**: "bland" or "unsavory," the opposite of *sapor*; it is used of distastefulness in both a figurative and actual sense, that is, applicable to food without flavor and people without good taste (and therefore not wise). Cf. note on *epig.* 12.2.

## 11.

Missing in 1597.
Meter: phalaecian hendecasyllable.

The Sophists were a favorite target for many Renaissance writers, mainly for their clever way of arguing convincingly for an issue irrespective of its veracity. Plato and Aristotle had billed them as hawkers of sham wisdom. Bèze himself would define their character in his commentary (*Novum Testamentum* [1582], part 2: 94) on 1 Cor. 1.17 (οὐκ ἐν σοφίᾳ λόγου):

Sed et nominatim Sophistae dicti sunt qui illam in rebus civilibus administrandis solertiam cum forensi facundia coniunxerat, et ab agendo sese ad dicendum contulerant, ut ait in *Themistocle* Plutarchus.

[They were termed "Sophists" who had combined a skill in administrating civil affairs with forensic eloquence, and had devoted themselves to talking instead of doing, as Plutarch says in *Themistocles*.]

But that was the ancient definition. Elsewhere in his New Testament commentary (*Novum Testamentum* [1582], part 2: 13, 14, 66, 166, 208, 387), Bèze attacks his Catholic opponents by calling them *Sophistae papistici*, and refers to their distortion of Scripture, their derisive manner, and the way they toy with fine distinctions. Here, however, the Sophists are right (we cannot be in two places at one time), but Bèze refutes them with his own verbal snares (*insidias locutionum*).

"Truchius" is Bèze's intimate friend Jean Truchon (1507–1578), to whom he addressed two more epigrams, 30 and 42 below. Truchon's life is fairly well documented. Meylan (*D'Erasme à Théodore de Béze*, 140) and Vindry (*Parlementaries*, 1: 69 and 196) give these details: he was born at Montfort l'Amaury, became master of the College of the Marche at Paris, then regent professor of Law at Orléans, where Bèze knew him. Soon he entered into the service of the king, who sent him into Bretagne, in spite of the complaints of the university which wanted him to come teach his classes. He was counselor of the Parlement of Chambéry in 1549 (ABM, 170, n. 6 give 1543 incorrectly), and second president in 1552; then in 1554 he became president of the court of Grenoble, where he died in 1578. Greater detail can be found at Herminjard, *Correspondance des réformateurs*, 6: 10 n.; Ridderikhoff, *Les livres des procurateurs*, 1: 366 n. 1. We have one poem addressed to Truchon by Bèze in the Orléans ms., mentioning that Truchon wrote poetry, some of which has survived in the Orléans ms.:

*De Truchio*

Nondum Virgilio Marone nato,
Primus Maeonides erat poeta.
Nato Virgilio Marone, coepit
Primus qui fuerat secundus esse.
At, nato Truchio, gradum secundum     5

Accepit Maro, tertiumque Homerus,
Primus autem Truchius locum occupavit.

[*On Truchon*

When Vergil was not yet born, Homer was the premier poet. But
when Vergil came on the scene, Homer had to take second place.
But now that Truchon has arrived, Vergil takes second place, and
Homer third. Truchon has taken the top spot.]

The conceit of *epig.* 11, namely, the division of Bèze's soul/mind,
figures in two other poems of his. In one poem (ABM, 171, *c.* 11),
Bèze complains that his mind has been quartered, with Truchon
taking one quarter, Dampierre taking two, and a third quarter that
is quartered among Vaillant, Popon, and Alexis Gaudin (who takes
two quarters of the quarter). Bèze himself is left with only a quarter
of his own mind. For the other poem, see *epig.* 42 below.

1. **malos**: Bèze had originally written *acres*, but Macrin pointed out that
   the quantity of the first syllable is long. Bèze was probably misled
   by a number of related words in Latin (*acus, acuo, aceo, acies, acer-
   bus*), which all have a short first syllable. At any rate, he changed
   *acres* here and in line 5 to *malos* in the second edition.
7. **victitet in locis duobus**: With this we can compare the sophistic ar-
   guments of the slave Tranio at Plautus *Most.* 791–92, insisting to his
   master that he was only late because he could not be in two places at
   the same time: "Simul flare sorbereque hau factu facilest. | Ego hic
   esse et illi simitu hau potui."

## 12.

### Missing in 1597.

In his play *The Country Wife*, Wycherley says, "Poets, like whores, are
only hated by each other," a truism often exemplified in Catullus and
Martial, who attack other poets mercilessly. This truism coupled with
Aristotle's maxim that "poets love their own work more than any other
worker," sums up the theme of this poem: Sapidus, whose name means,
"the wise," reckons himself an outstanding poet while Bèze considers
him stupid. The real occasion for the poem, however, is Bèze's desire to
make a play on several cognates: *Sapid-*, *desip-*, and *insip-*.

1. **Sapidus**: not an unreasonable name for a schoolmaster. In fact, during this period at Sélestat, a German-speaking town not too far from Strasbourg, a certain Johannes Sapidus (Witz) taught Latin and Greek, and was notorious for his old-fashioned methods and strict attention to propriety.
2. **insipidum**: A late word, built from *in* + *sapidus*, not occurring before Julius Firmicus Maternus (fl. 340) and this passage of Paulinus of Nola (d. 431), *Ep.* 39.4: "non ipsi sumus et ultra betam semicoctam insipidi." In his commentary on John 9.3 Augustine couples it to *fatuum*, which is the sense here.

13.

Bèze recognizes with Vergil that large estates require hard work and constant attention, but a small estate affords the owner some leisure time. The poem draws its inspiration primarily from *Georg.* 2.410–13:

> bis vitibus ingruit umbra,
> bis segetem densis obducunt sentibus herbae;
> durus uterque labor; laudato ingentia rura,
> exiguum colito.

[Twice the shade assails the vines, twice the weeds envelop the crop with numerous thorns; each toil is difficult; praise large fields, cultivate a modest one.]

It is interesting to note how Bèze varied the words of Vergil while still referring to him. The only real hint of Vergil's passage are in the words *laudare, colenda,* and *rura,* with only the latter appearing in the same form. No form of *spatios-* (here in place of *ingentia*) appears in Vergil anywhere, and Vergil's *exiguum* is replaced with *parva.* Vergil's *durus uterque labor* is echoed by Bèze's last two lines without duplicating a single word from this passage, but borrowing from a passage in the *Aeneid* almost whole (see note below).

Certainly the poem is not referring to fields and cultivation, but rather metaphorically to poetry as a field to be ploughed, since Tagliacarne was himself a writer of epigrams. A precedent for the poet as a plougher can be found at Juv. 7.48 and Mart. 1.107. Also to be compared is Apollo's advice to Tityrus (probably standing for Vergil himself) at Verg. *Ecl.* 6.4–5:

pastorem, Tityre, pingues
pascere oportet ovis, deductum dicere carmen.

[Tityrus, a shepherd ought to graze fat sheep, but aspire to a slender song.]

The context reveals that Tityrus had entertained the idea of singing about kings and battles, that is, epic poetry, but Apollo tugged at his ear and admonished him to reconsider and to prefer rural melodies; the *Georgics* were yet to be written.

As for the identity of Tagliacarne (sometimes "Teocreno" or "Tagliocarno"), ABM, 178 offer the following information: Benedetto Tagliacarne, "Theocrenus" (1480–1536), Italian humanist of Genoa, passed from the service of Robertet to that of the king and became preceptor of the children of France (1524–1535), whom he accompanied into Spain; he obtained as payment for his services the abbey of Fontfroide, then the bishopric of Grasse in 1534. He died on 18 October 1536, when he was going to publish the collection of epigrams (1536 at Poitiers)[6] that Bèze praises here so strongly, and several pieces of which were reprised by Henry Etienne in the second edition of the *Poemata* in 1569.

On Tagliacarne one may consult Pierre Jourda, "Un humaniste italien en France: Theocrenus (1480–1536)," *Revue du seizième siècle* 16 (1929): 40–57; and Jean Plattard, "L'humaniste Theocrenus en Espagne (1526–1530)," ibidem, 68–76. Jourda reviews his life and literary output. For other verses to Tagliacarne see Gilbert Ducher, *Epigrammatum libri duo*, 1538, p. 96, and Salmon Macrin, *Carm.* fols.4r, 64v. Furthermore, he was friend to Clément Marot, Nicolas Bourbon, and Jacques Colin. Hutton, *Greek Anthology in France*, 25, mentions his fondness for Hellenistic epigrams.

1. **Arva**: Certainly any poem about Vergil that begins with *arva* must be making a play on *arma* at *Aen.* 1.1; a typo in the 1713 edition even gives *Arma* for *Arva* (see apparatus).
3. **Qui volet, hic terram centenis vertat aratris**: An allusion to the Trojan Galaesus of *Aen.* 7.535–39, said to have been so rich that he plowed his Ausonian (Italian) fields with one hundred plows:

---

[6] *Benedicti Theocreni, Episcopi Grassensis, Regis Francisci liberorum praeceptoris, poemata quae juvenis admodum lusit*, Pictavii, ex officina Marnesiorum fratrum ... Anno M.D. XXXVI. The booklet contains lyrics, epigrams, and elegies.

> corpora multa virum circa, seniorque Galaesus,
> dum paci medium se offert, iustissimus unus
> qui fuit, Ausoniisque olim ditissimus arvis:
> quinque greges illi balantum, quina redibant
> armenta, et terram centum vertebat aratris.

For metrical purposes, Bèze replaced Vergil's *et* at line 739 with *hic* and had to expand *centum* to *centenis* to make up for the reduction of *vertebat*.

4. **Plus iuvat**: Again, Bèze reiterates the opinion expressed in *epig.* 1, that short, well-polished books are to be preferred to long ones.

## 14.

Missing in 1597.
Meter: phalaecian hendecasyllable.

The humor derives from the effect of the four lines ending in Philaenus's name: Philaenus, whose name fittingly means "conceited," loves himself without rival. We might say he's all "Philaenus this and Philaenus that" when he opens his mouth. Bèze would turn to the character of Philaenus a number of times in his poetry, and each time he fares very badly under his pen.

A recent investigation into the identification of Philaenus (M. Smith, "Théodore de Bèze and 'Philaenus'," *BHR* 52 [1990]: 345–53) concludes that he was Etienne Dolet, a native of Orléans known for his excessive ego and the calumnious character of his writings (see *epitaph.* 18). Not all of what Dolet wrote was poetry. He was involved back and forth in the Ciceronian controversy, he published translations, and he wrote commentaries on classical authors. After some success as a printer, he was executed in 1546. He published his *Carminum libri quatuor* in 1538, to which Bèze alludes in the following poem from the Orléans manuscript (ABM, 190, no. 114):

*In Philaenum*

> Omnes excellis vates, te teste, Philaene,
>     Et peream si non credo, Philaene, tibi.
> Nam cum te dicis vates excellere cunctos,
>     Te quoque credibile est dicere velle malos.

[*Against Philaenus*

On your word, Philaenus, you surpass all the poets, and may I
die if I don't believe you. For when you say that you surpass all
the poets, I think what you mean to say is all the "bad" ones.]

Again, as in the present poem, Philaenus's problem is that he thinks
much too highly of himself. This theme is carried into another,
unpublished poem by Bèze found in the Orléans manuscript (ABM 179,
no. 46):

> Philaenus Cicero videtur alter
> Et est: quippe superbus est peraeque.

[Philaenus seems and is a second Cicero: both are equally
haughty.]

In this apparent allusion to Dolet's *De imitatione ciceroniana* (1535),
Bèze is making a variation on the theme of Martial's epigram 1.41.
There Caecilius is charged with thinking that he is urbane when in fact
he is nothing more than an indiscriminately witty street vendor. Lines
14–15 are especially relevant:

> Quare desine iam tibi videri,
> quod soli tibi, Caecili, videris.

[So stop thinking you really are something that only you think
you are.]

No doubt Dolet fancied himself a first-rate scholar and poet, but reac-
tions to him among his contemporaries were mixed. Julius Caesar Scali-
ger later wrote a biting epigram about him entitled *Doletus iactabat se
habere Ciceronis animam*. See Smith, "Théodore de Bèze and 'Philae-
nus'," 347, n. 7. Cf. the similar reproach in a poem of Buchanan:

*In Steph. Doletum*

> Verba Dolet habet (quis nescit?) splendida: verum
>   Splendida nil praeter verba Doletus habet.
>           (appearing in Bèze's 1569 edition, 133)

But Visagier considered him both a good orator and a good poet (*Epi-
grammata* [1537], 8).

1. **facit**: this word is perfected, so to speak, by the *perficit* of the last line.
2. **Tersus ... elegans**: Quintilian, *Inst.* 10.1.93, makes a similar judgment of Tibullus: "Elegia quoque Graecos provocamus, cuius mihi tersus atque elegans maxime videtur auctor Tibullus." The idea must be that Philaenus reckons himself on a par with Tibullus.
3. **en tibi**: The word *tibi* here is an ethical dative, as if Bèze gives a sweep of his hand and ushers in Philaenus as a witness.
4. **haec**: a word that begs to be emended, but cannot be, since it appears in all editions. It must refer, then, to the string of adjectives in line two.

## 15.

Missing in 1597; Heywood, *Pleasant dialogues* . . . , ed. Bang, 267.
Meter: phalaecian hendecasyllable.

I have commented on this poem extensively in my article, "Theodore Beza's Classical Library and Christian Humanism," *Archiv für Reformationsgeschichte* 82 (1991): 193–207. The catalogue of books presented here likely reflects the actual contents of Bèze's classical library, given what we know about his early education and his use of these authors in his later career. Joannes Jacomotus alludes to this poem in a poem of his own addressed to the library of Bèze:

> *Ad Bibliothecam Reverendiss. D. Theodori Bezae*
>
> Magni Bibliotheca docta Bezae,
> Quo nil candidius, disertiusque
> Nil concinnius, eruditiusve
> Phoebi suspiciunt novem sorores,
> Et iunctus Charitum lepos choreae . . .
>> (appearing in Bèze's 1614 edition, 186r)

Jacomotus expresses the wish that Bèze will find a place for his book on his shelves.

5. **Cato, Columella, Varro**: The *editio princeps* of Columella was published in 1472 together with the other writers on agricultural matters, Cato, Varro, and Palladius (4th century A.D.) in Venice. Agricultural writers continued to be published together during the

sixteenth century, including important editions at Venice in 1533 and Basel in 1535.

11. **popularis aura**: Demosthenes, based on a rough etymology of the name: δῆμος + σθένος. The phrase is likely drawn from Vergil, *Aen.* 6.816 (*popularibus auris*). Similarly we find this in Pasquier:

> *Demosthenes*
>
> Qui populum flectit, demulcet, mitigat, urget,
>     Nominat hunc tellus Attica, vim populi. (*Icones,* 39)

[This one who motivates, calms, soothes, and spurs on the populace, Athens rightly called the "power of the people."]

13. **Timaee**: There was some confusion during the Renaissance concerning the name Timaeus. A Pythagorean Timaeus of Locri Epizephyrii appears as a character in Plato's work on the soul, *Timaeus*. But a relatively late work in a pseudo-Doric dialect, claiming to be composed by a Timaeus Locrus while merely paraphrasing Plato's work on the soul, allowed Timaeus to take on a life of his own. Both texts are edited together by C. F. Herman (Leipzig, 1852).

15. **Includi numeris Phaleuciorum**: that is, authors whose names do not fit into the constraints of the hendecasyllabic meter.

17. **Salvetote, iterumque, tertiumque**: Bonefon (*Delitiae,* 1: 685) appears to echo these lines in this address to Jacques and Francis Guellis: "Salvete o iterumque tertiumque." The interjection "o" in Bonefon's line appears to elide with the first syllable of *iterumque.*

25. **candido**: Perhaps a play on the name of Bèze's poetic girlfriend, Candida.


## 16.

Missing in 1569, 1576, 1597.
Meter: phalaecian hendecasyllable.


Bèze invites his companions to join him for a banquet to celebrate the arrival of his old mentor Melchior Wolmar, who has come to France on a diplomatic mission from Germany. Ceres and Liber (Bacchus) are invited as representatives of the best gifts that the gods have to offer, food and wine, but the preeminent seat of the classical seating arrangement is given to Wolmar. There's no need for anyone else to talk (no Mercury), recite their poetry (no Apollo), or make a show of their urbanity and wit (no Graces), because Wolmar himself will provide the most eloquent and entertaining conversation imaginable. The poem is somewhat reminiscent of Catullus *c.* 47 and Horace 1.37 (*nunc est bibendum ...* ). For classical arrangements of seating according to status see Pedar W. Foss, "Kitchens and Dining Rooms at Pompeii: The Spatial and Social Relationship of Cooking to Eating in the Roman Household," Ph.D. diss., University of Michigan, 1994, esp. 45-56. The locus classicus is Plutarch *Moralia* 619B-619F (and compare Suet. *Aug.* 74 and Pliny *Ep.* 9.5.3).

ABM, 180, define the occasion of this poem and identify its participants as follows: the diplomatic mission of Wolmar in France, at the side of count Guillaume de Furstemberg and of Christophe of Wenningen, took place in the autumn of 1539 (cf. *Catalogue des actes de François I*, 10 vols. [Washington, DC, 1978], 9: 92); the letter of the duke of Wurttemberg that accredits them is dated 9 August. The fellow-banqueters that Bèze invited to the banquet are his friends Rillerius, Jobertus, and Claude Framberge, who belonged to the group at Orléans. Of Rillerius, who figures already in the eulogy of Bourges, we know very little for certain. Two letters of his are preserved, the one to René Mairat, the son of the baillif of Orléans, dated from Bourges, 21 March 1535, where Rillier declares his intention of following his master Wolmar abroad (Bibl. de Berne, ms. 141, n. 221), the other to Maclou Popon, also from Bourges, on Palm Sunday (Bibl. Nat., ms. lat. 8585, fol. 110). Joubert was lord of Soupize, who would later be a renegade lieutenant of Bourges and denounced as a Protestant in 1562. We have his Latin verse for the performance of the Acts of the Apostles play at Bourges in 1536 (cf. R. Lebègue, *Le mystère des Actes des Apôtres* [Paris, 1929], 95).

8-10: Ironically recalls the liturgy for the dead, which expresses the hope that they are in a place from which all sadness and groaning have fled away.

13-15: Compare the proverb "Sine Cerere et Baccho friget Venus" (Terence, *Eunuchus* 732; Erasmus, *Adagia* 2.3.97)

14. Lyaeum: Lyaeus is a surname of Bacchus used often by the Roman poets, particularly in reference to Bacchus's function as a relaxer (Λυαῖος).

18. deambulones: a contraction of *deambulationes*.

24. in loco supremo: The place of honor, or *locus consularis*.

26. sūpplebis: does not fit the meter, as Macrin points out.

30. facundus ... nepos Atlantis: Mercury, or Hermes as the Greeks

called him, was the son of Zeus and Maia, the daughter of Atlas and Pleïone. According to Iamblichus (*De mysteriis Aegyptiacis* 1) Hermes was θεὸς ὁ τῶν λόγων ἡγεμών ["chief speaker among the gods"] and Luke tells us at Acts 14.12 that the inhabitants of Lystra mistook Paul, as the chief speaker among the missionaries, for Hermes.

## 17.

### Wright, *Delitiae delitiarum* (1637), 8.

Bèze has already counted Columella's *De re rustica* among the special books of his library (see note above on *epig.* 15.5), holding its place among the tomes of Cicero, Catullus, Vergil and the like. What edition Bèze had is not known, since several would be available to him, including the Aldines of 1514 and 1533. It is remarkable that Bèze heaps so much praise on a technical agricultural writer considering his own urban background, though in doing so he reflects a general interest among his contemporaries in the details of farm life and their nostalgic yearning to buy country estates to tie themselves to the land and to live off its produce.[7] Undoubtedly Bèze was also attracted to the citizen–soldier–farmer ideal prevalent in Roman literature (e.g., Pliny *NH* pref. 11). Bèze would allude to Columella once again in a letter dated 1558 to Francis Hotmann, excerpting a passage from 1.7: "Nae tu mihi praeclare Alfianum illud meminisse videris, Bona nomina non appellando fieri mala."

1. **Orphea mirata est Rhodope sua fata canentem**: From Verg. *Ecl.* 6.30, where, contrary to the impression left by Bèze, Vergil actually says that Rhodope and Ismarus never marveled so much at Orpheus's song as the woods do now at that of Silenus. Also cf. *Aen.* 8.499 ("fata canens") for the line-end.
3. **sylvestria rura**: Again an oblique reference to Verg. *Ecl.* 6, this time from line 8, where Tityrus (or Vergil; see note on *epig.* 13 above) says he will take up a rural melody (*agrestem ... Musam*), a clear reference to the *Georgics*, a work not unlike that of Columella.

---

[7] See the interesting discussion on this in Emmanuel Le Roy Ladurie, *The Beggar and the Professor: A Sixteenth-Century Family Saga*, transl. A. Goldhammer (Chicago, 1997), 140–41.

**4. Post te urbes ipsa in tua rura trahit**: The words in 1.6 of Columella's own work may have suggested this line to Bèze:

> Cum etiam si praedictarum artium professoribus ciuitas egeret, tamen sicut apud priscos florere posset res publica—nam sine ludicris artibus atque etiam sine causidicis olim satis felices fuerunt futuraeque sunt urbes; at sine agri cultoribus nec consistere mortalis nec ali posse manifestum est.

**5. Quirites**: another name for "Romans" after their treaty with thse Sabines, who were themselves called Quirites from their primary city Cures, as we learn from Servius[8] writing on Verg. *Aen.* 7.710: "Post foedus Tatii et Romuli placuit, ut quasi unus de duobus fieret populus. Unde et Romani Quirites dicti sunt, quod nomen Sabinorum fuerat a civitate Curibus; et Sabini a Romulo Romani dicti sunt." Cf. also Liv. 1.13.

18.

Missing in 1569, 1576.
Meter: phalaecian hendecasyllable.

Not unlike in the poem on Melchior Wolmar, where Bèze wondered if Wolmar was not greater than the gods since he restored sight to Homer, here he wonders if Manutius is not a god since he restored the poets to life, something only a god could do. Manutius had died in 1515, four years before Bèze was born, but his son Paulus kept the publishing house running, and the Aldine books were spread throughout Europe's "Republic of Letters."

**1-2. Didonis ... Maro**: Vergil wrote of Queen Dido's suicide in *Aen.* 4. Cf. *Icon.* 2.

**2. Pompeii rogum Lucanus**: Lucan's work *De bello civili* deals with the civil war between Caesar in Pompey, in which he makes Caesar out to be the villain. This line is hopelessly unmetrical, since there simply are not enough syllables. Perhaps he imagines "Pompeii" can be read as four syllables?

---

[8] *Servii Grammatici qui feruntur in Bergilii carmina commentarii*, edd. Georg Thillo and Hermann Hagen, 3 vols. (Lepizig, 1881-1902).

**12. sūblatam:** does not fit the meter, as Macrin notes.

**16. Vitam reddere mortuis:** For the same phrasing see *Scriptores Historiae Augustae: Flavi Vopisci Syracusii Divus Aurelianus* 24.8.3. Despite what Bèze says, traditionally the ancients imagined that even gods were forbidden by the fates from restoring life to the dead; so says Apollo in reference to his beloved Hyacinthus at Ovid *Met.* 10.202–3. Asclepius, son of Apollo, thought that his medical skills could override the fates, but he soon found out that it was not with impunity (Ovid *Fast.* 6.747). Hercules was able to bring Alcestis back from the dead, but only under special circumstances.

19.

Missing in 1569, 1576, 1597.
Meter: phalaecian hendecasyllable.

This first of the epigrams addressed to Candida, a fictitious girl of Bèze's literary imagination (see K. Summers, "Theodore Beza's Reading of Catullus," *Classical and Modern Literature* 15 [1995]: 233–45), employs the distinctive Catullan vocabulary: *ioci, deliciae, desiderium, invida, tenebricosum, carior,* words often employed in the context of Lesbia. Candida's name means "fair-skinned girl," and is used favorably as a descriptive term for females among the Roman poets; e.g., see Catullus's description of Caecilius's girlfriend at *c.* 35.8 and the girl whom Fabullus is supposed to bring to dinner at Cat. 13.4. Cf. also Cat. 68.70; 86.1; and Hor. *Epod.* 11.27, among many others (*TLL* s.v. 241.10). Ovid's use of the adjectival form at *Amores* 3.5–6 is clearly defined:

> Candida candorem roseo suffusa rubore
> ante fuit, niveo lucet in ore rubor.

> [Before she was fair, with rosy red mingling throughout her fairness; the redness glows on her snowy-white face.]

To modern tastes such paleness would make a girl less enticing, but for the ancients it was a mark of upper-class beauty: only girls who had to work outside and did not have the leisure of an easy life indoors would have tanned skin.

This poem begins along the lines of Ovid *Amores* 1.5, where that poet recounts how he was lying on his couch for a nap and was suddenly visited by his girl (Corinna). In contrast to Bèze's visit from Candida, though, Ovid's visit leads to a sexual episode that ends in exhaustion; Bèze, who began his nap exhausted, does not have a sexual episode with Candida. Instead, after some caressing and flirting with his girl, Bèze wakes up to find her visit was only a dream. He pleads with the gods of sleep and dreams either to make the image real or to put him to sleep forever. Another example of the dream topos in Ovid is *Am.* 3.5, which begins similarly to our poem: "Nox erat, et somnus lassos submisit ocellos; | terruerunt animum talia visa meum."

Although by almost any reading Bèze's poem has its own sexual undertones, the language is ambivalent enough that Bèze could and would alter a few words and lines here and there from his composition to make the subject of his dream his male friend Maclou Popon without it necessarily appearing homoerotic. He inserted the modified composition into a letter written to Popon in 1539 (*Corr.* 1: 34) and insisted to him—in a joking manner—that he was narrating a real dream. There the addition of the lines *Ni te plus oculis amo, Besaee* (twice) and *Meas delitias, meos amores*, show the Catullan affiliation of this poem even more definitively. While at first glance the latter line appears addressed to a lover, the words *delitiae* and *amores* did not always refer exclusively to the object of one's erotic love. Such is the case at Cic. *Div.* 1.79, where Quintus asks his brother Marcus, "Quid? amores ac deliciae tuae Roscius, num aut ipse aut pro eo Lanuvium totum mentiebatur?" Roscius was a male actor, but Quintus is not intimating that Cicero and he were lovers, only the closest of friends.

5. **iocos deliciasque factitare**: For the lovers' *ioci* cf. Horace *Odes* 3.21.2, *Epist.* 1.6.65f., 2.2.56; Ovid *Ars Am., passim*, esp. 3.365 has the following:

> Mille facesse iocos; turpe est nescire puellam
> Ludere: ludendo saepe paratur amor.

Catullus has a similar phrase with *delicias* at *c.* 74.1–2:

> Gellius audierat patruum obiurgare solere
> Si quis delicias diceret aut faceret.

Kenneth Quinn translates Catullus's phrase *delicas ... faceret* with "to indulge in funny business."[9] Adams, *Latin Sexual Vocabu-*

---

[9] Kenneth Quinn, *Catullus: The Poems. Edited with Introduction, Revised Text and Commentary* (London, 1973²), 405.

*lary* (161–62, 196–98), examines other passages with *iocari* and *deliciae* in amatory contexts.

**6. tractare manu**: Used of an especially skilled masseuse at Mart. 82.13:

> Percurrit agili corpus arte tractatrix
> Manumque doctam spargit omnibus membris;

[The masseuse with nimble art massages his whole body, and glides her skilled hand over all his limbs.]

**7. Et blaesa velut increpare voce**: The adjective *blaes-* is normally uncomplimentary in classical contexts, having to do with the inability to pronounce the sibilants *s* and *z*. Drunks are said to "slur" or "stammer" from the effects of alcohol (Ovid *Ars Amat.* 1.598; Mart. 9.87.2), a parrot is described as "throaty-toned" (Ovid *Am.* 2.6.24), and a child's babble receives the epithet "lisping" (Mart. 5.34.8). The only instance where the word can be said to have erotic overtones occurs at Ovid *Ars Amat.* 3.294, describing flirtatious women who feign a lisp. It is the latter connotation that Bèze intends here; the addition of *increpare* would indicate that the voice is being forced out with an extra amount of breath. Similarly, in an unpublished poem (ABM, 186), the lisping tongue of a woman holds a special attraction:

> *Ad Candidam*
>
> Ne canas mea mollicella Seiren
> Linguam istam, rogo, **blaesulam** coerce,
> Et guttur tremulum jube tacere.
> Nam si dicere voculam vel unam
> Si depromere verbulum vel unum                                    5
> Pergas, protinus ista vox suavis,
> Hoc guttur tremulum, ista lingua **blaesa**
> Suavi me facient perire morte.
> Tunc haec dicere, tunc loqui universi,
> Te visa, incipient: Ea est puella,                                10
> Haec est Candida, Candida illa Seiren,
> Voce quae tremula, ore quae canoro
> Bezam pessima nuper interemit,
> Bezam Candida cui placebat una.

Like Bèze, Bonefon uses the word in conjunction with *mollicella* to describe his girlfriend (*Delitiae* vol. 1, p. 658, *Ad Antonium Corellum*): *Illa blaesula mollicella verba.* The stress, therefore, must be on the effeminacy and softness of the girl's speech. Perhaps the best meaning comes to light through a line of Visagier (*Hendecasyllabi*, 1538, 16r): "Iamque puer blaeso murmure clamat, adest." In the latter instance the word gives the sense of "baby talk."

10. A mocking recall (in erotic context) of Philippians 1.23.
16. **Morphea ... Somnum**: Somnus, the god of sleep, and his son Morpheus, the personification of human forms in dreams, are implicated in the story of Ceyx and Alcyone (Ovid *Met.* 11.583ff.). Somnus, at the prompting of Iris, sent Morpheus in the guise of Ceyx to inform Alcyone in a dream that her husband had died at sea, at which news Alcyone was thoroughly grief-stricken.
20. **perennem | Inducas mihi somniationem**: Echoing the *perpetua nox* of Cat. 5.6, without duplicating any of the words.

**20.**

To this poem can be contrasted the admonishment of Horace that the critic be good and sensible (*AP* 445): "vir bonus et prudens versus reprehendet inertes." It is also in the *Ars Poetica* (esp. 295–322) that Horace makes the satirical claim, that, since he has lost the insanity needed to be a good poet, he will use his new-found sanity in his role as a critic. Apparently, many were taking insanity to be a mark of inspiration and a sufficient qualification for being a poet (Horace insisted on the combination of natural talent with strenuous training). Thus we understand that Sextus has not lived up to Horace's ideal critic, since he is not sane. He proves it by attacking everyone without discrimination, thereby breaking one of Horace's cardinal rules for the critic, namely, to allow some leeway in good poets for lapses: even Homer nods.

The poem is structured around the twofold meaning of *caecus* and *sanum*, which begin the lines. It is possible to be both blind in the eyes and blind in the mind (as was the case with Oedipus), just as it is possible to have a healthy head (not blind) and a sane head (mentally stable). I have tried to reflect Bèze's play by translating with a double entendre, "sick in the head." The double sense of *sanum caput* likewise seems to be at play in a poem of Martial (2.66.6), in which the poet describes how enraged a certain Lalage became toward her maidservant when the mirror revealed she had a hair out of place. In return for whacking her maidservant over the head with the mirror, Martial wishes she would become bald and ugly.

**2. reprensor:** continues the thought of *reprehendis* of the previous line. **sanum ... caput:** Echoes Horace's *caput insanabile* at *AP* 300. Horace is speaking of people who, influenced by Democritus's dictum ("excludit sanos Helicone poetas | Democritus," 296–97), pretend to be mad so they will be thought of as poets. These refuse to cut their hair as evidence that their mind is not right.

## 21.

Missing in 1569, 1576, 1597;
Kendall, *Flowers of Epigrammes*, 160–61.

Hutton (*Greek Anthology in France*, 117, 664) points to this poem as one of only two epigrams in which Bèze borrowed themes directly from the *Greek Anthology*, the other being the *Descriptio virtutis* (below). Here *AP* 9.11–13 are particularly relevant, but especially 9.12:

Τυφλὸς ἀλητεύων ξωλὸν πόδας ἠέρταζεν,
    ὄμμασιν ἀλλοτρίοις ἀντερανιζόμενος,
ἄμφω δ᾽ ἡμιτελεῖς πρὸς ἑνὸς φύσιν ἡρμόσθησαν
    τοὐλλιπὲς ἀλλήλοις ἀντιπαρασχόμενοι.

[The blind tramp carried the lame one, being repaid by the use of the other's eyes, and the two half-complete beings fitted together into one whole, each supplying the other's deficiency.]

Over a dozen Neo-Latin poets imitate the theme (see Hutton, *Greek Anthology in France*, 664).

**2. Convenīs:** unmetrical, as Macrin notes.
**6. Semiviro:** a derisive term most often used for the castrated, effeminate priests of Cybele, as at Mart. 3.91.2 ("semiviro Cybeles cum grege iunxit iter") and Verg. *Aen.* 12.99 ("semiviri Phrygis"). ἡμιγυναῖκα: Cf. Simon. 179.9. Pasquier concludes his imitation with this line: "Non ullus fuerit verior Androgynus" (*Epig.* 2.74).

## 22.

Meter: phalaecian hendecasyllable.

Lupus just so happens to have a name that means "wolf," the creature who is proverbially hungry in Greco-Roman literature (Aesop has thirty-seven fables involving a hungry wolf). No doubt Lupus made himself an attractive potential dinner guest by feigning sobriety and an interest in philosophical restraint, but once he arrived at Bèze's house he revealed himself to be the wolf he really was.

1. **sobrium Platonem**: Plato, like many other philosophers, urged the pursuit and practice of *sophrosyne*, i.e., moderation: σωφροσύνη μὲν διωκτέον καὶ ἀσκητέον (*Gorgias* 507D). Macrin notes that the original reading, *sōbrium mihi*, is unmetrical.
6. **sophia**: equivalent to the Latin *sapientia*, here it means "philosophy," as at Mart. 1.111.1 and 7.74.9.

## 23.

Missing in 1569, 1576, 1597; Tahureau (see below).

The two literary styles placed in antithesis in this distich catch our attention: *nugatur* and *seria faciet*. Unmistakably the word *nugatur* harks back to the Catullan programmatic *nugae* of c. 1.4, though here its appearance is so striking given the difference between the epigram and the lengthy satirical sketches like *Pantagruel* and *Gargantua*. Even so, for Bèze, what Catullus wrote, and for that matter what Martial wrote, has some affinity with these satires of Rabelais. The distinction drawn between the two styles represented by *nugatur* and *seria*, nevertheless, does not preclude some degree of overlap; here Bèze's *seria* hints at the moral significance of Rabelais's work underlying the more jocular surface, an arrangement that Visagier had called "spice added to the truth" ("adjunxit vero cum tua Musa sals" [1537], I, p. 61).[10] There appears also to have been a tradition that while *nugae* are suitable for one's early years,

---

[10] The labels "playful" or "soft" that the epigrammatists apply to their poetry do not preclude them from asserting a serious intent as well. Note, e.g., the sentiment in a poem of Bourbon: "Quod molleis faciam versus, quod temporis huius | Corruptos mores carmina nostra premant ..." (*Nugae* [1533], fol. 26v).

they must be abandoned eventually to be followed up by *seria*. Such is the sentiment expressed by Buchanan in a poem appearing in Bèze's 1569 edition (49):

> Ite leves nugae, sterilesque valete camoenae,
>   Grataque Phoebaeo Castalis unda choro.
> Ite, sat est: primos vobiscum absumpsimus annos,
>   Optima pars vitae deperiitque meae.

[Go, light *nugae*, and farewell, barren Muses, and Castalian Spring that pleases Phoebus's chorus. Go, it is enough. We consumed our early years with you, and the best part of my life has been lost.]

Bèze's poem, translated into French, appears in the *Premières poésies* of Jacques Tahureau, 1554 (see "Sources of Tahureau's Lycrics" in *Modern Language Notes* 54 [1939]: 339–47; Prosper Blanchemain, ed., *Poésies de Jacques Tahureau*, 2 vols. [Paris, 1870]; cf. Abel LeFranc, "Remarques sur la date et sur quelques circonstances de la mort de Rabelais," *Revue des études rabelaisiens*, 1 [1903]: 59–65, esp. 61):

> *De Rabelays, pris du latin de de Bèze*
>
> Puys qu'il surpasse en riant
> Ceux qui a bon esciant
> Traictent choses d'importance:
> Combien sera il plus grand
> (Je te pry dy moy) s'il prend                    5
> Un oeuvre de consequence?

Tahureau's translation of Bèze's poem is the first incontestable reference to the death of Rabelais.

On the sentiments of Bèze in regard to Rabelais, cf. Charles Bost, "Théodore de Bèze et Rabelais: Le passavant," *Revue du XVIᵉ siècle*, 19 (1933): 282–90. Rabelais was well-known to the *sodales* at Orléans, esp. Hubert Susannée. On this see Henri Clouzot, "Les amités de Rabelais en Orléanais," *Revue des études rabelaisiens* 3 (1905): 156–75. Bèze dropped this poem from later editions, influenced no doubt by Calvin's vicious attacks on Rabelais in the *De scandalis* (Geneva, 1550) and elsewhere. Reformers in general were fond of calling Rabelais an atheist: on this see Lucien Febvre, *The Problem of Unbelief in the Sixteenth Century* (Cambridge, 1992), esp. 101–51; our poem is quoted on 141, n. 78.

Finally, one must note poem 1.3 of Bourbon's 1540 collection of
*nugae* which this poem of Bèze closely echoes:

> Cum laude et fama volitem super aethera, scribens
> Nugas: si scribam seria, quantus ero?

[Since I fly to heaven with praise and glory while writing *nugae*,
if I write serious stuff, how impressive will I be?]

1. **nugatur**: cognate, as stated above, with the Catullan programmatic
   *nugae* of *c.* 1.4. The usual translation, "trifles," does not do full jus-
   tice to the word; obviously, Rabelais's work cannot be described as
   such. The *nugae* of Catullus evoke a long tradition of Greek and Ro-
   man satire, particularly as expressed in the biting iambs of Archilo-
   chus and Hipponax, Old Comedy, Atellan farce, mime, Fescennine
   verses, and the carnival spirit. A passage of Varro at *Saturae Menip-
   peae* 513 sums up much of the nugatory attitude:

> Quod si Actaeon occupasset et ipse prius suos canes comedisset,
> non nugas saltatoribus in theatro faceret.

[But if Actaeon had preempted his dogs by catching them and
eating them first, he wouldn't have provided nugatory material
for the mimes in the theater.]

*Nugae* depend upon the unexpected turn, the sudden reversal of the
mundane, the perverse observation of the ordinary. Many of the
Renaissance writers assumed the title *nugae* for their poetry, but not
always with merit.

**seria**: most often connected with *iocus* and its cognates in classical
authors; so Cic. *Off.* 1.37.134: "Ac videat in primis, quibus de rebus
loquatur; si seriis severitatem adhibeat, si iocosis, leporem;" Plaut.
*Poen.* 1320–1321: *Si quid per iocum | dixi, nolito in serium convertere.*
Likewise Cic. *Phil.* 2.7, *Fin.* 2.85, *Off.* 1.103; Ovid *Epist. ex Ponto*
2.4.9 and 4.3.13. Here, instead of some form of *iocus*, Bèze substi-
tutes *nugari*, a collocation reminiscent of Horace *AP* 451 (*hae nugae
seria ducent*; see *epig.* 2 above). To this also cf. the following poem of
Bourbon (*Nugae* [1533], fol. 112v):

> *Ad lectorem*
>
> Sic ut in immensum adsurgat crescatque volumen,
> **Nugari** tecum Lector amice iuvat:

Venerit (ut spero) nobis maturior aetas,
  Post ludos venient **seria**, parce precor.

[*To the reader*

I love to play the satirist with you, friendly reader, so I can make
my book fat and heavy. Should I ever reach old age, as I hope I
do, I promise you, be patient, I'll get more serious.]

### 24.

Missing in 1597; Wright, *Delitiae delitiarum* (1637), 9;
Heywood, *Pleasant dialogues* ... ed. Bang, 269.

In November 1530 François I married Eleanor, sister of Charles V, as
part of a conclusion to hostilities. The ceremony took place in Orléans,
so that Bèze probably had actually seen her. Bèze makes the point that
Eleanor's beauty, unlike Helen's proverbial beauty in the case of the
Achaeans and Trojans, led to peace and harmony between two warring
factions. He may be altering the thought of Propertius (2.3.32ff.) about
his girl Cynthia: "post Helenam haec terris forma secunda redit" ("the
beauty Helen once wore returns to the earth a second time"). Propertius
goes on to say that having seen Cynthia, to his mind another Helen, he
can understand why men could quarrel so over such a beautiful woman.
Propertius revisited the conceit and expanded on it at the end of 3.8.
The final two lines read:

> aut tecum aut pro te mihi cum rivalibus arma
>   semper erunt: in te pax mihi nulla placet.

[Either with you or for you I will always wage the battle with
my rivals: where you are concerned no peace pleases me.]

1. **Phoebus**: Apollo, as sun god, could see everything.
2. **pulchrius**: cf. Ovid, *Heroid.* 8.99: "te tamen esse Helenen, quod eras
   pulcherrima, sensi."
4. **ferit lites**: perhaps translating ἐρίσαντε ("quarreling") of *Iliad* 1.5, or
   an allusion to the goddess Eris, whose actions in part instigated the
   Trojan War. In Greek the name "Helen" was by a traditional ety-
   mology derived from "destruction," as in Aesch. *Agam.* 681–809.

## 25.

Missing in 1569, 1576, 1597.
Meter: phalaecian hendecasyllable.

As in other epigrams the name of the person concerned is instructive: Asinius is an ass. Apparently Bèze has made some sort of investment with Asinius which Asinius assured him would pay off big, but now that Asinius has the money he puts Bèze off. On the possible identity of Asinius, see the notes to *epig.* 6.

**1. Seu domi ... seu foris:** for the phraseology cf. Mart. 6.94.2: "sive foris seu cum cenat in urbe domi."

**8. horas ... nuntiabit omnes:** normally, *nuntiare horas* would mean "to tell the time of day," usually in reference to slaves who watch the *horologia* and *solaria*, as at Juv. 10.216, Mart. 8.67.1, and Pliny *Ep.* 3.1.8. Cf. also Buchanan's *Ecce, vigil subito quartam denuntiat horam* (in Bèze's 1569 edition, 50). The addition of *omnes* here indicates the emphasis on the individual hours that the clock (*quod*) sounds off.

## 26.

ABM (p. 184) report that a marginal note in the hand of Bèze in his own copy of the *Poemata* of 1597 reveals that the subject of the poem is the court reception of 1540. Again, as in several other poems by Bèze, the topic is François I and Charles V. Bèze uses the historical example of the Roman civil wars to remind the reader that wars have a devastating effect on power. What is interesting is the two states being compared: Rome and Europe. The title held by Charles V was Emperor of the Holy Roman Empire, and, together with France, which was controlled by François I, the two of them did indeed hold the reins of western continental Europe. The defining outside force was the Ottoman Turks who menaced Vienna in 1529 and the Habsburg territories (Germany) for the next few decades, until they were defeated at the battle of Lepanto in 1571.

**1. soceri generique:** Pompey the Great had married Julius Caesar's daughter Julia, and thus the two were related as father-in-law and son-in-law even though Pompey was older by six years than Caesar. Julia died in childbearing, however, in 54 B.C., several years before the Roman civil wars in 49–48 B.C. Note the close parallel at Mart. 9.70.3: "cum gener atque socer diris concurreret armis."

**2. suis ... gladiis:** i.e., by civil war; cf. Lucan 4.500.

**4. Martia Roma:** Mars, the god of war, as the father of Romulus and Remus, was considered the divine progenitor of the Roman people.

**5. fratrum:** François I and Charles V were not brothers by blood, but the former had married the sister of Charles V, Eleanor, in 1530, as was noted in reference to *epig.* 24 above.

**27.**

Missing in 1569, 1576.

François I was known for two things, his extravagantly expensive military pursuits against the territories of Charles V and his patronization of the arts, including architecture. He bestowed his royal favors on Robert Etienne, Marot, and Rabelais, all friends of Bèze, founded the Collège de France, and established the school of decorative arts headed by the Italians Rosso and Primaticcio. As in other poems, Bèze equates him with the gods, this time through a witty combination at the end of the poem. On the illness, ABM 184 write, "This illness of the king is probably that of the autumn of 1539 at Compiègne" (cf. Herminjard, *Correspondance des réformateurs*, 6: 466 and Guiffrey, *Oeuvres de Clément Marot*, 1: 461ff. and 4: 189).

**1. Pallas:** Athena as the patron goddess of the arts.

**2. Mavors:** an old poetic name for Mars, god of war, related to the Greek μάχη (+ Lat. *vor-*, "turner of war").

**7. Atropos:** the third sister of the Moirai (Fates), she was responsible for cutting the thread of a person's life at the point when it should end. Her name means "inevitable" or "no turning back." Bèze had originally printed *Hoc Atropos*, a reading corrected by Macrin for metrical reasons.

**28.**

Missing in 1597; Kendall, *Flowers of Epigrammes*, 159.

Ironically, after Marot died in 1544 and Bèze had published his *Iuvenilia* in 1548, then converted to Protestantism, John Calvin asked Bèze to complete the translation of the Psalms into French begun by Marot. Here, though, Bèze refers not to the Psalms but to his amatory verse (see C. A. Mayer, *Clément Marot*, [Paris, 1972]). He jokes that if people were so impressed by the vivid details and tone Apelles gave to his painting of Venus so as to imagine he saw Venus, then Marot's vivid amatory details and tone suggest that he saw Venus completely naked. Apelles was a fourth-century B.C. painter from Colophon and Ephesus; his Aphrodite Anadyomene depicts Venus rising from the sea and wringing out her hair. On the painter and his portrayal of Venus, Propertius (3.9.11) writes "in Veneris tabula summam sibi poscit Apelles" ("from his painting of Venus Apelles claims his highest glory"). References to Apelles's Venus abound in the Neo-Latin poets. E.g., Pasquier writes,

> Expressit Veneres tot et lepores,
> In una Venere exprimenda Apelles ... (*Epig.* 1.8)

And Bourbon:

> *Ad puellam*
>
> Olim qui Veneris vultum depinxit Apelles,
>     Maximus et primus fertur in arte sua.
> Ecce tamen genitor tuus est praestantior illo;
>     Cuius periculo sis Dea facta Venus.
> Ipsa quidem multos utebat Apellis imago,                     5
>     Atque aliquot iuvenes cepit amore sui.
> Non habuit tamen illorum unde restingueret ignes:
>     Tu simul inflammas, et medicamen habes.
>         (*Delitiae*, 1: 776)

This poem of Bèze echoes a conceit appearing at *AP* 16.168:

> Γυμνὴν εἶδε Πάρις με, καὶ Ἀγχίσης, καὶ Ἄδωνις·
> τοὺς τρεῖς οἶδα μόνους· Πραξιτέλης δὲ πόθεν;

[Paris, Anchises, and Adonis saw me naked; those three only did I know. So when did Praxiteles see me?]

4. **tota Venus**: i.e., Venus from head to toe, as indicated by the *tota*, as opposed to *omnis*, which by itself would not express the totality of the experience.

## 29.

Missing in 1569, 1576, 1597.
Meter: phalaecian hendecasyllable.

In other words, Candida's beauty could not be fully captured on canvas, even when the quality of the painting outstrips all others. A similar theme appears at Mart. 1.109, a poem about Publius and his beloved dog Issa. Lines 17–23 read as follows:

> hanc ne lux rapiat suprema totam,
> picta Publius exprimit tabella,
> in qua tam similem videbis Issam,
> ut sit tam similis sibi nec ipsa.      20
> Issam denique pone cum tabella:
> aut utramque putabis esse veram,
> aut utramque putabis esse pictam.

[Lest the final day should snatch her away whole, Publius paints her on canvas so realistically that it is more like Issa than Issa. Just compare Issa with the picture, and you won't know if both are real or both are painted.]

Poems about realistic paintings are common (cf. *AP* 9.604, 11.212–15, 233, 250), but Bèze has added his own twist: instead of this remarkably beautiful painting doing justice to Candida by being extremely lifelike, it falls short. Compare a similar play with words in the following epigram of Pasquier:

> *In Adonem*
> Qui voluit turpem cum formosissimus esses,
>     Formaeque effigiem pingere dissimilem,
> Tam vere expressit, magis ut non possit Apelles,
>     Nam nil dissimile est tam sibi, quam tibi tu.
>         (*Epig.* 1.61)

**1–3. Quanto ... tanto:** in order to express strongly the proportional relationships between the paintings and between Candida and her portrait, lines 1 and 3 are essentially the same, *mutatis mutandis*.

**3–4. pulchrior ... tabella:** perhaps it is coincidental, but similar phraseology appears at Mart. 10.32: "pulchrior in terris nulla tabella foret."

## 30.

### Kendall, *Flowers of Epigrammes*, 160.

ABM (185) report that in his personal copy of the 1597 edition Bèze writes that these New Year greetings were sent from Paris to Orléans, and were well received by Truchon and Dampierre. The poem expresses the close-knit circle the three of them had developed: Bèze is friends with both of them, and the two of them are inseparable. He closes the poem out with a subtle jest, that the two of them are so inseparable that one poem will do for both. Underpinning the gesture is Bèze's sly escape from writing more than one poem, comparable to the giving of one present to an entire family at Christmas rather than to every individual in it.

The ancient poets often sent newly composed poems to each other as gifts on holidays and birthdays. At *c.* 14 Catullus receives a book of bad poetry from Calvus as a Saturnalian joke. Martial at 10.18 insists to his muse that they must send the usual poetry to his friend Macer as a Saturnalian tribute. Martial implies at 10.87 that if people give presents each according to their own trade, as a poet he should send nothing but a poem for a present. Cf. Stat. *Silv.* 4.9 and pref., and 2.3.62.

The Neo-Latin poets often imitated the conceit. Cf. these two poems from Pasquier:

*Ad Scaevolam Sammarthanum*

Dant alii gemmas, smaragdos, adamanta, pyropos,
    Aurum, ebur, et locuples India quicquid alit.
Tu mihi qui versus, plus Sammarthane dedisti,
    Nam gemmas, quae tu carmina mittis habent.
      (*Epig.* 2.97)

*Ad Labienum*

Divitias tibi do, nobis Epigrammata mittis,
    Verum tu flocci munera nostra facis.
Iam variabo vices, siquidem tibi carmina mittam,
    Dum modo divitias des, Labiene, mihi. (*Epig.* 5.64)

**7–8. Nec temere ... mitto dona**: A reference to Martial's book 13, often entitled *Xenia*, which is a collection of couplets that would be attached to gifts, describing them in some way. Visagier also has a section entitled *Xenia* in his 1537 edition of epigrammata. Here, Bèze bows out from actually sending something material to his friends beyond a single piece of paper with a poem on it. In essence, he is being (among other things) cheap.

**31.**

Missing in 1569, 1576; *Tottel's Miscellany*, 1: 104, 2: 234–35
(= Merrill, *Grimald*, 389, 428–29);
McFarlane, *Renaissance Latin Poetry*, 34.

Hutton (*Greek Anthology in France*, 117) points out that this poem is an imitation of Lysippus's *Descriptio occasionis* at *AP* 16.275, along with the Latin version by Ausonius, but, as always, Bèze added original elements of his own. Bèze may have been influenced by a similar piece by Andrea Alciati (*Emblemata* 122) or by versions of Guillaume de la La Perrière (*Le théâtre des bons engins, auquel sont contenue cent emblemes moraux* [Paris, 1539], 63), Gilles Corrozet (*L' hécatongraphie* [1544], 166), or even Erasmus (*Adag.* 1.7.70). Other imitations of this poem from the *Greek Anthology* are listed by Hutton, *Greek Anthology in France*, 801. In the 1569 edition, Bèze would alter the title and text of the poem to a Christianized *Descriptio Religionis*. In the 1597 edition he attached it to his emblem XXXV (258), where appears an engraving of the personified *Religio* that he describes:

Quaenam sic lacero vestita incedis amictu?
   Religio, summi vera Patris soboles.
Cur vestis tam vilis? opes contemno caducas.

> Quis liber hic? Patris lex veneranda mei.
> Cur nudum pectus? decet hoc Candoris amicam.
> Cur innixa cruci? Crux mihi sola quies.
> Cur alata? homines doceo super astra volare.
> Cur radians? mentis discutio tenebras. (cf. Verg. *Aen.* 12.669)
> Quid docet hoc frenum? mentis cohibere furores.
> Cur tibi mors premitur? mors quia mortis ego.[11]

Among the epigrams of the 1597 edition Bèze includes yet another version (very close in content to emblem XXXV), entitled *Vera Religio* (218).

One poet not listed by Hutton who also imitated this dialogic style is the Scottish author George Buchanan, who, following Michael Marullus, changed the subject of inquiry to Cupid (in McFarlane, *Renaissance Latin Poetry* 58, poem XL). He begins as follows:

> Quis puer ales? Amor. genitor quis? blandus ocelli, etc.

Bèze turns Buchanan's ending on its head:

> non metuit mortem? non. quare? saepe renasci,
> saepe mori deciens hunc brevis hora videt ...

Pasquier has a poem similar to those of Marullus and Buchanan:

> *In amoris effigiem, ad pictorem*
>
> Quis puer hic nudus, caecus, pharetratus, et ales,
>   An Deus, an monstrum, dic mihi pictor? Amor ...
>       (*Epig.* 6.34)

**4. Cur gemina est facies? Tempus utrumque noto**: i.e., Virtue disregards fickle fortune, a major theme of philosophy, and already in Horace, *Odes* 3.29.49–56. See also Solon, fr. 4 (Diehl): ἐπεὶ τὸ μὲν ἐμπεδόν ἐστι, | χρήματα δ᾽ ἀνθρώπων ἄλλοτε ἄλλος ἔχει ["Virtue is a sure possession, but riches go now to this man, now to that one"].

**8. Nescio sola mori**: A common conceit; cf. Cic. *Am.* 27.102: "virtutem ... quae cum corpore non periit" ("virtue which does not perish with the body"); Plautus, *Captivi*, 690: "Qui per virtutem periit, at

---

[11] Cf. "O mors, ero mors tua," antiphon for Lauds of Holy Saturday.

non interit" ("He who dies for virtue's sake does not perish"); Sallust, *BC* 1.4: "Divitiarum et formae gloria fluxa atque fragilis est; virtus clara aeternaque habetur" ("The glory of riches and beauty is fickle and uncertain; virtue remains bright and eternal"); Tiberius Caesar, *Apophthegm*: "Vivet post funera virtus" ("Virtue lives beyond the grave").

## 32.

Wright, *Delitiae delitiarum* (1637), 9.
Meter: phalaecian hendecasyllable.

Bèze raises the question why Mercury should function as the god of such widely divergent areas, as eloquence and business. He answers that both are necessary to succeed in the marketplace. The word *mancipia* in the title puts a somewhat negative tinge on the poem, as if to say that those involved in money-making will do anything or say anything to make a sale. The 1597 edition has a significantly different version (152–53):

> Prisci quum fere sueverint Poetae
> Rebus quodque suis sacrare numen,
> Cur Lucrum, Forum, et Eloquutionem
> Uni Mercurio tamen sacrarunt?
> Vates scilicet hoc modo indicarunt          5
> Futurum, ut rabiosa quisquis arma
> Tractaret fori, haberet ille curam
> Lucri non minus ac loquutionis.

4. **lucrum, forum, et elocutionem**: Mercury, or Hermes as the Greeks called him, was the patron god of merchants and, as the herald god and as the god of thieves, was associated with cleverness of speech, especially the deceptive variety.

7–8. **arma ... fori**: Ovid (*Trist.* 4.10.17–18) used these words to indicate that his brother was more equipped for public speaking than himself: "Frater ad eloquium viridi tendebat ab aevo, | fortia verbosi natus ad arma fori."

### 33.

Missing in 1569, 1576, 1597.

The theme could have been suggested to Bèze from any number of sources, not least of which is the words of Jesus at John 4.23: "But the hour cometh, and now is, when the true worshipers shall worship the Father in spirit and in truth" (KJV). Remarkably similar to Bèze's poem is a passage from Seneca *Ep.* 115.5, *Ad Lucilium*:

> Colitur autem non taurorum opimis corporibus contrucidatis nec auro argentoque suspenso nec in thesauros stipe infusa, sed pia et recta voluntate.

> [Worship does not consist in the slaughtering of bulls with fat bodies nor in the hanging up of gold or silver, and not in pouring coins into the offering plate, but in a will that is pious and upright.]

At *De legibus* 24–25 Cicero argues that the gods should be approached with uprightness and purity of mind without a show of wealth and costly rites. Cf. also Hebrews 9.12–14.

**2. thura Sabaea**: i.e., Arabian frankincense and myrrh. Cf. *epig.* 71.

### 34.

Wright, *Delitiae delitiarum* (1637), 15;
Heywood, *Pleasant dialogues* ..., ed. Bang, 268.

Undoubtedly this poem takes its cue from the famous saying of Hesiod that the half is greater than the whole (*Works and Days*, 40): νήπιοι, οὐδὲ ἴσασιν ὅσῳ πλέον ἥμισυ παντός. The saying was repeated often in antiquity (Plato, *Laws*, 3.690E, *Republic*, 466C; Plutarch, *Moralia*, 36A; Diogenes Laertius 1.75 [attributed to Pittacus]); Erasmus includes it among his adages (1.9.95). Bèze may also have known the story told of Marcus Tullius Cicero at Macrobius 2.3.4, where it is reported that Marcus once said, on seeing an over-life-size portrait bust of his diminutive brother Quintus, that in this case the half was greater than the whole. In Bèze's version, however, the *half* of Erasmus is at least equal to the *whole* of the world. That Bèze had in mind Hesiod's maxim is indicated by the poem that follows this one in the manuscript collection (ABM 84) and appears in the 1569 edition (173) and in the *Icones* with Erasmus's entry:

De Erasmo, cingulo tenus depicto

Ἥμισυ τοῦ παντὸς εἶν᾽ Ἀσκραῖος ἔειπεν
Ἥμισυ δ᾽ ὡς οἶμαι, τοῦτο λογισάμενος.

Clearly Bèze has in mind a portrait from the waist up, i.e., half-length.

2. **dimidium**: Erasmus cites the Latin version of his proverb as *dimidium plus toto*.
   **picta tabella**: possibly refers to a portrait in a book of Erasmus, perhaps the *Opera* published by Beatus Rhenanus in 1540,[12] or to one of the famous Dürer portraits (1520 charcoal drawing, now in the Louvre; 1526 engraving). With this can be compared Martial's poem (14.186) on Vergil:

Quam brevis immensum cepit membrana Maronem!
   ipsius vultus prima tabella gerit.

[How small a quantity of parchment has accommodated immense Vergil! The first leaf bears his own portrait.]

Martial is amazed that such a small book could hold work so immense and vast, and also fit the portraiture of the man who created it on the first leaf. He expresses similar sentiments about a small book of Livy (14.190).

35.

Nicole, *Epigrammatum delectus* (1752), pp. 17–18 of appendix.
Meter: phalaecian hendecasyllable.

---

[12] Heywood (ed. Bang) weighs in with the following comment about an engraving, to which I can neither add nor subtract anything: "In dieser bekanntesten Fassung steht das Epigramm unter dem wundervollen Portrait des Erasmus (gestochen von Will. Marshall), das dessen Briefe schmückt, Lo., M. Flesher & R. Young, 1642."

That the poet is also in a sense a priest who can make sacrifices and perform religious rites, many passages of Latin literature illustrate, none, though, more clearly than Prop. 4.6, which begins with these austere, formulaic words taken directly from Roman religious practice:

> Sacra facit vates: sint ora faventia sacris,
>     et cadat ante meos icta iuvenca focos.

[The priest is making a sacrifice: Let our words be auspicious for the sacrifice, and let the heifer fall slain before my hearth.]

The *vates* is both priest and poet, the ambiguity of which is played with in the rest of the poem (for a discussion of the whole poem see Gordon Williams, *Tradition and Originality in Roman Poetry* [Oxford, 1968], 51–52). It is fitting that a poet-priest should invoke Calliope and her sisters for aid, as fitting as a farmer to Ceres or Liber, since the nine Muses (a.k.a. the Pierides or Camenae) give poetic inspiration. The only question is what sacrificial victim to bring. Bèze decides the best gift for the gods is the sacrifice of their greatest enemy, the bookworm, for it is she who destroys the works they inspire. But then the poem ends with a militaristic tone, as if Bèze has won a great victory over the worm and now in typical Roman fashion pays his vow by offering the spoils and trophies for display in the temple of the Muses.

1. **Cereremque, Liberumque**: Demeter and Dionysus. The two are often linked by virtue of their functions as gods of agriculture and viticulture. Vergil invokes them at the beginning of his *Georgics* (1.7): *Liber et alma Ceres.* Cf. note to *epig.* 16.
14. **tinea**: the problem of bookworms provides humor for many classical poems: Mart. 6.61.7–8; 11.1.14; 14.37; Horace, *Ep.* 1.20.12.
29. **monimenta**: cf. Cic. *Arch.* 9.21, "nostra sunt tropaea, nostra monimenta, nostri triumphi," also in reference to literature.
35–36: **cruento | Mucronem**: Macrin corrected Bèze's first version (*mūcronem | Cruenta*) for metrical reasons.
44. **exuvias**: typically a military term equivalent to *spolia*, used in reference to armor or arms stripped off the vanquished foe, and then hung in the temple with an inscription (Verg. *Aen.* 3.288); but also of the hide of animals, including the snake (Verg. *Aen.* 2.473).
    **trophaeum**: a monument to military victory, or the arms hung on the monument.

## 36.

Missing in 1597.
Meter: iambic senarius.

Apparently the abundance of wasps in the city of Orléans had become proverbial; in a journal entry dated August 1555 Felix Platter records a similar wasp problem in Montpellier to the south. Regardless, Bèze is not really concerned here with insects, as the reference to Attic wit and Philaenus as a drone make clear. Here, poets are wasps because they sting, and sting ferociously, though the talentless Philaenus is more like a drone: he wants to sting but has no stinger, so he must be content to serve as mate for his female master. The imagery of stinging poets is related to that of biting and stabbing. All three are used in antiquity to characterize satire, or more precisely, the urban wit and biting jests of drinking parties. It was at such a party that Juvenal (9.10) tells us his friend Naevolus once passed his time: *conviva ioco mordente facetus.* That this biting wit is satirical and directed against others is evident from the example of Martial's Cassiodorus (6.44), who, we are told, laughed and cracked his jokes during dinner parties against everyone. Epigrams, the same author asserts, should display the same mordant sensibility (7.25):

> Dulcia cum tantum scribas epigrammata semper
>     et cerussata candidiora cute,
> nullaque mica salis nec amari fellis in illis
>     gutta sit, o demens, vis tamen illa legi!
> nec cibus ipse iuvat morsu fraudatus aceti,          5
>     nec grata est facies cui gelasinus abest.
> infanti melimela dato fatuasque mariscas:
>     nam mihi, quae novit pungere, Chia sapit.

In a reference to his own poetry in the preface to the *Abraham Sacrifiant*, Bèze describes the epigrammatic genre with the words "trenchant à deux costez" (double-edged sword) and "picquant par le bout" (extremely stinging), so that it is reasonable to surmise that Bèze viewed himself as one of the wasps of Orléans.

Satirical verse did not have to be compared only to the sharp edges of swords or the biting mouth. The stylus itself, with which satires were composed, suggested to Horace once the pointed shape of the sword (*Sat.* 2.1.39–40), while Catullus seems to envision his epigrams as spears for hurling (fr. 4.1).

On the identity of Philaenus see *epig.* 14 above.

2. **nasum Atticum**: For the meaning "Attic wit," cf. the humorous treatment of Antony at Seneca Rhet., *Suasoriae* 1.6: "Nam cum Antonius vellet se Liberum patrem dici et hoc nomen statuis subscribi iuberet, habitu quoque et comitatu Liberum imitaretur, occurrerunt venienti ei Athenienses cum coniugibus et liberis et Dionyson salutaverunt. Belle illis cesserat si nasus Atticus ibi substitisset." Martial frequently uses forms of *nasus* and *nasutus* to denote an organ of criticism. Cf. Visagier's address to his book: "Posthaec nasutos contemnes, denique nasos, | Atque canum rabiem, Zoileasque notas" (*Epigrammata* [1537], 12).

4. **fucum**: the drone bee has no stinger and does not work; its sole function is to mate with the queen bee.

4–5. **pungas ... aculeum**: For the common phrase *pungere aculeis,* with the specific connotation employed here, cf. Cic. *Fin.* 4.7; *De partitione oratoria* 60.

37.

Missing in 1569, 1576, 1597.<br>Meter: phalaecian hendecasyllable.

This poem is usually considered to be a compliment to Léon Tripault (or Trippault), counsel to the mayor at Orléans. He was most famous for his work *Celt-hellénisme, ou étymologie des mots françois tirez du graec, plus preuves en général de la descente de nostre langue* (Orléans, 1580) and Ordonnances du roy François sur le faict de la justice, et abbréviation des procès, publiées en *l'an M.D. XXXIX* (Orléans, 1572). Besides law and etymology, Tripault had an interest in antiquities and history, especially that of Orléans, on which he also published a collection of *sylvae* in 1573. He was labeled a Protestant by the Parlement of Paris in 1563. He died sometime after 1584. In this poem, the greatest Roman legal minds surrender first place to Tripault when his book is shown to them, much in the same way Euripides tried to force Aeschylus to yield his position in Aristophanes's *Frogs.* Bèze wrote another hendecasyllabic poem to him that he did not publish (ABM 188):

*Ad Triputium, jurisconsultum*

Quae de jure habet hic tuus libellus
Triputi similis tibi parenti,

Hoc est perlepidus, pereruditus,
Fallor si tibi comparare laudis
Ulla praemia copiosa possint.                                   5
Quippe nil hodie solet probari
Quod non sit novum, at hoc tuo in libello,
Quamvis nil penitus sit invenustum,
Sit falsum nihil aut minus latinum,
Sic ut hactenus hisce veriora                                   10
Nemo scripserit aut magis latina,
Hoc tamen lepido tuo in libello
Nil possit merito novum videri,
Namque res vetus est et undiquaque
Nota, scribere posse te diserte.                                15
Res est certe oculis frequens parenti
Suo persimiles videre natos.

It is very odd, though, that Bèze mentions a book in these poems. Léon Tripault's earliest published work listed in the catalogues of the Bibliothèque Nationale of Paris is *Coustumes générales des bailliage et prévosté d'Orléans* (Orléans, 1570). The matter becomes more complicated and puzzling when one considers that Bimbenet (361–62), in discussing Léon Tripault, adds the following footnote: "Il avait un frère, Thomas Tripault, homme de lettres distingué, qui écrivit aussi sur le droit; ce fait n'a pas d'autre preuve qu'une épigramme que dirige contre lui Théodore de Bèze, aussi nous ne croyons lui devoir que cette courte mention." Of this Thomas Tripault I find no publications. ABM do not appear to have known the name. So how could a "distinguished writer on the law" to whom other famous lawyers in Hades give way, disappear into oblivion? Yet Brainne et al. (*Hommes illustres*, 2: 69) also know a Thomas Tripault, brother of Léon, and attributes to him the receipt of our poem: "Nicolas Trippault, avocat au bailliage d'Orléans, travailla, vers l'an 1509, à la rédaction de la Coutume: il eut deux fils qui se firent plus remarquer comme savants que comme jurisconsultes. L'aîné, Thomas, était avocat de la ville d'Orléans et ami de Théodore de Béze, qui composa en son honneur cette louangeuse épigramme . . ." Ultimately, it is of little consequence which brother is in view here.

1. **Doctum illum et lepidum tuum libellum**: a phrase gleaned from the two descriptions in Cat. 1: Catullus dedicates his charming book (*lepidum libellum*) to Nepos, writer of learned books (*doctis laboriosis*).

Tripault has combined the two in his work on law.

3. **Mercurius**: as the psychopompos, it was his duty to transport souls to the underworld; thus, by extension, the book also.

6. **Papiniano, Paulo, Scaevolae, et Ulpiano**: great legal thinkers of the past. Aemilius Papinianus (d. 212 A.D.), author of several works of jurisprudence, in particular the *Questiones* (ca. 198 A.D.) and *Responsa* (c. 204); Justinian (*Cod.* 6.42.30) called him "a man of keen intellect and unparalleled talent" ("acutissimi ingenii vir et merito ante alios excellens"). Paulus (fl. c. 210 A.D.), was a prolific writer and legal advocate; a popular anthology of his work is entitled *Pauli Sententiae*. Both Papinianus and Paulus were friends with Ulpian (d. 223), who like Paulus was an encyclopedic compiler and synthesizer of previous legal thought; the compilers of Justinian used him for nearly a third of the *Digesta*. Scaevola may refer to Quintus Mucius Scaevola, the eminent lawyer who was praetor c. 120 B.C., but more likely to Quintus Cervidius Scaevola, Roman jurist and teacher of Paulus. The names occur again in a list of Pasquier:

> *De Iure Civili Romanorum*
>
> Dum Latias meditor leges et Romula iura,
>   Quae sunt immensis aucta voluminibus,
> Nunc avide Paulum, nunc perlego Pappinianum.
>   Nunc mihi sese offert Scaevola Serbidius. . . .
>     (*Epig.* 5.85)

7. **Juris ... lucernam**: most probably Bèze means Moses. Other possibilities include Gaius or Tribonian (d. c. 542 A.D.). The latter was the director of the compilation that resulted in the *Digesta* for the emperor Justinian (see T. Honoré, *Tribonian* [Ithaca, 1976]).

## 38.

Wright, *Delitiae delitiarum* (1637), 9.

Philopater is apparently some sort of prude, who would not stoop to read Bèze's lascivious poems, though he will sneer at them. His sneering, however, has the effect of making the less prudish read them. Such a response to critics can be found often in Martial (1.91, 110; 2.8, 77; 9.50). In the Orléans ms. the addressee of this poem and the next is Louis Vaillant.

## 39.

Philopater is a critic, and no matter where he goes or what he says, negative words come out of his mouth. His criticisms are not necessarily unjustified (they are at least well-phrased), just constant. And so the poem builds to the final play on the slight alteration in *bene multa loquentem* and *bene loqui.* The first phrase, taking the accusative, refers to Philopater's eloquence, while the second phrase, without a direct object, says more about his character.

A poem of Martial (2.11) begins much the same way as this one, but concerns itself with the dining habits of a certain Selius:

> Quod fronte Selium nubila vides, Rufe,
> quod ambulator porticum terit seram ...

1. **Palatina ... aula:** the palace courtyard. In a letter to Maclou Popon, dated 7 December 1539, written at Paris, Bèze mentions that he frequented this place for relaxation and inspiration:

   > Si quid agam quaeris, nihil prorsus, nisi quod aliquoties nugor cum Musis meis, deinde animi gratia in Palatium ventito. Ibi omnium hominum mores velut in amplissimo theatro intueor.

   > [If you want to know what I am doing, nothing much, except that sometimes I play around with my poetry, then for relaxation I go to the Palace gardens. There I watch the pageant of people's lives, as if I'm in a vast and spacious theater.]

2. **utrumque:** an odd word at this point, the meaning of which is not clear. The related adverb *utrimque* would have meant "in both directions," but all editions have the reading given here. Machard translates the line, "Et foule d'un pied pédant les degrés de marbre," in which case he must consider *utrumque* to modify *marmor*. It could also refer to twin staircases, up and down.

11-12. **Sed cum ... loqui:** i.e., he speaks eloquently, but everything he has to say is negative.

## 40.

Missing in 1569, 1576, 1597; cf. *Tottel's Miscellany,* 1: 103, 2: 233–34
(= Merrill, *Grimald,* 388 and 428).
Meter: phalaecian hendecasyllable.

Bèze is particularly skilled in giving inexpensive gifts for New Year's
Day. Here he admits he cannot afford the usual finery, but gives some-
thing which to his mind is far more rare and desirable: his heart. A
poem of Visagier is very similar (*Epigrammata* [1537], 26):

*Ad Boyssoneum pro strenis*

Formosas violas, aurum, gemmasque Calendis
    Iani pro strenis det tibi, quisquis habet.
Non ego do flores, violas, pereuntia dona,
    Sed tibi, quod prius est, corque animumque meum.

The sentiment is touching, but among Bèze's epigrams one is always
tempted to see the lighter side. At any rate, the motif was common
among the epigrammatists. Martial is notorious for bowing out of ex-
pensive gift-giving. At 7.86 he loses his friend Sextus for failure to bring
expensive silver and clothes to his birthday feasts. At 9.53, Martial is
even asking for a present for himself on Quintus's birthday. Bourbon,
like Bèze, claims that he is too poor to send anything else:

Mittere non possum pro strena munera pauper,
    Qualia dat divers, qui dare magna potest . . .
        (*Nugae* [1533], fol. 15r)

Muret writes that he will not send expensive gifts to his friend either.
Then he poses the question, "What will I send?" to which he responds,
"*Nihil*" (appearing in Bèze's 1779 edition, 181).

3. **India . . . uniones**: usually called Erythraean pearls, as at Mart. 5.37.4
   and 10.17.5; but also *Indicae lapides*, as Mart. 1.109.4 and Petr. 55.6.
   Cf. Boissard's poem entitled *In Chilonem: O Indis preciosior lapillis!*
   . . . (*Hendecasyllaborum lib. II*, 261).
11. Recalls the formula *do dono dedico*.
14. **grande . . . munus**: a loaded phrase when one considers the same in
    Hor. *Odes* 2.1.11. There Horace, addressing Pollio who at the time
    is writing a history of the civil wars in Rome, encourages him to re-
    turn soon to the writing of tragedy, his lofty calling (*grande munus*).

## 41.

Bèze has read Plato's *Symposium,* and knows well the various theories about love there, all of which have to do with the union of two individuals (which is why *integer* is still the better reading in line 2; see note below): embracing, mingling hearts, friendship, and binding love. Most of these ideas can be found in Aristophanes's speech at *Symp.* 189c2–d6, where he relates the story of the origins of human love. Early humans, according to Aristophanes, used to be double, joined at the back, with four arms, four legs, two heads, and two sets of genitalia. Some of these double beings were male, some were female, and some were mixed, but all of them were very powerful and a threat to the gods. Zeus decided to split them, to weaken them, and after much rearranging of parts by Apollo, humans looked as they do today (though the moving of the genitalia to the front came after some time). Still, within them there was a burning desire for completeness (Bèze's *integer*), since now they were half. All humans spent their entire lives looking for their other half, and if they found it, would embrace it and refuse to let go. But Zeus warned that if humans remained a threat, he would again cut them in half, which would leave them a quarter of their original selves.

But Bèze does not invoke Plato to explain any of those well-known theories of simple union in love, but for a philosophical explanation of how he can divide his affections between two, or more precisely, how he can have a split heart (*anima*), and yet retain a single mind (*mens*). According to Aristophanes's story, he should have a heart that desires only one. To complicate matters more, though his heart is divided between his two friends, he still loves them with his whole heart (*integra anima*).

Structurally speaking, the poem develops around the words *anima* and *mens* in successive stages, with *anima* in line 4 followed by *mens* in line 11, then *animam* in line 13, *mens* in 15, and rounded off with *anima* in line 18. The interchange of the two, mind and heart, represents verbally the struggle within the soul of Bèze, a single individual with a single mind divided in his affections.

**2. integer:** *castus* (1597). The original poem, however, is not about purity but about wholeness.

**8. casti:** The 1548 reading, *sōbrii,* was unmetrical; cf. *epig.* 22.1 and the beginning of this very line.

**11. simplex atque una:** Cf. Horace's phrase for poetic unity at *Ars Poet.* 1.23: *simplex dumtaxat et unum.*

**14. Dimidiam Truchio, dimidiam Valido**: cf. Bonefon (*Delitiae*, 1: 678): *Panchari, pars animae dimidiata meae*; similarly Visagier:

> Tu sine me, sine te nect possum vivere: nam tu
> Pars vitae, atque ego sum dimidiata tuae.
> (*Epigrammata* [1537], 29)

The locus classicus for this is Hor. 1.3.8, *animae dimidium meae*.

**15. salva ... mens**: i.e., it has not taken on a split personality like the heart.

**18. Utrumque integra diligo, amoque anima**: the two ablatives comes from the 1597 edition; earlier editions read *integram ... animam*, in which case Bèze may have meant, "I love and cherish both of you *as* a whole heart." Machard translates, "J'aime et je chéris chaque part comme une âme entière."

42.

Meter: iambic senarius.

Hubert, one might think from the boiled cabbage and gluttons, is a bad cook, who does not realize it, i.e., he does not "know himself." The Latin formula for the phrase "know yourself" used the same words (see note on *epig.* 6 above): *ignosce sibi*. The boiled cabbage, however, must refer to Hubert's shabby poetry (see note on *crambe* [line 2] below), with which he vexed his teachers, since a note in the margin of Bèze's own copy labels him "truly a sorry poetaster" (*poetastrum vere nebulonem*), identifying him as Hubert Sussanneau (or Susannée; see Ruutz-Rees, "Some Sixteenth Century Schoolmasters at Grenoble and their Delectable Vicissitudes," *Romantic Review* 7 [1916]: 1–41, esp. 10–21), born in 1512, the French humanist who was part of the Rabelais circle at Lyons. In 1536 he published his *Epigrammatum libellus* and in 1538 *Ludorum libri*. He also wrote books on versification, accents, and Ciceronianism (a full bibliography can be found in Philippe Renouard, "Hubert Sussanneus," *Revue des livres anciens* 2 [1917]: 146–58). According to this poem, there was not a low life in town who did not know Hubert for what he really was (a bad poet). Judging from what I have seen of his poetry, particularly the *Ludorum libri*, I would surmise that Bèze was unimpressed with Susannée's excessive flattery and pious pretensions. Others, however, had a different view. Visagier often speaks admiringly of Susannée, while Girard speaks of his comic muse and delightful company (*H. Sussannaeo* [1752], 100).

Bèze wrote another poem to Susannée that he did not publish (see ABM 191), but which is worth repeating here as an illustration of Bèze's opinion of his literary output:

> Huberti illepidas cacationes
> Quum cognoscere nemo sustineret,
> Suas illepidas cacationes
> Hubertus populo explicare coepit.
> Cessent Caecilio Terentioque,                    5
> Cessent plaudere Roscio theatro
> Et laudare tuos, Latine, mimos.
> Plus est quod facit unus hic Hubertus
> Tantus histrio quantus et poeta.

Bèze views Susannée's attempts to explicate his deplorable poetry as nothing more than comic acting.

2. **Norunt magistri cocta quos crambe necat**: the smell of his poetry is pervasive and nauseating, like the smell of bad food wafting through the house. Juvenal, at *Sat.* 7.150–54, cites the proverb in reference to bad poetry:

> Declamare doces? o ferrea pectora Vetti,
> cum perimit saevos classis numerosa tyrannos.
> nam quaecumque sedens modo legerat, haec eadem stans
> perferet atque eadem cantabit versibus isdem;
> occidit miseros crambe repetita magistros.

Juvenal is merely repeating an old Greek proverb, "twice-cooked cabbage is death" (δὶς κράμβη θάνατος), which means essentially that too much repetition and rehashing of old themes is a bore. Erasmus reports the same proverb at *Adag.* 1.5.38 while referring to Suda (K 2318), where it says that recooked cabbage causes such nausea that the Greek made it proverbial. Contrast Horace's statement that something beautiful pleases even when repeated ten times (*AP* 365). **magistri**: Susannée's most noted teacher was Jacques Toussain.

3. **histrio ... scurrave**: actors in antiquity often had a bad reputation (Cic. *Pro. Arch* 5; Nepos *Praef.* 4; Suet. *Tib.* 35; Macr. *Sat.* 2.7), mainly because they were slaves, foreigners, or freedmen. Legally they were *infames* (*Dig.* 3.2.1; Aug. *Civ. Dei* 2.13, citing Cicero's *Rep.*). Note too the derogatory reference to mimes and clowns in Horace's lines at *Sat.* 2.1–2:

Ambubaiarum collegia, pharmacopolae,
mendici, mimae, balatrones, hoc genus omne
maestum ac sollicitum est cantoris morte Tigelli.

[The colleges of female flute players, quacks, beggars, actresses,
clowns, all this kind, are sad and dejected on account of the death
of the singer Tigellus.]

Even in Bèze's day their reputation remained sullied; cf. Montaigne,
*Essays*, 1.42:

Comme les joueurs de comedie, vous les veoyez sur l'eschaffaud
faire une mine de duc et l'empereur; mais tantost aprez les voylà
devenus valets et crocheteurs miserables.

**4. leno**: see note on lawyers in the next epigram (43).
**5. chiromantis**: Macrin suggests either *chiromantes* or *chiromanta*.

### 43.

Missing in 1569, 1576, 1597.
Meter: phalaecian hendecasyllable.

Bèze sarcastically refers to the consistency of his lawyer, who never fails
to cheat him, so much so that Bèze has come to expect it. The dishones-
ty of lawyers was always a given. For example, Mart. 4.5.1–3, puts the
lawyer on the same social plane as the pimp by assuming his friend Fabi-
anus is too honest to be either.

### 44.

Meter: dactylic hexameter followed by iambic quaternarius.

John Secundus was born 1511 at The Hague. He took his doctorate in
law at Bourges under Alciat in 1533 after a childhood of studying the
humanities. From 1533 he battled several illnesses, with a fever taking
his life in 1539. His poetry was all published posthumously at Lyons in
1539 under the title *Basia et alia quaedam*. On the poet and his literary
output one may consult Maurice Rat, *Oeuvres de Jean Second* (Paris,

1938); P. Godman, "Johannes Secundus and Renaissance Latin Poetry," *Review of English Studies* 39 (1988): 258–72; David Price, *Janus Secundus: Writing Love in the Renaissance*, MRTS 143, (Tempe, AZ, 1996). Bèze has written this poem in distichs consisting of a dactylic hexameter and an iambic quaternarian, after the style of Secundus himself.

According to this poem of Bèze, Secundus has pursued a broad range of poetic genres. To be sure, he did not attempt the grand genre of epic, but even so his short poems can rival the poetry of Vergil. By claiming that Secundus outshines even the great Vergil, Bèze extends to him a form of *recusatio*, an excuse for not writing longer epics. This tension between the serious social and political aims of the epic writers (or even writers of history) and the seemingly lighter themes of the epigrammatists and elegists, or between the big and the small, cropped up again and again in the ancient poets. Bèze alludes to it in *epig.* 1 above. Martial (8.3) plays with the tension as a way in his effort to justify why he is publishing yet another book of *nugae*; the Muse herself, he claims, scolded him with these words:

> Tune potes dulcis, ingrate, relinquere nugas?
>   Dic mihi, quid melius desidiosus ages?
> an iuvat ad tragicos soccum transferre cothurnos,
>   aspera vel paribus bella tonare modis,
> praelegat ut tumidus rauca te voce magister
>   oderit et grandis virgo bonusque puer? ...

[Are you able, you ingrate, to leave behind your sweet *nugae*? Tell me, what better will a lazy fellow like you do? Or maybe you plan to exchange the comic sock for the tragic buskins, to compose an epic about harsh wars in hexameters, so that the pompous schoolmaster will read it out loud in his coarse voice and the young lady and good boy will hate it?]

Martial ends the same poem much the way Bèze begins his, with a challenge to Vergil and the whole epic tradition: "dum tua multorum vincat avena tubas" ("while your reed outdoes the war trumpets of many"). Instead of epic in the manner of Vergil, Secundus perferred the elegiac couplets in the tone of Ovid, lyric odes after the manner of Pindar, and witty epigrams on the model of Martial. The *blandos sales* of line 7 is again reminiscent of the directives that the Muse gave to Martial: "at tu Romano lepidos sale tinge libellos" ["but you dip your charming little

books in Roman salt"]. Bèze would hark back to this precise deline-
ation of generic categories in reference to his own poetry in the preface
to his 1569 edition (see Summers, "Beza's Reading of Catullus" [1995]:
243); his aim was to respond to his critics by explaining that his poetry
was nothing more than a literary exercise, an imitation of ancient styles
and conceits.

The name of Secundus continued to provide obvious word-play for
other poets after Bèze; cf. the following poem of Pasquier:

> *In Iani Bonefii Basia*
>
> Iani Basia dum lego Secundi,
> Ianum censeo nemini secundum,
> Quod magnus quoque censuit Poeta:
> Iani Basia dum lego Bonefi,
> Secundo puto Iane te secundum,                                    5
> Et dum censeo Iane te secundum,
> Iane tu mihi totus es Secundus. (*Epig.* 6.52)

2. **Luminibus officere studet**: The iambic quaternarius allows for this
   kind of multiple resolution in the first three feet. Here, the first foot
   resolves into a dactyl, the third into a tribrach. Only the second and
   fourth feet are pure iambs (the last being a *brevis in longo*).

## 45.

Missing in 1569, 1576. Wright, *Delitiae delitiarum* (1637), 10.
Meter: phalaecian hendecasyllable.

Neo-Latin poets followed their ancient models in writing poetic dinner
invitations; here Bèze appears to have in mind Cat. c. 13 as well as
Mart. 5.78, 10.48, and 11.52; the entire mini-genre has its roots in Philo-
demus's invitation to Piso (*AP* 11.44, Sider 27) and his listing of a mod-
est menu in another epigram (*AP* 11.35, Sider 28). For discussion of the
genre see L. Edmunds, "The Latin Invitation Poem: What is it? Where
did it come from?" *AJP* 103 (1982): 184–88; E. Gowers, *The Loaded
Table: Representations of Food in Roman Literature*, chap. 4, "Invitation
Poems" (Oxford, 1993). The motif was useful for maintaining the con-
vivial ambience (wine, wit, and song) expected in the epigrams and for
emphasizing the simple pleasures of friendship. Fabullus here is merely

fictional, a stock name for the invitee drawn from Catullus's poem. Additionally, "Opimian" wine is present in the extravagant dinner of Mart. 3.82, the drunken revelry of 9.87, and the Amethystine cup of 10.49. With these hendecasyllabi Bèze has used the motif of the *cena*-invitation as a peg on which to hang a simple, witty word-play.

**5. Turtur:** See comment on *epig.* 88.1.

**6. casta ... uxor:** The fidelity of the widowed turtledove was proverbial. Cf., e.g., Bonefon's pleas for special kisses from his girl Pancharis: "Qualia dat casto turtur sociata marito | qualia amatori blanda columba suo ..." (*Delitiae*, 1: 678). A more detailed description of the phenomenon is recorded in the Aberdeen Bestiary, fol. 32r (first catalogued in the Aberdeen library in 1542):

> Fertur enim turtur ubi iugalis proprii fuerit amissione viduata per talem usum thalami et nomen habere coniugii eo quod primus amor fefellerit eam dilecti morte deceptam, [quoniam] et infidelis ad perpetuitatem fuit et amarus ad gratiam, qui plus doloris ex morte, quam suavitatis ex caritate generaverit. Itaque iterare coniunctionem recusat, nec pudoris iura aut complaciti viri resolvit federa, illi soli suam caritatem reservat, illi custodit nomen uxoris ... Turtur non uritur flore iuventutis non temptatur occasionis illecebra. Turtura nescit primam fidem irritam facere quia novit castimoniam servare, prima conubii sorte permissam.

> [They say that when the female bird is widowed by the loss of her mate, she holds the name and rite of marriage in such esteem that, because her first experience of love has deceived her, cheating her with the death of her beloved, and since he has become permanently unfaithful and a bitter memory, causing her more grief by his death than he gave her pleasure from his affection, therefore she refuses to marry again, and will not go back on her word to be faithful or the contract made with the man who pleased her. She reserves her love for her dead mate alone and retains her name as his wife. Learn, you women, how great is the grace of widowhood, when it is championed even among the birds ... The turtledove is not inflamed by the flower of youth and is not affected by chance temptation. It cannot go back on its first pledge of love because it knows how to preserve the chastity which it surrendered as the first duty of marriage.]

7. **mero**: i.e., wine that is undiluted. Catullus, c. 13.9 speaks of *meros amores*.

10. **Opimiana**: The finest vintage in Roman history reputedly occurred during the consulship of Lucius Opimius in 121 B.C. So much high quality *vinum Opimianum* was produced and stored that year that some still existed in Pliny the Elder's time, in the first century A.D. (*N.H.* xiv.55).

11. **Optimiana**: Obviously Bèze wants to say that the wine is not Opimian, exactly, but it is optimal; but he is also making a play on an event of Roman history: Opimius's struggles against the Gracchi brothers led to the formation of two parties within the senate, the Optimates and the Populares. So the wine is fit for upper-class people, as well.

## 46.

Missing in 1597; Wright, *Delitiae delitiarum* (1637), 9;
Heywood, *Pleasant dialogues* . . . , ed. Bang, 269–79.
Meter: iambic senarius.

A play perhaps on the adage of Persius, *Sat.* 1.1.27: "Scientia non visa, ut thesauri absconditi, nulla est utilitas" ["In knowledge unseen, as in hidden treasure, there is no usefulness"]. Cf. also Plaut. *Mil. Glor.* 572 and Ter. *Eun.* 721.

On the identity of Philaenus as Etienne Dolet, see *epig.* 14 with additional notes at *epitaph.* 18. Dolet had attacked Erasmus in his work on Ciceronianism in 1536. The following letter addressed to Guillaume Scève, and translated by Christie (*Etienne Dolet*, 197; see *epitaph.* 18), sums up his attitude toward Erasmus:

> I send you a dialogue concerning the imitation of Cicero against Erasmus, which you will hand to Gryphius. I shall be under very great obligation to you if you will see that it is printed as carefully as possible. Do not allow your kindness to me, which has never yet failed, to fail in this instance. The trivial crowd of grammarians who worship Erasmus as a deity, and place him before Cicero, will scarcely refrain from attacks upon me. Moreover I do not doubt that the old man (who is now almost childish with age) will ridicule the young man with his usual and persistent scurrility. But nothing troubles me less than the scur-

rility of a buffoon, nor do I fear any sharper bite from the tooth-
less old food for worms; while as to those who may accuse me of
insolence, and may cover me with reproaches because I attack
Erasmus, let them in the first place consider in what way they
can defend Erasmus himself from the charge of insolence and
scurrility in venturing to ridicule Cicero and those who strive to
imitate him.

**3. plumbeus**: on this meaning see Ter. *Heaut.* 5.1.4: "caudex, stipes,
asinus, plumbeus;" and Cic. *Tusc.* 1.29.71.

**6. latra**: Cf. *epig.* 2. Hor. *Sat.* 2.1.85. See Varr. *LL* 7.103 on *latrare* mean-
ing "to rage."

**6–7. quamdiu et quantum | ... quam tu**: Note the alliteration that
draws attention to the contrast betweeen these two lines.


## 47.

### Bèze's *Tumuli*, 16.

This verse, in honor of the birth of François II (b. Jan., 1543, d. 1560),
the eldest son of the dauphin Henri, brought Bèze his greatest fame
among fellow humanists in Paris. In the preface to his 1569 edition, ad-
dressed to A. Dudith (= *Corr.* 10: 90), Bèze writes:

> Reversus enim Aurelia Lutetiam, ibique velut in gymnasio totius
> orbis florentissimo, nactus quibuscum in omni studiorum genere
> me exercerem, prout sese variae offerebant animi a gravioribus
> studiis relaxandi occasiones, quaedam praeterea eiusmodi scripti-
> tarem; ita quidem (absit verbo invidia) doctissimis illius acade-
> miae hominibus, quos amicissimos habebam, comprobata (cuius-
> modi tum erant Joannes Stracelius, Adrianus Turnebus, Georgius
> Buchananus, Joannes Tevius, Antonius Goveanus, Mellinus San-
> gelasius, Salmonius Macrinus),[13] ut eos meminerim, cum Fran-
> cisci secundi Genethliacon scripsissem, uno consensu primas in
> epigrammate scribendo ultro mihi tribuisse.

---

[13] Strazel, Turnèbe, Buchanan, de Teive (probably Jacques rather than Jean), Gouvea,
Mellin de Saint-Gelais, Salmon Macrin.

Here Bèze predicts that he will benefit mankind even more than Hercules once did. But there must be recognized some ambiguity built into any comparisons with Hercules. Hercules held in tension two extremes: the greatness of the gods, and the faults of humanity. And while he was capable of unmatched feats, he was also capable of killing his wife and children in a fit of madness. In fact, François II, the first husband to Mary Queen of Scots, was a weak king who was mostly dominated by his mother; he died in 1560 after coming to the throne in 1559.

1. **Alcmenes**: In myth, Alcmene was the wife of Amphitryon, son of Alcaeus and king of Thebes. While Amphitryon was away at battle, Zeus disguised himself as the king and visited Alcmene's bed; he prolonged the night for his own benefit. The result of their union was the birth of the child Hercules (Herakles). The story is told in the following places: Homer, *Iliad*, 19.96-133; Hesiod, *Shield* 1-56; Plautus, *Amphitruo;* Ovid, *Met.* 9.273-323; Apollodorus, *Bibl.* 2.4.5-11.
2. **ter noctis**: Plautus, *Amph.* 112-113, has Mercury report, "Et meus pater nunc intus hic cum illa cubat, | et haec ob eam rem nox est facta longior."
11. Cf. Verg. *Aen.* 10.501 (of Turnus), "nescia mens hominum fati sortisque futurae;" Ovid *Met.* 15.559 (of the Etruscan soothsayer Tages), "edocuit gentem casus aperire futuros."

### 48.

Bèze's *Tumuli*, 16-17.
Meter: dactylic hexameter followed by iambic quaternarius.

François II (see previous epigram) and Isabella (= Elizabeth, b. April 1545, became Queen of Spain, d. 1568) were the first two of the ten children of Henri II (1519-1559) and Catherine de Medici (1519-1589). Poets often treat royal infants as heralds of a new golden age. Vergil's *Eclogue* 4 is the most obvious example.

1. **Catharina**: Macrin argues that the first syllable is short, not long, as it is in the original Greek. Despite Bèze's praise here, the two would later be at odds over the St. Bartholomew's Day massacre of Huguenots in 1572, which Catherine instigated and Bèze condemned.
11. **frontis honorem**: meaning her forehead is broad and open. In the

phrase, cf. the following lines of Muret to his girlfriend: "Pande oculos, pande stellatae frontis honorem | Queis doleat visis, invideat Venus ..." (appears in the 1779 edition of Bèze's poetry, p. 153).

17. **Gallica ... lilia**: i.e., the "fleur-de-lis" or "flower of the lily," which was used as a symbol of French royalty, especially among the Valois and Bourbon families. Its three petals were thought to represent various things, from the Trinity to "perfection, light and life." According to one legend, an angel presented Clovis, the Merovingian king of the Franks, with a golden lily as a symbol of his purification after he had converted to Christianity. The fleur-de-lis also became a symbol of military power. Joan of Arc, for example, carried a white banner that showed God blessing the design as she led French troops to victory over the English in support of the dauphin Charles VII in his quest for the French throne.

## 49.

### Bèze's *Tumuli*, pp. 17–18.

Henri, second son of François I, came to the throne on 31 March 1547 at the age of twenty-eight (see *epitaph.* 21–24); he died 10 July 1557, from a wound received in a jousting match during a festival meant to celebrate peace with England. The rivers mentioned here represent an extensive waterway system reaching throughout all of France and its bordering seas; the directions that Bèze gives them correspond to the flow of the waters.

5. **Sequana**: The Seine is the principal river in France, winding through Paris and northwest to the English channel after passing through Rouen and Normandy.

7. **Liger, Hesperiis Rheni, Mosa**: The Loire River flows northwest from the Cévennes mountains to Orléans, then southwest until it empties into the Bay of Biscay. The Meuse River flows through eastern France northward across Belgium and the Netherlands, then into the North Sea; the Rhine flows through Germany and the Netherlands until it empties into the North Sea near Rotterdam. The Meuse and Rhine flow close to each other as they approach the North Sea, just short of which they are connected by the Waal River (the "Vacalus" of Caesar's *Gallic War* 4.10).

**8. Rhodane:** The Rhone River flows through southern France after leaving Lake Geneva, and continues on until the Mediterranean Sea (and thus the reference to the Ethiopians).

## 50.

A close approximation to this poem appears in the 1597 edition with the following title: *Cl(arissimo) V(iro) Michaeli Quelino, Senatori Parisiensi, quum uxorem ducturus aegrotare coepisset.* The poem there exhibits Bèze's typical post-conversion alteration:

> Te, Michael, quodqumque malum tam laeta parantem
> Coniugia, e tristi vix sinit ire toro.
> Seu febris, seu rheuma hoc est, me iudice, dignum est
> Altera quod febris, rheuma quod interimat.
> Nam tua vel virtus, vel castae vota puellae,          5
> Materies iusti plena favoris erat.
> Perge, Queline, tamen, nec tam bene coepta morare,
> Finem etiam morbis tempora laeta dabunt.
> Perge puella simul: licet agrotante Quelino,
> Vix alius toto sanior orbe vir est.          10

On Michael Quélain, relative of Bèze's friend Jean Quélain, see *epitaph.* 14.

**8. Finem ... Di:** similar to Horace's well-known "finem di dederint" (sc. "vitae") (*Od.* 1.11.2), and, more apropos to the sense here, Vergil's hexameter, "O passi graviora, dabit deus his quoque finem" (*Aen.* 1.199).

**10. sanior ... vir:** a play on the double meaning of *sanus* in the adage, *mens sana in corpore sano* (Juv. 10.356).

## 51.

Missing in 1569, 1576, 1597.
Meter: phalaecian hendecasyllable.

The wealth to be found in the Tagus and the Pactolus rivers was proverbial, both in antiquity (Mart. 10.96.3, Hor. *Epod.* 15.20, Prop. 1.14.11, Juv. 14.299) and in the Renaissance (see, e.g., Pasquier, *epig.* 3.83:

"exigisque quicquid | Vel Pactolus habet, Tagus vel auri"). Poets often drew comparisons between a girl's beauty and the gold of those rivers. The passage of Propertius is especially interesting: "For if Cynthia lies with me by night in long-desired rest, or spends the day in kindly love, then the waters of Pactolus bring their wealth beneath my roof, and the Red Sea's gems are gathered for my delight; then does my joy assure me that kings must yield to me ... for who may have joy of wealth if Love be not kind? Never be the prize of riches mine if Venus frown!" (Loeb translation). It is likely that Bèze means to tell his friend that he struck it rich with a girl. Note his adoption of the treasure metaphors at *epig.* 70, esp. line 20: "meas divitias, opes, talenta ..."

7. **Pactolique, Tagique**: Pactolus was a celebrated river of ancient Lydia, whose golden sands provided the abundant wealth for that empire (Herod. 5.101 and Verg. *Aen.* 10.142); it was here that Midas washed away his legendary "golden touch" near the source at Mt. Tmolus. The Tagus River (Spanish Tajo, Portuguese Tejo) flows from central Spain to the Atlantic coast near Lisbon, Portugal (see Pliny, *NH* 4.115).

## 52.

This poem refers to the battle of Ceresole d'Alba (Cérisoles), in northern Italy, 14 April 1544, an episode of the fourth war with Charles V, and stemming from François's designs on Milan. The battle was considered a French victory only inasmuch as the imperial commander, Alfonso d'Avalos d'Aquino, Marquis[14] del Vasto (1502–1546), fled, having lost six thousand (by some accounts ten thousand) men and all his cannon. In reality, both sides suffered terrible losses, and the French commander, François de Bourbon, Prince d'Enghien, was about to commit suicide when news came that the imperialist troops were on the run. François I had to withdraw his army from Piedmont shortly thereafter when Charles V was threatening an invasion from the Low Countries, though Piedmont remained under French control until 1559. Ultimately, the battle did little to advance the cause of the French.

---

[14] French nobility during the period was arranged along the following lines, in descending order of prestige: *duc* (duke), *marquis* (marquis), *comte* (earl), *vicomte* (viscount), *baron* (baron).

**2. Franci ... ducis**: that is, Charles de Bourbon, a brilliant general who was obsessed with recovering his inheritance in Burgundy, which the king had confiscated in 1521. He defected to the Imperial camp in 1524 and was one of the commanders who defeated the French at Pavia in February of 1525, the battle that led to the humiliating capture and imprisonment of François I. In the treaty signed 14 January 1526, François was forced to restore Charles de Bourbon to his offices and land in Burgundy. See C. Hare, *Charles de Bourbon* (London and New York, 1911).

**5. aquilas**: The image of the eagle was central to the coat of arms of the Holy Roman Empire.

**6. lilia ... colubris**: On the lilies, see *epig.* 48 above. The *colubri* refer to the Visconti, prominent Lombard family of Milan, who used the imagery of a serpent devouring a child on their coat of arms.[15]

## 53.

Missing in 1569, 1576, 1597.

For a biographical sketch of Germain Vaillant (1516–1587), bishop of Orléans (from 1586) and able poet, see Brainne et al., *Hommes illustres*, 1: 369–70. There his relationship to Bèze is mentioned: "Théodore de Bèze ajoute qu'il était d'une belle taille et d'une physionomie intéressante." Also Moreri, *GDH*, 10: 408; Michaud, *Biographie universelle*, 42: 407. His poetry, as noted in the bibliography, appears in *Delitiae*, 3: 1112–23 under the name "Valens." Another poem to Germain survives in the Orléans ms. (ABM, 177). His brother Louis is the "Ludovicus Validus" of several of Bèze's epigrams.

**8. Ut canae tuti sint sub honore comae**: literally, "so that they may be safe under the honor of their hoary hair."

**9. At quid non didicit ...**: in other words, Germain has grown exceptionally wise in just twenty years, and therefore does not need a beard to earn respect.

**10. vicena videt bruma peracta senem**: because the beard makes him look like an old man.

---

[15] See A. C. Fox-Davies, *A Complete Guide to Heraldry*, rev. and annotated by J. P. Brooke-Little (London, 1985), 193–94, and ill. 484.

**12. quod**: namely, "scissors."

## 54.

As the expanded title from later editions reveals, this poem deals with a peace treaty signed between François I and Charles V. Given the absence of this poem from the Orléans ms., it is likely that the treaty in question is the one signed 18 September 1544, at Crépy-en-Artois, near Laon. By the terms of the treaty, which included another diplomatic marriage between Charles d'Orléans and a relative of Charles V, both parties renounced their territorial claims, with François abandoning Piedmont and Savoy, the emperor Burgundy.

**11. patriae patres**: Cf. *epig.* 49.12. The expression is frequently applied to rulers and great statesmen in classical literature, as is *parens patriae*. Quintus Catulus used it of Cicero after the Catiline conspiracy (*In Pisonem* 3); Plutarch calls Cicero πατέρα πατρίδος in his *Life*. Juvenal refers to the title also, using both father and parent:

> sed Roma parentem
> Roma patrem patriae Ciceronem libera dixit. (*Sat.* 8.243)

Martial, at *Liber Spectaculorum* 3.11, applies the expression to Vespasian; Seneca used it of Nero at *De clementia* 1.14.2. According to Suetonius, *Life* 76, Julius Caesar took it on as a kind of official title: "et abusus dominatione et iure caesus existimetur. non enim honores modo nimios recepit: continuum consulatum, perpetuam dictaturam praefecturamque morum, insuper praenomen Imperatoris, cognomen 'Patris patriae', statuam inter reges, suggestum in orchestra." Seneca succinctly captures the sentiment behind the phrase at *Octavia* 444: "Servare cives maior est patriae patri" ["To safeguard the citizens is the greatest virtue of the father of his country"].

## 55.

Missing in 1569, 1576.

When Paulinus comes to dinner, he talks incessantly until the wine is taken away and the party completely ended. Both Testilus and Paulinus appear to be purely fictional.

3. **depositis dapibusque, meroque quiescit**: The last verse would seem
to indicate that Paulinus had pontificated straight through dinner,
and could not have eaten. Therefore the phrase here would not
mean, "with the meal and wine served," rather, "with the meal and
wine removed," on the analogy of the idiomatic *mensae remotae*.
Verg. *Aen.* 1.723, with its addition of *quies*, may be the passage in the
back of Bèze's mind: "Postquam prima quies epulis mensaeque re-
motae" (cf. *Aen.* 1.216, where "mensa" is metonymy for "dapes").
It was not only tables that were removed, but dinner and wine also;
e.g., Val. Fl. 3.120, has the phrase *vina dapesque remota*. In contrast,
the word *ponere* was used to indicate the setting of the table: "qui
dapibus mensas onerent et pocula ponant" (Val. Fl. 1.706).
4. **immo venit**: i.e., he comes "already stuffed;" *satur* is made to do dou-
ble duty.

## 56.

Wright, *Delitiae delitiarum* (1637), 10.
Meter: phalaecian hendecasyllable.

Caecilius's sole criterion for choosing friends is personal gain, therefore
he does not really acquire friends. The sentiment occurs frequently in lit-
erature, as, e.g., at Ovid, *Pont.* 2.3.8: "Vulgus amicitias utilitate probat."

9. **servitur ... amatur**: *Servire*, as a verb that expects an object in the
dative, can only be used impersonally in the passive, with rare excep-
tion. In this case, both verbs appear to be impersonal, with the em-
phasis placed on the act considered *per se*.

## 57.

Missing in 1569, 1576, 1597.

Here the chiastic structure draws attention to the contrast between what
Posthumus says and what he does:

saepe        verbo

re        numquam

That chiasmus is mirrored in the second line. Bèze hopes that Posthumus will finally pay what he so often claims he intends to pay. On the name of Posthumus, who is a stock character among the poets, see *epig.* 60.

**1. solvis**: When used absolutely *solvere* often has the sense of "to pay," as at Cic. *Att.* 1.3.2: "misimus qui pro vectura solveret."

**58.**

The 1569 edition reveals that these verses are addressed to a certain M. Scaevola (unknown; certainly not Maurice Scève, author of the collection of highly-regarded amatory verse entitled *Délie*, published at Lyons in 1544; Scaevola Sammarthanus published his first poetry in 1564). Here Bèze accuses him of writing poetry so shrill and supercilious as to become laughable.

**1. censoris**: In ancient Rome the censorship was the highest office one could obtain. Here Bèze refers to one particular duty of the office, *regimen morum*, the oversight of conduct. The censors had the right to attach a stigma to anyone for offenses that were not ordinarily punishable by law, but were considered morally reprehensible, such as the ill-treatment of children or neglect of religious duties. Sometimes the stigma resulted in a loss of the right to vote or a change of status that might include the imposition of a tax. Censors could also deny entrance into the senate or expel members for misconduct.

**3. o mores, o tempora!**: Bèze succinctly characterizes Bergedus by alluding to Cicero's famous exclamation of indignation at *Cat.* 1.1.2: *o tempora! o mores!* Cf. Mart. 9.70, where the theme of hypocrisy is similarly developed with reference to this exclamation.

**6. Sīleni vector qualia nempe rudit**: for metrical reasons the 1548 version of this verse was changed. The phrase *Sileni vector* refers to the ass of Silenus, usually called *asellus pandus* (note that in Bèze's 1548 version Silenus himself is addressed with *pande*). Silenus, who was an attendant of Dionysus, needed to ride the ass because he was so often drunk and could not support himself (Ovid *Ars Amat.* 1.543–448). At *Fasti* 1.415–40 Ovid tells the story of how the braying of Silenus's ass saved the nymph Lotis from being raped by Priapus. Verses 433 and 444 provided Bèze with the appropriate terms: "ecce rudens rauco

Sileni vector asellus | intempestivos edidit ore sonos." At 6.342 the ass's untimely blast saved Vesta from a similar fate: "intempestivo cum rudit ille sono."

7. **gemunt calami crasso tractante bubulco**: The ox-plougher often served as the archetypal ignorant rustic in literature (see, e.g., Juv. 7.116), and therefore could not be expected to produce beautiful sounds from a syrinx or other such reed instrument. Lucretius, 5.1401, mentions the inability of such country bumpkins to keep time.

8. **viridi**: Wheels made from green wood would be especially creaky.


## 59.

Missing in 1569, 1576, 1597.

4. **reddet**: Bèze is reporting the claim of Jean, i.e., "you insist that he will repay ..."

5. **Graecorum ... Calendis**: "On the calends of the Greeks" = never (see Augustus ap. Suet. *Aug.* 87.1, with the same theme of settling debts), because unlike the Romans the Greeks did not have "calends" as a date. Bèze may have known this phrase from Erasmus, *Adagia* 1.5.84. Dorat makes clever use of the proverb in the following poem:

*Ad Carolum Lotharingiae Card.*

Hebraicis, Graecis, Latiis lectoribus, anno
    Carole debentur praemia pro triplici
Haec numerare velis aut adsignare, Kalendis
    Sed Latiis: Graecis nolo, nec Hebraicis.
    (*Delitiae*, 1: 282)


## 60.

Missing in 1569, 1576, 1597.
Meter: phalaecian hendecasyllable.

Daedalus engages in a full range of activities (as in other poems, the distinction between *seria* and *ioci* is prominent), but no matter what he does, he is compulsive about reporting everything he hears and sees to his father. Bèze wonders what Daedalus would do, then, if he did not have a father. The structure of the poem, with its the anaphora (four lines beginning with *seu*) and the two tricola, one in the first three lines (*seu ... seu ... seu ...*) and one in the fourth line (*seu ... -ve ... -ve*), throws special emphasis on *cuncta* at the beginning of the sixth line: "*Everything that Daedalus does ...*" The reader is then left to anticipate the question posed in the final line, to which there is no obvious solution.

1. **seria ... ioci**: yet again these two words are placed in antithesis.
6. **Posthumus**: or "Postumus," a fairly common Roman surname; literally it should mean, "coming after." Machard points to Aulus Gellius (2.16.5) as somehow related to the thrust here: "Postuma proles non eum significat qui patre mortuo, sed qui postremo loco natus est." But Gellius is reporting the opinion of Caesellius on Verg. *Aen.* 6.760ff., only to cast doubt on his interpretation. It is important to look at the entire passage:

> Haec enim uerba significare uideri possunt Aenea uiuo ac iam sene natum ei Siluium et educatum. Itaque hanc sententiam esse uerborum istorum Caesellius opinatus in commentario lectionum antiquarum: "postuma" inquit "proles" non eum significat, qui patre mortuo, sed qui postremo loco natus est, sicuti Siluius, qui Aenea iam sene tardo seroque partu est editus. Sed huius historiae auctorem idoneum nullum nominat; Siluium autem post Aeneae mortem, sicuti diximus, natum esse multi tradiderunt.

> Gellius insists that the surname means the child is born after the death of the father, *post ... mortem ... natum*. It is clear from the context of our poem that Bèze also understands that the surname would be applied to those whose father had died.

**fuisses**: the contrary-to-fact protasis assumes the apodosis, "What would you do then?"

## 61.

A reference to the breaking of the siege of Landrecies, the news of which brought much rejoicing to Paris. The city had been occupied by François's commander Claude d'Annebault in 1543, but was soon thereafter besieged by the Imperial army and the English army under Sir

John Wallop, governor of Guisnes. François marched to relieve the city, and Charles and his allies withdrew without incident. On the siege, see Adolphe Delécuse, *Essai historique sur la ville de Landrecies; comprenant son origine, sa description, ses neuf sièges ...* (Jemappes, Belgium, 1866), pp. 41–45, and Paulin Giloteaux, *Histoire de Landrecies des origines à nos jours* (Le Quesnoy, 1962), 49–58.

8. Cf. "O magnum pietatis opus," antiphon for Vespers of the feast of the Finding of the Cross (3 May). The phrase colors in turn "dilecto sanguine ... emi" in line 6.
9. **nolens**: François's hand was forced by a secret alliance between Henry VIII and Charles V that lead to the invasion of France.
9-10. **tui ... victor eras**: i.e., "you controlled your passion" when you could have been expected to take revenge (cf. the similar phrase at *icon.* 1). In fact, it was François's patience, along with the coming winter and a separating river, that prevented a pitched battle between his troops and those of Charles V, eventually forcing a withdrawal of the enemy (see esp. Giloteaux, *Landrecies*, 57).

**62.**

Wright, *Delitiae delitiarum* (1637), 11;
Wright, *Sales epigrammatum* (1663), 42.
Meter: phalaecean hendecasyllable.

The name "Zoilus" was a fictitious cover for any carping critic of poetry (as above, *epig.* 2 comm.). Many of Bèze's contemporaries wrote poems to and about this character. Dolet (*Delitiae*, 1: 869) describes him as *rabido frendens ... ore*. But he also appears in Bonefon, Visagier, Bourbon, and countless others. To say that "Zoilus" was a mere stock character is not the same as saying that poets did not have an enemy in mind when they used the name. Visagier could ask, *quis sit Zoilus in meis libellis?* ("Who is this Zoilus in my books?" [*Hendecasyllabi* (1538), fol. 42]), then refuse to tell on the grounds that his enemies would expose themselves without names being named. At any rate, Zoilus was a universally reviled figure. Cf. the treatment by Bourbon:

> Ossa tegat modicus tua Zoile pulvis, ut illa
> Effodiant citius dilanientque canes.
> (*Nugae* [1533], fol. 8v)

[May only a handful of dust cover your bones, Zoilus, so the dogs may dig them up more quickly and gnaw them to bits.]

Such is the attitude toward Zoilus in a nutshell.

Bèze's poem revives the theme of *epig.* 1, though now it is turned on its head. He replaces his former confidence in the book's brevity with anxiety over whether readers will find the collection too long. This was another motif common with the epigrammatists; cf. the following of Bourbon:

> *Ad Lectorem*
>
> Nostra tibi nimium si carmina longa videntur;
>     Dimidium legito; sic minuetur iter.
> Quod si dimidium esse vides prolixius aequo;
>     Dimidium longi perlege dimidii. (*Delitiae*, 1: 793)

> [*To the Reader*
>
> If our poems seem too long to you, reader, read half; this cuts the journey short. But if half seems more drawn out than it should be, read half of the long half.]

# 63.

Meter: phalaecian hendecasyllable.

We have several examples of poets who send their books around to be refereed, so to speak, by their friends. Before publication they are much more willing to accept criticism than they are after the book leaves the press. Buchanan had addressed such a poem to Bèze:

> *Ad Theodorum Bezam, Vezeliensem*
>
> Praesul optime, sacra Christiana
> Qui caste colis et facis canisque,
> Ad te carmina mitto nec Latino
> Nec Graio sale tincta, sed Britannis
> Nata in montibus, horrida sub arcto,                    5
> Nec caelo neque seculo erudito.
> Quae si iudicio tuo probentur,
> Ut classis modo in ultimae referri
> Possint centurias, nihil timebo

Censuram invidiae, nihil morabor                                    10
Senatus critici severitatem,
Nihil grammaticas tribus: mihi unus
Beza est curia, censor, et Quirites.
(appearing in 1569 edition, 106)

Buchanan imagines that after his poems have passed under Bèze's criti-
cal pen, they will have nothing to fear of the censorship of the public.

Bèze gives the motif his own original twist: he is anxious that his
friends mark up his poems, even if it means that the work is more theirs
than his in the end; after all, he concludes, the poet himself belongs to
them.

**1-2. illepidus ... perlepidi**: These words carry a double meaning. The
friends are called _perlepidi_, "sophisticated and charming," as opposed
to the book in the first verse, which is _illepidus_, "unsophisticated and
lacking in charm." The alliteration of *l*'s and *m*'s in the first verse
makes for a very smooth introduction.

**4. perlegite usque ad umbilicum**: The *umbilicus* (or ὄμφαλος) was a
thin piece of wood applied to the last leaf of a rolled book. Hence to
read *ad umbilicum* means "to read to the end." Bonefon also read his
poets cover to cover:

Misisti geminos mihi poetas,
Quos ego geminos ad umbilicum
Legi attentius ... (*Delitiae*, 1: 689)

**13. Stellulisque obelisque virgulisque**: *stellulae,* from the Greek
ἀστέρισκοι, that is, "asterisks," were used to mark formulaic lines;
on *obeli* (†) which marked spurious lines, see *epig.* 2.2; *virgulae*
("spits") are essentially the same as *obeli*, critical marks in the shape
of a rod, also used to indicate that a line should be rejected; see
Quint. 1.4.3: "quo quidem ita severe sunt usi veteres grammatici ut
non versus modo censoria quadam virgula notare et libros ..."

**15. titulo tenus**: a stock phrase, bearing the connotation of a title used
nominally, and so translated here, "at least in name;" cf. Suet. *Claud.*
25; idem, *Jul.* 76. The idea is that, although his friends will have to
make substantial changes, so that technically this is *their* work, the
title page will nonetheless bear Bèze's name. Thus in line 18 the idea
is repeated with *praeter titulum*.

**18. praeter titulum**: And note how uncolorful Bèze's title is: *Poemata*.

## 64.

Missing in 1569, 1576, 1597.
Meter: phalaecian hendecasyllable.

Philene's Greek name means "the lover," which Bèze hopes will reflect her disposition. Among the Roman and Hellenistic poets girls bearing Greek names typically come from the class of courtesans and slave girls, the kind of less-than-respectable demimondaines one would expect to find at drinking parties and on the city's seamier side. There is no question here of a long-term love-affair; rather, Bèze has in mind a one-night stand or the occasional amorous tryst. We are to assume that Philene will change her mind again in the future.

**14. subito:** This word, the very position and sound of which evokes the impression of the arrow's sudden strike, likewise signals the unexpected shift in the poem, both in subject (Philene only now appears in the nominative in a main clause) and in the girl's attitude. It also echoes the *subito* of line 4, as if to emphasize the startling rapidity with which the change came about.

**16. levis:** The poets usually reserved this word for girls who change from yielding to unyielding. At any rate, the inconstancy of a woman had long become proverbial (esp. Verg. *Aen.* 4.569–70).

## 65.

Missing in 1569, 1576, 1597.
Meter: iambic senarius.

With all his anxious running about, Poardus looks like an upstanding citizen checking on the condition of the republic, but in reality his intent is less than patriotic: he's more interested in locating one of the city's more popular inhabitants. On the significance of Doris's Greek name, see note on *epig.* 64. Pasquier appears to have borrowed the punch line in the following:

*De uxore Aviti*

Torpentem iuvenis cum cerneret uxor Avitum,
   Stertere in ignavo nocte dieque toro,
Nec privata illi nec publica commoda curae,

Hoc sibi supplendum munus utrumque putat.
An non exercet privata et publica vere,
Quae rem cum servis, cum populo facit? (*Epig.* 4.84)

1-2. **illam ... scortillum**: The alliteration of *l*'s and *m*'s of the first line, together with the flattering words, crescendos to the jarring *scortillum* in the second line and the antithetical description that follows it.

3. **Illam Dorida Poardus ille**: The chiasmus provides a smooth transition between Doris and Poardus, while throwing the spotlight on *deperit* at the end of the line.

6. **uno ... in loco**: The hyberbaton serves to emphasize Poardus's restlessness.

7. **Rem ... publicam**: a double-entendre, drawing on both the literal meaning of the words ("the public thing"), and the technical meaning ("the republic"). Because Doris belongs to every man, she can be considered public property, i.e., the republic.

### 66.

Missing in 1569, 1576, 1597.

Structurally this poem is built around a tension of contrasts that is eventually resolved in the last two lines by Candida herself, who is able to balance what is otherwise incompatible. Line 3 mirrors line 1 by repeating the *quoties* and duplicating *tunc -o totus*, thus focusing attention on the distinctions between hot and cold, nearness and distance. In line 2, Aetna and its sulfuric fires are countered in line 4 by the Caucasus and its snowy peak, while *ut cum ... fremit* is echoed by *ut cum ... anhelat*. Finally, line 6 unites these discordant elements of hot and cold under the single umbrella of "Candida," which as a word hovers above them in the previous line.

### 67.

Missing in 1569, 1576, 1597.
Meter: phalaecian hendecasyllable.

It is nearly impossible to duplicate the word-play here into English. The joke revolves around the diminutives of *cor* and *mens*. The former creates, by some stretch of the imagination, a reference to the anus (*corculum*, which by an obviously false etymology, Bèze derives from *culus*),[16] while the latter becomes the word for the penis.

**5. mentula**: used frequently in Catullus and Martial, and common in graffiti, but purposefully avoided by Cicero (*Fam.* 9.22.3) as being too obscene. It is unlikely that *mentula* is related to *mens*, though the connection has been suggested (see P. Chantraine, *Dictionnaire étymologique de la langue grecque* [Paris, 1968–1980]), 3: 692–93, s.v. μῆδεα. At any rate, Bèze is more concerned with making a play on the word than drawing a correct etymology.


### 68.

Missing in 1569, 1576, 1597.

Structurally the poem develops around *arcum*, the third word of the first line, and *telum*, the third word of the last line. While it is true that Candida has the bow, Bèze says, he himself has the weapon.

**2. aptus ad arma puer**: a common motif; cf. Ovid, *Am.* 1.10.19: "nec Venus apta feris Veneris nec filius armis."

**3. Nempè supercilii nobis sic forma notata est**: It was a commonplace to compare the eyebrow to a bow; so Bonefon remarks, "Me supercilii nigellus arcus" (*Delitiae*, 1: 657, line 20).

**8. telum**: naturally used as a metaphor for the penis; cf. esp. Mart. 11.78.6. Adams, *Latin Sexual Vocabulary*, 20, cites the following story from Justin: "According to Justin (38.1.9), Mithridates, on being frisked by a representative of the younger Ariarathes, gave the warning, 'caveret ne aliud telum inveniret quam quaereret' ['he should be careful lest he find a weapon other than the one he was looking for']. The remark provoked mirth ..."

---

[16] On the scatologic uses of *culus* see Adams, *Latin Sexual Vocabulary*, 110–12.

### 69.

Missing in 1569, 1576, 1597.
Meter: phalaecian hendecasyllable.

The occasion of this poem is the same as that of *epitaph*. 11, which one may consult for background. The poetry of Maclou Popon was not published, but undoubtedly C(h)loris was his imaginary love interest, given the comparisons here to Catullus's Lesbia and Ovid's Corinna. Her name is Greek (Chloris, Χλῶρις; cf. Hor. *Od.* 2.5.18 and 3.15.8), and equivalent to "Flora," the goddess of flowers and plants. Ovid, *Fast.* 5.195–200, makes the connection between Chloris and Flora, and at the same time explains that Latin pronunciation corrupted the spelling of the former:

> Chloris eram quae Flora vocor: corrupta Latino
> nominis est nostri littera Graeca sono.
> Chloris eram, nymphe campi felicis, ubi audis
> rem fortunatis ante fuisse viris.
> quae fuerit mihi forma, grave est narrare modestae;
> sed generum matri repperit illa deum.

1. **Chloris, o Chloris**: The repetition of a name is used in classical literature to add pathos. Cf. Hor. *Od.* 2.14: "Eheu fugaces, Postume, Postume ..." The device is used with great effect in the Scriptures: 2 Sam. 19:4, "he cried with a loud voice, o my son Absalom, o Absalom"; Matt. 23.37, "O Jerusalem, Jerusalem, you that kill the prophets ..."; Luke 10.41, "Martha, Martha."
12. **infacetiarum**: These are "coarse jokes" that accompany mourning. Ancient Roman funeral processions, like the triumphs, often included dancers and mimes who dressed as the deceased and imitated their gestures while telling lewd jokes (see Suet. *Iul.* 84 and *Vesp.* 19). The idea behind the practice seems to be that such humor can reaffirm life in the face of an otherwise gloomy occasion.

## 70.

Missing in 1569, 1576, 1597.
Meter: phalaecian hendecasyllable.

This epigram is a variation on the "lover-shut-out" (*exclusus amator*) theme, in which the poet is typically kept from his sweetheart by an un-yielding gate or doorkeeper. Examples abound; cf., e.g., Horace, *Od.* 1.25, 3.10; Prop. 1.16.17-44; Tib. 1.2; Ovid *Am.* 1.6. See Frank O. Copley, *Exclusus Amator* (Madison, WI, 1956; repr. Chico, CA, 1981). Lucretius, 4.177ff., gives a classic description:

> at lacrimans exclusus amator limina saepe
> floribus et sertis operit, postisque superbos
> unguit amaracino et foribus miser oscula figit.
> quem si, iam ammissum, venientem offenderit aura    180
> una modo, causas abeundi quaerat honestas,
> et meditata diu cadat alte sumpta querella ...

The *querella* here refers to the plaintive love poems, such as the one at hand.

1. **fibula**: possibly a clasp or brooch used to fasten the breastband. Note the first-occurring diminutive (recurring in line 29).
3. **niveum ... flammas**: The poets loved this antithesis between hot and cold, ice and flames, since they marked the extremes of the lover's emotional and physical experience. Cf. lines 16-17: "nix ... nimio calore."
4. **globulos**: often of breasts, to emphasize the roundness and largeness. Cf. Bonefon: "Hos inter globulos papillularum," and

> Sinisterne globus globusne dexter
> Figura placeat rotundiore:
> An dexter globus, an globus sinister
> Papilla rubeat rubentiore? (*Delitiae*, 1: 665–66)

11-15. **carcere ... claustra**: The description of the confinement here is reminiscent of Vergil's description of Aeolus's imprisonment of the winds at *Aen.* 1.50ff. (note "luctantis ventos, vinclis et carcere, indignantes ... circum claustra").
24. **et illam**: "even her," an outrage, because the goddess of love did not often conceal her treasures. The affair between Mars and Venus figures in *epig.* 4 above.

29. **fibulula**: the diminutive, which until now has been used in a cajoling manner, has here taken on a sinister tone, as when the fairy-tale witch says, "Come here, my little dearie."

71.

Missing in 1569, 1576, 1597.
Meter: phalaecian hendecasyllable.

Many of the poets address poems to their sick sweethearts (e.g., Monier to Corinna, *Delitiae*, 2: 676: "Virgineum potuit macies violare ruborem?" ... ). The subject of illness seems to be a metaphor for the mortality of human relationships in general. See D. R. Hofstadter, *Le Ton Beau de Marot* (New York, 1997). For the medical ingredients, it is useful to look at J. M. Riddle, *Dioscorides on Pharmacy and Medicine* (Austin, 1985) and J. Scarborough, "Early Byzantine Pharmacology," *DOP* 38 (1984): 213–32 (also noteworthy in the same volume [95–102] is Riddle's "Byzantine Commentaries on Dioscorides"). All references to Pliny the Younger's *De medicina* are from the edition of Alf Önnerfors (Berlin, 1964).

7. **Ubi purpura, quae genis sedebat**: i.e., "blushing cheeks"; cf. Pasquier's *purpureusque pudor* (*Epig.* 1.79).
9. **sanguisuga**: often used of leeches, but here it is the fever that sucks away the blood.
17. **pixidas**: properly, *pyxidas*, they are boxes for carrying medicines. In addition to using them for storage, Pliny relates that many drugs should be aged in special *pyxides* made of such exotic materials as horn or copper.
18. **emplastica**: from ἐμπλαστικός, "causing to adhere," and related to "emplastrum," a favorite medium for the external application of medicines. See *TLL* 5.2.530–31.
20. **Butyrumque**: Butter was considered an all-purpose cleansing agent and astringent (Pliny, *NH* 28.133–34). Cf. Pliny the Younger's (*De Medicina* 1.21 and 2.23) "butyro aut adipe ursino perfricantur" and "omnia in his locis ulcera purgantur, complentur, persanantur butyro ac medulla cervina, item felle taurino cum cyprino oleo aut irino."
   **oleumque**: Oils were used both to add consistency to plasters, ointments, and cerates, and for their own properties when ingested or

applied topically. Oils could come from any number of plants or seeds (see example in the previous note), and there were numerous ways to extract them, including pressing and distillation.

**lac:** Pliny (*NH* 28.123ff.) gives a long list of uses of milk from sheep, goats, cows, and donkeys, mostly for complaints involving ulcers and dysentery.

**adipesque:** Pliny (*NH* 28.136ff.) says that pig's fat or lard was especially coveted for external application on fatigued limbs, aching joints, and wounds. Its effectiveness was believed derived from the fact that pigs consumed roots that in themselves had healing properties.

**cassiamque:** from the *Lauraceae* family, sometimes called "Chinese cinnamon," this plant is still valued for the medicinal properties of its sweet and aromatic bark (its oil is the only oil officially remaining in the United States Pharmacopoeia and German Pharmacopoeia). It is prescribed for various digestive disorders and colic, and is also said to promote menstrual discharge and to be capable of decreasing the secretion of milk.

22. **crocus:** Saffron was mixed with wine or water as a remedy for various kinds of inflammation, both internal and external (Pliny, *NH* 21.137).

   **amomum:** probably *Elletaria cardamomum*, now commonly called cardamom. An Egyptian papyrus dating to around 1550 B.C. mentions cardamom as having numerous medical properties. In antiquity it was valued second only to saffron among the plants from the East. Cleopatra found the odors of the crushed seeds so enticing that she scented the rooms of her palace with them when Marc Antony paid her a visit. According to Pliny (*NH* 12.48) it was obtained from Indian wild vines and bundled tightly as soon as it was gathered. Elsewhere, he prescribes it as a treatment for stomach conditions that involve the spitting of blood (26.34) and for joint ailments in general (26.105).

23. **thura:** Frankincense and myrrh were used from antiquity until the development of morphine as an analgesic (Jesus was given wine mixed with myrrh while on the cross). Myrrh was also effective for treating inflammations, coughs, and infections. For a recent study of its effectiveness as a painkiller, see the newsbrief in *Archaeology* 49.3 (May/June, 1996): 25 (Brett Leslie Freese). Similar antiseptic and anti-inflammatory properties are attributed to frankincense, a gum resin derived from trees of the genus *Boswellia* in Arabia and Africa (see F. N. Hepper, "Arabian and African Frankincense," *JEA* 55 [1969]: 66–

72). It was usually prescribed for diarrhea, menstrual problems, digestive tract ulcers, and skin problems.

**rosaeque:** The coolness of rose oils were thought to alleviate hot rashes, ear aches, and burns (Pliny the Younger, *De medicina* 1.6, 3.9).

**cinnamomumque:** commonly used for stomach problems.

**29-30. Erit, pharmaca ... Convervasse duos:** i.e., Bèze would pine away if he loses his girl. Ovid, *Am.* 2.13.15, entreats Isis on behalf of Corinna with the same conceit: "huc adhibe vultus, et in una parce duobus."

**32-33.** Cf. Catullus *c.* 5.7-8, again below lines 37-38.

**36. labore amantum:** The "toil of lovers" is to write amatory poetry.

**39. singula singuli:** Bèze has already promised that the doctors will receive commendation for saving two at once and will gain a kind of immortality through being celebrated in his poetry. Therefore, the sense of *singula singuli* must be that the doctors will receive the reward of physical contact with Candida too, which will make the task worth the effort (short of the money, which such poets always refuse to pay).

**57. cito:** not metrical, as Macrin notes; cf. *epig.* 53.3, where it is used correctly.


## 72.

Missing in 1576, 1597.
Meter: iambic senarius.


Again, as in *epig.* 65 above, the joke centers around the double-entendre of *res publica.* Here the punch line is given a new dimension by the legal-political language employed.


**4. evincere:** In strict legal terms of Roman law, an eviction would imply the recovery of one's own property. The joke, then, is that Ligurinus's wife is public property, and so a public official has every right to remove Ligurinus, the tenant, from the premises, so to speak.

## 73.

Missing in 1569, 1576, 1597.
Meter: phalaecian hendecasyllable.

The Neo-Latinists often addressed body parts. Bonefon, for example, has
a poem that begins "O dens improbe" . . . Such poems tend to follow a
pattern. The poet registers his complaint, then he takes to cursing, then
making promises, and finally resorting to a threat. While at first glance
Bèze's poem appears to be merely a trite, extended exercise building to
a simple word-play based on the double meaning of "foot," it also re-
flects an epigrammatic attitude that brings it very close to Bakhtin's car-
nival and to what he called the "unfinished, grotesque" body. Here the
world is viewed upside down, in a parody filled with hyperbole and
exaggeration: Bèze addresses not the head of Candida, where one would
normally focus one's attention, where the brain operates and decisions
are made, but approaches her from another, odd angle, from the lower
stratum, the earth-bound. The entire poem is addressed to the foot, and
it is to the foot that entreaties are made, promises are offered, and curses
are hurled, as if the foot is dismembered and acting on its own accord.
There is something here of the *exclusus amator* motif also (see *epig. 70*).
Yet, even though the foot has a chance to achieve immortality by itself
among the stars, we are also given faint reminders that the foot is at-
tached to Candida too (the foot cannot be hurt without hurting the
whole; the foot cannot depart without taking Candida with it), and that
it possesses the power to destroy their relationship or to sustain it. Thus
we are left with something comic. This is not the classic image of the
beautiful female body, complete, well-proportioned, harmonious. Solo-
mon's express admiration of his beloved's feet, for example, is only a
small part of a larger picture (*Cant.* 7.1 Vulg.). This glimpse at Candida
is an oddity, a weird focusing of the eye's lens on something less than
the perfected whole, something turned bottom up, as one would expect
in carnivalesque humor.

1. **pes**: The singular stands for the plural, as the phrase *geminae colum-
   nae* indicates. Yet Bèze wants to maintain the singular throughout so
   that the punch line will be more effective at the end.
   **columnae**: For legs as columns, cf. *Cant.* 5.15 Vulg.: "crura illius co-
   lumnae marmoreae quae fundatae sunt super bases aureas."

23. **quadruplum**: such is the punishment prescribed often in the code of Justinian.

31. **sublimis**: The first syllable should be long by position, as Macrin notes; cf. *epig.* 87.14, where it is used correctly.

34-35: **unum pedem**: a foot of poetry. A similar poem appears in Pasquier:

*In Iberum*

Nescio quid foetere tibi succenseo, tu me,
    Nasum, vellem te non habuisse pedes. (*Epig.* 3: 48)


## 74.

### Missing in 1569, 1576, 1597.

The title of the poem, *ad quandam*, indicates that Bèze has left aside the Candida cycle for a time to delve into subjects he could not otherwise broach. What he has in mind with this poem is not exactly clear. Prescott ("English Writers and Beza's Latin Epigrams," 87) believes this poem shows a certain "sexual ambivalence" on the part of Bèze, who is shocked that a girl could have apertures for making love. Yet the shock of the poet derives from the fact that the girl is missing her aperture, not that she has it. One must ask rather what girl could be missing her "crack" (*rima*) so unexpectedly. Is she very young perhaps, and that is why she has such a faint line? Is Bèze addressing a statue of a girl, akin to Ovid's Galatea, which would explain the missing genitalia? One compelling solution to the nature of this mysterious girl comes by way of comparison with Juvenal's reproach of effeminate actors at 3.93-97. There the satirist complains of foreign actors in Rome who are able to play the parts of women so perfectly because they are physically similar to women, even down to their "crack":

an melior, cum Thaida sustinet aut cum
uxorem comoedus agit vel Dorida nullo
cultam palliolo? mulier nempe ipsa videtur,     95
non persona, loqui; vacua et plana omnia dicas
infra ventriculum et tenui distantia rima.

Bèze's *quaedam* has not quite achieved such perfection in mimicking the female genitalia as Juvenal's actors, only enough to have fooled the poet for a moment. In line 9, Bèze wonders if the *quaedam* has any aperture at all, while the addition of *monogramma* in line 10 is not meant to be the definitive resolution of the problem, but only a possibility, maybe even wishful thinking.

Montaigne (*Essays*, 678 [III.5, on Vergil]) was interested in the poem, and thought that he at least understood the tone of it. While discussing the eagerness of people to take care of the vices of appearance while overlooking the ones of reality, and at the same time bemoaning the fact that his detractors attack him for delving sometimes into risqué language, he protests that even famous churchmen are forgiven for the same deviations, merely because they write in verse:

> And it is not right that they should refuse me, because I lack rhyme, the dispensation that even Churchmen, and some of the most proudly crested at that, enjoy in our time. Here are two of them:

> "May I die if your crack is more than a faint line."
>
> Beza

> "A friendly tool contents and treats her well."
>
> Saint-Gelais

> And what about the many others? I like modesty, and it is not by judgement that I have chosen this scandalous way of speaking; it is nature that has chosen it for me. I do not commend it, any more than I do any forms that are contrary to accepted practice; but I excuse it, and by particular and general circumstances I make the accusation lighter.

Montaigne ignores the fact that Bèze repudiated much of his own early efforts, including this poem.

7. **Aurea ... descendunt ... fluenta**: Probably an allusion to the story of Danaë, whom Zeus visited in the form of a stream of golden rain (Apollod. *Bibl.* 2.2.2, 2.4.1ff.; Ovid, *Met.* 4.611ff.). The imagery is one of the girl locked up and shielded from intercourse with the male.

9. **rimula**: used of the female genitalia in Juvenal (noted above) and Ausonius; see Adams, *Latin Sexual Vocabulary*, 95.

## 75.

Missing in 1569, 1576, 1597.
Meter: phalaecian hendecasyllable.

The theme is the same as that of *epig. 77*. Gellia must be a prostitute
who has many clients. She has every right to call those clients "sons,"
since they spend as much time, even more, *in utero* as real sons do.
According to Greek sources, it was the habit of prostitutes to use such
familial terms with their clients. See, e.g., the following of Xenarchus
(4.13–15, ed. T. Kock, *Comicorum Atticorum Fragmenta* [Leipzig, 1880–
1888, repr. Utrecht, 1976], 2:469):

> αὗται [sc. prostitutes] βιάζονται γὰρ εἰσέλκουσι τε
> τοὺς μὲν γέροντας ὄντας ἐπικαλούμεναι
> πατρίδια, τοὺς δ' ἀπφάρια, τοὺς νεωτέρους.

[They apply force and drag them in, calling the older
men, "Daddy," and the younger ones, "Boy."]

Machard cites a poem from the *Touches* of Etienne Tabouort that is a
close translation of this poem of Bèze:

> Candide appelle ses enfants
> Ceux auxquels elle s'abandonne,
> Dont il ne faut pas qu'on s'étonne,
> Car si ceux qu'on porte le temps
> De neuf mois, ainsi l'on surnomme,
> Elle peut bien dire à un homme
> "Mon fils" l'ayant porté dix ans.

2. **Gellia**: This character appears frequently in Martial, especially as an
   old woman who tries to appear young (cf. esp. 4.20).
5–6. **tulere ... tulit**: That *ferre* can refer to the bearing of children is
   well-attested in classical authors; for its use as a metaphor for inter-
   course cf. Aristophanes, *The Knights* 1056: καί κε γυνὴ φέροι
   ἄχθος, ἐπεί κεν ἀνὴρ ἀναθείη ["A woman will bear any weight
   when it is placed upon her by a man"].

## 76.

Missing in 1569, 1576, 1597.
Meter: phalaecian hendecasyllable.

Bèze admonishes Candida to expect ups and downs in their relationship, just as everything in human experience comes in cycles. Bèze may have in mind Terence, *Eun.* 276 ("omnium rerum vicissitudo est") and many other similar passages cited by Erasmus, *Adag.* 1.7.62.

4. **turturilla**: Doves (including *columbae*) were a fairly common metaphor for the tender girl. Cf. Bonefon (*Delitiae*, 1: 679):

> Nunc te possideo alma Pancharilla,
> Turturilla mea et columbulilla ...

Visagier (*Hendecasyllabi* [1538], iii, fol. 68r) uses the adjective *blanda*:

> Et quae sum modo blandior columba,
> Saeva ero tibi sevior leaena.

Macrin was uncertain whether this form was permissible (he had no doubt about *turturillo*, though, which is even more questionable); the feminine diminutive is in fact a hapax legomenon in classical literature, occurring at Sen. *Ep.* 96.5, though it appears several times in glosses (see index of G. Goetz, *Corpus Glossariorum Latinorum* [Leipzig and Berlin, 1888–1923]).

6. **Tot doli exagitent calumniarum**: These slanders are not unlike those of the harsh old men of Catullus (5.2) and Propertius (2.30.13). The idea is that those who are not able to enjoy love for themselves often try to destroy it for others.

18. **Tanto fervidior futurus ignis**: The idea is that embers (as in lines 1 and 13) conceal a raging fire (cf. Horace, *Od.* 2.1.7–8).

## 77.

Missing in 1569, 1576, 1597.

This epigram is to be compared with 75 above, the notes of which apply here too.

3. **commercia**: a word of business, but often applied to prostitution, as most certainly here. See Adams, *Latin Sexual Vocabulary,* 203.

## 78.

Missing in 1569, 1576, 1597.

Commiseration with a sick lover was commonplace in this genre of writing, as noted in reference to *epig.* 71 above, and appropriate to the origins of the elegy in the lament. Cf. also Visagier, *Hendecasyllabi* (1538), 50:

> De Clinia aegrotante
>
> Flete vos, iubeo, meae Camoenae,
> Flete cum domino, simulque adeste
> Cum luctu comites mei doloris ...

**4. Binas vicisset**: In the judgment of Paris, Venus was chosen over Juno and Minerva as the most beautiful of the goddesses.

## 79.

Missing in 1569, 1576, 1597.
Meter: phalaecian hendecasyllable.

Gillius is proud of himself for having an accommodating girlfriend, but Bèze warns him that he found a prostitute, not a girlfriend.

**2. facili**: Horace, *Sat.* 1.2.119 speaks of his preference for easy and available sex, as opposed to the girl who flees and plays hard-to-get: "Non ego: namque parabilem amo venerem facilemque." He then cites Philodemus, who chooses girls who are inexpensive and who come when ordered.

## 80.

Missing in 1569, 1576, 1597.

Bèze turns a confession to Candida into a succinct statement about his internal struggle between the lust of the flesh and the will of the spirit.

**4. cupiam ... nolo**: The word *cupere* denotes an involuntary desire for some object or action, while *velle*, the positive of *nolle*, indicates that the will has been actively engaged and applied to the desired outcome. Cf. Cic. *Mil.* 12, 32; Sen. *Ep.* 116.2. The difference between the desire and the will, between wishing and wanting, figures in many a theological discussion about the extent of the atonement. The *loci classici* are 1 Tim. 2.4 and 2 Pet. 3.9. The question that has vexed theologians is why, if God does not wish that anyone should perish, his will is not done. Bèze preferred to translate both passages with forms of *velle* and *nolle*, while explaining in his commentary (*Novum Testamentum* [1582], part 2: 300 and 422) that the statement does not apply to every individual universally and must be balanced against God's secret decree. The distinction between "desire" and "will" toyed with here has interested later commentators.

## 81.

### Missing in 1569, 1576, 1597.

Candida is in Paris, while Bèze is in Vézelay. Candida is fretting over their separation, as suggested by the three occurrences of *abesse* throughout the poem and the *longum intervallum* of line 3; but Bèze offers her reassurance, the nature of which depends mostly on the meaning carried by the rather cryptic *video* at the end of line 6. He appears to be echoing Verg. *Aen.* 4.83, where Dido is said to "see" Aeneas even though he is absent: "Illum absens absentem auditque videtque." In the mind's eye, at least, absent loved ones are ever present.

2. **Hedua:** The Aedui were a tribe that in Roman times lived between what is now the Loire and the Saône, in the Nivernais and Burgundy regions, where Bèze's childhood town of Vézelay is located.

5. **requiram:** picked up by *quaero* in the next line and countered with *video.* The word does not always indicate a physical searching for something; it also denotes simply a need or lack of something that is absent. Cicero (*Tusc.* 1.87), explaining that the dead do not miss anything because they have no sensation, sheds light on the meaning of this word: "Triste enim est nomen ipsum carendi, quia subiicitur haec vis: habuit, non habet, desiderat, requirit, indiget. Haec, opinor, incommoda sunt carentis ..." Here *requirere* falls in with "desiring" and "needing," as does *quaerere* in the next line (cf. Ovid *Met.* 2.239

for *quaerere* in this sense), both with a touch of sorrow or regret added. Probably, then, Candida wonders, not whether Bèze is asking for her or looking for her, but whether he is missing her.

7. **terris involvat Juppiter astra**: i.e., cause a general conflagration of the universe, of the sort the Stoics expect.

8. **absit ... absit**: a play on the figurative and concrete senses of the word.

### 82.

Missing in 1569, 1576, 1597.

The allusion may be to the advance of Imperialist forces on Paris in 1544, which caused general panic among the people there (thus the *attonitos* of line 1); the late date is suggested by the absence of the poem from the Orléans ms. At any rate, the national uproar serves as a nice antithesis to the peaceful love that Bèze and Candida enjoy.

1. **Caesaris**: Bèze consistently uses this title to denote Charles V. The tone of panic here is meant to evoke that experienced in Rome as Julius Caesar crossed the Rubicon.

2. **Absentis praesens**: The juxtaposition of the two words sums up the contrasting realities of this scenario succinctly: The fear is at hand within the city (*praesens*), though Charles is at some distance (*absens*), as he campaigns in the countryside around Paris. *Absentis* here must be mildly concessive in force, giving the sense, "When the fear of Caesar, though absent, was present among the panicked people ..." Ultimately, Mars will spare Paris the actual experience of occupation (Caesar will never be *praesens*) out of concern for Candida as Venus.

3. **Saturnique sequens propius vestigia Mavors**: The conjunction of Mars and Saturn was thought to be an ill-omen. See, e.g., Cic. *Div.* 1.85: "Quid astrologus cur stella Iovis aut Veneris coniuncta cum luna ad ortus puerorum salutaris sit, Saturni Martisve contraria?" Note also Pliny, *NH* 2.139 and Seneca, *NQ* 7.12.4.

## 83.

### Missing in 1569, 1576, 1597.

Bèze succinctly captures the irony of poetic inspiration so predominant in Classical and Renaissance amorous poetry: it is the elusive girl who inspires the poet to write (the elegiac couplet has its origins in the lament for lost loved ones), not the one who has been attained.

## 84.

### Missing in 1569, 1576, 1597.

Bèze's detractors used this poem to disparage his wife Claudine Denosse by claiming that she had become pregnant before their marriage. Bèze addresses the matter in the preface to the 1569 edition (= *Corr.* 10: 91):

> At istis bonis viris non pudet quicquid de poeticae Candidae amoribus lusi (lusi autem certe pleraque veteres illos imitatus, priusquam etiam per aetatem, quid istud rei esset, intelligerem) ad castissimam et lectissimam foeminam accommodare. Id autem non aliter se habere quam dico, non ii tantum testari possunt quibuscum per id tempus vixi, verum etiam res ipsa declarat: cum nullos unquam liberos ex uxore susceperim, in meis autem illis carminibus, Candidam praegnantem superis commendem; quod tum mihi nimirum illud fictitium argumentum, ut alia subinde multa, occurreret.

2. **Sequana**: The Seine river flows northwest through Paris and empties into the English Channel.
5. **et Yona tibi, et concedat Matrona nomen**: The Yonne and Marne "yield their name" in the sense that they empty into the Seine, and thus become part of that river. The Marne flows westward from northeastern France and joins the Seine near Paris. The Yonne flows in from the south. The Latin river name "Matrona" also punningly conveys the idea of "matrona," a married woman ("let it concede the name 'wife' to you").
6. **victis Isarae ... vadis**: the Isère river flows into the Rhône, southwest of the Seine. *Victis* is a prolepsis.

## 85.

Missing in 1569, 1576, 1597.

According to *epig.* 81, Candida is in Paris, Bèze in Orléans. There are close parallels to this poem in the following poem of Pasquier:

*Ad Gallam*

Arderem cum te, si te non Galla videbam,
   Una dies mensis, mensis at annus erat.
Nunc te non video, quia nunc evanuit ardor,
   Si videoque, dies, mensis, et annus erit.
Forma eadem tamen est quam cum te Galla peribam,
   Prisca tibi forma est, non mihi priscus amor.
Nec residet nostris male suada libido medullis,
   Hei mihi, quae miserum me mihi surpuerat.
Quisquis amat, formam matrem ne credat amoris.
   Nam formae pater est, si mihi credis, amor.
   (*Epig.* 1.19)

2. **sidera**: probably meaning "eyes," as does *lumina* often. Cf. Ovid *Am.* 2.16.44: "per me perque oculos, sidera nostra, tuos"; 3.3.9: "radiant ut sidus ocelli."

3. **diem ... mensemque ... annum**: accusatives of the extent of time; *moratus* is intransitive.

7. **lunaque ... una**: i.e., the monthly cycle.

   **numerabitur**: The idea is that time will no longer matter: hours, days, months and years will all be counted the same once Bèze is with his sweetheart.

9–10. **Sic tempus ... tibi**: The *sic* signals the coming result clause (*ut*), while *haec eadem* looks back to *mea tempora*. Bèze hopes that time will restore lost hours to him so he can give those hours to Candida.

## 86.

André Tiraqueau (1488–1558), a humanist and jurist, originally from Fontenay-le-Comte, was associated with humanists and poets there, including Salmon Macrin and Rabelais. For the latter, see M. Perrat, "Autour du juge Bridoye. Rabelais et le *De nobilitate* de Tiraqueau," *BHR* 16 (1954): 41–57. This poem of Bèze, along with those of several other well-known humanists, appears as a dedication in Tiraqueau's monumental legal treatise entitled *Ex commentariis in Pictonum consuetudines ... sectio de legibus connubialibus* (Paris, J. Kerver, 1546). Two other poems of Bèze's appear there as well (see below), but all were cut from later editions of Tiraqueau's work, most likely because Tiraqueau showed himself not to be a friend of the reform movement. At any rate, Bèze identifies him here as a second Varro, the polymath of the late Roman Republic, undoubtedly because of the encyclopedic nature of what Tiraqueau accomplished. For more on Tiraqueau cf. *Corr.* 1: 194–95 and M. Jacques Brejon, "André Tiraqueau, 1488–1558," diss., Université de Poitiers, 1937.

The poem itself reprises an old motif, that of the book bringing abiding fame to its author (as Catullus *c.* 1.10: "plus uno maneat perenne saeclo"; cf. Horace *Od.* 1.1 and 3.30). Bèze also seems to be making a tacit play on the words *libri* (books) and *liberi* (children), indicating that while one's progeny may fade, a well-written book keeps—Bèze hopes—its author's glory intact. Note that the library, like Tiraqueau's wife, gives birth (*parit*) to children (*natos*), and from them glory is born (*nata est*).

As mentioned, Bèze wrote two other poems honoring Tiraqueau and his *De legibus connubialibus* that appeared as dedications in the book itself. The first attributes to Tiraqueau the union of humanistic learning (represented by Athena) with legal knowledge (represented by Hermes as patron of assemblies in the agora). The child of this union is the book itself. The second merely proclaims the difficulty of abiding by the marriage laws in the book while stating that the level of erudition contained therein is not likely to be duplicated.

ΕΠΙΓΡΑΜΜΑ εἰς τὸ περὶ γαμικῶν νόμων σύνταγμα τοῦ
Ἀνδρέα Τιρακέλλου, ἐπισημοτάτου καὶ ἐπεικεστάτου βου-
λευτοῦ τῇ τῶν Παρρισίων συγκλήτῳ

Πάλλαδα μισόγαμον Ἑρμῆς ἀγοραῖος ἔγημεν,
Πειθεῖσαν νοεροῖς σοῖς, Τιρακέλλε, λογοῖς.
Καὶ δὴ τόνδε τόκον μιχθέντ᾽ ἐπονήσατο ἄμφω,
Γνήσιον οὐρανίου σπέρματος ὄντα τόκον.
Ἀλλ᾽ αὐτὸν μετέπειθ᾽ Ἑρμῆς σοι δῶρον ἔδωκεν,
Τὸν μισθὸν μεγάλης ἔμμεν᾽ εὐεργεσίας.

[*An epigram on the treatise about marriage laws of André Tiraqueau, most wise and capable advisor to the Parlement of Paris*

Hermes, patron of the agora, married Pallas Athena, hater of marriage, when she was persuaded by your learned arguments. And what is more, the two of them struggled to produce this child of their union, a genuine child of heavenly seed. But thereafter Hermes gave him as a gift to you, the eternal reward of a great service rendered.

> Quas in conjugio leges, Tiraquelle, requiris,
>     Qui servet, nostro tempore, rarus erit.
> Sed tamen ex hominum forsan tot millibus olim
>     Illarum custos unus et alter erit.
> At qui tam docte mores, legesque sequendas
>     Conjugibus possit tradere, nullus erit.

Rare will be the person in our day and age who will abide by the rules you require in marriage. Even so, perhaps someday there will be someone here or there who will keep them. But there will be no one able to communicate with such erudition the mores and rules to be followed in marriages.]

1. **agmina**: not exclusively a military term, though it is often used figuratively even in non-military contexts. The following poem of Monier counts, undoubtedly with much exaggeration, thirty children:

> *In imaginem And. Tiraquelli*
>
> Triginta ingenio libros, tot corpore natos
>     Edidit hic, cuius conspicis ora, senex.
> Omnia potor aquae: Nunc die potoribus istis
>     Nil gigni, quamquam est haec rata fama, boni.
>         (*Delitiae*, 2: 622)

3. **Fortunate senex!**: a phrase gleaned from Verg. *Ecl.* 1.46 and 51.
   **oblivia mortis**: The neuter plural from *oblivium* is preferable to the original *oblivio* (*-onis*) for reasons of scansion. The form also recalls Vergil's description of the shades at the river Lethe (*Aen.* 6.715): "longa oblivia potant."

4. **avara dies**: *dies* here = *tempus.*

5. **ex illis . . . ex his and illi . . . haec**: i.e., *ex illis natis . . . ex his libris,* and *illi nati . . . haec gloria.* Note the same conceit in Scévole de Sainte-Marthe, in his eulogy on Tiraqueau (*Opera*, 33–34): . . . "Andreas Tirquellus, quem hominem undecunque ad immortalitatem

fuisse natum diceres: cum et numerosam sobolem ex honestissima uxore susceperit que genus propagaret, et ingentem librorum numerum ediderit, qui nomen aeternitati consecrarent."

## 87.

Meter: phalaecian hendecasyllable.

Pious Spurinna and his wife have not been able to have children, so he decides to make pilgrimages to all the major Christian shrines to ask both saints and God for a fertile marriage. He scales high mountains, braves treacherous seas, and crosses bandit-infested deserts to reach them. The journey is an enormous undertaking that keeps him away from home for years. When he finally does return home, he finds his home full of children! It seems the neighbors were lending a helping hand during his protracted absence.

1. **Spurinna**: an Etruscan name used as a surname by many Romans (including the haruspex who warned Caesar to beware the Ides of March: Cic. *Div.* 1.119; Suet. *Caes.* 81). The word, however, with its first syllable long, does not fit the hendecasyllabic meter at this point: *Spūrinna*. Macrin did not notice it, but Bèze eventually did. In later editions he changed it to *Toleno*.
2. **superat jugum Pyrenes**: i.e., from France into Spain.
3. **Divo ... Jacobo**: Tradition has it that James went to northwestern Spain (Galicia) to evangelize. Later, after King Herod Agrippa ordered him beheaded in Jerusalem in 42 A.D. (Acts 12.2), James's body and head were transported back to northwestern Spain in a stone coffin. The spot was forgotten until the year 812 when a hermit followed a star to a field where he discovered the coffin. Inside, James's head and body were miraculously reattached. A shrine was built and named Santiago de Compostela (St. James of the Star's Field), where the faithful from all over the world make pilgrimages. Roads to the shrine run through Vézelay (Bèze's birthplace) and Orléans (where Bèze studied law), so the site must have been well-known to Bèze. According to instructions given in *Codex Calixtinus*[17] (5.7) in the

---

[17] For a transcription of the Latin text see W. M. Whitehill, *Liber Sancti Iacobi—Codex Calixtinus*, 3 vols. (Santiago de Compostela, 1944).

archival library of the Cathedral of Santiago de Compostela, pilgrims coming to the shrine from Paris via Tours should first stop at Or-léans to visit the Church of the Holy Cross, where they would see wood from the cross and the chalice of St. Euverte. Those coming via Saint-Gilles (5.8) should stop at the Church of Saint-Marie-Madeleine in Vézelay to honor the tomb of Mary Magdalene. See William Melczer, *The Pilgrim's Guide to Compostela* (New York, 1993); Maryjane Dunn and Linda Kay Davidson, *The Pilgrimage to Compostela in the Middle Ages: A Book of Essays* (New York and London, 1996).

4. **Alpes**: into Italy.
5. **Petri ... limina ... Pauli**: the well-known Basilica of St. Peter at the Vatican, which sits over the tomb of Peter, was undergoing major renovations during Bèze's lifetime. Paul's shrine, built just southwest of Rome on the Ostian Road by Constantine the Great, is called the Basilica of St. Paul-Outside-the Walls. Paul was beheaded on the Ostian Road, and, as was the case with many saints, was buried near where he died.
6. **reflexus**: upward along the coast of Italy on the Adriatic side.
7. **Laureti**: A major shrine of the Holy House of the Blessed Virgin exists at Loreto, a small town in the Marches, Italy, overlooking the Adriatic. Tradition says that angels transported Mary's house there from Nazareth sometime around 1295. Miracles are thought to take place in the church that houses the shrine.
9. **Idumen**: poetic form for *Idumaea(m)*. Specifically, Spurinna goes to Jerusalem to see the empty tomb of Jesus.
15. **Divae Catharinae**: a reference to the remote Orthodox Monastery of St. Catherine on Mt. Sinai, where later Tischendorf discovered Codex Sinaiticus.

## 88.

Meter: phalaecian hendecasyllable.

Pierre Caillard was named professor at the University of Orléans before 1552; see J. Doinel, "Anne du Bourg à l'Université d'Orléans," *Mémoires de la Société archéologique et historique de l'Orléanais* 18 (1884): 457–62. In later editions the poem has the title *Cl[arissimo] V[iro] Callartio I[uris] C[onsulto] Aureliensi*. It is not clear whether in some ironic way the *patronus* of line 5 refers to Callartius or not. If it does, Bèze may be dropping the hint to his lawyer that he will receive rich rewards if Bèze wins his case. In the 1597 edition Bèze altered lines 9–11 significantly for religious reasons:

> Obtestorque Deum simul, beato
> Ut senis tibi messibus peractis,                                    10
> Fas sit coniuge de tua pudica ...

The poem has mild sexual undertones, especially when one thinks of Catullus's sparrow (see note on *pippiones* below) and the many erotic associations of the dove in antiquity.

1. **pippiones**: properly *pipiones*; Bèze may have been influenced by the Italian *pippione*. Macrin doubted whether this word would have been allowed by Italian critics. In fact, it only appears in extant Latin literature relatively late, not before its use in *Alex. Sev.* 41.7 ("Lampridius"), and then often by Plinius Valerianus in the fifth or sixth century. The thirteenth century physician Matthaeus Silvaticus defines it as follows: "sunt pulli columbarum, et est nomen formatum a proprio sono animalis." Thus *pip(p)iones* were hatchlings of pigeons (or turtledoves), which Romans often raised on their farms (Varro, *RR* 3.7–8). Undoubtedly, with the use of this word Bèze looks back to Catullus's *pipiabat* at *c.* 3.10. If, as it appears, Bèze is thinking of Catullus's sparrow as a metaphor for the penis, then the connection of the birds to six children at the end of the poem makes perfect sense. For the dove as penis see, e.g., Mart. 1.7.
**En senos tibi mitto pippiones**: Bonefon has an almost identical opening line (*Delitiae*, 1: 674, *c.* 26): "En flores tibi mitto discolores ..."

12–13. **Tot ... pippientes**: The *natos vagientes* of line 12 is counterbalanced by the *foetus pippientes* of line 13.

89.

Missing in 1569, 1576, 1597.
Meter: dactylic hexameter followed by iambic quaternarius.

To the simple theme of this poem one may compare Horace *Od.*1.13 and Mart. 11.8. Horace writes to Lydia, whom Venus has imbued with a special portion of her nectar. Martial likens the morning kisses of his

favorite to the sweetest and most pleasant scents of the world, including
a Sicilian meadow of flowers where bees come to draw their nectar. For
other poems on the sweetness of kisses see *AP* 5.32 (Marcus Argenta-
rius), 5.295 (Leontius), and 5.305 (anonymous).

1. **rores**: dew is often an erotic image in antiquity. W. M. Clarke, "The
   God in the Dew," *L'Antiquité classique* 43 (1974): 57–73, argues that
   Eros (Cupid) himself has his origin from the dew. Arguments are
   based on literary sources, vase paintings, comparative mythology,
   and etymology. See also D. Boedeker, *Descent from Heaven. Images
   of Dew in Greek Poetry and Religion* (1984). Paulus Silentiarius (*AP*
   5.270.7) mentions his girlfriend's dewy lips (χείλεα δροσόεντα) as
   a sign of her natural beauty. Pontano had used dew (and honey) as a
   metaphor for the cooling effects of his girl's kisses:

   > E labris mihi ros, ex ore recentiore aura
   >    spirat, Stella, tuo, stillat et ipse liquor.
   >    (*Erid.* 1.13.11–12)

   Dew also creates an image of softness. For Bonefon, however, it is
   the moistness of the lips that hold special attraction: "De rore humi-
   duli tui labelli ..." (*Delitiae*, 1: 665). Sussannée adds the epithet "am-
   brosial": "labra ambrosio rore purpurantia ..." (1538, 8v).
1-2. **aurea ... Venus**: just as gold is alluring, so is Venus. Cf. Homer
   *Iliad* 3.64, χρυσέη Ἀφροδίτη; Verg. *Aen.* 10.16; Ovid *Met.* 10.277,
   15.761.
3. **cannis incluse liquor**: i.e., sugar extracted from the cane. Both Arabia
   and India supplied cane sugar in antiquity (mostly for medicinal pur-
   poses). E.g., Pliny *NH* 12.17: "Saccaron et Arabia fert, sed laudatius
   India. est autem mel in harundinibus collectum, cummium modo
   candidum, dentibus fragile, amplissimum nucis abellanae magnitu-
   dine, ad medicinae tantum usum"; Lucan 3.237 (concerning people
   from India): "Quique bibunt tenera dulces ab harundine sucos." The
   choice of *liquor* instead of *sucus* is somewhat unusual, though similar
   descriptions of honey at Lucr. 1.938 (*mellis dulci flavoque liquore*)
   and Vergil *Aen.* 1.432 (*liquentia mella*) may have influenced Bèze
   here. And as noted above in the discussion of *rores*, Pontano also ap-
   plies *liquor* to honey. Bourbon refers to Indian sugar cane using the
   Latin word *humor* (*Delitiae*, 1: 790):

   *De melle Indico quod in arundinum foliis colligitur*

> In foliis est ros, et dulcis arundinis humor.
> Talia mella ferens India, spernit apes.

4. **mensis secundis**: Roman dinners were divided into three parts: the hors d'oeuvres, at which a sweet was offered; the main course; and, after a libation to the gods, a dessert, the "second table." So Varro *RR* 3.16.5: "mel ad principia convivi et in secundam mensam administratur." See also Cic. *Att.* 14.6.2, 14.21.4; Verg. *Georg.* 2.101; Horace *Sat.* 2.2.121.

5. **coelestia mella**: It has become proverbial to say that nectar/ambrosia is the food of the gods. See Erasmus *Adag.* 1.8.88, θεῶν τροφή, *deorum cibus*. Nero perverted its use to refer to Agrippina's mushrooms with which she killed Claudius (Suet. *Nero* 33). At Mart. 13.108, Attic honey mixed in wine is said to be fit for Ganymede to serve to the gods. The imagery is then often transferred to the lips; cf. examples from Bonefon:

> Tam dulcem **ambrosiam** mihi labella
> Propinant tua?

> Et tot prodiga basiationes,
> Uni **nectareo** propinat ore,
> Quot nec Lesbiolam suam poposcit,
>         (*Delitiae* 1: 656–70, *passim*)

and,

> Tune Pancharidis mea labellis
> Infelix, Anime, ausus incubare?
> Ausus sugere mella basiorum?
> Ausus nectare delicatiore
> Tete prolucre? heu miselle parce:
> Nam dum sugere mella, dumque nectar
> Credis ebibere, ebibis venena,
> Et incendia sugis et furores.
>         (*Delitiae*, 1: 670, *c.* 19, lines 1–8)

Bourbon says of the kiss of Rubella, *Basiolum, dulci nectare dulce magis* (*ibid.* 766).

13. **verna ... labella**: in other words, "lips that blossom like flowers in the spring;" so Macedonius the Consul (*AP* 5.231.1): τὸ στόμα ταῖς Χαρίτεσσι, προσώπατα δ' ἄνθεσι θάλλει.

15. The spondaic line emphasizes the sudden interruption.

## 90.

Missing in 1569, 1576, 1597;
Perosa and Sparrow, *Renaissance Latin Verse*, 387–88.
Meter: phalaecian hendecasyllable.

No poem caused Bèze more grief in his later years than this one, a target for his many Catholic critics. The Parisian theologian Claude de Sainctes cites this poem in his *Responsio ad Apologiam Theodori Bezae* (1567) as proof of Bèze's homosexuality. He is echoed by Gabrielis Fabricius, a student of an old enemy of Bèze, François Bauduin, in his *Responsio ad Bezam Vezeliam Eceboliam* (1567). The latter's uncle had written an attack in 1564 (see *Corr.* 5: 17, n. 7). Many others afterward joined the chorus (for a full account of attacks on Bèze's morality, see Machard, *Juvenilia*, xi–lxxiv; Geisendorf, *Théodore de Bèze*, 23–29). In 1569 Bèze responded to both de Sainctes and the Fabricii in the preface to his second edition, denying any validity to the claim that he had a sexual relationship with Audebert:

> Habui tum mihi, ut et alios multos, Lutetiae coniunctissimum sodalem, iam tum maximae spei iuvenem, nunc vero summae eruditionis et integerrimae famae virum, Germanum Audebertum, Aureliae, in patria sua videlicet electum quem vocant. Scripsi ad eum forte Vezeliis ludibundus aliquot hendecasyllabos, quibus singulare illius videndi et repetendorum scilicet meorum amorum desiderium (ita enim inter nos ludere poeticis istis iocis consueveramus) declarabam. Ad istos perditos non pudet (quid enim Ecebolium, quid monachum pudeat?) illum quidem ea tum autoritate tum dignitate virum in Adonidem transformare: mihi vero id sceleris impingere, ad quod depellendum nulla me indigere apud quemquam honestum hominem defensione mihi persuasi. (*Corr.* 10: 91)

Back then I had, among many others, a very close friend at Paris, already at that time a young man of great promise, but now a man of the highest erudition and unblemished reputation, Germain Audebert, of Orléans. In his homeland they call him "Elect." By chance while playing around at Vézelay I wrote to him a few hendecasyllabics, declaring to him my strong desire for seeing him and renewing our affection (this was a constant poetic game of ours). Those lost souls are not ashamed to transform him into an Adonis, although he is a man of authority and rank. But me they charged with that foul deed [sc. homosexuality], which I chose not to dignify with a response.

And in his second apology to Claude de Sainctes he writes:

Quid cum eo usque proveheris ut meam cum honestissimo viro, et iam tum in Senatu Parisiensi Advocato, quem vocant, nunc vero in civitate Aureliensi magna cum dignitate versanti, amicitiam et familiaritatem summam ad nefarium et execrandum illud scelus transferas, quod a nobis ne nominari quidem sine horrore potest, a vobis autem in vestris illis gurgustiolis, ut omnes norunt, pro ludo et ioco ducitur, quis te ipsum vir honestus non execretur? (*Opera*, 1: 360)

For an interesting discussion of the exchange of homosexuality charges between Catholics and Protestants during this period, including the dispute over this poem, see Winfried Schleiner, "That Matter Which Ought Not To Be Heard Of: Homophobic Slurs in Renaissance Cultural Politics," *Journal of Homosexuality* 25 (1994): 41–75. Schleiner compares the motif of Bèze's poem to Vergil's *Ecl.* 2, where a certain Corydon is attracted to *candidus* Alexis, a catamite, and *tristis* Amaryllis at the same time. H. Dannreuther, "A propos de Théodore de Bèze," *Bulletin de la Société de l'Histoire du Protestantisme français* 52 (1903): 282, interprets the poem as a pastiche of Catullus and Horace, asserting that friendship with a male is more fulfilling than love with a woman. If so, Bèze may be thinking of Phaedrus's speech in Plato's *Symposium*, in which the love between men is given preference over that between a man and a woman. But homosexual love is often treated as abnormal among Greek and Roman poets: *AP* 5.208, 12.41, and 12.86 (Meleager); 5.19 (Rufinus); 5.116 (Marcus Argentarius); 5.277 (Eratosthenes Scholasticus); 5.278 and 10.68 (Agathias) (the last three are Byzantines); Ovid *Ars Amat.* 2.683.

On the erudite jurisconsult, Germain Audebert, born 1518, close friend of Bèze's youth and "premier élu de l'élection d'Orléans" (i.e., President in the Election or Court of Assessors of Taxes and Subsidies in Orléans),[18] see the following: Brainne et al., *Hommes illustres,* 1: 186; Moreri, *GDH,* 1.2: 498; Bayle, *Dictionnaire,* 1: 554; Jean-Pierre

---

[18] According to Léon Tripault, *Celt-Hellenisme,* 136 (cf. above, p. 373).

Niceron, "Germain Audebert," *Mémoires pour servir à l'histoire des hommes illustres dans la republique des lettres* 24 (1733): 84–90 (our poem is mentioned on pp. 88–89); *Dictionnaire de biographie française* (Paris, 1933–1999): 4, col. 346–47; Bagenault de Viéuille, "Germain Audebert le Virgile orléannais," *Mémoires Soc. Orléans* 5 (1860): 56–86; and L. Pertile, "Un poemetto inedito sulle guerre di religione: 'L'Erynne françoise …' di G. Audebert," *BHR* 38 (1976): 299–300. He studied at Bologne under Alciat, and, returning to France, excelled in poetry and politics. He composed various works in verse, including a eulogy of Venice, on the merits of which Pope Gregory XIII and the Lord of Venice made him a knight in the order of St. Mark. Henry III honored him by giving him permission to place the fleurs-de-lis on his coat of arms as an ornament. Audebert died at Orléans on 24 December 1598, and his son Nicolas died a few days later; they were buried together in the cemetery of the Church of the Ste. Croix in Orléans. His poetry includes the aforementioned eulogy on Venice (1583), as well as ones on Rome (1585, and cf. Bèze's epigram on pp. 189–90 in the 1597 edition: *In Romam, poemate Germani Audeberti Aurelii, pulcherrime descriptam*) and Naples (1585), but not one on his native Orléans, for which he was criticized. He left two books of *sylvae* unpublished at his death. The three travel poems, based on an extended trip he made to Italy from 1539 to 1544/45, were collected and printed at Hannover in 1603 under the title *Germani Audeberti Aurelii … Venetiae, Roma, Parthenope, postrema editio ab auctore ante obitum recognita et emendata*. Some of his poems appear in the *Delitiae*, vol. 1, and one poem appears at the head of Scévole de Sainte-Marthe's 1597 collection of poetry. Another work with which Audebert was involved has gone largely unnoticed. Using his knowledge of Italy and his travel notes, he edited a manuscript of the Florentine poet Ugolino Verino containing a poem in three books on his native city; the work is entitled *De illustratione urbis Florentiae libri tres. Nunc primum in lucem editi ex bibliotheca Germani Audeberti Aurelii: cuius labore atque industris multae lacunae, quae erant in manuscripto, repletae; ac multi loci partim corrupti, partim vetustate exesi, restituti et restaurati sunt* (Paris, 1583).[19] Audebert added a preface to Verino's work with a poem

---

[19] The work receives brief mention in Cosenza, *Dictionary of the Italian Humanists*, 4: 3622, esp. card 2 (cards 3 and 6 mention a 1636 edition edited by Carlo di Tommaso Strozzi); Renouard, *Estienne*, 184: 3 (s.v. Mamert Patisson's press); Emile Picot, *Les Français italianisants au XVIᵉ siècle*, vol. 2 (1907), 153–80, esp. 157–58 and n. 1; Alfonso Lazzari, *Ugolino e Michele Verino* (Turin, 1897), 185–89.

addressed to Catherine de Medici, which begins:

> Cui potius regina potens, regumque creatrix,
> Quam tibi sacrentur Verini carmina vatis
> Syllanae veteres urbis celebrantia cunas,
> Illustresque viros, totamque ab origine prolem,
> Maioresque tuos? quorum tu maxima iure
> Gloria censeris: sunt haec tibi propria dona
> Magnanimum Heroum genus alta e stirpe trahenti,
> Summosque augenti Medicaeae gentis honores ...

At his death, Audebert was eulogized by Scévole de Sainte-Marthe (*Elogia* [1602], 191–93). In addition, Pasquier was an intimate friend to him, as the following poem reveals:

> *Ad Germanum Audebertum Aurelianum*
>
> Quid sit quod veneremur atque amemus,
> Et quid quod cupide colamus omneis,
> Certant Grammatici tumultuantes:
> Sed has censeo disputationes
> Mere ridiculas et otiosas:
> Qui te sic adamo ut colam, deinde
> Sic colo, ut venerer magis magisque:
> Ergo Grammatici valete, nec vos
> Vestras vendite somniationes:
> Unus nam docet Audebertus esse
> Quod simul venerer, colamque, amemque. (*Epig.* 5.56)

**3–4. amores ... lepores:** The difficulties inherent in these lines have been skirted by those treating this poem. In the preface cited above, Bèze places Audebert in Paris, where, in fact, he lived and worked as a lawyer from 1545 to 1548. Audebert's manuscript collection of Bèze's poems has been dated to that same period. But one should note that no poem to Audebert appears there, which is strange in light of the fact that Audebert procured it. That fact alone would seem to date this particular poem to the period from 1545 to 1548, when the two of them were in Paris and may have met for the first time (despite Meylan's unsupported claim that they knew each other in Orléans, Audebert's hometown). It is odd, too, that Bèze never mentions Audebert in his early correspondence. So is Candida in Orléans, while Audebert is in Paris? But in *epig.* 81, Bèze laments that

Candida is away in Paris, while he is in "Heduan country" (Véze-lay); and in *epig.* 85, he places her on a boat in the Seine. A break-down of the structure of the first few lines perhaps sheds some light on the problem:

| 1. Candida | 3. Paris — *amores* | 5. Candida & *amores* |
| 2. Audebert | 4. Orléans — *lepores* | 6. *lepores* & Audebert |

Lines 5 and 6 are in a chiastic arrangement, and within each line the words are conjoined by -*que*. Still, one cannot say whether these lines are a repetition of one another (Candida and Audebert, Audebert and Candida), or each referring to a separate person. Yet the align-ment of 1, 3, and 5 appears to make Candida *amores*, while that of 2, 4, and 6 makes Audebert *lepores*, which seems to this author the best solution. Audebert, being from Orléans, could be there on a visit, while Candida, figment of Bèze's imagination, could be anywhere he wants (and again, *epig.* 81 places her in Paris).

**Aurēlii:** Macrin points out that the antepenult here is long, not short.

**32. imo:** Mysteriously, Sparrow prints *uno*, but without authority. One little kiss will not keep Candida quiet as effectively as a deep kiss. It is to be noted that Bèze is implying that he can kiss Candida, but not Audebert, a fact which mitigates somewhat the charge of homo-sexuality.

## 91.

Missing in 1569, 1576, 1597; *Tottel's Miscellany*, 1: 95–96; 2: 226
(= Merrill, *Grimald*, 378, 419–20).

This poem and the next one must be read together as a point/counter-point. For the device cf. *AP* 5.292 and 293; and cf. the 1597 edition, 206 and 211 for other instances. Bourbon had utilized the point/counter-point scheme in his own *Nugae* (*Delitiae*, 1: 787):

> *Ad Amicum*
>
> Dum tu Graecaris, nos pergraecamur: et alter . . . ,

which is countered with,

> *Respondet pro amico*
>
> Dum pergraecaris tu, nos graecamur; et alter

The question at hand is whether Cornelius should take a wife, an idea that Ponticus objects to because he sees it as a no-win proposition. Whether she is ugly, beautiful, or average, unhappiness is sure to follow. Ponticus's advice to Cornelius follows the reasoning of Bias, one of the wise men of Greece (c. 566 B.C.), of whom we have several surviving apophthegms. Asked by a man whether he should marry or stay single, Bias responds, "You will surely marry either an ugly woman or a beautiful one. The ugly one will be a curse around your neck, while the beautiful one you will share with many men. Therefore, do not marry [οὐ γαμητέον ἄρα]." When Socrates was asked the same question, he replied, "Whichever you do you will repent it" (Diogenes Laertius 2.33).

The theme of the merits of marriage was a fairly common one in antiquity. We have fragments of Lucilius from a work to which the title *De nuptiarum et matrimonii modestiis* has been attributed (see Wendy Raschke, "The Early Books of Lucilius," *JRS* 69 [1979]: 78–89). Aulus Gellius (1.6) reports a speech of the censor Metellus (102–1 B.C.), who takes up the question of the advantages and disadvantages of taking a wife. Stobaeus (4.22.3.68) provides an anthology of quotations on the topic, with the general conclusion that a wife is a necessary evil because she provides children (as per the sentiment in Hesiod's account of Pandora in the *Theogony*, 570–612). Varro, *Sat. Men.* 167, appears to be responding to Menander (fr. 59, οὐ γαμεῖς ἄν νοῦν ἔχεις) when he writes, γαμήσει ὁ νοῦν ἔχων. Juvenal wonders why his friend Postumus wants to marry when he can commit suicide instead (6.30–32), and so on. Centuries later Poggio wrote a dialogue entitled *An seni uxor est ducenda* on the matter. Walter Haddon's *Poemata* (1567), 70–72, contains two such poems: "Uxor Non est Ducenda," and "Uxor Est Ducenda"; so too Turbervile's *Epitaphes, Epigrammata*, etc. (1567), 130–32: "To a Yong Gentleman, of Taking a Wyfe," and "The Aunswere, for Taking a Wyfe." Nicholas Grimald for the most part translates Bèze in his two poems on the theme: "N. Vincent, to G. Blackwood, agaynst Wedding," and "G. Blackwood to N. Vincent, with weddying." The first begins,

> Sythe, Blackwood, you have mynde to wed a wife:
> I pray you, tell, wherefore you like that life.
> What? that henceforth you may live more in bliss?
> I am beguylde, but you take mark amisse ...

Perhaps related also is the common joke among the Neo-Latin poets that a wife brings happiness only twice during the marriage: on the wedding night and at her funeral (see, e.g., Pasquier, *Epig.* 4.87).

The tendency to debate the pros and cons of important topics runs rampant through the literature of the period, and reveals the ambivalency of the educated elite toward major questions of the meaning and nature of human existence. Here Bèze is satisfied to degrade such serious business into a joke, a kind of declamatory exercise from schoolboy days gone awry. The joke, however, is not devoid of insight. Often people take different sides of an issue, not because of the merits or demerits of the case, but because of some overriding personal motive.

**1. velīs**: Macrin points out that the ultima is long, not short.

**uxorem, Corneli, ducere**: so Juvenal launches into his diatribe against women at 6.28: "certe sanus eras; uxorem, Postume, ducis?"

**4. hac lege**: i.e., "under these terms," alluding obliquely to the marriage contract itself. But note too the phraseology Bonefon uses to describe his relationship to Pancharis (*Delitiae*, 1: 675, *c.* 29, lines 15–18):

> Ah mihi tu poteras victrix praefigere leges:          15
> Iura mihi poteras imperiosa dare.
> Nec leges mihi turpe tuas, et iura subire:
> Parere imperiis nec mihi turpe tuis.

**8. subito deperit iste modus**: The idea is that, if beauty fades fast, average looks must disappear almost immediately.

**12. mille**: Bèze uses the word three times in four lines with mystical, carnival exaggeration: the woman will hurt him in a myriad of indescribable ways. Cf. also Cat. *c.* 5.

**18. celebs et sine lite torus**: i.e., a man will not be able to sleep because his wife is constantly bitter. Cf. Juv. 6.268ff.:

> semper habet lites alternaque iurgia lectus
> in quo nupta iacet; minimum dormitur in illo ...

So too Varius Germinius ap. Jerome *Adv. Juvin.* 1.28, *qui non litigat caelebs est*. Ovid (*Ars Amat.* 2.155) considers it the dower of a wife to quarrel: *dos est uxoria lites*. See also Plaut. *Men.* 765–71. But Lattimore notes that *sine ulla querella* was an extremely popular phrase in epitaphs (*Themes in Greek and Latin Epitaphs*, 279, esp. n. 107).

**19. felicis semita vitae**: appears to be modelled on Horace's *Ep.* 1.18.103: "an secretum iter et fallentis semita vitae."

## 92.

Missing in 1569, 1576, 1597; *Tottel's Miscellany*, 1: 96–97; 2: 227
(= Merrill, *Grimald*, 379, 420–21).

This poem is a retort to the previous one. Cornelius repeats the objections of Ponticus about marriage, and then adds his own rejoinders. She will not be ugly or unfaithful, he insists, and really her faults are tolerable, just as we permit thorns on a rose. It would seem, at first glance, that Cornelius has taken the high road, ready to accept his wife for better or worse, always to look on the bright side of this so-called necessary evil. But in the last two lines his integrity is stripped away to expose his real motivation for taking a wife: better to marry than to burn (1 Cor. 7.9).

17. **Semita virtutis stricta est**: an echo of Matt. 7.14 (*Novum Testamentum* [1582], part 1: 33), "Narrow is the road which leads to life." Although the Vulgate has "arcta via est quae ducit ad vitam," Bèze translates the passage "stricta via quae ducit ad vitam" in his own version of the New Testament. Bèze's note on his choice of the word indicates that he interprets the word to mean, "tight" or "narrow" rather than "difficult." He argues that the emphasis of the passage is on how few can find the path, not on how arduous it is (cf. "strictissima ianua" in Ovid *Rem. Am.* 233).
18. **stricta via**: a double-entendre. He hopes the "narrow path" of his wife's vagina will transport him to heaven and eternal happiness.

## 93.

Missing in 1569, 1576, 1597.

Damon and Phillis are two fictitious characters drawn from an eclogue that Bèze wrote but never published (ABM 279). There Damon and Coridon discuss a mutual friend, Lycidas, who has fallen on hard times. Once rich in cattle, now he can barely keep up a small herd of goats. The source of his problems proves not to be a plague, but, to the dismay of the interlocutors, his preoccupation with his new wife Phillis. Damon is made to express an attitude toward Phillis quite antithetical to the sentiment of our poem:

O Lycida, cum post aliquot decrescere menses          40

Phillidos incipiet facies, quam saepe tuorum
Fatorum seriem frustra clamabis iniquam.

[Lycidas, after time Phillis's beauty will begin to fade, and you
will be left to curse in vain the cruel chain of events untwined by
the fates.]

**1-2. Bis ... gelu**: Damon's heat (*accensus*) is juxtaposed to the wintry
cold (*hiemes*), so that in the balanced expression of line 2, he endures
the torches (*faces*) of his desire, and the ice (*gelu*) of the weather.
**7. Damōn**: Macrin points out that the final syllable should be long, not
short as the meter here demands.
**eras ... dedissent**: contrary to fact clause with the conclusion in the
indicative to show certainty of fulfillment; cf. Verg. *Aen*. 6.358 for
the same imperfect indicative/pluperfect subjunctive arrangement.

## 94.

### Missing in 1569, 1576, 1597.

The poem makes a clever pun by integrating Phoebus Apollo's function
as the sun god with his indomitable sexual appetite. Italy is hotter than
France because the beautiful women there inflame Apollo so. Machard
makes the following observation:

> Brantôme cites this last verse and invokes the authority of Beza
> to resolve this important question: "In which provinces and re-
> gions of our Christianity and our Europe are there more co-
> quettes and whores?" They say that in Italy the women are hot-
> ter, that is to say, there are more prostitutes in Italy, as Beza said
> in an epigram, since the sun is so much hotter and intense, it
> heats up the women more.
> (*Dames Galantes*, Discours I, *sub fine*.)[20]

---

[20] Pierre Bourdeille, Abbé Brantôme (1527–1614), *Vies des dames galantes*. One may find
the passage in *Oeuvres* (Paris, 1857) 1: 145. See also *Lives of the Fair and Gallant Ladies*,
transl. A. R. Allinson (Paris 1901) 1: 223: "Before making an end, I will say yet one word
more, how that I have seen a dispute raised that is still undecided, to wit, in which prov-
inces and regions of our Christendom and Europe there be most cuckolds and harlots? Men
declare that in Italy the ladies are exceeding hot, and for that cause very whorish, as saith
M. de Bèze in a Latin Epigram, to the effect that where the sun is hot and doth shine with

But Bèze says nothing about whores and coquettes, nor does he say that the women are hotter *because* of the sun, rather, that they make the sun hotter.

4. **astrologus:** An astrologer would argue that Italy is hotter because it is closer to the equator, but Bèze refuses to accept such mendacious reasoning.

## 95.

Missing in 1569, 1576, 1597.
Meter: phalaecian hendecasyllable.

Bèze warns the west wind not to be seduced and trapped by Candida's hair as he has been.

3. **verno Phoebo:** In antiquity it was axiomatic that the west wind is a gentle, temperate breeze that accompanies the spring (Cat. 46.1–3; Verg. *Georg.* 1.44; Hor. *Odes* 1.4, 4.7; Ovid *Fasti* 2.220; Pliny *NH* 18.337). The west wind was chosen here simply because of the erotic associations of springtime (see Richard Inwards, *Weather Lore* [London, 1869; repr. 1994]).
5. **lactoleae:** She avoids the sun, and so she is fair-skinned; cf. Catullus's "milky girls" at 55.17. Candida's name itself indicates her light complexion.
6. **aureolosque, crispulosque:** Curly-haired blondes were the ideal for the Romans. See Kenneth Quinn, *Latin Explorations* (London, 1963), 66–67.
14. **cincinnique:** used of well-primped hair, as in Cic. *Pis.* 25.
16. **veloci ala:** As with the thunderbolt, the wind is often depicted as winged.
   **misera:** Since *Aura* has been addressed directly in line 12, this form is to be preferred to *miser*, though both fit the meter.

---

most power, there doth it the most heat women, inditing a verse thus conceived: *Credibile est ignes multiplicare suos* [Tis to be believed he doth there multiply their fires]." Here the *suos* is being translated as if it were *earum*, which seems to be how Bourdeille himself took it.

20. **plagae**: probably viewed as such because of the curls. Cf. the line from Pasquier: "Et per retia [sc. 'iuro'] tortilis capilli" (*Epig.* 1.11). Likewise, Bonefon warns his own breath about the hair of his girl Pancharis: "Non sunt aureolae comae videntur | Sed sunt vincula, compedes, catenae" (*Delitiae*, 1: 661).

22. **Arachne**: She challenged Athena to a weaving contest and lost. Distressed, she hanged herself, and Athena changed her into a spider (Ovid *Met.* 6.1–145).

## 96.

Wright, *Delitiae delitiarum* (1637), 11;
Kendall, *Flowers of Epigrammes*, 161.

There is an interesting resonance here with Bèze's view of the vatic poet on the one hand and the urbanity and wit required of an epigrammatist on the other. The priest unites the two for one purpose. Here the *sacerdos* is present to perform a religious task, but he is *nequissimus*, that is, "naughty" or "mischievous." This corresponds to Martial's aspirations for his own poetry, as he explains at 11.15.3–4:

> hic totus volo rideat libellus
> et sit nequior omnibus libellis.

The association with laughter is telling. The priest is not evil in a moral sense, he is a jokester, or more precisely in this instance a lampooner of a certain effeminacy of character exhibited by this hermaphrodite.

2. **propexique ... capilli**: Well-groomed hair was often seen as a sign of low morals and femininity: cf. Cicero's attack on Gabinius's *compti capilli* (*Pis.* 25) and Vergil on the Phrygian *semiviri* (*Aen.* 12.99–100). Contrast the standards for manliness delineated at Hor. *Od.* 1.12.41–43 on Camillus, and the following advice of Ovid to girls seeking a mate (*Ars Amat.* 3.133):

> non sint sine lege capilli
> admotae formam dantque negantque manus.

Martial has an interesting take on the matter at 1.24:

> Aspicis incomptis illum, Deciane, capillis,
>   Cuius et ipse times triste supercilium,

Qui loquitur Curios adsertoresque Camillos?
Nolito fronti credere: nupsit heri.

In Rome, prepubescent boys let their hair reach their shoulders as a sign of their prettiness and interest in or availability for same-sex involvement. When they began to grow hair on their bodies, they would trim their hair as a mark of their interest in heterosexuality. Such is the sense of Mart. 1.31.6: "fusae lactea colla iubae." Recent scholarship on the question of Roman homosexual practices have all noted that of prime importance among the Romans was one's degree of masculinity. Homosexuality *per se* did not diminish one's masculinity, so long as you had the insertive and not the receptive role during sex. Any womanly habits, such as depilation or the wearing of perfume or female clothing, could expose one to the charge of being effeminate. See Craig Williams, *Roman Homosexuality: Ideologies of Masculinity in Classical Antiquity* (Oxford, 1999), esp. 125–59; Saara Lilja, *Homosexuality in Republican and Augustan Rome* (Helsinki, 1983), esp. 127–33.

3. **tersa cute**: According to Ovid *Ars Amat.* 1.506, smooth skin is unbecoming to a man, unless he wants to be like the eunuch priests of Cybele: "nec tua mordaci pumice crura teras."
   **blaesula**: See note on *epig.* 19, line 7.
4. **paetis oculis**: "leering-eyed" was an epithet of Venus, because she often gave a sidelong, sexually inviting look; cf. Ovid *Ars Amat.* 2.659 (Kenney, following 1502 Aldine; some edd. have *straba*, i.e., "squinting"): "si paeta est, Veneri similis;" Varro, *Men.* fr. 344: "non haec res de Venere paeta strabam facit;" Priap. 37: "Minerva flava, lumine <est> Venus paeto."
   **molli**: with the double sense of both "soft" and "effeminate."
9. **utra**: the feminine, because both seem to be girls.
**Utra sponsus foret rogare coepit**: Note the subtle imitation of this conceit by Monier (fl. c. 1573):

> *In leporem a puero cursu captum*
>
> Dum pede longinquos emensi praepete cursus
>     Pene darent animas hinc puer, inde lepus:
> Pernici pernix succumbens praeda puello,
>     Audiit adstantes dicere, uter lepus est?
>                 (*Delitiae*, 2: 590)

## 97.

Missing in 1569, 1576, 1597.

The comparison of a lover to other analogous occupations has a long pedigree. For example, lovers are like pleaders at the bar. Ovid is fond of using military metaphors, saying that "love is a species of warfare" (*Ars Amat.* 2.233, "militiae species amor est"), and that "every lover is on active duty" (*Am.* 1.9, "militat omnis amans"). He delineates the many toils that the soldier–lover must endure as he braves the weather, makes long marches, and lays siege to his lover's house. But Bèze follows another train of thought from Ovid's *Ars Amatoria*, that convention has established that the male must pursue the female (1.277). From this stems many a predatory metaphor from the realm of hunting and fishing (traps, nets, dogs, bait, trolling, spearing, and so on). Men are called upon to be cunning and persistent as they engage in the sport, while the girls will naturally run to dens and hiding places like scared animals. The girls dread capture—though there is some indication that their fear is feigned: they say "no" when they mean "yes"—because ultimately it means that they will be subdued, dominated, speared, and treated as a trophy. Ovid does not want the metaphor pushed too far, though, since the secret art he is revealing aims at simplifying the task (*Ars Am.* 2.193–95):

> Non te Maenalias armatum scandere silvas
> Nec iubeo collo retia ferre tuo,
> Pectora nec missis iubeo praebere sagittis.

Machard compares this poem with Pliny the Younger, *Epist.* 1.6, to Tacitus. It is more likely, though, that the theme was suggested to Bèze from the following series of poems in Bourbon's *Nugae* of 1533 (fol. 25v):

> *Venator et amator*
> Ut saepe incassum venator retia tradit,
> Sic frustra infelix saepe laborat amans.

> *Idem*
> Retia saepe solet venator tendere frustra;
> Non raro miseram ludit amans operam.

> *Idem*
> Saepe fit, ut frustra venator retia ponat,
> Saepe operam perdit, quem ferus urit Amor.

Bourbon himself may have taken the idea from Horace, *Sat.* 1.2.105–6, where the lover is compared to a hunter chasing a hare: "Leporem venator ut alta | in nive sectetur, positum sic tangere nolit."

The notion that the hunter and lover often labor in vain and come back empty-handed becomes the turning point of Bèze's poem in lines 7–8. True, the hunter-lover may fail to catch the prey, but in the case of the lover, even if he should catch his prey, he has still lost the game.

5. **Ille etenim leporem sectatur, et iste leporem**: One chases a *lepus* (hare), the other his *lepor* (girlfriend). I have tried to reflect the pun on the similarity of the two words in my translation. Bourbon has a list of such puns, including this one, in a poem entitled *In Hugonem* ([1533], fol. 27r–v). Hugo has a problem pronouncing words, and so at line 4 we read: "Hugo qui lepores vocas lepōres" (i.e., who calls hares [accusative with short o] "darlings/bunnies" [accusative with long ō]). There was also a tradition that eating a hare (*lepus*) gives one charm (*lepor*) for several days: Mart. 5.29; Pliny, *NH* 28.79.260; *Scriptores Historiae Augustae*, Alexander Severus 38.

7. **venator ... amator**: Even the words denoting "hunter" and "lover" are similar in Latin.

9. **pluvias et ventos**: Among the Roman poets the "shut-out lover" (*exclusus amator*) often curses the weather as he waits by the locked (or guarded) gate of his beloved. Ovid (*Am.* 1.9.15–16) says that both the soldier and the lover are willing to endure the elements:

> quis nisi vel miles vel amans et frigora noctis
> et denso mixtas perferet imbre nives?

10. **canes**: Ovid draws on the dog-hare image also: "Maenalius lepori det sua terga canis" (*Ars Amat.* 1.272). For *canes* as a metaphor for the male penis (esp. κύων = πέος) see Aristoph. *Lys.* 158, *AP* 5.105.4 (Marcus Argentarius), Strato *AP* 12.225.2.

14. **praeda**: Cf. Ovid *Amores* 1.2: "En ego confiteor! tua sum nova praeda, Cupido," where Ovid uses the word not of a hunter's prey, but of a soldier captured in battle. Also *Amores* 1.3: "Iusta precor: quae me nuper praedata puella est ..."

## 98.

Missing in 1597.
Meter: phalaecian hendecasyllable.

The Janus Garnerus of this poem refers to Jean Garnier of Orléans rather than the more famous Jean Garnier, the printer of Bourges during the years 1530 to 1562, although Bèze could have known him also while staying at Bourges in the house of Wolmar in the early 1530s (Bèze knew another Jean Garnier among the Calvinists). In fact, ms. Lat. 8143 of the Bibliothèque Nationale in Paris records two poems by Bèze on the drowning death of the Orléans Garnier, one an epitaph for Garnier himself that concludes with the notation, "Theodorus Beza moerens faciebat," and the other a consolation for Marguerite. The first line of the latter poem suggests that the death came early in the marriage: "Quum Janum iuvenem iuvenis coniuxque maritum . . ." In this earlier poem, though, Bèze is certain that Jean's marriage to Marguerite spells doom for his friendship with himself. He effectively conveys his contempt for his rival, Marguerite, by piling up a string of diminutives (lines 4–7 all end in a diminutive body part, while in line 9 Marguerite herself receives a diminutive), by allying her with the *anus scelesta* who answers the door (old people typically undermine a poet's love), and by exposing the games (*ioci*) she plays in lines 30ff. in order to manipulate Jean. But in the end Bèze has to concede that in truth Marguerite has swallowed his friend whole, so he takes the opportunity to make a play on the name of *Ianus* and the Roman god by the same name, who ushers in the new year and gives his name to the first month. Instead of expecting that he will ever get his friend back, Bèze instead wishes that every year the couple will have a new baby, or "another Janus."

# *Appendix 1*

Bèze's sketch of the life of Melchior Wolmar
from the 1580 *Icones*:

*Melior Wolmarius Rotuillensis, iuris civilis et Graecarum literarum
in academia Tubingensi professor*

Meliorem Volmarium (sic enim eius nomen, cum antea Melchior vocare-
tur, vir doctissimus, et eius in academia Tubingensi collega, Ioachimus
Camerarius probitatem hominis admiratus, emolliit) genuit Rotuilla ci-
vitas Helvetiis confoederata, puerum aluit Berna, bonis literis imbuit
Lutetia, eundemque mox Graeca Latinaque facundia excellentem est ad-
mirata, ut et Aurelia, et Biturigum civitas: ubi, Margaretae Valesiae Na-
varrorum Reginae ac Biturigum Ducissae stipendiis, utramque linguam
profitens, simulque Andraeae Alciati, iurisconsultorum aetatis nostrae
facile Principis iudicio, legum doctor creatus, domum ipsius bonis ac piis
quibusque frequentantibus, inter quos Ioannem quoque Calvinum non
puduit pro Graecae linguae praeceptore Volmarium agnoscere, cum pri-
vatam quoque scholam ingenuis et selectae indolis pueris aliquot aperuis-
set, hoc est consequutus ut nemo erudiendae iuventuti magis idoneus,
nemo plures bonae frugis discipulos aluisse videretur: maiores multo
fructus inde collectura Gallia, nisi partim saevities adversus pios recru-
descens, partim Ulrichi ducis Wirtenbergensis eum invitantis auctoritas,
illum Tubingam anno Domini millesimo quingentesimo tricesimo quin-
to evocasset. Ibi vero annos amplius viginti ius civile et Graecos etiam
authores maxima cum laude interpretatus, tandemque rude donatus, cum
suam. Margaretae uxoris patriam, familiam transtulisset, vitam finiit,

postquam aliquot menses ex paralysi decubuisset, eodem etiam die uxore ex animi aegritudine defuncta, ut simul elati eodem tumulo conderentur quos sanctus amor totos 27 minimum annos coniunxerat. Fuit autem vir iste omnibus tum corporis tum animi dotibus excellens, ac praesertim eximia in pauperes munificentia insignis, et ab omni ambitione tam remotus, ut, quamvis Graece et Latine scribendo excelleret, nihil tamen praeter unicam perelegantem praefationem grammaticae Graecae Demetrii Chalcondylae[1] praepositam ediderit: quem ego a pueritia unicum praeceptorem nactus, et vivum ceu parentem alterum semper colui, et mortuum una cum ipsius uxore sic deploravi.

> Coniugii exemplum rarum certumque beati,
>  Spectate cuncti coniuges.
> Una dies nobis Meliorem sustulit, una
>  Et Margaritam sustulit.
> Sic uno quos vita thoro coniunxerat, uno
>  Mors una tumulo condidit:
> Una ambos donec reddat lux unius olim
>  Beatitatis compotes.

## IN EOSDEM

> Mi Melior, quo nec melior nec doctior ullus
>  Nostrum beavit seculum,
> Tu ne iaces, mutique taces sub more sepulcri?[2]
>  Et Beza stat, Beza loquitur?
> State certe et loquitur: sed cui nec vivere dulce,
>  Nec dulce posthaec sit loqui:
> Verum dulce mori fuerit, tecumque sepulcri
>  Uno latere sub specu.
> Nanque iacent tecum Charites, iacet ipsa venustas,
>  Et omnis Aonidum chorus.

---

[1] Demetrius Chalcondyles (1423–1511), a Greek refugee who taught Greek at Perugia, Padua, Florence, and Milan. Around 1493 he produced a Greek textbook for beginners, *Erotemata,* meant to be an improvement over that of Theodorus. On the popularity of the text throughout Europe, see J. E. Sandys, *A History of Classical Scholarship* (Cambridge, 1908), 3: 64, and N. G. Wilson, *From Byzantium to Italy* (London, 1992), 95–98.

[2] Note the conscious rhyming in *melior/doctior* and *iaces/taces.*

IN EOSDEM

Cum tumulo lateat Melior Volmarius isto,
    Cui Margarita adest comes,
Est illi cur invideas, Mausole, diuque
    Celebrata pyramidum strues.
Namque nihil melius Meliore, nec India quicquam
    Fert Margarita carius.

Obiit Isnae anno Domini millesimo quingente-
simo sexagesimo primo, anno aetatis sexage-
simo quarto.

# Appendix 2

Epitaph on Bèze by Joseph Justus Scaliger,
from the 1606 *Epicedia*, fols. 9r–11r

*Epicedion venerandi patris Theodori Bezae*

Magne senex, miti quem funere nuper ademptum
    Allobrogum molli cespite velat humus,
Quamvis aeterna caeli regione receptum
    Te seposta piis manibus aula tenet,
Iamque es decurso spatio delatus in ipsum,           5
    Semper anhelabat quo tua vita, locum:
Quod tamen haud pridem caris ereptus amicis,
    Atque illis nunquam conspiciendus abes,
Solvimur in lacrimas. Omnes tua signa secuti,
    Et commilitii strenua membra tui,           10
Aut memorem clara testantur voce dolorem,
    Aut contracta notis tristibus ora gerunt.
Bezam matura solverunt fata senecta:
    Longius ast nobis Beza fruendus erat.
Excipitur Bezae cognatis spiritus astris:           15
    Ast Bezae in terris utile pectus erat.
Non caelo admissum (quid enim felicius illo?)
    Sed terrae ereptum femina virque dolent.
Est aliquid longae finem promittere vitae,
    Et dare discessus pignora certa sui,           20
Cum sensim moriens senior longaevus, amicis

Moerendum linquit post sua fata nihil,
Et moriendo magis, quam mortuus, afficit illos.
    Nam longum senium funeris instar habet.
Quis tamen in patrem, quem summa senecta resolvit,                    25
    Impendi lacrimas iure, negare potest?
Vixerit innumeros, aequarit Nestoris, annos,
    Implerit vitae tempora longa suae:
Immaturus obit. Pietatis iura, parentum
    Non vitae, lacrimis non posuere modum.                          30
Nullus ut optandi longaevae tempora vitae,
    Sic nullus stendi funera finis adest.
Cum tua, summe virum, pietas exegerit, ut te
    Possemus iusti patris habere loco,
Quis nostras damnet lacrimas? quis flere parentem                    35
    Intempestivum dixerit officium?
Stabat Olympiadum, fateor, iam meta tuarum,
    Atque bis undecimae tertius annus erat,
Emeriti quando te post stipendia cursus
    Composuit placido sine beata quies,                             40
Qualiter autumni cocto flaventia succo
    Pendula poma suo pondere fessa cadunt.
Festinata tamen quaerimur tua fata, neque ultra
    Nostra tuos cursum tendere vota dies.
Sed tamen hoc melius, quam si felicius aevum                         45
    Rupisset vitae stamina longa tuae,
Indelibato pietas cum flore vireret,
    Et sacer afflaret pectora casta calor,
Nec caperet tellus examina tanta piorum,
    Divinae laudis quos stimulabat amor:                            50
Cum veri studiosa tuae de flumine linguae
    Ora rigaturas turba sitiret aquas:
Et quae non modico murorum clauditur orbe,
    Vix satis hospitiis ampla Geneva foret,
Totque peregrinis coleretur gentibus illa,                          55
    Pene quot indigenas vel satis esse fuit.
Felix, qui tali vivens interfuit aevo.
    Hei mihi, quas aetas nunc rotat ista vices.
Aurea saecla Dei mutans peiore metallo
    Infecit nostros decolor aura dies,                              60
Quaeque incendebant caelesti pectora flamma,

Dilapsae in cinerem nunc tepuere faces.
Qui vix signavit prima puer ora iuventa,
   Cui pius imbuerat flammea corda timor,
Transfuga castrorum meliores abdicat artes,                    65
   Militiae calcans foedera prima suae.
Nec minus interea, serae sub fine senectae[3]
   Sunt qui deserto terga dedere Deo.
Omnibus incessunt sinceri taedia cultus:
   Et nova materies, et nova causa subest.                70
Illum dira trahit blandi pellacia quaestus.
   Hunc rapidus vortex ambitionis agit.
Quid loquar, ut nigris grassans insania chartis
   Probra venenato lurida felle iacit,
Atque latrocinii sub imagine plurima vulgo                     75
   Invadunt lectos scripta proterva viros?
Vixque ipsum ficto tutum est a crimine caelum.
   Pene Deum rabido provocat ore furor.
Tu, qui perfidiae primordia videris huius,
   Hoc melius, quod non his graviora vides.                80
Utque Dei famulo non Hippo superstite capta est,
   Cum quateret Libycas Vandalus hostis opes,
Indulsit tibi sic praesentia Numinis, isto
   Cernere ne posses ulteriora malo.
Atque utinam celeres rapiant procul omina venti,              85
   Et potius mendax finxerit ista metus.
Sed te felicem, qui non spectacula praesens
   Ista gemis, vel non deterriora times.
Nos infelices, tua quos absentia curis
   Urit, et immemores non sinit esse tui.                  90
O quoties animo venerandae frontis imago,
   Et pulchri species oris honesta subit,
Et placidi mores, et fandi lactea vena,
   Et non moroso tincta loquela sale.
O quoties plenae moderantem frena coronae                     95
   Obstupuit verbis pendula turba tuis.
Ut te spectaret, patriam non linquere Graecus,
   Sarmata non longas horruit ire vias.

---

[3] Cf. Verg. *Aen.* 1.633.

Mollivit tantos spectandi causa labores:
    Et Bezam merces sola videre fuit.               100
At quia nec nobis doctae dulcedine linguae,
    Praesentis vivo nec datur ore frui,
Nunc superest cultis mentes advertere libris,
    Et quodcunque vigil cura paravit opus.
In quibus et foetus supra caput extulit omnes       105
    Ille tuorum operum summa caputque liber,
Quo penetrale Novi referatur Foederis, in quo
    Discussa lucem nocte videre datur.
Hic nobis Beza est, Bezam spectamus in illo.
    Totus in hoc speculo Beza videndus adest.      110
Non alia est, quae te praesentiaque ora reducat,
    Usurpanda oculis picta tabella meis.
Iamque vale. Toties mihi mens te fingat adesse,
    In libris quoties haeserit illa tuis.

      Iosephus Scaliger Iulii Caesaris a Burden P.
      memoriae aeternae maximi viri D. D.

# Appendix 3

From *Ugolini Verini poetae Florentini de illustratione urbis Florentiae libri tres* (Paris, 1583), fols. 2r–3v:[4]

*Ad serenissimam ac Christianiss(imam) reginam Catharinam Medicaeam, Henrici III, Galliae et Poloniae regis Christianiss(imi) matrem, Germani Audeberti Aurelii carmen*

Cui potius regina potens, regumque creatrix,
Quam tibi sacrentur Verini carmina vatis
Syllanae veteres urbis celebrantia cunas,
Illustresque viros, totamque ab origine prolem,
Maioresque tuos? quorum tu maxima iure
Gloria censeris: sunt haec tibi propria dona
Magnanimum Heroum genus alta e stirpe trahenti,
Summosque augenti Medicaeae gentis honores.
   Nobilis ut fulvo decoratur gemma metallo,
Ut radiis magis illa suis illuminat aurum:
Sic splendente domo, et claris natalibus orta

---

[4] Renouard, *Estienne*, 184: 3 (s.v. Mamert Patisson's press). Emile Picot, *Les Français italianisants au XVI* siècle, 2 vols. (Paris, 1906–7): he refers to Ugolini's book in 2: 157–58: "Pour célébrer Florence, le docte Orléanais se contenta de compléter et de retoucher un poème inachevé d'Ugolino Verini, dont il possédait le manuscrit, et il le mit au jour avec une dédicace à Catherine de Médicis" [this is accompanied by a footnote identifying Ugolini's book, and citing several copies at the BN]. The NUC locates one copy in America, at the Newberry (Case Y 682 V 5958). There also was a reprint: Florence, 1636 (copies at the University of Chicago, Columbia, and Yale).

Scintillas, raraque tuos virtute parentes
Illustras magis, atque magis: moderatio magno
Magna licet fuerit Cosmo, prudentia solers
Laurenti primo, generoso mira Leoni
Ingenii cultura, et cui clementia nomen
Conveniens peperit, virtusque invicta secundo
Laurenti, quo tu quanto genitore fuisses
Fortunata magis; tenerae nisi filia iuventae
Rupissent fata ante diem! fata invida terris.
    Sed quid ego reliquos nequicquam prosequar ultra,
Una tuos cum tu meritis superaveris omnes,
Nilque unquam tulerit tua te Florentia maius?
Nec decus esse suum te Thuscia sola fatetur,
Sed tota Italiae tellus sibi vendicat, et te
Ut pridem assuetum veneratur Gallia numen.
    Altera nobilitas materna ab origine surgit
Ducta Bolonaeum Comitum de semine claro
Regibus antiquo iunctorum sanguine Gallis.
Unde tibi dudum locuples Arvernia cessit.
Nunc etiam cedunt tibi Lusitanica regna,
Debita pacifico, sed non possessa Roberto;
Qui quondam Rege Alphonso, Arvernaque Mathilde
Editus haud vetitis, inconcessisque Hymenacis,
Legitima ad seros transmisit iura nepotes:
Liligerae sed regna foves potiora coronae
Coniugio Henrici Regis dignata, secundi
Nomine, at haud cuiquam bello, vel pace secundi.
Ecquis pace etenim fuit observantior aequi?
Quis bello melior, sumptisque audentior armis?
    O felix una ante alias Regina, frequenti
(Altera ceu Cybele mater fecunda deorum)
Tot Regum partu, Reginarumque superba!
Praecipue Henrici, gemino cui regia late
Gallo, et Sarmatico diademate tempora fulgent.
Virtuti et meritis hoc Sarmata detulit ultro,
Haeredemque amplexa absentem Gallia, fratre
Defuncto: quo non Regum praestantior alter
Dotibus ingenii, et facundae munere linguae.
    Quantas Franciscus Gallis spes excitat ingens,
Dum Belgam oppressum iuvas auxiliaribus armis,

Ventososque nova virtute exterret Iberos
Intrepidus: belloque ad Scaldim fulminat amnem
Assuetus magnis caput obiectare periclis,
Nec dubius merita letum pro laude pacisci!
Felicem eventum coeptis date numina iustis.
 Unica restat adhuc caelo demissa benigno
Regina, auratos inter tria lilia flores
Flos apprima nitens, gemma pretiosior omni
Margaris,[5] astringens fraternos unio nexus,
Bellorum impatiens, tranquillaeque arbitra pacis.
Casta Venus, prudens Iuno, formosa Minerva,
Orta Iovis cerebro, sed non sine matre Deorum.
Dignus uterque parens nata, digna illa parente
Utroque; ingenium referens utriusque parentis
Et genium; vultum Francisci, animumque virilem
Neptis avi: par eloquium, par gratia frontis.
 At tibi tam multis genitrici Heroibus auctae
Quid tantis dignum titulis feret iste Poeta,
Mortali quanvis sonet immortalia voce
Enthea Pierio praecordia concitus oestro?
Nam licet innumeros urbi, varieque nitentes
Aspergat flores; nullo tamen, inclyta, flore
Culta magis, quam flore tuo Florentia claret,
Aurea quae globulis miscet tria Lilia senis.
 O talem si te Verini secla tulissent,
Quantis ille tuos cumulasset laudibus ortus!
Tu contra quales stimulos sub pectore vatis
Vertisses: quantoque afflasses numine mentem!
 Nanque excepisset tua cum te Aurelia nuper,
Et nos, alloquio non dedignata, beasses:
Insolitum experti sacro te agnovimus ore
Laeta infundentem nostro tua lumina cordi,
Accendere novos animo quae protinus ignes:
Sensimus et vegetas commoto sanguiine vires,
Ut Deus in nobis stupefacta per ossa cucurrit[6]

---

 [5] For this variant on *margarita*, see Serv. *Aen.* 1.655 (= μαργαρίς). Note the pun with
*unio* in the same line.
 [6] Cf. Verg. *Aen.* 8.390.

Languida labentis reparans fomenta senectae.
Usque adeo Divae potuit praesentia! reddant
Abs te igitur sumptam mea nunc tibi carmina lucem,
Ulla tamen decorare valent si carmina lucem
Ornantem reliquas, et nulla luce minorem,
Reflexamque in se Phoebei luminis instar.
Sic, dando accipies, dignis si lumina fundas.
Si vero, quod habes renuis, quae munera sumes,
Cum sola accipiant superi, quae dona dedere?

# Bibliographical Notes

## Editions of Bèze's *Poemata* Consulted

1547    *Tumuli Francisci Valesii primi, christianiss. Francorum regis, et duorum eius liberorum, Francisci, Carolique, alterius Galliarum delphini, alterius Aureliorum ducis. Querela de Caroli, Aureliensium ducis, morte Gallicis rythmis conscripta. Epigrammata in Henricum Valesium, II, christianiss. Francorum regem, et duos eius liberos, Franciscum et Isabellam* (Paris, 1547). Long considered anonymous (see below, Lachèvre, *Bibliographie*, 1922, 230), until studies by Droz, "Notes sur Théodore de Bèze," and Shaw, "Tumuli." There are only seven known copies in existence; I have used the Newberry copy: Wing ZP 539 B12. Contents: 2, royal privilege, granted 8 August 1547; 3–6, epitaphs 21–24 of our collection; 6–15, "Complainte au nom d'une dame, sur le trespas de seu monsieur d'Orleans" in French verse; 16–18 (= ms. Bibl. nat. fr. 22561, fols. 239–40), epigrams 47–49 of our collection.

1548    *Theodori Bezae Vezelii poemata* (Paris, 1548). First edition of the *iuvenilia*. Detailed descriptions can be found at Renouard, *Imprimeurs*, 2: 308–9 and Gardy, *Bibliographie*, no. 1. See also Renouard, *Estienne*, 72: no. 16.

1569    *Theodori Bezae Vezelii poematum editio secunda, ab eo recognita. Item, ex Georgio Buchanano aliisque variis insignibus poetis excerpta carmina, praesertimque epigrammata* (Geneva, 1569). Contents: 3–20, letter to Andre Dudith; 21–31, poems in Hebrew,

Latin, and Greek, by Henri Stephanus (the printer of the collection) et al., about Bèze and his book, including a poem *In cucullatos Bezomastigas* by Bèze himself; pagination starts anew, with Bèze's poetry on 1–174 (errata sheet on 174); pagination starts anew again, with the poetry of George Buchanan on 3–138, Pontano, 139–46; Sannazarius, 146–50; Antonius Flaminius, 152–81; other Italians (Molsa, Cotta, Bembo, Castilion, Casanova, Vital, Tibaldeus, Theocrenus), 182–98; John Secundus, 199–207; Henri Stephanus, 208–55. See Renouard, *Estienne*, 132: 4.

1576　　*Theodori Bezae poemata ... omnia, in hac terrtia editione, partim recognita, partim locupletata* (Geneva, 1576).

1580　　*Poemata.* Not included in Gardy, *Bibliographie*; a surreptitious reprint of the 1548 ed.

1580　　*Icones, id est verae imagines virorum doctrina simul et pietate illustrium, quorum praecipue ministerio partim bonarum literarum studia sunt restituta, partim vera Religion in variis orbis Christiani regionibus, nostra patrumque memoria fuit instaurata: additis eorundem vitae et operae descriptionibus, quibus adiectae sunt nonnullae picturae quas Emblemata vocant* (Geneva, 1580).

1597　　*Theodori Bezae Vezelii poemata varia. Sylvae, elegiae, epitaphia, epigrammata, icones, emblemata, Cato Censorius* (Geneva, 1597).

1713　　*Poemata Theodori Bezae, Vezelii: Quibus continentur sylvae, elegiae, epitaphia, icones, epigrammata* (London, 1713).

1757　　*Theodori Bezae Vezelii poemata* (Lyons, 1757).

1779　　*Amoenitates poeticae: Theodori Bezae, Marci Antonii Mureti, et Johannis Secundi Juvenilia; tum Joannis Bonefonii Pancharis; Joachimi Bellaii Amores,* etc. (Lyons, 1779). Bèze's poems appear on 1–118; Muret, 121–208; John Secundus, 211–306; Jean Bonefon, 309–52; Joachim du Bellay, 355–89; three more poems of Muret, one of Peter Lotichius, and one of Famianus Strada, 390–96.

1879　　Machard, Alexandre, *Théodore de Bèze: Les Juvenilia* (Paris,

1879). Essentially the 1548 edition with French translations of epitaphs and epigrams. Especially valuable for its discussion of the *Nachleben* of Bèze's first edition, v–lxxiv.

## Anthologies Consulted

Canoniero, Pietro Andrea. *Flores illustrium epitaphiorum ex praeclarissimarum totius Europae civitatum et praestantissimorum poetarum monumentis excerpti per Petrum Andream Canonherium, in hac secunda editione multis pulcherrimis epitaphiis aucti* (Antwerp, 1627). Canoniero (d. ca. 1620) conceals the names of Protestants throughout.

Duchesne, Léger. *Flores epigrammatum ex optimis quibusque authoribus excerpti* (Paris, 1555). Among French writers contains poems of Bèze, Claude Roselet, Dolet, and Duchesne himself. Poems of Secundus also appear.

——, *Farrago poematum* (Paris, 1560). Among French writers contains poems of de l'Hôpital, Turnèbe, Germain de Brie, Dorat, du Bellay, and "Chr. Aulaeus." Buchanan receives thirty pages.

Gruter, Jean (pseud. R. Gherus), ed. *Delitiae C Poetarum Gallorum*, 3 vols. (Frankfurt, 1609), cited as *Delitiae*. Bèze's poetry appears in vol. 3, pp. 587–743, including his *iuvenilia*, under the pseudonym "Adeotatus Seba."

Heywood, Thomas, ed. *Plesant dialogues and drammas selected out of Lucian, Erasmus, Textor, Ovid, etc. ... As also certaine Elegies, Epitaphs and Epithalamions ... Anagrams and Acrostichs ... with other fancies translated from Beza, Buchanan, and sundry Italian poets* (London, 1637). I have used the edition as reprinted in W. Bang, ed., *Materialien zur Kunde des älteren Englischen Dramas*, vol. 1 (Louvain, 1902); the poems of Bèze are on 267–71.

Kendall, Timothy. *Flowers of Epigrammes* (London, 1577; repr. Manchester, 1874). Bèze's poems are on 156–66; translates eight of the secular poems into English.

McFarlane, I. D. *Renaissance Latin Poetry* (Manchester and New York, 1980).

Merrill, L. R. *The Life and Poems of Nicholas Grimald* (New Haven, 1925); to be compared with *Tottel's Miscel.* (see "Rollins," below) and H. H. Hudson, "Grimald's Translations from Beza," *Modern Language Notes* 39 (1924): 388–94.

Nicole, Pierre. *Epigrammatum delectus ex omnibus tum veteribus, tum re-*

*centioribus poetis accurate decerptus, etc., cum dissertatione, de vera pul-*
*chritudine et adumbrata, in qua ex certis principiis, rejectionis ac selec-*
*tionis Epigrammatum causae redduntur* (Paris, 1659; London, 1683).
On 374–76 gives three of Bèze's epitaphs with notes. Later editions
(the 1752 twelfth edition was also available to me) append *epig.* 35 and
remove the harsh criticism leveled against Bèze (see introduction).

Nichols, F. J. *An Anthology of Neo-Latin Poetry* (New Haven and Lon-
don, 1979).

Perosa, A. and J. Sparrow. *Renaissance Latin Verse: An Anthology*
(London and Chapel Hill, 1979).

Rollins, H. E., ed. *Tottel's Miscellany (1557–1587)*, 2 vols. (Cambridge,
MA, 1928).

Wright, James, ed. *Sales epigrammatum: being the choicest disticks of Mar-*
*tials fourteen books of epigrams; and of all the chief Latine poets that*
*have writ in these two last centuries* (London, 1663). Includes five of
Bèze's poems (both in English and Latin) on 42–45.

Wright, Abraham, ed. *Delitiae delitiarum, sive epigrammatum ex optimis*
*quibusque huius et novissimi seculi poetis amplissima illa Bibliotheca*
*Bodleiana, pene omnino alibi extantibus* ἀνθολογία, *in unam corollam*
*connexam* (Oxford, 1637). Bèze's poems appear on 6–15.

## Neo-Latin Authors

Works and editions of authors consulted for this study in addition to
the authors included in the 1569 and 1779 editions of Bèze (especially
George Buchanan).

Audebert, Germain: *Delitiae*, 1: 89–256.

Bellay, Joachim du: *Delitiae*, 1: 390–487.

Boissard, Jean-Jacques: *Delitiae*, 1: 548–652.
  *Ioan. Iacobi Boissarti . . . Poemata. Epigrammatum libri III. Elegiarum*
    *libri III. Epistolarum libri III* (Basel, 1574).
  *Iani Iacobi Boissardi . . . Poemata.* (Metz, 1589). Bound with *Disticha*
    *in icones diversorum principium* (Metz, 1587).

Bonefon, Jean: *Delitiae*, 1: 656–707.

Bourbon, Nicolas: *Delitiae*, 1: 766–93.
  *Nicolai Borbonii Vanderoperani Nugae, eiusdem Ferraria* (Paris, 1533).
  *Nicolai Borbonii Vanderoperani Lingononnsis nugarum libri octo*
    (Basel, 1540).

*Les Bagatelles de Nicolas Bourbon*, ed. V.-L. Saulnier (Paris, 1945).

Brie, Germain de: *Delitiae*, 1: 720–66.

Duchesne, Léger (Leodegarius à Quercu): *Delitiae*, 3: 188–203.

Espence, Claude d': *Delitiae*, 1: 896.

Dampierre, Jean: *Delitiae*, 1: 833–61.

Dolet, Stephan: *Delitiae*, 1: 863–70.

Dorat, Jean (= Auratus): *Delitiae*, 1: 264–384.

Duchat, Luc-François le: *Delitiae*, 1: 870–92.

    *Poemata* (Paris, 1554)

Girard, Jean: *Delitiae*, 1: 946–55.

    *Stichostratia* (Lyons, 1552)

    *Poemata* (Lyons, 1558)

    *Poemata nova* (Paris, 1584)

Macrin, Jean Salmon: *Delitiae*, 2: 453–573.

    *Carminum libellus* (Paris, 1528).

    *Carminum libri quatuor* (Paris, 1530).

    *Epigrammatum libri duo ad Franciscum Mommarantium* (Poitiers, 1548).

Monier, Martial: *Delitiae*, 2: 584–711.

Montaigne, Michel de: *The Complete Essays of Montaigne*, trans. by David Frame (Stanford, 1957).

Muret, Marc-Antoine de: *Delitiae*, 2: 738–814.

Pasquier, Étienne: *Delitiae*, 2: 843–1021.

    *Epigrammatum libri VI* (Paris, 1585).

    *Les Oeuvres d'Estienne Pasquier, contenant ses Recherches de la France ... son plaidoyé pour M. le Duc de Lorraine ... clarorum virorum ad Steph. Pasquierium carmina; epigrammatum libri sex et epitaphorum liber; iconum liber cum nonnullis Theod. Pasquierii in francorum regum icones notis; ses lettres ...* (Trévoux, 1723).

Roillet, Claude: *Delitiae*, 3: 253–54.

    *Varia poemata* (Paris, 1556)

Ronsard, Pierre de: *Oeuvres complètes*. Texte établi et annoté par Gustave Cohen. Bibliothèque de la Pléiade, 2 vols. (Paris, 1950).

Rousselet, Claude: *Delitiae*, 3: 254–62.

Sainte-Marthe, Scévole de: *Delitiae*, 3: 262–502.

    *Gallorum doctrina illustrium, qui nostra patrumque memoria floruerunt, elogia. Recens aucta et in duos divisa libros quorum alter nunc primum editur* (Limoges, 1602).

    *Scaevolae Sammarthani opera, tum poetica, tum ea quae soluta oratione scripsit* (Paris 1616).

Scaliger, Joseph Justus: *Delitiae*, 3: 502–77
    *Scaligerana, editio altera, ad verum exemplar restituta, et innumeris iisque foedissimis mendis, quibus prior illa passim scatebat, diligentissime purgata* (Cologne, 1667).
Scaliger, Julius Caesar: *Iulii Caesaris Scaligeri viri clarissimi, poetices libri septem* (Heidelberg, 1594).
Scévole de Sainte-Marthe: *Scaevolae Sammarthani opera, tum poetica, tum ea quae soluta oratione scripsit* (Paris, 1616).
Sussanée, Hubert: *Huberti Sussanei ... Ludorum libri nunc recens conditi atque aediti* (Paris, 1538).
Vaillant, Germain de Guélis (Valens): *Delitiae*, 3: 1112–23.
Voulté, Jean (Visagier, Vulteius): *Delitiae*, 3: 1131–47.
    *Ioannis Vulteii Remensis Epigrammatum libri IIII, eiusdem Xenia* (Lyons, 1537).
    *Io. Vulteii ... hendecasyllaborum libri quatuor* (Paris, 1538); bound with *Ioan. Vulteii ... inscriptionum libri duo* (Paris, 1538).

## General

The following bibliography includes only those items that are mentioned more than once in the commentary, in which case they are referred to by the name of the author with short title.

Adams, J. N. *The Latin Sexual Vocabulary*. Baltimore, 1982.
Aubert, F., J. Boussard, and H. Meylan. "Un premier recueil de poésies latines de Théodore de Bèze." *Bibliothèque d'Humanisme et Renaissance* 15 (1953): 164–91, 257–94; extracted and published with index in 1954 at Geneva by the Société du Musée Historique de la Réformation.
Bernier, Jean. *Histoire de Blois*. Paris, 1682. Contains map of the region.
Bèze, Th. de. *Iesu Christi D. N. Novum testamentum, sive Novum foedus. Cuius Graeco contextui respondent interpretationes duae: una, vetus: altera, nova, Theodori Bezae, diligenter ab eo recognita. Eiusdem Th. Bezae annotationes, quas itidem hac tertia editione recognovit, et accessione non parva locupletavit.* Geneva, 1582.
——. *Correspondance*. Recueillie par H. Aubert, publiée par H. Meylan, A. Dufour, et al. Geneva, 1960– . 20 vols. to date, covering 1539–1579.
Bietenholz, Peter. *Contemporaries of Erasmus: A Biographical Register of the Renaissance and Reformation*. Toronto, 1980.

Bimbenet, Jean-Eugène. *Histoire de l'Université de Lois d'Orléans*. Paris and Orleans, 1853.

Boussard, Jacques. "Le ms. 1674 de la Bibliothèque d'Orléans." *Bibliothèque d'Humanisme et Renaissance* 5 (1944): 346–60.

——. "L'Université d'Orléans et l'humanisme au début du XVI^e siècle." *Humanisme et Renaissance* 5 (1938): 209–30.

——. "Un poète latin, directeur spirituel au XVI^e siècle, Jean Dampierre." *Bulletin philologique et historique* (1946–1947): 33 58.

Brainne, C., J. Debarbouiller, and Ch.-F. Lapierre. *Les hommes illustres de l'Orléanais*. 2 vols. Orleans, 1852.

Chavannes, Frédéric. *Notice sur un manuscrit du xvi^e siècle appartenant à la bibliothèque cantonale: Poésies inédites de Clément Marot, de Catherine de Médicis et de Théodore de Bèze*. Lausanne, 1844.

Clark, John E. *Élégie: The Fortunes of a Classical Genre in Sixteenth Century France*. The Hague and Paris, 1975.

Cosenza, M. E. *Biographical and Bibliographical Dictionary of the Italian Humanists and the World of Classical Scholarship in Italy, 1300–1800*. 4 vols. Boston, 1962.

Droz, E. "Notes sur Théodore de Bèze." *Bibliothèque d'Humanisme et Renaissance* 24 (1962): 392–412, 589–610.

Faye, Antoine de la (Antonius Fayus). *De vita et obitu clariss. viri D. Theodori Bezae Vezellii*. Geneva, 1606. Bound together with *Epicedia, quae clarissimi aliquot viri, et D. Theodoro Bezae carissimi: sicut et illis ipse Beza vivus carissimus, et mortuus est honoratissimus: scripserunt in ipsius obitum*. Geneva, 1606. The latter contains a collection of Hebrew, Greek, and Latin epitaphs in honor of Beza (including ones by Joseph Scaliger, Jacques Lect, and Isaac Casaubon).

Gardy, Frédéric. *Bibliographie des oeuvres théologiques, littéraires, historiques et juridiques de Théodore de Bèze*. Geneva, 1960.

Geisendorf, Paul-F. *Théodore de Bèze*. Geneva, 1949.

Grant, W. Leonard. "The Shorter Latin Poems of George Buchanan, 1506–1582." *Classical Journal* 40 (1945): 331–48.

Grant, William Leonard. *Neo-Latin Literature and the Pastoral*. Ann Arbor, 1963.

Groot, D.-J. de. "Melchior Wolmar Rot, de Rottweil." *Bulletin de la Société de l'Histoire du Protestantisme français* 83 (1934): 416–39.

Hackett, Francis. *Francis the First*. New York, 1935.

Hallowell, Robert E. *Ronsard and the Conventional Elegy*. Urbana, IL, 1954.

Hanisch, Gertrude S. *Love Elegies of the Renaissance: Marot, Louise Labé and Ronsard.* Stanford French and Italian Studies 15. Saratoga, CA, 1979.

Herminjard, A.-L. *Correspondance des réformateurs dans les pays de langue française.* vol. 16, *1539–1540.* Paris, 1883.

Hutton, James. *The Greek Anthology in France.* Ithaca, 1946.

Jarry, L. "Une correspondance littéraire au XVIᵉ siècle: Pierre Daniel et les érudits de son temps." *Mémoires de la societé archéologique et historique de l'Orléanais* 15 (1876): 343–430.

Lachèvre, Frédéric. *Bibliographie des recueils collectifs de poésies du XVIᵉ siècle.* Paris, 1922. Covers collections from 1502 to 1609.

Laing, James. *De vita et moribus Theodori Bezae, omnium haereticorum nostri temporis facile principis, et aliorum haereticorum brevis recitatio.* Paris, 1585.

Maigron, L. *De Theodori Bezae poematis.* London, 1898. Originally a dissertation presented to the literary faculty at the University of Paris.

Maire, François le. *Histoire et antiquitez de la ville et duché d'Orleans.* Orleans, 1646. The first 566 pages treat "temporal history"; pagination begins anew with an overview of the University of Orleans, and runs up to 108; then a second volume is attached, entitled *Antiquitez et choses memorables de l'eglise et diocese d'Orleans*, and pagination begins again to 144; then is added *Histoire et vies des evesques d'Orleans*, with pagination running from 1 through 108.

McFarlane, I. D. "Jean Salmon Macrin (1490–1557)." *Bibliothèque d'Humanisme et Renaissance* 21 (1959): 55–84; 311–49; 22 (1960): 73–89. Reprints a letter from Macrin to Antoine de Lion in which the former criticizes Bèze's poetry and offers information concerning vowel quantity.

———. "La poésie néo-latine et l'engagement à l'époque des guerres de religion." In *Culture et politique en France à l'époque de l'humanisme et de la Renaissance*, ed. by Franco Simone, pp. 387–411. Turin, 1974,

———. *A Literary History of France: Renaissance France, 1470–1589.* London and New York, 1974.

McNeil, David O. *Guillaume Budé and Humanism in the Reign of Francis I.* Geneva, 1975.

Meylan, H. "Bèze et les 'sodales' d'Orléans, 1535–45." In *Actes du Congrès de l'Ancienne Université d'Orléans* (Orléans, 1962): 95–100; repr. in Meylan, *D'Erasme à Théodore de Bèze* (Geneva, 1976), 139–44.

———. "La conversion de Bèze ou Les longues hésitations d'un humaniste chrétien." *Geneva*, n.s. 7 (1959): 103–25; repr. in Meylan, *D'Erasme à Théodore de Bèze* (Geneva, 1976), 145–67.

Michaud, J. Fr. *Biographie universelle ancienne et moderne.* 45 vols. Paris, 1843–1865.

Moreri, Louis. *Le grand dictionnaire historique . . . nouvelle édition, dans laquelle on a refondu les suppléments de M. l'Abbé Goujet; le tout revu, corrigé & augmenté par M. Drouet.* 10 vols. Paris, 1759.

Nivet, J. "L'humanisme orléanais au XVIᵉ siècle." *Bulletin de la Société historique et archéologique de l'Orléanais,* 1, 7 (1960): 339–50.

Pineaux, Jacques. "Poésie et prophétisme: Ronsard et Théodore de Bèze dans la querelle des 'discours'." *Revue d'histoire littéraire de la France* 78 (1978): 531–40.

Prescott, A. L. "English Writers and Beza's Latin Epigrams: The Uses and Abuses of Poetry." *Studies in the Renaissance* 21 (1974): 83–117.

Reineke, Ilse. *Julius Caesar Scaligers Kritik der neulateinischen Dichter.* Munich, 1988.

Renouard, A.-A. *Annales de l'imprimerie des Estienne ou Histoire de la famille des Estienne et de ses éditions.* 2nd ed., New York, 1960.

Renouard, Philippe. *Imprimeurs et libraires parisiens du XVIᵉ siècle.* Ouvrage publié d'après les manuscrits de Philippe Renouard. 3 vols. to date. Paris, 1969– .

Ridderikhoff, Cornelia, et al. *Les livres des procurateurs de la nation germanique de l'ancienne Université d'Orléans 1444–1602.* "Texts," 2 vols., and "Biographies," 3 vols. Leiden, 1971–1985.

Scollen, C. M. *The Birth of the Elegy in France 1500–1550.* Geneva, 1967.

Sider, David. *The Epigrams of Philodemos: Introduction, Text, and Commentary.* New York and Oxford, 1997.

Smith, Malcolm. *Ronsard and du Bellay versus Bèze.* Geneva, 1995.

Shaw, David J. "Les *Tumuli Francisci Primi* de Théodore de Bèze." *Bibliothèque d'Humanisme et Renaissance* 40 (1978): 567–73.

Sparrow, John. "Renaissance Latin Poetry: Some Sixteenth-Century Latin Anthologies." In *Cultural Aspects of the Italian Renaissance: Essays in Honour of Paul Oskar Kristeller,* ed. by Cecil Clough, pp. 386–405. Manchester and New York, 1976.

Spitzer, Leo. "The Problem of Latin Renaissance Poetry." *Studies in the Renaissance* 2 (1955): 118–38.

Summers, Kirk. "Theodore Beza's Reading of Catullus." *Classical and Modern Literature* 15 (1995): 233–45.

Thomson, T. "The *Poemata* of Théodore de Bèze." In *Acta Conventus Neo-Latini Sanctandreani,* ed. I. D. McFarlane, MRTS 38, 409–15. Binghamton, NY, 1986.

Van Tiegham, Paul. "La littérature latine de la Renaissance. Etude d'histoire littéraire européenne." *Bibliothèque d'Humanisme et Renaissance* 4 (1940): 177–418.

Vindry, Fleury. *Les parlementaires français au XVI^e siècle.* 2 vols. Paris, 1909–1910.

# MRTS

MEDIEVAL AND RENAISSANCE TEXTS AND STUDIES
is the major publishing program of the
Arizona Center for Medieval and Renaissance Studies
at Arizona State University, Tempe, Arizona.

MRTS emphasizes books that are needed —
texts, translations, and major research tools.

MRTS aims to publish the highest quality scholarship
in attractive and durable format at modest cost.